The Riddle of Amish Culture

Center Books in Anabaptist Studies

Donald B. Kraybill

CONSULTING EDITOR

George F. Thompson

SERIES FOUNDER AND DIRECTOR

Published in cooperation with the Center for American Places,
Santa Fe, New Mexico, and Harrisonburg, Virginia

REVISED EDITION

The Riddle of Amish Culture

Donald B. Kraybill

The Johns Hopkins University Press | *Baltimore and London*

© 1989, 2001 The Johns Hopkins University Press
All rights reserved. Published 2001
Printed in the United States of America on acid-free paper

2   4   6   8   9   7   5   3   1

The Johns Hopkins University Press
2715 North Charles Street
Baltimore, Maryland 21218-4363
www.press.jhu.edu

Library of Congress Cataloging-in-Publication Data

Kraybill, Donald B.
The riddle of Amish culture / Donald B. Kraybill—Rev. ed.
p.   cm.—(Center books in Anabaptist studies)
"Published in cooperation with the Center for American Places,
Santa Fe, New Mexico, and Harrisonburg, Virginia."
Includes bibliographical references and index.
ISBN 0-8018-6771-1 (acid-free paper)
ISBN 0-8018-6772-x (pbk. : acid-free paper)
1. Amish—United States. 2. Amish—Canada.
3. Amish—Pennsylvania—Lancaster County. I. Title. II. Series.
E184.M45 K73 2001
305.6'87—dc21   00-013054

A catalog record for this book is available from the British Library.

For Gid (1913–1997)
who taught me the secrets of the riddle.

CONTENTS

The Amish are thriving in the twenty-first century despite their rejection of many contemporary values. From a meager band of 5,000 in 1900, they have blossomed to more than 180,000. Indeed, they are doubling about every twenty years. How do a tradition-laden people manage to flourish in a post-modern era? That enchanting riddle inspires this story. Apart from the big puzzle of Amish survival, smaller Amish riddles baffle us as well. Why, for example, do the Amish freely ride in cars but refuse to drive them? And why, pray tell, are tractors used at the barn but not in the field? Moreover, why would God smile on rollerblades but not on bicycles?

When the Amish look at contemporary society, they are equally perplexed by the riddles of "progress." Why, they wonder, do civilized people deposit their aging parents in retirement centers, isolated from children and grand-children? Why do professionals move around the country in pursuit of jobs, leaving family and neighbors behind? And, why do suburbanites sit on riding mowers to cut their lawns and then go to a fitness center for exercise? Each culture, to be sure, has its own set of riddles.

This book initiates a conversation between the riddles on both sides of the cultural fence. Such a dialogue not only explores the riddles of Amish culture but also prods us to ponder the puzzles of our own society. In this sense, the following pages are both a venture in cultural analysis, that is, an attempt to understand the dynamics of Amish society, and an exercise in social criticism—a reflective critique of contemporary culture. I hope these conversations across the cultural fence will help us understand both the Amish and ourselves in new and better ways.

Social scientists seek to maintain an objective, neutral stance when they analyze human societies. Yet social analysis always involves interpretation and judgment. In many ways it resembles storytelling. Creating a narrative from interviews and historical documents involves selection, omission, inter-pretation, emphasis, and embellishment. Stories have limits; certain frag-ments must be snipped. Some episodes are enriched by the yarn teller to underscore a theme or the teller's special interest. And stories, of course, have a slant. They are told from a perspective—a particular vantage point.

The setting for this story is Lancaster County, Pennsylvania, home of the oldest surviving Amish settlement in the world. In addition to its age, the Lancaster Amish community holds several other distinctions. It is the world's most densely populated Amish settlement, hosting the largest group of Amish who share similar religious practices. Moreover, it rests on the fringe of the urban sprawl in the eastern megalopolis—a region undergoing rapid suburbanization. These factors make Lancaster County an ideal setting to explore the Amish encounter with mainstream culture in the twenty-first century. The details of Amish practice vary from settlement to settlement across North America, but the basic values described in this book are widely shared in other Amish communities as well. In general, the Lancaster Amish tend to use more advanced technology than their ethnic cousins in some of the other North American settlements.

I have chosen to tell the Amish story for several reasons. First, it is a fascinating tale of a traditional people navigating their way through the swirling rapids of modern life. The outcome of their journey over the last century was perilous at every turn. This book introduces the basic features of Amish culture and charts their intriguing voyage in the context of the larger society in recent years.

Second, Amish culture is easily misunderstood. Despite inordinate publicity, misunderstandings of Amish life abound. We applaud them for caring for their elderly but are bewildered by their rejection of telephones in their homes. We will discover that many of their perplexing puzzles are reasonable solutions to the problems faced by a traditional group in the throes of social change. Putting the puzzles together will also help us solve the larger riddle of how they manage to thrive in a postmodern age.

Third, the Amish story clarifies the contemporary story—our story—in a new way. Venturing across the fence that separates the two cultures allows us to glance back and see our own society from a different angle. In the same way that learning a foreign language teaches us the grammar of our native tongue, so an excursion into Amish society informs us about our own culture. In short, exploring the Amish story enables us to understand our own story better.

And indeed, we have much to learn from the Amish and the wisdom in their reservoir of experience. They remind us that there are other ways to organize social life. They have coped with progress in radically different ways than has the broader society. And in the process, they have distilled some insights that can enlighten those of us swimming in the mainstream of contemporary culture.

This book is a comprehensive revision and updating of the first edition, published in 1989. The Amish community has changed in many ways over the fifteen years since the fieldwork was done for the first edition. I have gathered new information on nearly nine hundred people and have updated all the demographic and historical data. The text has been lightly reorganized and carefully rewritten, line for line, word by word. Chapter 6 is a new chapter that explores the ways in which Amish society creates social capital to address individual needs and the broader welfare of their community. The research methods and data sources for the investigation are described in Appendix A.

Although this book provides an introduction to Amish culture, it is not a comprehensive study of Amish life. I have focused on those aspects of Amish society that are particularly relevant to solving the riddle of their growth and success. Topics such as courtship, weddings, funerals, foods, crafts, health, and medicine are treated lightly or not at all. Sources in the Select References will aid those who want to pursue such topics in depth.

Finally, a word on writing style. As much as possible, I have dispensed with technical sociological jargon. In some instances, I have used German words that are basic to understanding Amish culture and I discuss some theoretical and technical issues in the Notes. Because they speak a German dialect, the Amish typically refer to non-Amish people as *English*. However, for stylistic consistency and clarity, I have used the terms *outsiders, non-Amish,* and *Moderns* to refer to those of us living on the contemporary side of the cultural gap.

The term *Modern* begs for clarification. In many ways the larger society is moving toward what many observers are calling a postmodern era. However, the exact distinction between modern and postmodern social organization is still emerging because these changes reflect long-term shifts in values and patterns of social life. Despite the movement toward a postmodern era, the Amish struggle has focused on issues prompted by modernity—individualism, formal education, industrialization, and mass media. Thus, I use the word *Moderns* as a broad label to refer to non-Amish people who have been shaped by contemporary culture. I also use the term *modern* to refer to contemporary forms of culture and social organization in American society.

Modernity, of course, means 'the state of being modern.' I use the term *modernity* in two ways throughout the text: to describe the historic changes produced by the Age of Enlightenment, and as a descriptor of contemporary society. I use these slippery terms, not in opposition to postmodern, but as a convenient label for contemporary culture and society, and I trust that their meaning will be clear in the context of their use.

ACKNOWLEDGMENTS

First and most importantly, I am deeply indebted to dozens of Amish people whose kind and generous sharing of their time and ideas have made this book possible. I have honored their requests to remain anonymous throughout the text. Moreover, I am grateful to numerous public officials and professional people who work closely with the Amish and who graciously granted interviews that have enriched the scope, accuracy, and depth of the story. A senior research fellowship from the National Endowment for the Humanities provided financial support for the archival research and fieldwork for the first edition.

The following people provided valuable counsel in the preparation of the first edition and their influence lingers in this edition as well: Carl F. Bowman, Ivan Glick, John A. Hostetler, James W. Hostetter, Gertrude Enders Huntington, David Luthy, Stephen Scott, David J. Rempel Smucker, Mervin Smucker, and Diane Zimmerman Umble. Staff of the following institutions kindly assisted me in many ways: The Heritage Historical Library, the High Library of Elizabethtown College, The Lancaster Mennonite Historical Society, the Murray Library of Messiah College, and the Pequea Bruderschaft Library.

I am especially thankful for the expertise of the following persons whose collaboration undergirds the project in many ways: Noah G. Good translated many of the original source materials from German; Linda Eberly created all of the graphic art throughout the book; and Charles Beyl sketched the cartoon in Chapter 9. I was fortunate to have the superb assistance of Louise Stoltzfus, who worked closely with me as a research associate in the preparation of the second edition. She coordinated the data-gathering effort on nearly nine hundred people in ten church districts. Moreover, she conducted numerous interviews and assisted me in the analysis and interpretation of the story in an always-gracious manner. Ed Klimuska has provided a steady source of suggestions, support, and encouragement over the years. My colleague Richard Stevick generously shared his knowledge of Amish youth and critiqued Chapter 6. Professor Steven M. Nolt collaborated with me in our study of Amish businesses, which has informed this revised edition. His scholarship and knowledge of Amish history have enhanced the interpretation and accuracy of my work. Nolt, as well as Michele Kozimor-King, Torveig Karina Strai, and Theron F. Schlabach, offered critical comments on the first edition that have significantly improved this revision.

Krista Malick, with a cheerful spirit, performed many of the tedious tasks of data analysis, historical documentation, and clerical assistance. My assistant, Michele Gómez, provided excellent clerical support for the endless revisions, as well as helpful administrative aid. Mark Lacher read the revised manuscript and offered valuable suggestions for improving it. And my long-time friend Dennis Hughes spent endless hours searching for photographs to illustrate particular sections of the story. I also thank Messiah College for providing space and time to complete the project. As always it has been a pleasure to work with my editors, George F. Thompson and Randy Jones, at the Center for American Places. They have been a continuing source of wise counsel and support. I have been fortunate to be blessed with many wonderful and gracious colleagues whose efforts and thoughtful advice have helped to improve the book in so many ways.

The Riddle of Amish Culture

The Amish Story

We wish especially that our descendants will not forget our suffering.
—Anabaptist writer, 1645

SOCIAL RIDDLES

The tale of modern life is mixed. From laser surgery to genetic engineering, science has produced astonishing advances. But modernization is also a story of traditional cultures eroding beneath the swift currents of change. The Old Order Amish have demonstrated an amazing resilience to such cultural devastation. Their distinctive dress and horse-drawn buggies set them apart as a people who have dared to snub the tide of progress. How have they managed to tame the powerful forces of history?

Idyllic from afar, Amish culture is teeming with riddles upon closer inspection. Outsiders are often baffled by the logic, or apparent absence of it, in Amish culture. Many Amish practices seem to defy common sense. Contradictions and inconsistencies abound, bewildering admirers and skeptics alike. Even some of their neighbors, understandably, call them hypocrites for using the services of doctors and lawyers while forbidding their own children to pursue such vocations. Banning telephones from their homes but permitting them in an outdoor booth mocks common sense. By what rationale do the Amish permit electronic calculators but prohibit computers? And by what mystery does God smile on the use of electricity from batteries but not from public utility lines? What system of logic makes it plausible to pull modern machinery with horses? And why would owning a car lead one to hell, whereas it is perfectly permissible to ride in one? These riddles of Amish life appear silly and downright ridiculous to many Moderns.

The puzzles of Amish culture are baffling not only to outsiders but sometimes to the Amish as well. When asked why bicycles are off limits, a young Amish farmer said: "I really can't give you an answer to that." But before we criticize the Amish for not solving their own riddles, we should remember that Moderns would likely give the same answer when asked why men wear ties and women wear skirts.

Before the arrival of cars, tractors, and electronic technology, the Amish blended more smoothly into the surrounding society than they do today. They were, of course, different even then, with hook-and-eye fasteners on their coats, wide-brimmed hats, distinctive dress, and austere buggies. Many of their riddles, however, emerged in the twentieth century as they coped with the growing forces of industrialization. Is there a system of logic beneath this cultural hodgepodge—a hidden web of meaning that explains the confusing conundrums?

The big riddle, however, eclipses all the smaller ones: How is it that a tradition-laden people who spurn electricity, computers, automobiles, and higher education are not merely surviving but are, in fact, thriving in the midst of modern life? By all expectations such a group should be fading in the face of a hi-tech, consumer society, but the Amish are booming. Why? That is the basic question addressed by this book.

POSSIBLE CLUES

There are some clues that may help us solve the mysteries of Amish culture. First, many of the apparent inconsistencies become intelligible when viewed in historical perspective. Amish practices did not suddenly drop out of the sky. Like the behavioral codes of other societies, Amish norms were socially constructed over time as the group grappled with material changes in its social environment. Viewed in the light of their history, many of the perplexing practices begin to make sense. If tractors had been used before cars, for example, it is possible that the Amish would be plowing their fields with tractors today. But the car came first, and its arrival shaped the Amish reaction to tractors.

Second, although the Amish advocate separation from the world, they do not live in a social vacuum. Members of other Plain churches live among the

Amish in Lancaster County. Some of these churches branched off from the Amish. Many of the groups within the larger Plain community draw symbolic lines to distinguish themselves from one another. Some distinctive Amish practices emerged from the historical interplay between the Amish and their Plain-dressed cousins.

Third, some of the puzzles play important social functions in Amish life. The prohibition on photography, inexplicable to Moderns, helps to bridle individualism and build community solidarity. Refusing to use electricity from public utility lines eliminates access to mass media and helps to preserve traditional values. What appear as odd practices to outsiders often make sense within the purview and purposes of Amish society.

Fourth, other apparent quirks in Amish practice are actually bargains that the Amish have struck with the larger culture. The common impression that the Amish never change is false. They have stubbornly resisted some aspects of modernization, but in many ways they are quite up-to-date. Squeezed by the pressures of progress, they have been forced to strike some deals in order to survive. Although their cultural compromises may appear odd, they are often ingenious arrangements that enable the Amish to retain their distinctive identity and also thrive economically. These negotiated cultural compromises allow them to have their cake and eat it too, so to speak—to protect their traditions while using the benefits of modern technology.

Our journey into Amish life will not solve all of the riddles. But as we go backstage to begin to unravel them, we will discover that the logic of Amish culture makes more sense behind the curtain than it does in front of it. Cultural practices that stupefy outside observers become sensible and reasonable when seen in the dim light of Amish history. From behind the curtain, many of the puzzles appear to be ingenious solutions to the practical dilemmas faced by a group struggling to retain its traditional values amidst a rapidly changing world.

THE ANABAPTIST LEGACY

The Amish trace their religious heritage to the Swiss Anabaptists of sixteenth-century Europe, who emerged in the wake of the Protestant Reformation. Disgruntled with the practices of the Catholic Church, Martin Luther led a protest in 1517. His revolt inaugurated the Protestant Reformation, making Protestantism a permanent branch of Christendom. A few years later in

Zurich, Switzerland, students of the Protestant pastor Ulrich Zwingli became impatient with the pace of the Protestant Reformation. They argued that Christian practices should be based solely on Scripture, not on church tradition and civic custom. They called for a sharper break from Catholic traditions and a separation of church and civil government. After several heated consultations with the Zurich city council, the dissidents illegally rebaptized one another in a secret meeting on 21 January 1525. This simple service of baptism initiated a new movement, sometimes called the Radical Reformation, that became another branch of the Protestant Reformation.

The young renegades believed that baptism should only be conferred on adults who were willing to live a life of radical obedience to the teachings of Jesus Christ. Adult baptism became the public symbol of the Radical Reformation, but the implicit issue was one of authority. Did government officials have the right to interpret and prescribe a Christian practice such as infant baptism, or was the Bible the sole and final authority for the Christian church? The answer was clear for the rebaptizers. For them, Scripture was the ultimate authority. They felt compelled to obey the teachings of Christ even when such obedience placed their lives at risk.[1]

The young reformers were nicknamed Anabaptists, meaning "rebaptizers," because they had already been baptized as infants in the Catholic Church. Their refusal to baptize infants, to swear oaths of allegiance, and to use the sword in armed conflict incensed civil authorities. The Anabaptists were a political threat because they challenged the historic marriage between the church and civil government. They shook the pillars of civil authority because infant baptism conferred citizenship, which helped determine taxation and conscript soldiers for war. Civil authorities as well as Protestant and Catholic leaders were not about to be mocked by a small group of young radicals.

Within five months of the first rebaptism, an Anabaptist was killed for sedition, and the heretics began to flee for their lives. Meetings were often held at night in caves. The Anabaptist movement soon spread northward into Germany and eventually into the Netherlands. Thousands of Anabaptists were executed by civil and religious authorities over the next two centuries. Civil authorities commissioned special hunters to torture, brand, burn, drown, imprison, dismember, and harass the religious rebels. Describing the persecution between 1635 and 1645, an eyewitness wrote: "It is awful to read and speak about it, how they treated pregnant mothers, women nursing infants, the old, the young, husbands, wives, virgins, and children, and how they took their homes and houses, farms and goods. Yes, and much more, how they made widows and orphans, and without mercy drove them from their homes and scattered them among strangers . . . with some the father died in jail for lack of food and drink."[2]

In Switzerland the killing subsided by 1614. Nevertheless, other forms of persecution continued intermittently until the early eighteenth century. As the persecution waxed and waned, Anabaptists found refuge in Moravia, Alsace, the Palatinate, the Netherlands, and eventually in Russia and North America.[3] Even today, stories of the harsh persecution remain alive among the Amish. The *Martyrs Mirror,* a book of 1,100 pages found in many Amish homes, chronicles the bloody carnage. Stories of the persecution also appeared in the back of the Amish hymn book, the *Ausbund.*

The severe persecution had a profound impact on the theological views of the early Swiss Anabaptists. Some of their common convictions were artic-

A drawing from the second Dutch edition of the *Martyrs Mirror* (1685) depicting an Anabaptist martyr, Jan Bosch, burning at the stake in Maastricht, 1559.

ulated in a statement written in 1527.[4] This confession of faith emphasizes, among other issues, the authority of the New Testament as a guide for everyday life, and it highlights the following religious beliefs:

> Adult, or "believers," baptism
> The church as a covenant community
> Exclusion of errant members from communion
> Literal obedience to the teachings of Christ
> Refusal to swear oaths
> Rejection of violence
> Social separation from the evil world

One scholar has argued that the core of the Anabaptist vision contained three distinctive features: a radical obedience to the teachings and example of Christ that transforms the behavior of individual believers, a new concept of the church as a voluntary body of believers accountable to one another and separate from the larger world, and an ethic of love that rejects violence in all spheres of human life.[5]

In any event, the bloody persecution etched a sharp distinction between the church and the larger world in the Anabaptist mind. Propelled by persecution and missionary zeal, the Anabaptist movement spread into northern Europe. In the Netherlands, Menno Simons became an influential proponent of Anabaptism. Ordained as a Catholic priest in 1524, Menno Simons soon found himself caught between the authority of the Catholic Church and the new interpretations of Scripture taught by the Anabaptists. By 1531 he opted for the Anabaptist view of Scripture, and he left the Catholic Church in 1536. Menno Simons soon became a powerful leader, writer, and preacher for the Anabaptist cause.[6] He was so influential that many Anabaptists were eventually called Mennists or Mennonites.[7]

The relentless persecution drove many Anabaptists to remote mountainous areas, where they could more easily elude their tormentors.[8] As the persecution dwindled, many Anabaptists turned to farming, and over the generations their religious fervor mellowed as congregational life developed into routine patterns. Renewed persecution near Bern, Switzerland, in the 1660s spurred some Anabaptists to head northward to more tolerant areas along the Rhine River. By the late 1600s clusters of Swiss Anabaptists had emigrated from Switzerland to the Alsace region of present-day France, which lies between the Rhine River and the Vosges Mountains. In the early 1690s a controversy erupted among some of the Alsatian immigrants as well as among various factions back in Switzerland. The quarrel came to a head in 1693 and gave birth to the Amish church.

AMISH BIRTH PANGS

The Amish take their name from Jakob Ammann, a Swiss Anabaptist leader who moved to the Alsace region to escape persecution. Banned from Switzerland by civil authorities, Ammann was considered a "roving arch-Anabaptist." He was a recent convert who, according to civil authorities, had become "infected" by the Anabaptist sect.[9] In the 1690s, Ammann called for change and renewal in church life. He proposed holding communion twice a year rather than annually, according to the Swiss Anabaptist pattern. Following the lead of Anabaptists in Holland, he argued that footwashing should be literally observed in the communion service in obedience to Christ's command. Other issues—the excommunication of liars, the role of church discipline, the salvation of Anabaptist sympathizers—also hovered over the dispute.

The decisive issue that polarized the debate, however, was the shunning of excommunicated members. Following the teaching of Menno Simons, Ammann taught that expelled members should not only be banned from holy communion but also shunned in daily life. Some of the more lenient Swiss

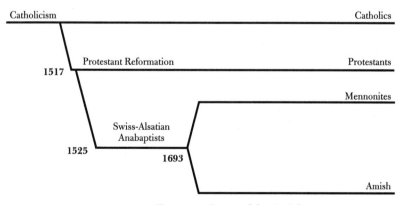

FIGURE 1.1 European Roots of the Amish

Anabaptists excluded wayward members from communion but did not ostracize them socially. Cultural and regional factors as well as personality conflicts amplified the theological differences. However, differences over the shunning of excommunicated members drove the final wedge between various clusters of Swiss and Alsatian Anabaptists in 1693.[10]

The charges and countercharges between Jakob Ammann and the senior Swiss bishop, Hans Reist, became rather harsh. Ammann's boldness was matched by Reist's stubbornness. Ammann's recent conversion to Anabaptism may have encouraged his boldness and zeal for the church. Several Swiss leaders resisted his attempt to reform the church and increase its purity, and to their surprise Ammann excommunicated them. Numerous ministers in various locations supported Ammann's leadership and formed what eventually became the Amish church. Several years later the Amish group apologized for excommunicating the elders, but by then it was too late to heal the wound. A series of conciliatory meetings continued until 1711 but failed to repair the breach. Many of Ammann's proposed reforms reflected early Swiss Anabaptist teaching as well as practices advocated by Menno Simons in Holland. Thus, the formation of the Amish movement was, in many ways, an effort of church renewal.[11]

The emergence of the Amish created a permanent division among Swiss and Alsatian Anabaptists. Shunning was the pivotal issue in this family quarrel, but Ammann also taught against trimming beards, rebuked those with fashionable dress, and administered a strict discipline in his congregations. Although dress styles were not the catalyst for the schism, they gradually became distinctive among the Amish, possibly because Ammann was a tailor. The Amish were sometimes called "hook-and-eyers" because they considered buttons too ostentatious, and some Mennonites were nicknamed "button people." Ammann left no books and only a few letters for his followers. For theological guidance, the Amish to this day rely primarily on Anabaptist literature written before Ammann's time.

The followers of Ammann gradually became known as Amish, while many other Anabaptists were called Mennonites. Thus, Swiss Anabaptism, originating in Zurich in 1525, had two branches after 1693: Amish and Mennonite. Nourished by a common heritage, Amish and Mennonite life has flowed in separate streams since the division.[12]

THE *CHARMING NANCY*

Social upheaval, political turmoil, and intermittent persecution prompted the Amish and Mennonites to leave their homelands in the Alsace and Palatinate and emigrate to the New World. A few Mennonites had already established a settlement near Philadelphia in 1683, ten years before the Amish-Mennonite division. In 1710 Mennonite settlers purchased some 10,000 acres bordering the Pequea Creek, several miles south of the present-day city of Lancaster, Pennsylvania. Between 1717 and 1732, several contingents of Swiss–South German Mennonites followed the early pioneers and settled in the Lancaster area.

It is possible that some early Amish immigrants accompanied these Mennonite settlers, but the first Amish may not have arrived until the 1730s. In any event, about five hundred Amish came to the New World in the 1700s.[13] The *Charming Nancy,* the first ship to carry a large group of Amish, docked in Philadelphia in 1737 after an eighty-three-day voyage. Some twenty-seven years after the first Mennonites arrived in the Lancaster area, the Amish established two settlements. One of these, known as Old Conestoga, or West Conestoga, formed a few miles northeast of the present-day city of Lancaster. However, most of the *Charming Nancy*'s passengers made their home in the Northkill colony in southern Berks County, thirty miles northeast of Lancaster. An Amish historian concludes: "These two settlements can rightly be called the mother colonies of our present districts in Lancaster County."[14]

The early settlements were fledgling communities, loosely organized around family lines. They were vulnerable to Indian attacks, drought, and crop failures. An Indian raid, evangelization by the Dunkards, and other factors eventually dismantled the Northkill settlement.[15] The Old Conestoga colony near Lancaster also dwindled for unknown reasons, and the survivors of the two settlements scattered to more friendly places, where they joined new Amish immigrants.

Several new congregations took root in Lancaster after the Revolutionary War, but they remained rather small until the end of the nineteenth century. The Conestoga Congregation began in about 1760, and the Pequea Congregation formed in about 1790. The Lancaster Amish community consisted of these two congregations, with probably no more than 150 adult members, until 1843, when a third congregation emerged. A fourth group blossomed in 1852, and by 1880 there were six congregational clusters in the Lancaster region. Although the Mennonites had settled the best land in Lancaster County before the Amish arrived, the Amish had the last word as they steadily bought more and more fertile farmland in the last half of the twentieth century.

THE LANCASTER SETTLEMENT

Over the years, Lancaster County has provided a pleasant habitat for the Amish, who helped to forge its distinguished reputation. Known locally as the Garden Spot of the World, the county tops the nation in agricultural production among nonirrigated counties. Fertile soils, a moderate climate, ample rainfall, and the hard toil of farmers have transformed the 946-square-mile area into an agricultural paradise. With some four thousand farms and 65 percent of its acreage in farmland, the county leads all nonirrigated counties across the nation in the total value of its agricultural products and other key indicators.

Situated 65 miles west of Philadelphia and 135 miles north of Washington, D.C., Lancaster rests on the western edge of the sprawling eastern megalopolis stretching from Norfolk, Virginia, to Boston, Massachusetts. Lancaster City is surrounded by a quiltwork of farms, small towns, and suburban developments. The county is one of the fastest growing of Pennsylvania's thirteen metropolitan areas. Its population of 470,000 will likely top 500,000 by 2010. Agriculture continues to thrive in spite of urbanization. Conservation, farmland preservation, manure pollution, traffic congestion, tourism, and intense development pressures dominate the county's public agenda.

Despite its robust agriculture, not all Lancastrians are Amish or farmers. Today less than 2 percent of the county workforce is farming, but agroindustry creates about 20 percent of all county jobs.[16] Nearly eleven hundred businesses dot the Garden Spot, twenty of which have more than five hundred employees. Twelve major shopping centers and 2,300 retail outlets serve the county. Each year, Lancaster Countians host some 4 million tourists, who spend over $1.2 billion. Tourism involves over 1,800 facilities and creates more than 8,600 jobs for local people, including some Amish. In fact, there are six tour industry employees for every farmer in Lancaster County.

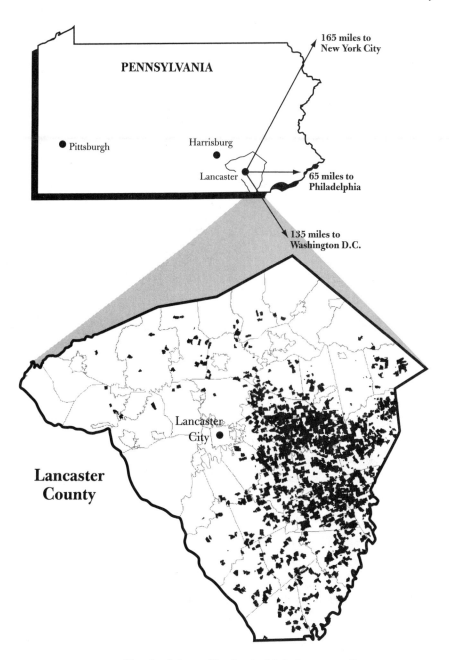

FIGURE 1.2 Farmland Owned by the Amish in Lancaster County.
Source: Lancaster County Geographic Information Systems

Lancaster's Amish have easy access to large department stores and shopping malls.

This commercialized Garden Spot is the home of Lancaster's Old Order Amish community, the oldest Amish settlement in North America, with some 22,000 children and adults.[17] More than 90 percent of Lancaster's Amish are affiliated with the Old Order Amish. Several more progressive Amish-related groups number about a thousand members. These groups splintered off over the years, leaving the Old Order Amish as the sole guardians of traditional Amish culture.[18]

Their distinctive garb and use of horses distinguish the Amish from their modern neighbors. Unlike their Anabaptist cousins, the communitarian Hutterites, the Amish own private property.[19] Despite private ownership, a strong tradition of mutual aid and communalism permeates the Amish community. Barn raisings, "frolics," and other forms of assistance are routine expressions of community life. Although they borrow money from banks, the Amish hesitate to accept government subsidies in the form of farm supports, Social Security, and Medicare.

Many small industries and businesses have sprung up alongside farming within the Amish community. Indeed, more than half of the adult men are employed in some type of trade or business. For others, farming remains their primary occupation. Dairying, the chief type of farming, is often supplemented by tobacco, poultry, and produce farming. Married Amish women typically work at home, but increasingly many are involved in craft shops and other businesses. Some single women work in restaurants and as domestics in motels and private non-Amish homes. Others serve as teachers, clerical workers, and clerks in retail stores and produce markets.

Extended families spanning two or three generations often live in adjoining houses on a farmstead. Other Amish own single dwellings along country roads or in small towns. Children are usually born at home, and grandparents typically retire on the farm. Amish youth walk to one-room schools, where Amish teachers stress practical skills and teach English as well as German. The primary language of the Amish is a dialect known as Pennsylvania German, which the Amish call *Deitsch*. The English they learn in school enables them to communicate fluently with their English-speaking neighbors. Amish social life revolves around family, home, and church. Membership in "worldly" organizations such as service clubs, professional organizations, and political parties is prohibited.

Amish society is organized around three basic social units: *settlement, district,* and *affiliation*.[20] A *settlement* encompasses the Amish families living in a common geographical area and may range in size from a dozen families to several thousand, such as the settlement in Lancaster County. Amish and non-Amish homes are interspersed throughout the settlement. The density of the Amish population increases toward the settlement's center, where they own most of the farms. In some townships the Amish own 90 percent or more of the farmland. However, even in the hub of their settlement, they are outnumbered by non-Amish, who live beside them in small villages and along country roads.

The congregation, or church *district,* is the basic organizational unit above the family in Amish society. A church district typically includes some twenty-five to thirty-five families that live in the same immediate locale. Because church services are held in the home, houses need to be large enough to accommodate all the district's members. As the membership grows, districts divide. Four or five new districts are added each year in the Lancaster settlement. About fifteen of the settlement's 131 church districts spill over into Chester County to the east as well as two in York County to the west.

A family heads for a favorite sledding spot. An Amish homestead frames
the background.

A cluster of Amish congregations that are in spiritual fellowship is called
an *affiliation*. Congregations in an affiliation follow similar religious practices
and cooperate with each other. The 131 Old Order Amish congregations
in the Lancaster area constitute one affiliation. A smaller, more progressive
group of New Order Amish and the Beachy Amish are outside the Old Order
affiliation because of their different practices.[21] These organizational patterns
are typical across the nation as well.

Today in North America, some 1,300 Amish congregations are scattered
throughout twenty-four states and the Canadian province of Ontario, as
shown in Appendix C. The national Amish population totals nearly 180,000
adults and children.[22] Extinct in their European homeland, the Amish are
prospering in the United States. Of the 250 settlements across the nation,
some 70 percent were founded after 1960. Geographic settlements vary considerably in size. Many contain only one congregation, whereas the largest
settlement in Ohio has more than 150 congregations. Approximately 70 percent of the Amish live in three states: Indiana, Ohio, and Pennsylvania. Moreover, about half of Pennsylvania's Amish live in the Lancaster settlement.

PLAIN COUSINS

There are about thirty different Anabaptist-related groups in Lancaster County organized into some 370 congregations as shown in Table 1.1. The Old Order Amish represent about 20 percent of the adult Anabaptist membership in the county.[23] About a dozen of the county's religious groups are dubbed "Plain" because of their traditional dress and austere lifestyle. The Plain groups consist primarily of conservative Mennonites and Amish-related groups. The Plainer churches maintain strict standards of dress and behavior, whereas the more assimilated Mennonite and Brethren groups have largely blended into the surrounding culture in recent years. The mainstream Mennonites number about 16,000 members in several different church affiliations. The Old Order Mennonites, with more than six subdivisions, have about 6,000 members.

The colorful array of religious practices in Lancaster County perplexes outsiders and insiders alike. Although many of the groups have similar theological and cultural origins, they have split into factions with spirited fervor over the use of cars, tractors, televisions, Sunday schools, and shunning. Some Plain churches permit central heating in their homes, and others oppose it. Telephones and electricity, found in some conservative Mennonite homes, are condemned by other groups. One Old Order Mennonite group prefers black cars to avoid ostentatious display. A New Order Amish church

TABLE 1.1
Anabaptist-Related Churches in Lancaster County

	Affiliations	Congregations	Members[a]
Old Order Amish	1	131[b]	10,650
Other Amish Groups	3	9	1,033
Old Order Mennonites	6	34	6,057
Other Mennonite Groups	11	139	18,598
Old Order Brethren Groups	3	3	255
Other Brethren Groups[c]	6	57	13,314
TOTAL	30	373	49,907

SOURCE: Various denominational directories and informants.
[a] Includes adult baptized members, not unbaptized children, as of January 2000.
[b] Includes seventeen church districts (1,416 members) in Chester and York counties that are part of the Lancaster County settlement.
[c] Includes Church of the Brethren, Brethren in Christ, Grace Brethren, and United Zion Churches.

permits tractors in the field and on the road but forbids the use of cars. Each group specifies a dress and behavior code that helps to distinguish it from its Plain cousins living nearby. Meanwhile, mainstream Mennonites and Brethren dress in contemporary styles; own Internet companies; and work as surgeons, stockbrokers, and attorneys. Beneath the endless distinctions lies a fervent piety because these cultural expressions, in the eyes of believers, symbolize spiritual loyalty and obedience to the will of God.

A FLOURISHING PEOPLE

The floundering Amish congregations that gradually took root in Lancaster County after the Civil War flourished in the twentieth century. Ironically, they grew as the larger society left the farm and embraced the industrial revolution. Families in preindustrial societies are typically large, and the Amish are no exception. Their long agricultural tradition has nurtured sizeable families. When asked how many children they think are ideal for an Amish family, older women answer, "As many as come"; but young women on the average want about six children.[24] Although the Amish live in the midst of a spreading urban region, rife with temptations of all sorts, their dropout rate is surprisingly low. More than 90 percent of their children join the church as adults.[25]

The combination of a high birthrate and low attrition has produced vigorous growth as shown in Figure 1.3. Lancaster's settlement expanded from merely six church districts in 1878 to sixty-five by 1980. In the twenty-year period between 1980 and 2000, the number of districts more than doubled. By the end of the twentieth century, Lancaster's Amish population of 22,000, including children, was thirty times larger than at the beginning of the century.[26]

The combined pressures of their own high growth and the shrinking farmland have squeezed the Amish demographically. As a result, some families have moved to more remote sections of Lancaster County, to more rural counties in Pennsylvania, and to other states as well. The Lancaster settlement has spawned at least sixty new congregations in twenty-eight other settlements since 1940. A group of families migrated south to St. Mary's County, Maryland, in 1940. A year later a second outpost opened in Lebanon County, bordering the northern edge of Lancaster County. The migrations halted for two decades but began again in the 1960s when new settlements

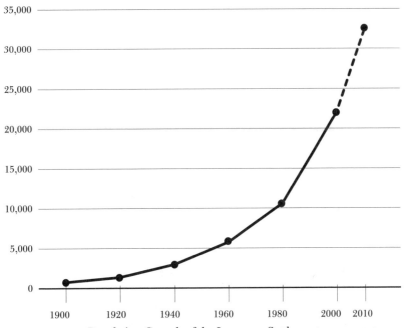

FIGURE 1.3 Population Growth of the Lancaster Settlement, 1900–2010. *Source:* Various directories of the Lancaster Settlement. *Note:* Includes children and adults. Children under 18 years of age constitute 52 percent of the population. The 2010 estimate is based on current trends.

were planted in a half dozen other Pennsylvania counties. In the 1990s settlements sprouted in Kentucky, Indiana, and Wisconsin.[27]

Today nearly 10,000 people in twenty-eight settlements trace their roots back to the parent community in Lancaster. A listing of all the settlements originating directly or indirectly from Lancaster appears in Appendix D. In addition, some Lancaster families occasionally join settlements of other affiliations in other states as well. The pattern of emigration from Lancaster is shown in Figure 1.4.

MODERN TRADITIONALISTS

The Amish are often portrayed as social antiques who have withdrawn from the modern world. This simplistic stereotype depicts them as a fossilized subculture—a relic of bygone days.[28] Folks who read by lantern light, ride in buggies, and shun high school in the twenty-first century are obviously not modern. Or are they? Walk into a booming Amish shop and you

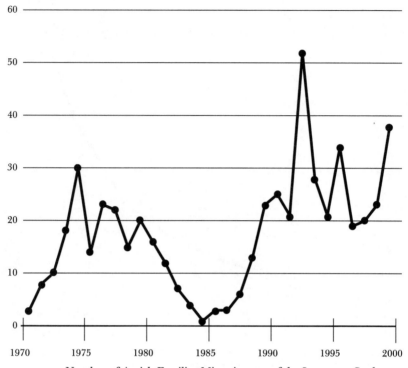

FIGURE 1.4 Number of Amish Families Migrating out of the Lancaster Settlement, 1970–2000. *Source: The Diary*

will see sophisticated manufacturing equipment powered by air and hydraulic pressure. Visit a dairy farm and you will witness an efficient operation using the latest feed supplements, vitamins, fertilizers, insecticides, artificial insemination, and state-of-the-art veterinarian practices. Wander through a new Amish home in Lancaster County and you will discover up-to-date bathroom facilities, a modern kitchen with lovely wood cabinets, and the latest gas refrigerator and stove. Despite our cherished stereotypes, the Amish are quite modern in many ways.

The Amish do indeed cling to social customs and religious rituals that hark back to the past. Without electricity, their homes have no blow-dryers, dishwashers, microwaves, toasters, doorbells, televisions, VCRs, or computers. But does the absence of these gadgets make them diehard traditionalists? Their unusual mixture of progress and tradition poses interesting questions about the meaning of modernization.[29] What strategies have the Amish used to cope with the pressures of modern life? Why have they accepted progress in some areas of their culture and resisted it in others? Are they happier than Moderns who indulge themselves in the latest technological fads?

Throughout the twentieth century, the Amish tenaciously sought to preserve their traditional way of life. They have obviously benefited from the products of industrialization, although remaining skeptical of the long-term impact of technology. The Amish are suspicious that beneath the glitter of modernity lurks a divisive force that in time might fragment and obliterate their close-knit community. The fear that modernization might pull their community apart is not an idle one. Indeed, some analysts argue that social separation has been a major consequence of industrialization.[30]

The technological age has brought the World Wide Web and high-speed travel, multiplying the number of possible ties individuals might have around the globe. But in other ways modernization is also a process of separation that pulls things apart and partitions whole systems—psychological, social, and organizational—into smaller parts in the name of efficiency. Many of the social bonds of modern life are abstract, rational, complex, and detached from a particular social context. The fragmentation of modern life is often experienced on the personal level as alienation when ties with meaning, work, and place evaporate. Modernization often segments social relationships and activities. Working in a factory instead of at home, going away to college, and moving to a retirement center break up family units and separate members. Living in one city, commuting to work in another, and vacationing in a third separates family, work, and play. This pervasive process of separation threatens to rupture the traditional ties of close-knit communities.

The process of modernization also pulls people and things out of their social context. In a small village everyone knows almost everything about everyone else. Modernity decontextualizes. A photograph pulls people out of context. In a telephone conversation, especially with a cell phone, it's impossible to know the social context of the other person. Television portrays floating images without context. Virtual reality on the World Wide Web literally has no context. On the Internet, lovers are unhitched from social reality. When things are taken out of context, we lose perspective, meaning, and clarity.

The hallmark of Amish society has been a close-knit, highly integrated community, where the threads of social life are woven into a single fabric that stretches from cradle to grave. To avoid the fragmentation of modernity, the

Children learn to work together at an early age. An Amishman developed
this machine which lays plastic on rows of vegetables to prevent weeds
and preserve moisture.

Amish have tried to separate themselves from the larger society. In order to
stay whole, to preserve their snug community, they have sought to separate
themselves from the Great Separator—modernity.

One reason to remain separate is to preserve their distinctive identity as
well as their *social capital*. Analogous to financial capital, social capital entails the social resources that can be mobilized for the well-being of the community. Social capital consists of the structures, traditions, networks, and
rituals that have been invested in the social bank, so to speak, and that can
be used to serve the entire community as well as individuals. In a similar
fashion, *cultural capital* consists of the knowledge—the values, beliefs, trust,
and obligations—within the reservoir of Amish life. These cultural resources
help to motivate and inspire individuals to act on behalf of their fellow members and community. Both social and cultural capital—networks and values—are valuable resources that the Amish have tried to preserve and use to
strengthen their community.

When a child is born in an Amish home, several adult women mysteri-
ously appear. A grandmother, sister, or aunt typically assists the new mother
for several days. They know the folklore and wisdom surrounding the care

of newborn babies. Within two or three days of a fire, the community erects a new barn. This gigantic task happens ritualistically, seemingly almost without effort. A young mother in need of babysitters can easily find safe care across the lane or fencerow. In these ways the values and structure of Amish society generate an abundant supply of cultural and social capital that serves the common good.[31]

In many ways the Amish emphasis on separation from the world enables them to preserve their cultural and social capital. Understanding the link between the fragmentation of modern life and the integration of Amish society unlocks many of their riddles; for only by being a separate people have they been able to remain together, and only by shunning modernity have they been able to survive. Many of the odd Amish riddles that perplex outsiders are in fact social devices that shield their society from fragmentation, protect their ethnic identity, and preserve their social capital.

Cultural minorities use a variety of strategies to protect their way of life. When things get too bad, groups may migrate in search of a more serene setting. From the early days of European persecution, the Amish have done exactly that when faced with harsh conditions. Despite a trickle of migrations over the years, most of Lancaster's Amish have chosen to resist and negotiate with modernity, rather than run from it. *Resistance* and *negotiation* are the two primary strategies that the Amish have used to protect their identity and preserve their community in the face of modernization. The traditional side of Amish life, maintained by resistance, tilts backward toward the past. But had they only resisted, they would surely be social antiques. By contrast, their willingness to negotiate with modern life reflects an openness to change and progress. How do they both resist and negotiate?

RESISTING MODERNITY

When athletic teams, armies, corporations, and ethnic minorities face adversaries, they use defensive tactics to resist being overwhelmed by their opponents. A group under cultural attack typically develops an exclusive set of beliefs—an ideology—to justify its existence and motivate its members. Finding ways to rally members behind collective goals is a pressing problem for threatened groups. The aspirations, whims, and rights of individual members must be sacrificed for the common good if a group is to survive. Personal aspirations must give way to collective ones if armies, sports teams, corporations, and marriages are to succeed. Defensive groups must find ways to suppress individualism or at least to persuade individuals to find personal fulfillment through collective goals. Groups on the defensive tend to emphasize obedience, surrender, sacrifice, commitment, and discipline in order to harness personal resources for the collective mission and purpose. To resist being swallowed up by their cultural opponents, minorities must develop social controls to keep members in line with group objectives and to preserve the cultural barricades that ward off outside influences.

Two cornerstones of Amish religious doctrine are *obedience* to the church's teachings and *separation* from the world. Only members who are obedient to the church and separate from the world will receive God's blessing of peace and eternal life. These cardinal beliefs funnel individual energy toward the shared goal of preserving a disciplined and distinctive community.

Groups such as the Amish that believe the surrounding culture threatens their survival will likely engage in at least five defensive tactics.[32]

1. *Decisive leadership.* Threatened groups often welcome decisive leadership because it speeds decision making and offers a sense of security. Clear lines of authority more easily marshal collective resources against a perceived threat. Diffused authority, on the other hand, cripples a group's ability to respond quickly to external threats.

2. *Comprehensive socialization.* Like other defensive groups, the Amish must find ways to pass their worldview on to their offspring as well as to newcomers. Indoctrination in the group's "story," through formal and informal schooling, must start early in life and be repeated again and again in order to build allegiance and loyalty.

3. *Controlled interaction with outsiders.* The fewer the opportunities to mingle with outsiders, the less likely that members will become contaminated with foreign values and leave the fold. When interaction with outsiders is necessary for economic survival, the time, place, and mode of interaction must be carefully regulated. A special dialect, private schools, taboos on public behavior, restrictions on marriage, and limited use of public media are some of the ways the Amish stifle interaction with outsiders. Such cultural fences make it more difficult for members to leave and join the larger society.

4. *Social sanctions.* A system of social rewards and punishments is necessary to bolster conformity to group standards. Leaders must establish the standards and administer the sanctions (both formal and informal) to keep members compliant with group norms.

5. *Symbolization of core values.* Cardinal values are symbolized by objects and rituals that call for group loyalty and accent ethnic identity. Uniforms, badges, flags, special jargon, rituals, and ceremonies help to strengthen the cohesive ties that bond members to the group and their common destiny.

The Amish have used these defensive tactics and others to preserve and safeguard their distinctive cultural heritage. Defensive ploys are not distinctive Amish practices; they are generic social strategies used to some extent by virtually all groups. The emergence of defensive tactics intensifies in direct relation to the amount of *perceived* hostility in a cultural environment. Thus, teams facing aggressive opponents, corporations battling stiff competition, and armies engaged in combat will likely fortify their defensive stance. The Amish have simply applied to community and religious life the standard techniques of social control that are routinely used by other groups for different objectives.

NEGOTIATING WITH MODERNITY

If the Amish were only waging a war against progress, they would likely be relics in a cultural museum. In addition to resistance, they have also been willing to negotiate. They have struck compromises that have led to many changes. On some issues—education, for example—they have stubbornly refused to concede to modern ways. But on many other fronts, Lancaster's Amish have been willing to change dramatically. Seeking a balance between strict isolation and wholesale accommodation to the larger society, they have struck compromises that blend aspects of both cultures. Concessions are traded back and forth in a social bargaining process until a compromise of sorts is reached. When the negotiable items are values, ideas, beliefs, and ways of thinking—cultural phenomena—we can call the process *cultural bargaining.* When patterns of social organization are on the negotiating table, the exchange involves *structural bargaining.* Over the years the bar-

Children wash the family carriage. They develop a distinctive ethnic identity
at a young age.

gaining sessions have created many of the perplexing puzzles of Amish society that appear silly to outsiders—using telephones but not in the house,
riding in cars but not owning them, and using rollerblades but not bicycles.

The negotiating metaphor implies a dynamic process of give-and-take
both within Amish society and *between* the Amish and the larger world. This
has indeed been the case, for sometimes the Amish have acquiesced to the
demands of modernity, whereas in other instances modern society has bent
the rules or made special ones for the Amish. This way of viewing their
struggle identifies the negotiable issues as well as the nonnegotiable ones that
form the lines of resistance. The concept of negotiation captures the dynamic
interaction between Amish society and the larger society and solves many of
the baffling puzzles, the cultural compromises that have been hammered out
at the bargaining table.[33] These cultural "settlements" have both safeguarded
Amish society and spawned the many intriguing riddles of Amish life.

THE ULTIMATE STRATEGY

What happens when resistance and negotiation fail? The Old Order
Amish experienced three internal divisions in Lancaster County after the

Civil War: in 1877, 1910, and 1966. In one sense, the three schisms represent a failure of Amish policies. The refusal of Amish leaders to bargain prompted progressive factions to leave the Amish family on all three occasions. The expulsion of detractors is the ultimate strategy for the preservation of Amish culture. By unloading the activists, the elders were able to slow the drift toward mainstream society.

The first of three divisions erupted in 1877. Following Amish divisions in the Midwest, two progressive factions withdrew from the main Lancaster body and formed independent congregations.[34] Within five years each group built a meetinghouse for its worship services. Sometime after this division, the traditional Amish became known as the Old Order, or House Amish, because they continued to worship in their homes. The splinter groups, labeled Amish-Mennonite, or "Meetinghouse Amish," held their worship services in church buildings and eventually became full-fledged Mennonites.

The second rupture occurred in 1910, as cars, telephones, and electricity were beginning to revolutionize the social landscape of rural America. Disturbed by a strict interpretation of shunning, a liberal faction formed an independent group eventually known as the Peachey church.[35] Although very similar to the Old Order Amish in dress and outlook, the group embraced Protestant religious practices such as Sunday school and tolerated technological innovations—telephones, electricity, tractors, and, eventually, cars. To-

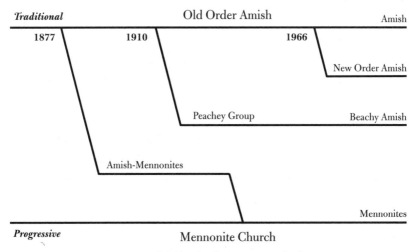

FIGURE 1.5 Divisions in the Lancaster Settlement

day this group is affiliated with the Beachy Amish Church and has six congregations in Lancaster County.

The third breach came in 1966 when a group of about one hundred progressive-minded families left the fold over differences related to the use of modern farm machinery.[36] This faction subsequently splintered into several Amish-related groups that vary in dress, in the use of cars, tractors, and electricity; and in other matters. The various pockets of progressive Amish groups in the Lancaster area have fewer than a thousand members.

The three divisions—1877, 1910, and 1966—are crucial benchmarks in Amish history. Memories of the schisms, alive in the minds of leaders, function as turning points in Amish oral history. The residual effects of these schisms touch the decision-making process in the Amish community even today. The three divisions released social steam in periods of rapid change as the church grappled with technological innovations. Interestingly, no divisions have led to more conservative Amish factions in Lancaster County.

In retrospect, the expulsion of dissidents served useful social functions over the years. The offshoots of 1877, 1910, and 1966 provide negative reference groups for the Old Order Amish—living demonstrations of the corrosive effects of worldliness. Through their ownership of cars and use of electricity, the progressive groups have displayed the folly of worldliness to several generations of Amish. By extracting the progressives, the Old Order Amish were able to tighten their grip on traditional practices—the ban on electricity, cars, and tractors—because they no longer had to placate the liberal agitators. Thus the divisions left the Old Order Amish as the sole guardians of tradition, a role they gladly assumed.

Safeguarding their religious traditions and rituals is a major concern of Old Order leaders because the larger culture poses a direct threat to their religious identity and community. Expressions of modernity—"worldliness," as the Amish would say—ranging from cars to television, are viewed as vices that, if not deflected, will eventually demolish their religious community. As social engineers of sorts, they have masterminded an effective program of cultural survival without the benefits of higher education, computerized technology, or the advice of professional consultants. How have they accomplished such a feat?

The Quiltwork of Amish Culture

I completely abandoned myself to the Lord.
—Anabaptist martyr, 1527

SACRED PATCHES

Amish women are noted for their lovely quilts.[1] They symbolize the complex patchwork of Amish culture—the beliefs, myths, and images that shape their world. Symbolic patches of soil, martyrdom, obedience, family, work, and community, stitched together by history, form a cultural quiltwork of Amish life. These patches of meaning, quilted into a single fabric, fill daily routines with significance. Religious threads hold the quiltwork together. Silent prayers before and after meals embroider each day with reverence. Daily behavior, from dressing to eating, is transformed into religious ritual with eternal significance. An Amish farmer's description of springtime events shows how the patches are woven together in his mind:

> Spring is coming to the Pequea when:
> horses start to lose their hair
> first silo is about empty
> milkman is glad it didn't snow much
> folks talking about high mule prices
> milk price is coming down
> alfalfa and rye fields greening up
> you should read John 14–15, Matt. 26–27 and
> practice pages 727, 481, 655, 284 in the *Ausbund,*

> you should help your wife move furniture and clean
>   ceilings
> grease the harness and plow the garden[2]

The Amish subscribe to basic Christian doctrines—the divinity of Christ, heaven and hell, the inspiration of Scripture, and the church as the body of Christ in the world today. Yet the practical expressions of Amish faith diverge from mainline Christian churches. Contemporary religious practice is often restricted to brief episodes of life—an hour on Sunday morning, a wedding, or a confirmation. Amish faith has not been separated from daily living; it penetrates their entire way of life. Amish beliefs, worship services, and religious rituals remain virtually untouched by modern influences. Basic Amish doctrines are found in the Dordrecht Confession of Faith, an Anabaptist statement written in 1632, some sixty years before the Amish emerged as a separate group.[3] Nevertheless, the Amish emphasize the practice of faith more than doctrinal details.

Although the Amish revise their practical definitions of worldliness in response to social change, their fundamental religious tenets have remained intact over the years. This chapter describes the religious values of Amish

Women enjoy the delights of community and artistic expression at a quilting bee.

culture—the patches of meaning stitched together in their quiltwork. These resources provide the cultural capital that undergirds the operation of Amish society.

YIELDING THE RIGHT WAY

The solution to the riddle of Amish culture is embedded in the German word *Gelassenheit* (Gay-la-sen-hite). Roughly translated, Gelassenheit means 'submitting, yielding to a higher authority.' Rarely used in speech, it is an abstract concept that carries a variety of specific meanings—self-surrender, resignation to God's will, yielding to God and to others, self-denial, contentment, a calm spirit. Various words in the Amish vocabulary capture the meaning of Gelassenheit: obedience, humility, self-denial, submission, thrift, and simplicity. In short, Gelassenheit is a master cultural disposition, deeply bred into the Amish soul, that governs perceptions, emotions, behavior, and architecture.[4]

In Pennsylvania German, the phrases *uffgewwe* (to give up) and *unnergewwe* (to give under) best capture the meaning of Gelassenheit. Members are asked to "give up" things and to "give themselves under" the authority of the church. One member said "to give yourself under the church means to yield, to submit." Baptismal candidates and contrite church members before a confession sit in a bent posture with hand over face, signifying their willingness to "give up" and to "give themselves under" the authority of the church. One member, writing to another one facing excommunication, said, "My heart just bleeds for you, all cause you cannot *give yourself up* to church rules and those set above you in the church by God" (emphasis added).

Gelassenheit stands in sharp contrast to the bold, aggressive individualism of modern culture. The meek spirit of Gelassenheit unfolds as individuals yield to higher authorities: the will of God, church, elders, parents, community, and tradition. Gelassenheit reveals that Amish culture is indeed a subculture whose core value collides with the heartbeat of modernity, individual achievement. Modern culture tends to produce individualists devoted to personal fulfillment. By contrast, the goal of Gelassenheit is a subdued, humble person who discovers fulfillment in the service of community. In return for giving themselves up for the sake of community, the Amish receive a durable and visible ethnic identity.

The meaning of Gelassenheit penetrates many dimensions of Amish life—

values, symbols, ritual, personality, and social organization. "The yielding and submitting," said one member, "is at the core of our faith and relationship with God." The faithful Christian yields to divine providence without trying to change or influence history. Gelassenheit is also a way of thinking about one's relationship to others. It means serving and respecting others and obeying the consensus of the community. It entails a modest way of acting, talking, dressing, and walking. Finally, it is a way of structuring social life so that even organizations remain small, compact, and simple. Like a social equation, Gelassenheit spells out the individual's subordinate relationship to the larger ethnic community. It regulates the tie between the individual and the community by transforming the energies of the individual into cultural capital. However, rather than pitting the individual against the community, the Amish tend to see the primary tension as being between two social systems: the church, which calls for obedience and self-denial; and the outside world, which exalts individual fame and achievement.[5]

The early Anabaptists used the term *Gelassenheit* to convey the idea of yielding fully to God's will with a dedicated heart—forsaking all selfishness.[6] They believed that Christ called them to abandon self-interest and follow his example of suffering, meekness, humility, and service. True Christians, according to the Anabaptists, should not take revenge on their enemies but should turn the other cheek in the face of hostility. They should pray for their persecutors and love their enemies, as commanded by Christ. Self-will obstructs obedience to God's will. Jesus' words, "Not my will but thine be done," became their script of faith. Hence, yielding to God's will was the test of true faithfulness.

Thousands of Anabaptist martyrs yielded to the sword as the ultimate test of their willingness to mortify self and submit to God's will. The blood of martyrs seared Gelassenheit into the sacred texts of Amish history. It is not surprising that such a bloody history would leave the indelible print of Gelassenheit on the quiltwork of Amish culture. What is surprising is that the imprint remains vivid, even centuries after the persecution.

Yielding to the right way—God's way—is the stance of Gelassenheit. Although the Amish rarely use the term in everyday speech, the principle of Gelassenheit orders their whole social system. All things being equal, the higher the cost of joining a group, the more attractive it becomes to its members. In other words, groups that demand very little will not be valued very

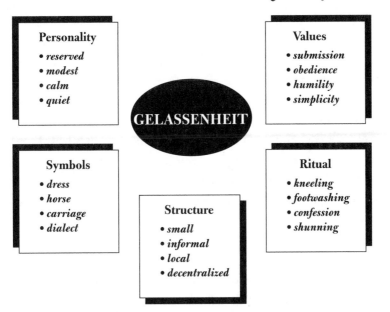

FIGURE 2.1 The Dimensions of Gelassenheit

highly by their members. Amish values of simplicity, humility, and austerity entail personal sacrifice. They provide the cultural capital to build commitment to community and mobilize social capital.

The nonresistant stance of Gelassenheit forbids the use of force in human relations. Thus the Amish avoid serving in the military, holding political offices, filing lawsuits, serving on juries, working as police officers, and engaging in ruthless competition. Legal and personal confrontation is avoided whenever possible. Silence and avoidance are often used to manage conflict. Indeed silence is an important mode of communication in Amish life.[7] A lowly spirit denies luxuries, worldly pleasures, and costly entertainment. Purging selfish desires means yielding to the Plain standards of Amish dress as well as to restrictions on transportation, technology, and home appliances. The submissive posture of Gelassenheit discourages higher education, abstract thinking, competition, professional occupations, and scientific pursuits.

An Amish petition to state legislators concerning a new school law depicts the lowly tone of Gelassenheit: "We your humble subjects . . . do not blame our men of authority for bringing all this over us. . . . We admit, we ourselves are the fault of it. We beg your pardon for bringing all this before you, and worrying you, and bringing you a serious problem."[8] The yielded person submits to the authority of God-ordained leaders, engages in mutual aid activities, respects the wisdom of tradition, and washes the feet of others in a sacred rite of humility.

Amish attempts to harness selfishness, pride, and power are not based on the premise that the material world or pleasure itself is evil. Smoking, for example, is a common practice among some men, though it is dwindling.[9] Sexual relations within marriage are enjoyed. Good food is savored. Recreation, humor, and play, in the proper time and place, are welcomed. Evil, the Amish believe, is found in human desires for self-exaltation, not in the material world itself.

THE PARADOX OF GELASSENHEIT

Talk of self-denial defies modern culture, which is saturated with endless dreams of self-fulfillment. Although Gelassenheit seems repressive to Moderns, it is a redemptive paradox for the Amish. They believe that the followers of Christ and the martyrs of old were called to lose their lives in order to save them. The death of Christ redeemed the world, and the sacrifice of the martyrs fertilized the growth of the true church. The Amish believe that people who deny self and submit to divine precepts bring honor and glory to God. Members who yield to their neighbors are ultimately revering God. The person who forgoes personal advancement for the sake of family and community makes a redemptive sacrifice that transforms the church into the body of Christ. Gelassenheit is a social process that recycles individual energy for community purposes, a recycling empowered by the words of Jesus, the blood of the martyrs, and the blessing of ancestors. This deep conviction to yield self-interest for the sake of the community provides a powerful resource of cultural capital.

Etched into Amish consciousness, Gelassenheit regulates the entire spectrum of life from body language to social organization, from personal speech to symbolism. The cultural grammar of Gelassenheit blends submission to God's will, personal meekness, and small-scale organizations together in Amish life. All of life embodies religious meaning as people place themselves on the altar of community, a sacrifice that brings homage to God. The Amish are urged to "patiently bear the cross of Christ without complaining."[10] Bearing the cross of Christ is not an abstraction, but in the words of one leader,

"We wear an untrimmed beard and ear-length hair because we are willing to bear the cross of Christ."[11] Dressing by church standards, raising a neighbor's barn, cooking for the family, pulling weeds in the garden, forgoing electrical appliances, plowing with horses, and using a carriage are ritual offerings of sacrifice and service to the community—the incarnation of God's will on earth.

THE YIELDED SELF

The size and prominence of mirrors in a society signal the cultural value attached to the self. Given concerns about pride and bloated selves, it is not surprising that the mirrors in Amish homes are typically smaller and fewer than those in non-Amish homes. While Moderns are preoccupied with "finding themselves," the Amish are engaged in "losing themselves."[12] Either way, it is hard work. Uncomfortable to Moderns, who cherish individuality, losing the self in Amish culture brings dignity because its ultimate redemption is the gift of community.

Children learn to "give up" and "give in" at an early age. Parents teach their children that self-will must be purged if they want to become children of God.[13] The large size of families teaches young children to wait their turn as they yield to siblings and prepares them for living a yielded life. Amish children are less likely to use first person singular pronouns—*I, me, mine, myself,* and *my*—than non-Amish children.[14] A personality test administered to children in several settlements found that Amish personality types differed significantly from non-Amish ones. The Amish personality exemplified Gelassenheit: "Quiet, friendly, responsible, and conscientious. Works devotedly to meet his obligations and serve his friends and school . . . patient with detail and routine. Loyal, considerate, concerned with how other people feel even when they are in the wrong."[15]

The Amish believe that the quickest way to spoil children is to let them have their own way. Parents and teachers are encouraged to "work together so that bad habits . . . disobedience, disrespect, etc. can be nipped in the bud so to speak."[16] For young children, a spanking may help to stop misbehavior. Children are taught to yield, to wait, to submit. An Amish leader noted: "By the time that the child reaches the age of three the mold has started to form and it is the parents' duty to form it in the way that the child should go. When the child is old enough to stiffen its back and throw back its head in temper it is old enough to gently start breaking that temper."[17] "Spanking," said one mother, "is what makes Amish children so nice." Visitors to Amish homes often remark about the nice and quiet children.

The Amish think the children of Moderns are often spoiled by being driven from club to club and lesson to lesson in hope that they will discover their true selves. In contrast, Amish children are washing dishes by hand, feeding cows, pulling weeds, and mowing lawns. They are learning to lose their selves, to yield to the larger purposes of family and community. JOY, a widely used school motto, reminds children that *Jesus* is first, *you* are last, and *o*thers are in between. The essence of Gelassenheit is tucked away in a favorite school verse:

> I must be a Christian child,
> Gentle, patient, meek, and mild;
> Must be honest, simple, true
> In my words and actions too.
> I must cheerfully obey,
> Giving up my will and way.[18]

It would be wrong to conclude that losing one's self in Amish society is demeaning or dehumanizing. Bending to the call of community does not smother individual expression. The Amish neither wallow in self-contempt nor champion weak personalities. Within limits, creative self-expression flourishes—from quilting patterns to stickers on lunch pails, from gardening to hobbies, from farming to crafts. As in other societies, Amish personality styles, preferences, and habits vary. The constraints of Amish culture would certainly suffocate the "free spirits" of the modern world. But Amish children, taught to respect the primacy of the community, usually feel less stifled by the constraints than Moderns who cherish individuality.

The grammar of Gelassenheit regulates interaction with others. How one smiles, laughs, shakes hands, removes one's hat, and drives one's horse signal Gelassenheit or its absence. A boisterous laugh and a quick retort betray a cocky spirit. An aggressive handshake and a curt greeting disclose an assertive self that does not befit Gelassenheit. Rather, a gentle chuckle, a hesitation, and a refined smile embody a yielded and submissive spirit. A slow and thoughtful answer, a deference to the other's idea, and a reluctance to interrupt a conversation are signs of Gelassenheit. In a small community, individu-

The contented smile of Gelassenheit.

als know one another well enough that there is no need to "sell" themselves. Thus, the yielded self does not flaunt itself in everyday life. An Amish bishop ended his letter to one of his members with these words: "Remember us in your prayers, for we are likewise minded in weakness. Only me."

The goal of Amish life is a tame, gentle, and domesticated self—one that yields to the community's larger goals. But even in Amish society there is room for manipulation. A clever person may learn subtle ways of presenting a "yielded" impression to others for personal gain. A yielded self is especially valued in church life and with elders and others in authority. Men who are assertive and boisterous with outsiders will suddenly become meek and mild in the presence of their bishop. Bold, untamed selves are more likely to flare up with outsiders in business deals, at play, around the barn, and especially among teenagers.

WAITING ON DIVINE PROVIDENCE

As a master disposition, Gelassenheit also regulates religious experience and practice. In the broader world, religious doctrines are often packaged in theological formulas designed to hold the faithful and convince nonbelievers of the truth. Some formulas imply that one can "find the answers," "be sure of salvation," and have "no doubts" about religious faith. In this view, eternal salvation can be achieved by believing and acting properly. This religious logic separates ends from means, for example, "I must be saved in order to achieve eternal life." Such a calculation assumes that one can decide, that one must decide, and that ultimately one controls one's own destiny.

It is precisely at this point that Amish faith bewilders those with evangelical religious persuasions. Amish faith is holistic. The Amish resist separating means and ends—salvation and eternal life. They are reluctant to say that they are sure of salvation. They focus on living faithfully while waiting on providence—trusting that things will turn out well. Announcing that one is certain of eternal salvation reveals a haughty attitude that mocks the spirit of Gelassenheit. The faithful, in the Amish view, are called to yield to God's eternal will and rest in hope that things will turn out for the best. After all, "not everyone who calls on the name of the Lord will be saved." Indeed it is God, the Amish believe, that makes these weighty decisions. Boldly declaring oneself "saved" is a pretentious self-assertion that borders on idolatry in Amish thinking, for only God can make such claims.

Amish ministers talk of "the hope of salvation" and of a "living hope." Salvation is linked to obedience and faithful practice rather than to belief and emotion. "Feeling and experience is bubble and froth," explained one bishop. Because salvation is tied to faithful living throughout a lifetime, the Amish hesitate to talk of assurance of salvation. In fact, to say that one is certain of eternal salvation is considered pride. "Humility," said a bishop, "never exalts itself. Humility never boasts about salvation. There are two ditches along every road, and it's easy to fall off."

The code words of the evangelical mind-set—personal salvation, personal evangelism, and personal devotions—accent the *individual* rather than the *community* as the center of redemptive activity. In refusing this vocabulary, the Amish bring a much more holistic, integrated view that does not separate the individual from community or faith from action. Evangelical and Amish vocabularies are analogous to two foreign languages describing the same sentiments of love. One is a communal language of patience, humility, community, and practice; the other is an individualistic language of beliefs, certainty, feelings, and experience. Whereas evangelical Christians want to know, control, plan, and act to guarantee their salvation, the Amish outlook is a more modest and perhaps a more honest one.

The Amish view the Bible as a trustworthy guide for living, but they do not quote it incessantly. Those who do so are accused of being "Scripture smart," for showing off their biblical knowledge. Personal interpretations of Scripture and small group Bible study are downplayed. Individual interpretation of the Scripture is considered dangerous. The Bible is considered trustworthy enough to speak for itself without interpretation. The Scripture is read aloud in church and in family settings where it is heard and interpreted in a communal context. Beyond their religious worldview, social control issues also come into play. Individual interpretations would quickly splinter uniform beliefs and, more importantly, the authority structure of the entire community.

Much is at stake here because this theological understanding undergirds the entire cultural system. A shift toward individual belief, subjective experience, and emotionalism would cultivate individualism and undermine the total package of traditional practices. By linking salvation to obedience and lifelong living, the Amish accent the importance of *practicing* the traditions of faith. Members are chastised if they attend Bible study groups or fellowship with "born again" Christians who boast of their personal faith and certainty of salvation. One member said it simply, "If you believe in assurance of salvation, you are not Old Order Amish. You are New Order." Ex-Amish are often quite critical of the Amish emphasis on practice. A former member who joined an evangelical charismatic fellowship said the Amish promote "works and a way of life that makes the Amish religion just that, a religion. In our church we don't need man-made rules, we just follow the Bible."

Some religious groups seek to transform or save the world by seeking converts and engaging in missionary programs. Indeed, groups can only grow in two ways: by making converts or having babies. Evangelism is foreign to the Amish. Rather than trying to save the world, they wait on divine providence. In tandem with this, they are surprisingly tolerant of other religious groups. Although firmly committed to their faith, they are reluctant to judge or condemn other people. They yield to the brotherhood, live faithfully in community, and trust that their offering of a yielded self will, in time, be acceptable to God.[19]

THE HABIT OF OBEDIENCE

Paired oppositions—obedience and disobedience, church and world, low and high, humility and pride, slow and fast, work and idleness—provide clues to the structure of meaning in Amish consciousness. Abundant throughout the culture, these code words permeate the training of children. Obedience tops the hierarchy of Amish values. Yielded individuals are obedient. Obedience to the will of God is the cardinal religious virtue. Disobedience is dangerous; it signals self-will and, if not confessed, leads to eternal separation from God. The confession for baptismal instruction predicts that the unbelieving, disobedient, and headstrong will receive eternal damnation.[20]

Obedience to church regulations signals an inner obedience to the will of God. Those who are willing to crush selfish desires will gladly comply with church standards. The belligerent and headstrong, who challenge the order of the church, lack spiritual submission. Various religious phrases and Bible verses are used to underscore the importance of obedience and submission throughout the life cycle.

The Amish emphasize the importance of rearing (*die Zucht*) a child properly. Childhood training ingrains obedience into daily routines making it a taken-for-granted habit. Learning obedience at an early age is a powerful means of social control. Children are taught from the Bible: "Obey your parents in the Lord for this is right."[21] "Spanking," said one young mother, "is a given. We start at about a year and a half, and the majority of it is done before they turn five."

An Amish booklet on child rearing speaks of the "habits of obedience." The Amish believe that parents should be "ready to punish disobedience," "insist on obedience," "allow no opposing replies," and realize that "if orders are disobeyed once and no proper punishment given, disobedience is likely to come again." Parents are expected to make children "understand that they

Children learn the virtues and habits of work at a young age.

must obey you."[22] Retorts and challenges from children, sometimes considered amusing forms of self-expression in mainstream culture, are not tolerated in Amish life. The child obeys the teacher in the Amish school, for "the teacher's word is the final authority and is to be obeyed."[23] Learning to yield at an early age is a crucial step in preparing for a life of obedience.

Adult members are expected to obey church rules and customs. A husband and a wife discuss many issues together, but in the end a wife is expected to obey her husband. Deacons and ministers are obedient servants of the bishop. Younger bishops defer to senior bishops. Obedience to divine and human authority regulates social relationships from the youngest child to the oldest bishop, who in turn is called to obey the Lord. To disobey at any level is tantamount to rebellion against God.

These rites of surrender are sacrifices for the larger goal of an orderly and unified community. While expectations for obedience are firm and final, loving concern permeates the social system. A father spanks his child out of love. The bishop expels and shuns a member in "hopes of winning him back." There are, of course, ruptures in the loving concern, but a tone of reverent obedience governs community life.

THE VIRTUE OF HUMILITY

Humility and pride frame Amish consciousness. Humility is rooted in biblical teachings. *Pride,* a religious term for the sinister face of individualism, has its own share of biblical condemnation. An Amish devotional guide says: "Read much in God's Word and you will find many warnings against pride. No other sin was punished more severely. Pride changed angels to devils. A once powerful king, Nebuchadnezzar, was transformed into a brute beast to eat grass like an ox. And Jezebel, a dominant queen, was eaten of dogs as the result of her pride."[24]

The Amish make a sharp distinction between *Hochmut* (high-mindedness) and *Demut* (humility). High-mindedness is pride. On a cultural ladder, the Amish equate high-mindedness with arrogance and worldliness. Lowliness reflects humility and weakness—the true spirit of Gelassenheit. Consequently, the Amish speak of "high" individuals and "high" church districts, meaning those that are more worldly and more assimilated into the larger culture. By contrast, low families are the Plainer ones that "hold back" to the traditions of the past. The high and low distinctions are important symbolic boundaries in Amish culture.

A cancerous threat to group commitment, pride elevates individuals above community. Proud individuals display a spirit of arrogance, not of Gelassenheit. The Amish view the proud person as "showing off," "making a name for himself," "taking care of herself," and in all of these ways hoisting him- or herself above others. Proud people "call attention to themselves"; they are "pushy," "bold," "forward," and "always jumping the fence." A persistent threat to the common good, pride must be rooted out promptly by church leaders, for if left to sprout and grow, it will spread and debilitate the community. "It was pride," said one minister, "that brought down the world the first time at the Flood." The Amish cite numerous scriptures that condemn pride—the exaltation of self.

> A high look and a proud heart is sin. (Prov. 21:4);
> God hates a proud look. (Prov. 6:17);
> A proud heart is an abomination to the Lord. (Prov. 16:5);
> God resisteth the proud. (Jas. 4:6)

Pride has many faces. The well-known Amish taboo against personal photographs is legitimated by a biblical command: "You shall not make for yourself a graven image or a likeness of anything" (Ex. 20:4). In the latter part of the nineteenth century, as photography was becoming popular, the Amish applied the biblical injunction against "likenesses" to photographs. Their aversion to photographs of individuals was a way of suppressing pride. If people pose for a photograph, they want to exalt themselves and are taking themselves too seriously. They might "think they are somebody." Such people are obviously "out to make a name for themselves." With religious sanction, this taboo suppresses individualism and cultivates Gelassenheit.[25]

The Amish also believe that public recognition of personal achievement erodes humility. Moderns committed to self-advancement eagerly take credit for anything that will enhance their résumés. The legal apparatus of copyrights, credits, permissions, and acknowledgments is designed to assure that individuals receive proper recognition for their efforts. Just as Moderns work hard at earning credit, the Amish work hard at disavowing it. Amish people who yield properly are careful not to make a name for themselves, for that would lead to pride. If recognition comes, it must be modestly shared with others.

Amish writers often write anonymously to avoid attracting attention (pride) to themselves. An Amishman who started using his name at the end of published articles said: "I got my wings clipped and so I just stopped using my name." An Amishman who published an essay under his name in a local newspaper was disciplined by the church with a six-week probation. Another member, who posed for a photograph to accompany a newspaper story about his use of computers, had clearly overstepped several taboos at once. Scrambling for cover, he took the unprecedented action of sending a letter of apology to a public newspaper. The Amish believe that proud individuals tack their names on everything, draw attention to themselves, and take personal credit for everything. The humble individual, by contrast, freely gives time and effort to strengthen the community and, in the spirit of Gelassenheit, declines public recognition.

The Amish abhor publicity, which is the delight of modern organizations. They leave their public relations to the imagination of outsiders. When Amish achievements do appear in newsprint, names are conspicuously miss-

Faced with prosecution for not sending their children to high school in 1953, Amish fathers show the resignation of Gelassenheit in the office of a district magistrate.

ing. This happened when one Amishman was designated "most improved" dairy farmer of the year. Tagging names on accomplishments turns them into acts of idolatry for human praise and applause. The Bible teaches that "pride comes before a fall," and in Amish eyes, publicity leads to pride, which may make the community stumble. However, although the Amish deplore public recognition, they warmly recognize and gently praise personal contributions in face-to-face conversation.

The presentation of the self is particularly vulnerable to pride. Vocabulary, dress, and body language reveal a proud or humble self. Modern society provides individuals with an astonishing repertoire of props for making up and presenting a self for every occasion. Hairstyles, clothing, jewelry, cosmetics, and suntans enable individuals to "package" themselves in a multitude of ways. These same tools of modernity, ironically, provide the means of conforming to the latest fads and fashions. The Amish believe that preening rituals, repeated morning after morning in suburban bathrooms, are infested with pride. Self-exaltation is diametrically opposed to the core values of Amish culture. Consequently, all cosmetic props are considered signs of pride, showing off "number one" and scorning the spirit of Gelassenheit. Moreover, the false mask of the "made up" face is seen as a lie, of sorts, that covers up the real face.

In the close interaction of friends and family, the authentic Amish self becomes known and accepted without cosmetic props. Thus all jewelry (including wedding rings and wrist watches) is taboo, because it reveals a proud heart. Any form of makeup, hair styling, showy dress, commercial clothing, flashy color, or bold fabric that calls undue attention to the self is off-limits in Amish culture. Makeup is proscribed, even in the casket. The rejection of outward adornment is rooted in biblical teaching.[26]

Pride, however, pops up in virtually all avenues of Amish life. Traces of it appear in professional landscaping around houses, showy furniture, fancy harnesses, and windshield wipers on carriages. An artist worried that she was becoming too high-minded, or *Hochmut,* because of her paintings. One farmer described another as "horse proud," that is, too concerned about the appearance of his horses. Another man noted, "You can easily tell the difference between the horses and carriages of well-to-do businessmen and everyone else." Unnecessary trappings are considered pretentious signs that individuals are clamoring for self-attention, elevating themselves above others.

Humility is a barometer of Gelassenheit. The Amish are taught: "If other people praise you, humble yourself. But do not praise yourself or boast, for that is the way of fools who seek vain praise. . . . In tribulation be patient and humble yourself under the mighty hand of God."[27] Jesus, the meek servant, is the model of true humility. The Amish ritualize the virtue of humility by washing one another's feet during the fall and spring communion services. According to the command of Christ (John 13:4-7), they teach that stooping to wash the feet of a brother or sister "is a sign of true humiliation."[28] One member, writing to another member facing censure by the church, pleaded, "Humble yourself and stoop low enough so that you can forgive others . . . and make peace with the church."

SEPARATION FROM THE WORLD

Taking their cues from the Bible, the Amish divide the social world into two categories: the straight, narrow way to life and the broad, easy road to destruction. The Amish seek to embody the straight and narrow way of self-denial, while the larger social world represents the broad, easy path of vanity and vice. To the Amish, the term *world* refers not to the globe but to the entire social system outside Amish society—its people, values, vices, and institutions—in short, to modernity itself. Sectarian groups typically oppose the dominant social order. The Amish contrast church with world, Amish with non-Amish, and "our people" with "outsiders." A leader put it simply: "If you're not Amish, you're English and part of the world." Even the five-year-old son of an Amish hat maker said: "We sell most of them to *our people,* but a few of them to *the English.*" Such a simple division of the social terrain is common even in the modern mind, where capitalism is pitted against socialism, Republican against Democrat, and alien against citizen.

The values of a worldly system that savors individualism, relativism, and fragmentation threaten the spirit of Gelassenheit. The larger social system serves as a negative reference point for perverted values. Daily press reports of government scandal, drug abuse, violent crime, divorce, war, greed, homosexuality, and child abuse confirm again and again in the Amish mind that the world is teeming with evil. Asked one Amish writer, "If we have to read the sickening details of one more war, rape, robbery, murder, riot or famine, or hear the gory report of one more senseless automobile crash, what shall it profit us if we hear of a thousand more?"[29] Just as the fear of aggression intensifies American patriotism, so the fear of an evil world strengthens Amish solidarity.

This sharp dualism between church and world crystallized in the sixteenth century, when many Anabaptists were tortured and executed. An early Anabaptist theological statement, written in 1527, underscored the deep chasm between the church and the world: "All of those who have fellowship with the dead works of darkness have no part in the light. Thus all who follow the devil and the world, have no part with those who are called out of the world into God."[30]

The split between church and world, imprinted in Amish consciousness by decades of persecution, is legitimated by Scripture. Using biblical imagery, the Amish see the church as "a chosen generation, a royal priesthood, a holy nation, a peculiar people . . . who were called out of the darkness" (1 Pet. 2:9).[31] The Scripture admonishes them not to "conform to the world" (Rom. 12:2), and to "love not the world or the things of the world" (1 John 2:15). Moreover, "Whosoever . . . will be a friend of the world is an enemy of God" (Jas. 4:4). One Amishman said: "Jesus through his direct plea has commanded us to come out from the world, and be separated, and touch not the unclean things. . . . In other words, we shall not be conformed to this world, but be transformed."[32]

To the Amish, worldliness denotes a whole host of specific behaviors, objects, and lifestyles. High school, cars, computers, cameras, video recorders, television, films, showy houses, and bicycles, all tagged "worldly," are censured. However, the term *worldly* is a slippery one, for its meaning evolves over time. White enamel stoves and bathtubs, for instance, were obvious signs of worldliness in the 1940s. Today modern gas stoves and bathtubs are common in Amish homes. Many children and even some adults wear sneakers, which were once forbidden. The term also provides symbolic boundary markers for the Amish moral order. For example, white commercial cigarettes are forbidden but thin "Winchester" cigars in brown wrappers are acceptable.

Pliable over time, the term *worldly* is a convenient way of labeling changes, products, practices, and beliefs that appear threatening to the welfare of the community. The stigma of this label stalls the acceptance of some products and keeps them at arm's length. However, not all new things are dubbed worldly. For example, battery-operated calculators, synthetic materials, solid-state gasoline engines, hot dogs, rollerblades, plastic toys, and fiberglass have escaped the stamp of worldliness because they pose little threat to the community.

The Amish fear of worldliness is rooted in a spiritual concern to preserve the purity of the church. The drama between church and world is a battle between good and evil, between the forces of righteousness and those of the devil. It is the ultimate struggle, and to succumb to worldliness is to surrender the community to apostasy. This key unlocks many of the riddles in Amish society. The impulse to separate from the world infuses Amish consciousness, guides personal behavior, and shapes institutional structures. The sectarian suspicion of the world confounds Moderns, who are enchanted by inclusivity, acceptance, diversity, and religious pluralism. If social separation is indeed a by-product of technological progress, the Amish believe they can only preserve their community by separating from the Great Separator, modernity itself.

THE JOY OF WORK

In contrast to some Moderns who hate their jobs but love to shop, the Amish enjoy their work and despise conspicuous consumption. Theirs is an economy of production, not consumption. Although mischief, play, and leisure flourish in Amish life, work dominates. Often hard and dirty, it is good and meaningful work that for the most part builds community. Amish work integrates; it binds the individual to the group, the family, and the church. Work is not a personal career but a calling from God, and in this sense, it becomes a redemptive ritual.[33]

Housework, shop work, and fieldwork are offerings that contribute to a family's welfare. Family, community, and work are woven together in the fabric of Amish life. Work is not pitted against the other spheres of life as often happens elsewhere. The rhythms of work are pursued for the sake of community, not just for individual profit and prestige. A great deal of work is done in small groups, where it blends effort and play in a celebration of togetherness. The profits of Amish work typically support family and church, not exotic hobbies and expensive cruises. Children are expected to "help out" soon after they can walk, and some will learn to drive a team of mules by the age of eight. Because of the communal nature of work, labor-saving technology poses a threat to the social order.

Idleness is deplored as the "devil's workshop." If there is any doubt that work is a sacred ritual, there can be no doubt that the Amish despise idleness. They are told: "Detest idleness as a pillow of Satan and a cause of all sorts of wickedness, and be diligent in your appointed tasks that you not be found idle. Satan has great power over the idle, to lead them into many sins. King David was idle on the rooftop of his house when he fell into adultery."[34] Idle minds fill up with vulgar thoughts and become dangerous. An Amishman from another settlement grumbled that the Lancaster Amish "don't even have time to visit" because "they just work, work, work." An Amish businessman worries that with more people working in shops, there will be too much free time in evenings and weekends, which will lead to mischief.

An Amishman was vexed by the sloth he saw in a state-funded road crew: "I had the privilege of seeing with my own eyes the total disregard of any work ethic. Eight men and women showed up for the project. . . . And folks, this was one of the laziest and unmotivated crew of bums you ever saw gathered for a job." He concluded that it took eight state employees three days to do what three Amishmen could have done in one.[35]

Amish work is "hands-on," practical work. Plowing, milking, sawing, welding, quilting, and canning do not involve the manipulation of abstract symbols and data like work in an information society. The farmer or carpenter sees, touches, and shapes the final product and holds responsibility for it. Manual work breeds a pragmatic mentality that values "practical" things and eschews abstract, "impractical" theories derived from "book learning." Historically, farm life provided abundant work in the context of family, neighborhood, and church. The strong work ethic that provided enormous energy for farming has fueled the dramatic growth of Amish businesses as well.

A consistent theme in the Amish opposition to high school was the fear that academic life would teach Amish youth to despise manual work. The goal of Amish schools is "to prepare for usefulness by preparing for eternity" rather than to spoil children with the abstractions of philosophy.[36] Quoting a Bible verse (Col. 2:8), the Amish caution: "Beware lest any man spoil you through philosophy and vain deceit after the rudiments of the world and not after Christ."[37] "Children," according to one leader, "should grow up to be useful men and women, useful in the community and also useful members of the church of Christ."[38]

Decorative artwork displayed on walls is disdained because it is not useful and because it encourages vanity. Embroidered family registers, calendars, and genealogical charts are more likely to hang on Amish walls. Some Amish write poetry, keep journals, and decorate crafts with pastoral scenes. Art that exalts the individual artist is unwelcome, although a few folk artists have always found expression in Amish society.[39]

Practical expressions of art are encouraged in quilting patterns, recipes, flower gardens, artistic lettering in Bibles, toys, dolls, crafts, and furniture designs. The Amish spend an enormous amount of creative energy making crafts for gifts and family needs as well as to sell to neighbors and tourists. Many of the older artistic restraints eroded in the 1990s with the rapid growth of the craft market.[40]

An Amish quilt shop displays artistic expression. Electric lights are permissible because the property is owned by a non-Amish person.

The artist is always on the fringe of Amish society and needs to work within its moral boundaries, for example, by not painting faces on images of people. Public art shows that call attention to the artist are generally not allowed because they would cultivate pride. One artist complained: "It's okay to paint milk cans but not to display your work at art shows." Artistic impulses in their modern forms are considered worldly, impractical, and self-exalting—a waste of time and money. However, church leaders will sometimes grant artists special freedoms to display their work because of disabilities or economic hardships in their families.

THE PRACTICE OF THRIFT

When things become too practical and handy, they border on luxury. A hay baler is practical, but an automatic bale thrower to load bales on wagons is considered "too handy" and thus worldly. Automatic devices generally are considered too handy. Sacrifice is a sign of the yielded self, but luxury signals pride. No longer content to work and sacrifice for the common good, the pleasure seeker is preoccupied with self-fulfillment. The Amish are urged to "suffer affliction with the people of God rather than to enjoy the pleasures of sin for a season."[41] Pleasure and self-denial, ease and discipline, and fancy and plain are symbolic oppositions that pinpoint the difference between self-enhancement and Gelassenheit.

The yielded self does not seek pleasure, buy luxuries, make things too handy, or pay for "looks." In the Amish economy rags are recycled into carpets, clothing is patched rather than tossed away with every passing fad, and clothing and toys are passed down to younger children. The exaltation of thrift is not a masochistic drive to win divine favor or guarantee eternal life. It is an acceptance that the habit of austerity—developed over the decades—has produced a wholesome life. In short, it works by stifling vanity and spiking productivity.

One expression of thrift is a strong saving ethic. A financial advisor to the Amish has 750 Amish clients who invest in mutual funds on a monthly basis. The dollars are transferred electronically from their checking accounts to the mutual funds. Some may save as little as twenty-five dollars a month, and others several thousand dollars. Instead of investing in college, young adults often save carefully so they can buy a home or business. One young adult earned $24,000 a year, saved half of it, and in several years bought a small house with virtually no mortgage. Another young man saved $200,000 by the time he was twenty-eight to invest in a farm. A hard work ethic, combined with an impulse to save, an austere lifestyle, and a strong economy, make it possible for some young people to buy property with a very modest mortgage.

THE VALUE OF TRADITION

Amish culture tilts toward tradition. In the modern world, where new is best and change equates with progress, the Amish offer a different view. They see tradition as a healthy brake that "slows things down." A young minister noted:

> We consider tradition as being spiritually helpful. Tradition can blind you if you adhere only to tradition and not the meanings of the tradition, but we really maintain a tradition. I've heard one of our members

say if you start changing some things, it won't stop at some things, it will keep on changing and there won't be an end to it. We have some traditions, that some people question and I sometimes myself question, that are being maintained just because they are a tradition. This can be adverse, but it can also be a benefit. Tradition always looks bad if you're comparing one month to the next or one year to the next, but when you're talking fifty years or more, tradition looks more favorable.

Another Amishman said: "Tradition to us is a sacred trust, and it is part of our religion to uphold and adhere to the ideals of our forefathers."[42]

The spirit of Gelassenheit calls for yielding to tradition. Economic pressure, expansion, curiosity, greed, and youthful innovation foster social change. Although suspect, change is not necessarily all bad. New things are not rejected out of hand by the Amish just because they are new. Innovations are cautiously evaluated to see where they might lead and how they might influence the community. Traditional sentiments, however, regulate everything from clothing to education.

Modern societies look forward and strategically plan their future. The Amish glance backward and treasure their tradition as a resource for coping with the present. Tradition slows the dangerous wheel of change. Some entrepreneurs are increasingly looking forward as they plan and strategize to find new markets for their products. Despite these forward glances, the Amish have not lost sight of their past and its precious legacy. While Moderns are preoccupied with planning, the Amish hearken to the voice of tradition. Echoes from previous generations and concerns for future ones merge and enlarge their sense of the present.

A SLOWER PACE

Perceptions of time vary enormously from culture to culture. Time organizes human consciousness as well as everyday behavior.[43] Anyone stepping into Amish society suddenly feels time expand and relax. The battery-operated clocks on Amish walls seem to run slower. From body language to the speed of transportation, from singing to walking, the stride is slower. Traveling by buggy, plowing with horses, and going to church every other week create a temporal order with a slower, more deliberate rhythm. Time is marked by half-days and seasons, not by thirty-second commercials and fifteen-minute interviews.

An Amishman described an Amishwoman who had her yard professionally landscaped as "a little on the fast side." "Fast" families and church districts stretch the boundaries of tradition. The spirit of Gelassenheit is reserved—slow to respond, slow to change, slow to push ahead. An Amishman noted: "Our way of living differs greatly from those living in the fast pace of this world."[44] The Amish separated themselves from the pace of modernity in the mid-twentieth century by not turning their clocks to daylight saving time but following "natural" standard time.[45] Although increased interaction with the outside world has led many families involved in business to comply with daylight saving time, other families still follow standard time as a symbolic practice of separation from the world. Church services, of course, usually follow "God's (standard) time."

Fast tempos, quick moves, and rapid changes are suspect in Amish culture. The torturously slow tempo of Amish singing in church reflects an utterly different conception of time.[46] Holding church services every other week stretches the temporal span of Amish life. The rhythm of the seasons and the agricultural calendar of planting and harvesting widen the temporal brackets and slow the pace of Amish life. These "wide" intervals of time contrast sharply with the abbreviated slices of modern time dictated by news clips, sound bites, and half-hour television programs diced up by commercials.

The great irony here is that in Amish society, with fewer labor-saving devices and technological shortcuts, there is much less "rushing around." In general, the perception of rushing seems to grow directly with the number of "time-saving" devices one uses. Although much time is "saved" in modern life, for some reason there seems to be less of it. Rushing increases as the number, complexity, and mobility of social relations soar. Thus, the simplicity, overlap, and closeness of Amish life slow the pace of things and eliminate the need for time-management seminars. Visiting, the popular Amish "sport," is often spontaneous. Drop-in visits without warning are welcomed. There are, of course, planned family gatherings, but spontaneity generally prevails in Amish socializing. Children are sometimes told to "hurry up," but all things considered, the stride of life is slower.

There are, however, some impending changes. Time clocks, appointment books, and telephones springing up around Amish shops reflect a livelier tempo. Appointments, unheard of in the past, are now commonplace among Amish businessmen, who must synchronize their work with the patterns of the larger society. A "punch-in" time clock in some Amish shops is a sure sign of a new temporal order. Telephones near Amish work sites make it easier to arrange appointments. One person complained: "Now you even have to make an appointment to have your horse shod by an Amish blacksmith. In the past you could just take it there and wait." Patient waiting, a virtue of Gelassenheit, is now at risk. Moderns, of course, also have moments of waiting and yielding, but they are few. In Amish society, pausing at the yield sign is *the* way of life.

UPSIDE-DOWN VALUES

The social organization and practices of a society constitute an argument about its fundamental values and worldview. The quiltwork of Amish culture is upside down in many ways. The cultural capital and basic values of this community challenge the taken-for-granted assumptions of modernity.[47] The implicit arguments flowing from Amish culture contend that:

> The individual is not the supreme reality.
> Communal goals transcend individual ones.
> Obeying, waiting, and yielding are virtuous.
> The past is as important as the future.
> Tradition is valued more than change.
> Personal sacrifice is esteemed over pleasure.
> Work is more satisfying than consumption.
> Newer, bigger, and faster are not necessarily better.
> Preservation eclipses progress.
> Local involvement outweighs national acclaim.
> Technology must be tamed.
> Staying together is the supreme value.

In all of these ways, the Amish have not capitulated to modernity. Their core value system has withstood the torrents of progress. There is, of course, slippage from the ideal of Gelassenheit. Egocentrism, pride, envy, jealousy, and greed sometimes fracture community harmony. This is not heaven. Sin stalks this community as well as others. There are sporadic cases of sexual abuse and drug use. There is pain, suffering, and depression in this community. At times family or church feuds splinter an otherwise peaceful social order. Even leaders sometimes balk when asked to yield to the authority of elder bishops. Business owners in a competitive world find it hard to abide by the spirit of Gelassenheit. Moreover, the conformity to explicit rules cultivates an attitude of hollow conformity among some members who look and dress Amish but have left the community in spirit. After all, this is a human community and these people are people.

Despite aberrations and episodes of self-enhancement, Gelassenheit remains the governing principle, the core value, that solves the riddle of Amish culture. Definitions of worldliness and pride are cautiously updated to permit a slow drift forward. But submission, simplicity, obedience, and humility still prevail. They continue to structure the Amish worldview—a sure sign that Gelassenheit has not faded from the quiltwork of Amish culture.

3

Symbols of Integration
and Separation

Telephones, electricity, cars, and tractors set us off from the Mennonites,
and then, of course, there is television and all the other stuff.
—*Amish farmer*

THE FLAGS OF ETHNICITY

The Amish share many cultural objects with other Americans. They read newspapers, jump on trampolines, and barbecue hamburgers on gas grills. Other aspects of their material culture—lanterns, harnesses, bonnets—are unique. Such artifacts serve both *symbolic* and *practical* functions in Amish culture. They symbolize Amish identity and also shape daily life. Lanterns, for instance, not only announce the ethnic affiliation of Amish homesteads but also make a practical difference in daily living. Without electricity for television or air conditioners, Amish homes are remarkably quiet. Without dishwashers, manual work increases. Without microwaves, the family usually eats meals together. Amish families are often found gathered in the common room of their home because they use space heaters and have fewer sources of light. And they typically go to bed earlier—often by eight or nine on winter evenings. In these and other ways, the absence of electricity shapes Amish behavior. This chapter focuses on four important symbols—language, dress, horse, and buggy—that shape Amish identity and impact daily life.[1]

Like other people, the Amish live in a symbolic world of their own creation. The symbols of Gelassenheit articulate surrender, bond the community together, and mark off boundaries with the larger society. Symbols stir deep emotions. Just as a nation's flag is not just another piece of cloth to be burned or trashed at will, the horse in Amish culture is not merely another animal; it evokes special memories and meanings. Like flags, Amish symbols represent the very essence of Amish life. Over the years dialect, dress, horse, and buggy have crystallized into durable symbols of Amish identity.

THE DIALECT OF SEPARATION

In many ways, people are captives of their language. Vocabulary and grammar construct images of reality in our consciousness. These perceptions of reality, embedded in the mind of a child, are taken for granted as "the way things are." Because language defines the "way things are," it is the most powerful means of social control. Language also integrates and separates. It unites those who speak a common tongue and excludes those who do not.

The Amish speak English and a German dialect known as Pennsylvania German or Pennsylvania Dutch. This dialect, which the Amish call *Deitsch*, is their native tongue and should not be confused with the Dutch language of the Netherlands. The dialect was once spoken by most Germanic settlers in southeastern Pennsylvania.[2] The Amish across North America speak Pennsylvania German and can identify themselves by various regional accents.

Except for the Amish and a few related Plain groups, the dialect has declined in recent years. In Amish culture, the dialect is the language of family, friendship, play, and intimacy. Most children live in the world of the dialect until they learn English in the Amish school. Students learn to read, write, and speak English from Amish teachers, who learned it from their Amish teachers as well. But the dialect prevails in friendly banter on the playground. The dialect functions primarily as an oral language; however, idioms of it are frequently mixed in with an old form of German in Amish sacred writings.

By the end of the eighth grade, young Amish have developed basic competence in English, although they often speak with a slight accent. Adults are able to communicate in fluent English with their non-Amish neighbors. When talking among themselves, the Amish sometimes mix English words— *chance, surprise, birthday party, refrigerator, hydraulic, computer*—with the dialect. A word such as *embalm* may be mispronounced *embam*. Some "high" Amish may use English among themselves to show off their vocabulary by adding an English phrase such as "Well I don't know" amidst a sentence of dialect. Letters between Amish people are often written in English, with salutations and occasional phrases in the dialect.

Competence in English varies directly with occupational roles and interaction with outside speakers. Amish businessmen, for example, develop an extensive English vocabulary. They talk about marketing strategies and use legal terminology with ease. But even they stumble when searching for English words to communicate religious ideas. Finally, with a tone of frustration, an Amish person might say: "I could just say it much better in German." Such acknowledgments underscore the importance of the dialect in creating and perpetuating a different worldview. Numerous Amish note an increased use of English in everyday speech and worry that some children are learning too much English too early. And clearly the dialect itself is changing, drifting farther from formal German and incorporating more and more English words.

If English is a trade language and the dialect is the mother tongue, German is God's voice. Old German with Gothic letters is taught in schools and used for religious documents. An editor of an Amish publication noted: "Our policy forbids the publishing of Amish church revered matter in English."[3] Scripture verses, church regulations, religious booklets, and sayings of respected leaders are usually printed in German. Although the Bible, the *Martyrs Mirror*, and other inspirational materials are read in German, the ability to speak German varies considerably.[4] Church leaders speak and read German to the best of their ability. Preachers read from a German Bible or prayer book with the flavor of local idioms, but most sermons are delivered in the dialect. A few English words may even slip in. One preacher, reciting the biblical story of John the Baptist's execution, referred to Herod's "birthday party" in his sermon. Concerned that fewer and fewer young people could read German, an Amish publisher printed a book of prayers in both English and German, signaling a shift toward English even in religious writings.[5]

Amish schools have been crucial in preserving the dialect and expanding the use of the German. Although all members of the community speak the dialect fluently, the use of written English and German varies considerably by training, occupation, intelligence, and personal motivation. A weekly Amish newspaper, *Die Botschaft* (The message); a business newspaper, *Plain Communities Business Exchange;* and a monthly periodical, *The Diary,* are all published in English. Many Amish receive a daily newspaper and subscribe to the *Reader's Digest* as well as other magazines that relate to their work.

English is viewed as the currency of high culture and worldly society, a language of sophistication at odds with the lowly spirit of Gelassenheit. The Amish note that when "high" families leave the church, they eventually drop the dialect and drift in worldly directions. Knowing that the dialect helps to preserve their ethnic identity, the Amish have refused to concede it to modernity.

The dialect preserves Amish identity in several ways. It provides a social glue that binds and unites the community into a world of their own. It also links members to their religious roots and to the martyrs of the past. Reading the Bible, the *Martyrs Mirror,* and other religious materials in the "original" tongue creates a sacred discourse. English is the language of the modern world, the verbal currency of a vain society. To use English in prayers or religious services is considered worldly. A shift to English would erode many oral traditions because the dialect also serves as a depository for folklore, a vehicle for transporting Amish traditions.

The dialect also separates. Although most Amish can speak English, they are never quite at ease with it. There are moments of hesitation when they grope for an English translation or stumble on an English word. It is difficult to tease, dream, and communicate intimate emotions in a foreign language. The dialect provides a prudent way of keeping the world at bay. It controls interaction with outsiders and stifles intimate ties with non-Amish neighbors. Progressive Amish leaders and businessmen subscribe to magazines such as *Newsweek, U.S. News and World Report,* and *Farm Journal,* but the advanced vocabulary of such media keeps it out of the hands of many. In all these ways, the dialect creates a worldview, a way of perceiving reality that obstructs the discourse with modernity.

THE GARB OF HUMILITY

Dress speaks. It communicates membership, commitment, and social status. Their dress unites the Amish as a community and also sets them apart. Dress has provided a means of separation since their beginning.[6] As manufactured clothing became popular in the twentieth century, dress became an even more distinctive badge of Amish identity, a defensive tactic that sharpened their cultural boundaries.

Both Amish and Moderns dress for success, but the standards of success differ radically. In fact, the two cultures use dress in opposite ways. In modern society, dress is used to express individual preference, social class, and wealth. It is a tool of self-adornment that communicates individual taste, highlights the body, and signals social status. In Amish society, dress signals group membership and submission to the moral order. Amish people forgo the right of self-expression and don the communal garb that serves as an ethnic name tag. Modern dress accents the individual, whereas Amish dress builds group solidarity.

The number of outfits in contemporary wardrobes reflects the complexity of modern social structure. Multiple roles require specialized outfits—swimming trunks, sweat pants, casual wear, and tuxedos. The more simple Amish social structure requires fewer outfits that loosely fit around three occasions: work, dress up, and church. The church's ability to dress its members in the "company uniform" reveals the strength and scope of religious control. Because their world is sacred and they are always "on duty," the Amish always appear in uniform.[7]

Amish dress serves a variety of functions. The ethnic garb: (1) signals that a member has yielded to the collective order, (2) prevents dress from being used for self-adornment, (3) promotes equality, (4) creates a common consciousness that bolsters group identity, (5) increases social control because members are expected to "act Amish" when in uniform, (6) projects a united public front, which conceals diversity in other areas, and (7) erects symbolic boundaries around the group—the equivalent of a cultural moat.

Relinquishing control over the presentation and ornamentation of one's body is a fundamental offering—the supreme sign that the self has yielded to a higher authority. Dressing in prescribed patterns day after day symbolizes one's surrender to the supremacy of the group. Indeed, the details of Amish dress provide subtle clues to an individual's conformity to the standards of the church. The width of a hat brim, the length of hair, the length of a skirt, the size of a head covering, and the color of shoes and stockings quietly signal a member's compliance with the church. Subtle variations announce whether one is liberal or conservative, showing off or obeying the church, "jumping the fence" or falling in line.

The language of dress communicates without words. Common dress unites members and makes it impossible to blend into the cultural main-

Amish garb unites members and separates them from the non-Amish, as a crowd observes the filming of *Witness* in the village of Intercourse.

stream. Dressed like their parents, children learn to act, think, and feel "Amish" from birth. Dress regulations have been encoded in the oral tradition of the church and are usually not justified by moral or biblical arguments. Thoughtful leaders sometimes offer explanations based on biblical principles of modesty or simplicity, but regulations are not tied to specific scriptures.[8] Central to both self and group identity, Amish dress is the language of loyalty and belonging. The dress code is usually accepted as simply "the way our people dress."

The style and color of dress signify a host of meanings related to at least nine dimensions of Amish life: (1) gender, (2) age, (3) marital status, (4) Plainness, (5) membership, (6) authority, (7) mourning, (8) sacred-profane boundaries, and (9) private-public domains. The cultural maze of these dimensions creates a complicated grammar of dress that specifies what is appropriate in a particular setting for a person in a certain role. The recipe for a particular role provides psychological clarity and identity for the individual and com-

municates acceptance of the role to others as well. However, within the prescribed recipe there is some freedom for flexibility. A mother can dress her
young boys in shirts of various colors. Young women have some choice in
the style of the aprons they wear. To the outsider the Amish appear to dress
alike, but a closer glance reveals a mosaic of details that signal important
meanings within the culture.

Many items in the Amish wardrobe are homemade. A member described
the process: "The Amish mother sews all the dresses, capes, aprons, and
head coverings for the girls and herself as well as the pants and shirts for the
men and boys. Most of the underwear is bought except some slips and pant-
ies may be homemade for the girls. Men's overcoats and dress suits are made
by a seamstress, usually an older single woman who makes a living by sewing
for other folks." In recent years more and more women are buying ready-
made clothing from Amish dry goods stores.

THE WOMAN'S WARDROBE

Baby girls wear a small head covering when they first come to church at
six weeks of age. At about the age of four, girls begin wearing an adult-style
head covering for Sunday services but not for other activities.[9] The coverings
are made of Swiss organdy and are almost always white, with one exception.
From age thirteen until marriage, most girls wear a black covering when
attending church services. The coverings vary slightly in style and size.
Younger girls and more liberal women wear a covering with a larger, heart-
shaped back, narrower front, and longer, narrower tie strings. Ministers'
wives and women age fifty and older wear a covering with a wider band at
the bottom of the back. Older women have the pleat through the middle of
the back pressed rather than sewn in. One member said, "The covering is a
symbol of subjection to God and to man. Amish women wear them, or at
least a bandana or scarf to cover the head at all times, especially while praying
or in the presence of men."

Small girls often wear their hair in braids, which do not hang loose but
are fastened together around the back of the head. When girls are four years
of age, their hair is twisted into rolls and arranged into a bun at the back of
the head. Adult women part their hair in the center and also wear it in a bun.
Cutting or curling hair, shaving legs, and trimming eyebrows are prohibited
because they are viewed as irreverent tampering with God's creation.

The dresses of little girls button in the back. For dress-up occasions little girls wear a black *Schatzli,* a little pinafore apron that flows around the dress and matches its length. Church dresses for little girls are solid colors— purple, dark green, dark blue, maroon, pink—covered with a white organdy pinafore.

Adult women close their dresses in the front with snap fasteners or straight pins. Sleeve lengths vary. Younger girls and more liberal women wear shorter skirts, lower necklines, and puffier sleeves. The skirts of older women may touch the tops of their shoes, whereas those of younger girls are often just below the knees. Dresses are usually a solid color of gray, blue, green, purple, or wine. A black dress is worn by adult women to communion services and funerals as well as to other religious services during periods of mourning.

Except for young girls at play, Amish females usually wear aprons over their dresses. A belt sewn at the top of the apron encircles the waist and is fastened with pins. The width of the belt varies from one to four inches; progressive women wear wider ones. A bib apron is often worn by younger and more progressive women when they go to town or other public places. A black apron may sometimes have a fine white polka dot print. Women also wear capes that cover the top half of their dresses. The cape is cut like a triangle, and its apex is fastened with pins at the waistline in back. The sides are brought over the shoulders, overlapped in front, and connected with pins.

A young girl begins wearing a cape and apron in daily activities at about age eight. The cape and apron worn to church are white organdy, but those for other occasions are black. Young girls typically only wear head coverings and capes to church and other dress-up occasions—not to school or in casual settings. From age twelve to about age forty, women wear a cape and dress of the same color. In church services single girls wear a white cape and apron, symbols of virginity. Unmarried women wear a white cape and apron to church until about age thirty, when they begin wearing a colored cape and black apron, as do married women. After age forty a black cape and apron are worn over any color dress. Ministers' wives always wear a black cape and apron. Capes are worn mostly for dress-up occasions, but aprons are worn at all times.

Black stockings are worn by all females, except babies under two years of age, who wear white. Teenage girls and progressive women wear service-

These two women illustrate typical dress at a summer public gathering.

weight nylon stockings, but younger girls and older women often wear cotton stockings. Black tie shoes are usually worn to church and other dress-up events. Brides and ministers' wives as well as older women always wear high shoes in winter. Children, youth, and even some adults wear athletic sneakers to informal events.

A shawl and bonnet complete the woman's distinctive wardrobe. Babies of both sexes wear a bonnet when they are first brought to church at six weeks of age. Little girls wear colored bonnets until age nine, when they begin wearing black bonnets, as do adult women. The style of the woman's bonnet is fairly consistent, but differences in size signal a Plain or progressive attitude. There is a growing tendency for some women to appear in public without a bonnet, to the consternation of some leaders.

Woolen shawls are worn by Amish women of all ages—except young girls, who usually wear a homemade coat for school. The black shawl is draped over the shoulders and fastened in front at the neck with a hat pin or safety pin. A homemade woolen coat with a quilted lining is usually worn under the shawl by adult women. The coat is always black and is fastened with either buttons or snaps in the front. Teens and some adults wear the coat without a shawl.

Dress also signals stages of mourning for a loved one. Women carry the symbolic burden of grief by wearing black capes and aprons for various lengths of time for different relatives: one year (spouse, parent, child, brother, or sister), six months (grandparent or grandchild), three months (uncle, aunt, niece, or nephew), and six weeks (first cousin). This symbol of mourning enables the community to grant the solitude and support that is fitting for a particular loss.

OUTFITTING THE MEN

In the past, baby boys wore dresses until about age one, making it easier to change their diapers. Today some progressive mothers outfit their child in pants and shirt throughout the week and bring them to church in a dress only once or twice as a courteous nod to tradition. More traditional mothers, on the other hand, may wait a year before ever dressing a boy in pants. The boy's first pants have buttonholes at the waistline, which fasten to large buttons on the shirt. At about four years of age, boys wear adult-styled suits, which include a vest, suspenders, coat, hat, and "broadfall" trousers.

The debate about appropriate dress for baby boys is interesting. Conservative parents, holding to older ways, may say sarcastically, "Soon the little boy babies will be born with pants." More progressive parents will confess that they can hardly bear to put their baby boys in dresses because "out in the world such things happen with grown men, and we may be encouraging bad things if we don't dress them like boys." Although the Amish are not preoccupied with the lives of gays and lesbians as in the larger culture, some of them do connect this particular tradition to such issues in American society.

The hair of Amish males is cut about even with the earlobe. Hair is not parted, and bangs are cut in front about halfway down the forehead. Sideburns without a beard are prohibited for members. Men shave until marriage, at which time they grow a beard, which serves the symbolic function of a wedding ring in the larger culture and as a rite of passage to manhood as well. Single men over forty also grow a beard. An untrimmed, full beard from ear to ear is encouraged for adult men; however, many trim their beards for neatness. The upper lip is shaved even after marriage because the mustache,

These young men sport the typical vest and hat en route to a youth gathering in their open buggy. The lack of beards indicates they are unmarried. Sunglasses are acceptable but not jewelry or wrist watches.

once associated with European military officers, is forbidden by the church. Some young Amish men wear their hair in a "shingled" style by getting it cut in a commercial barber shop, but upon baptism they must return to the traditional Amish bowl cut with bangs.

For males the distinctive wide-brimmed hat is the foremost tag of Amish identity. Hats are worn whenever men are outside the house. Amish boys begin wearing a hat at about age two. Straw hats are worn in the summer; black woolen hats, in the winter. At about age ten, boys begin wearing a "telescope" hat with creases pressed into the crown's inner edge. Little boys, older and more conservative men, and ministers wear a black hat with a plain or rounded crown. Around age forty most men give up their telescoped hats for plain crowned hats. Sunglasses, gloves, and scarves are worn seasonally.

Hook-and-eye fasteners close the suit coats and vests worn at church services. Buttons are worn on work coats. In some cases, Velcro is used as a fastener. Shirts are usually pocketless. "Broadfall" trousers without hip pockets or zippers are the norm for males of all ages. The wide opening on the front of pants is closed with buttons. Trousers are held by suspenders, for belts are prohibited. For work, men and boys wear a black sack coat often fastened with snaps or buttons. Men wear a frock coat with divided tails and a V-neck shirt for church and special occasions. Boys receive their *Mutze,* or frock coat, at age sixteen. For other cold weather dress-up occasions, men wear a plain-cut, notched-collar suit coat instead of the *Mutze.* A black vest is usually worn under the coat. In summer months males may attend church or other dress-up occasions without a coat but rarely without a vest. Vest, hat, and suspenders, prime markers of ethnic identity, must never be left behind.

Although black is the dominant color for men, dress shirts are typically green, purple, blue, or wine. The color of death, however, is white. Both males and females are buried in white. Special white pants and a vest are made for the man, who is also dressed in his best white shirt. A white dress is fashioned for the woman, and she also wears the white bridal cape and apron worn at her wedding. Single women will often put away, in safekeeping for their burial, the last white cap and apron they wore before joining the ranks of adult women.

DRESSING OVER THE DECADES

Some aspects of Amish dress can be traced back to European peasant traditions, others to early American customs. Many traits of Amish garb simply jelled over the years as the church sought to remain separate from the world, preempt pride, avoid fashions, and preserve tradition. The Amish dress code is justified by appeals to tradition, as simply the way things are, in the same way that ties for men and skirts for women are justified in the larger culture. Modesty is often given as the reason for many of the practices. Amish dress, the central code of moral order, has been blessed by the church and wisely passed on by the forebears of the faith. Conforming to the code is a redemptive ritual that binds one to the group and reveals a willingness to yield to history, to church, to God—a yielding that places one in touch with divine mysteries.

Some Amish leaders and thoughtful lay people offer religious reasons for some of the practices. One member stated:

> There is significance in the Amish garb other than mere tradition. The broadfall trousers worn by the men are designed for the sake of modesty. Suspenders are worn so that the trousers need not fit so tightly. The head covering is a symbol of the woman's subjection to the man and to God. It is worn at all times, especially in the presence of men and while praying. The cape is designed for the nursing mother and the apron for the pregnant woman. So that no woman has to expose herself, all women wear clothes designed in this manner. The length of the hair for men and the width of the hat brim are established for the sake of uniformity.

Despite minor changes in Amish dress in the twentieth century, the styles have been rather resilient. An elderly member noted that around 1910 men wore different colors of corduroy trousers—brown, gray, and blue—and they rarely had a suit coat that matched their pants. Gradually, male dress suits became a uniform black, and corduroy became taboo. A sharper line between dress and work clothes emerged after the Depression. Until this time, many males had only one pair of shoes and would merely "blacken" them before going to church. The separation of clothing for work from that for dress-up occasions reflects a growing division between activities as well as a more affluent lifestyle.

A threat to Amish identity appeared in the 1970s when a federal regulation required employees in construction industries to wear protective hard hats. Although most Amish were in farm-related occupations, those in public construction firms in several states were affected by the regulation. The broad-brimmed hat had served as an important badge of ethnicity for many years. Church leaders, dismayed by the regulation, feared that Amish men in other jobs might also leave their hats at home.

A Lancaster representative for the Amish National Steering Committee made several trips to Washington, D.C., to plead the Amish case with the Secretary of Labor and Industry. The representative explained that dress is part of their religious testimony against worldliness and hence wearing the traditional hat was a religious issue. According to a firsthand witness, the secretary asked the Amish spokesman to pass his hat around the table of bureaucrats. When it reached the secretary's hands, he tested its rigidity and wryly remarked: "This hat is pretty stiff by itself; it is no use in us fighting you. We'll see what we can do." The secretary's staff designed an exemption form to excuse Amish men from the regulation. And so, according to Amish lore, the traditional hat trumped the powers of bureaucracy.

YOUTH AND DRESS

Although the broad contours of the dress code are firmly established, minor variations abound. Church leaders are unhappy that boys occasionally go hatless. Some girls have coverings that do not cover their ears and strings that are rarely tied except for church. One layman worries about the shrinking size and shape of the head covering worn by teenage girls. He believes it is a pattern that might follow the trend of some Mennonite groups where, as the strings come off, more hair is exposed and soon the covering shrinks to a small "flat doily" on top of the head. However, he concluded almost triumphantly, "We still have the strings on and the ear covered by the corner of the cap."

Some young men use their hairstyle to taunt church authorities and assert their independence. In the 1950s and 1960s, teenage boys cut their hair short to defy church standards. In the 1970s and 1980s some young males wore long hair to stir the ire of Amish elders. Several members date the flip-flop in hairstyles to the popularity of the Beatles. Leaders cite the change as an example of worldly influence. A minister stated: "We used to have trouble with short hair, and now we have to tell them about long hair. As the world changes so we have to change our teaching." By the turn of the twenty-first century, short hair was back.

The time when men begin growing the beard has also changed over the years. In 1880, the beard was a requirement at baptism. By 1920, it was no longer required at baptism, but a young man had to grow one before he could apply for marriage. Today the beard symbolizes marriage and manhood rather than church membership. Now young men are expected to have a "full stand" by the time of the first communion service, usually in the spring, after they are married. In the 1950s, young men who trimmed their beards in defiance of church rules had to make public confessions. "Today," one leader said, "the beard isn't much of an issue since so many outside people have one." But he lamented, "We have troubles with the mustache sometimes. Some boys will go away deer hunting for a week and come back with a mustache on and be daring enough to come to church with it." Deer hunters have conformed to hunting regulations by wearing fluorescent orange vests and hats over their black coats and broad-brimmed hats, making a colorful confluence of old and new.

Some teenage boys look like mirror images of their dads, and others experiment with "dressing around" by getting a "shingled" haircut and wearing commercial shirts of all styles and patterns. They have a fondness for black jeans as well as for baseball caps and sneakers. Dressed in this attire, they can easily disguise their Amish identity and melt into the larger society. At baptism, of course, these worldly symbols must be trashed for the sacred garb of the church.

DRESSING FOR COMMITMENT

Although Amish dress is important throughout the life cycle, it is carefully scrutinized at baptism. Families vary in their compliance with church regulations, but at baptism everyone must conform. One minister estimated that half of the families do not have to change the dress of their children at baptism. "But then," he said, "there are a portion that have to be kind of coaxed, kind of brought into line." He explained: "We have to work harder to get our young ladies in line with regulations than we do with the boys. Our girls get jobs away from home in restaurants, and their coverings get smaller, dresses are shorter, stockings are almost flesh-colored, and the shoes get fancy."

Hair and dress styles are a barometer of church loyalty. A minister noted: "You can single your people out, your families out, which way they are leaning by the cut of their hair. After twelve years of age, you can just about tell what they're thinking by their hair. You can almost tell which boys are driving an automobile by the cut of their hair; they have it shingled, you know." "How a child is dressed," said one mother, "gives away the mother's heart."

Dress also reflects role changes in ministerial leadership. In general, the higher the level of authority, the greater the expectations for conservative dress. At the time of ordination, both husband and wife are expected to make changes. Men wear a crown wool hat with a wider brim, a more plainly tailored suit, high top shoes for Sunday services, and a distinctive overcoat over the *Mutze* on cold days. The spouse of an ordained man always wears a black cape and black apron, a bigger covering with wider strings, high top shoes for Sunday services, and more plainly tailored dresses, capes, and aprons always attached with pins. Ordained men and their spouses are expected to serve as models of faithful compliance.

NEGOTIATED PATTERNS OF DRESS

One of the more subtle changes in dress has been a shift to double- and single-knit polyester materials. There are some restrictions on the type of material used for clothing. Corduroy, rib-knit, prints, and certain colors—yellow, for example—are off limits. The acceptance of synthetic materials saves considerable labor in washing and ironing. The traditional styles present a standard "front" to the public eye. Moreover, common patterns on the front stage allow the latest type of synthetic materials to be adopted backstage without alarm. Striking a bargain, the Amish have accepted labor-saving synthetic materials but have insisted on making their own clothing in order to preserve the symbolic patterns that protect their ethnic identity.

A variety of other negotiations have been underway as well. The Amish have long eschewed buttons and have used hooks and eyes to fasten the clothing of men and pins to attach dresses and aprons for women. However, this practice has increasingly become a ritual of deference to tradition only on Sunday. On many everyday garments for both men and women, snaps are used in lieu of buttons. Still avoiding the forbidden buttons, and more practical than hooks and eyes and straight pins, snaps make a perfect compromise. Buttons are used for men's shirts and to close their broadfall trousers. However, hooks and eyes on dress-up coats keep the traditional symbols front stage. On Sunday the traditional hooks and eyes and pins prevail. All of these arrangements reveal a delicate compromise between the patterns of tradition and the interests of convenience.

In modern culture, dress fads, designer labels, and seasonal fashions provide the means to conform to consumer styles. In this sense, both modern and Amish wardrobes are tools of social conformity. At first glance, the Amish appear preoccupied with dress. Their code of dress seems complicated and restrictive. Their garb does indeed restrict individuality, but it also frees them from the burden of choice. They do not have to sort through their wardrobe in a frenzy each morning looking for matching outfits, nor do they spend endless hours shopping to stay abreast of current fads. So, ironically, while the Amish appear to be engulfed by dress, they in fact spend much less time, money, and worry on clothing than Moderns do. Conformity to prescribed dress standards not only unites them and marks off their social turf, but it also frees them from incessant choice. Moreover, their symbolic codes are controlled by the church, not by fashion designers in faraway cities.

THE HOOFBEATS OF TRADITION

The horse and buggy are silhouetted on road signs, tourist brochures, and billboards as the archetypes of Amish identity. As society turned to cars in the early twentieth century, the horse became the prime symbol of Amish life by default. Although the Amish do not worship the horse with cultic rituals or fetish charms, it approximates a sacred symbol in some ways.

Lighter road horses pull buggies to town, but draft horses and mules tow farm equipment across the fields. The driving horses are often obtained from commercial race tracks. The heavier workhorses and mules are bought from jockeys, horse dealers, or at public auctions. Although farmers will occasionally ride horseback to and from fields, horseback riding is generally discouraged because it borders on a worldly form of sport.

The typical Amish farm family has one or two driving horses and six to

A young man changes into a baseball uniform inside the back
of his carriage.

eight draft horses or mules for fieldwork. Families who no longer live on a
farm also have one or two horses for transportation. New Amish homes, built
along rural roads or in villages, can be identified by their small horse barns.
Although the Amish are not required to own a horse, it is the typical mode
of travel because car ownership is forbidden. Single adult sisters living to-

gether in a village home, for example, stable their driving horse in a barn at the back of their property. Parents will often buy a horse for their son's sixteenth birthday. A good driving horse will cost from $2,500 to $3,500.

As a symbol of Amish culture, the horse articulates the meaning of several key values: tradition, time, limits, nature, and sacrifice. As a sacred link with history, the horse provides hard evidence that the Amish have not completely succumbed to progress. It heralds the triumph of tradition and signals faithful continuity with the past. A counter-symbol to the worldliness embodied in cars, the horse is tangible proof that the Amish have not sold out to the glamour and glitter of a high-tech society. A striking symbol of nonconformity, the horse separates the Amish from the modern world and anchors them in the past. Over the years, the church has forbidden fancy harnesses and decorative tack in hopes of keeping the horse undefiled. To be content with horse-drawn travel is a sign of commitment to tradition, faith, and the church. In this way, the horse becomes a sacred symbol.

Horses not only symbolize the slower pace of Amish society but also actually retard its speed. It takes longer to plow with horses, and driving time on the road increases fivefold. A horse culture places other limits on social life as well. At best, on level roads, travel is limited to twenty-five miles a day. Hilly terrain imposes additional burdens. By restricting travel, the use of the horse curtails the size of the settlement and holds the community closely together. It intensifies face-to-face interaction in local church districts. In short, it builds social capital by keeping people together.

Horses impose other curbs as well. Amish farmers yield to nature's clock because horses cannot be used in fields at night. Using horses and mules for fieldwork requires additional labor and slows the pace of farmwork. It restricts the number of acres that can be plowed and controls both the size and the number of farms that a family can cultivate. Modern farmers with large tractors can till several hundred acres, whereas the typical Amish farm has less than fifty acres. The horse limits the expansionist tendencies of modernity. In all these ways, horses temper the pace of Amish life.

The horse is important in other ways as well. The Amish have always been a people of the land. By living close to nature, they believe they are closer to God. The Amish feel that the rhythms of nature, the changing seasons, and the daily struggle with weather provide opportunities to experience divine presence. The horse preserves this link with nature in the midst of modernity. Horse care brings daily contact with nature—birth, death, illness, grazing, excrement, and unpredictable temperaments—a never-ending dialogue with the Creator. The horse has also held the Amish close to nature by keeping them out of cities.[10] With the rise of Amish shops, the horse may preserve one of the few bonds with nature for those involved in business.

Dependence on the horse requires daily sacrifice, a cogent reminder that identity and tradition supersede convenience in Amish life. Horses must be fed morning and evening. It takes time to hitch and unhitch them. Stables must be cleaned and manure hauled to the fields. Horses must be shoed regularly, and they also kick and bite. In some towns, it is difficult to find hitching posts. Moreover, driving a horse on high-speed highways is dangerous.

Non-Amish motorists sometimes grumble about buggies clogging the roadways of Lancaster County. One local citizen, responding to the complaints of a non-Amish motorist, noted that if the Amish sold their farms for development, each fifty-acre farm might bring 400 more cars to the county. So he concluded, "The next time you are behind a buggy, picture 400 cars ahead of you. That could very well be what each buggy is keeping off our roadways."[11]

The use of workhorses has taken an ironic twist in recent years. In speed and power, they obviously lag behind tractors. However, a different picture emerges when viewing financial investments on small farms. Although a good pair of mules may cost $7,000, mules and horses may have gained on tractors as the cost of machinery has soared. If labor costs are subtracted, Amish farmers on small farms can compete with modern farmers who use $60,000 tractors and $200,000 harvesters to harvest crops. The Amish contend that on small farms the horse is superior. One Amish farmer argued that "the horse farmers can produce milk, hogs, and poultry cheaper than the large tractor farmers."[12] Because horses pack the ground less than tractors, Amish farmers can begin plowing earlier in the spring. And although horses plow slowly, modern farmers marvel at how the Amish always seem to get their planting and harvesting done on time, if not first.[13]

The horse creates another benefit in Amish society: a subculture filled with lore and labor. Horse stories abound. Articles on horses appear in Amish publications. Horse tales preserve and perpetuate this distinctive symbol of Amish identity. But more importantly, the horse culture creates work. Small industries that manufacture, sell, and repair horse equipment provide jobs for many Amish.

As a front-stage symbol, the horse projects a conservative public image that conveniently camouflages a multitude of differences in income, lifestyles, and hobbies on the backstage of Amish life. The Amish businessman who travels in a hired truck all week supervising a multimillion-dollar business bends to tradition by driving his horse to Sunday services. Progressive Amish who read *Newsweek,* limit the size of their families, and landscape their homes can nod with affinity to their more conservative neighbors as their horses pass each other on country roads. The horse offers compelling proof that the Amish are still Amish while permitting a host of changes in other areas of Amish life.

The horse slows things down, imposes limits, and symbolizes some of the deepest meanings of Amish life. Riding in a horse-drawn carriage is a visible symbol of ethnic identity, unmistakable to insiders and outsiders alike. As a good ethnic badge, the horse both integrates and separates; it leaves no doubt about the symbolic boundaries of Amish society. It would be foolish to concede the horse to modernity or carelessly place it on the bargaining table. Although retaining the horse, the Amish have been willing to negotiate the use of the car and tractor—a story we will explore in Chapter 9.

THE CARRIAGE OF SIMPLICITY

The carriage also symbolizes Amish identity in several ways. At least seven different vehicles are used by the Lancaster Amish: the open buggy, the spring wagon, the market wagon, the cab wagon, the two-wheeled cart, the standard carriage, and a combination (open or closed) carriage. Each is pulled on the road with a single driving horse and rolls on wooden wheels wrapped in a steel band. Sleighs are also used in winter.[14]

The term *buggy,* often used for many of these vehicles, technically only designates the one-seat open vehicle. The open buggy, sometimes called the "courting buggy" by outsiders, is used by young and old alike, but its use has declined in recent years. The spring wagon, named for its extra spring suspension, is an open wagon used for hauling heavy supplies on the road. The market wagon, an enclosed carriage, is the Amish version of the station wagon, with a tailgate that swings upward, a removable back seat, and heavier suspension. Historically, it was used to haul produce to city markets. Its roof and enclosed sides protect both driver and produce from the weather. The cab wagon, the Amish edition of the pickup truck, has an enclosed cab for the driver and an open bed for hauling materials. The basic and most widely used vehicle is the standard carriage. Having undergone several changes in the twentieth century, the standard carriage today is a gray, enclosed, box-like, two-seated vehicle.[15]

The carriage functions as the family car for most Amish families. Its two seats may carry six or more passengers. Sliding doors with glass windows provide openings on both sides near the front of the carriage. The front is enclosed by a glass windshield. In contrast to the faddish designs of modern cars, the exterior form of the carriage has resisted change. Gray became the standard color in the early twentieth century, and apart from the enclosed front, the basic form and style jelled at that time. Today's carriage is equipped with battery-operated front lights, turn signals, flashing rear lights, and a large triangle reflector. These modern accouterments are required by state law.

Older carriages were open in the front and had no dashboard, windshield,

A young mother drives a spring wagon to the bank. Many Amishwomen are adept at handling horses.

or sliding doors. Roll curtains covered the open doorways, and a canvas tarp was fastened across the front to shield the driver from flying mud. Sliding doors and permanent windshields, called storm fronts, began appearing on a few carriages in the late 1920s. An expanding settlement required longer trips in harsh weather, which prompted the use of enclosed carriages. Storm fronts and sliding doors came into use over three decades and were officially permitted in the 1960s. As enclosed carriages gained acceptance, those with open fronts became symbols of tradition. The conservative districts in the settlement's southern region, always dragging their feet, were slower to accept the fully enclosed carriage. Ministers generally do not enclose the fronts of their carriages. In extremely cold weather some ministers may use an enclosed market wagon, but usually, in deference to tradition, they drive a carriage without a storm front.

THE SYMBOLIC BUGGY

The Amish buggy serves a variety of social functions. Its gray color and box-like form are public symbols of Amish identity. Gray symbolizes Gelassenheit, for it quietly blends into its surroundings; it is the unpretentious color of modesty. However, there is nothing quite as obtrusive on a modern highway as a horse-drawn vehicle. When some buggy makers began producing darker buggies in the 1930s, Amish leaders insisted on keeping the traditional gray. There was another reason as well for staying with gray: Old Order Mennonites drove black buggies. Thus, over the years, gray became the signature of Amish identity in the Lancaster settlement.[16]

Like garb, the buggy is a visible ethnic badge that shapes social interaction. Stepping out of a buggy is a public announcement of one's religious identity. On the road, the carriage provides a mobile stage for enacting the drama of separation. The rolling stage separates the Amish from the larger world. With few windows, the ethnic travelers are insulated from the outside world even while in transit. Indeed, on the front stage of public roadways, passengers inside the carriage can remain backstage.

Whereas the car in modern society accentuates social status and inequality, the Amish carriage is a symbolic equalizer. It signals the egalitarian ideals of Amish society. Although there are minor variations, carriages are quite uniform. The church has staunchly prohibited ornamentation and ostentatious display on buggies. People of all sorts—farmers, homemakers, laborers, and millionaires alike—drop the trappings of status and prestige as they step into similar buggies. And for the moment at least, the carriage levels them symbolically. Unlike the car, the carriage imposes a community standard that transcends individual choice, preference, and status.

Although the carriage suppresses individuality, it is not unusual to find carriages owned by teenagers decorated with creative stickers and plastic reflectors. Some have shrill air horns, boom boxes, and CD players run by batteries. An adult described some buggies owned by Amish youth: "Some have wall-to-wall carpeting, insulated woolly stuff all around the top, a big dashboard, glove compartment, speedometer, clock, CD player, buttons galore, and lights and reflectors all over the place. There's one that even has little lights all the way around the bottom. They even have perfumed things hanging up front, and at Christmas time, some have tinsel and little bells. If they have the money, that's what they do and that's pride."

On the outside, at least, the carriage summarizes a host of Amish values: separation, simplicity, frugality, tradition, equality, and humility. The carriage protests the high-tech fads of modern transportation. Clashing with the sleek style of modern cars, its stark rectangular form symbolizes the stalwart nature of Amish society. Its shape and accessories are governed by local tradition rather than by market research driven by consumer desire. Like the horse, the carriage has spawned an infrastructure of related industries. Amish shops manufacture, repair, and service carriages. Locally produced, the carriage ignores the flux of oil prices, imports, and strikes. It is, in short, a summary statement of Amish values and identity.

THE CHANGING BUGGY

On the outside the carriage appears resilient to change, but modernity has intruded beneath its shell. These changes, in many ways, are a metaphor of social change in Amish society at large. While external images hold firm, change percolates beneath the surface. The buggy has been a bargaining table of sorts, where the forces of tradition and technology have waged a quiet debate. In the early twentieth century, Amish carriages were rarely driven at night. When they were, a kerosene lantern provided light. After World War I, enterprising Amish youth began hooking up electric lights, powered by small batteries. Church leaders were adamantly opposed to the use of electric lights, believing they would speed the use of lights elsewhere.

Moreover, the lights made the buggies look too worldly—too much like cars. Upon baptism, many youth had to scrap the lights on their buggies.

In the 1920s, to the church's consternation, state laws required electric lights on vehicles at night. The use of lights became a contentious issue because the church forbade them. However, the church gradually acquiesced, and in the 1930s, most carriages traveling at night had battery-powered lights. In the 1950s and 1970s, flashing red lights and large reflective triangles, respectively, were required by law.[17] For a people who detested publicity, these requirements were most unwelcome. Flashing lights and bright triangles mocked the modest spirit of Gelassenheit. But acknowledging the need for safety, the Amish agreed to use them.[18]

Although safety concerns prevailed, the Amish carried some weight because they were fast becoming a prime tourist attraction. Thus, over the years an informal bargain emerged. The Amish could drive on public roads without paying gas taxes or license fees, but their buggies would carry the trappings of modernity—electric lights, turn signals, flashers, and fluorescent triangles. Buggies would not be inspected or licensed, and drivers would not need a license. Horseshoes could continue to chop up public roads at the taxpayers' expense. Tourists would pay gas taxes and bring enough money into the local economy to offset the cost of Amish "freeloading." Representatives on both sides of the bargaining table knew that they had struck a good deal.

Although the buggy's exterior has stabilized over the years, its interior has undergone many changes. Hidden to the outsider, these discreet changes make today's buggy a rather up-to-date vehicle. In addition to the safety features stipulated by law, other enhancements have slipped in as well. Beginning in the mid-1970s, fiberglass replaced wood in the bottom shell of the frame as well as in the shafts that connect to the harness. Vinyl tops—in gray, of course—cover the carriage. The wheels spin on ball bearings, and hydraulic brakes slow them down. Some carriages even have battery-operated windshield wipers. Thermopane windows, to deter fogging in cold weather, are also an option.

A young man purchasing his first buggy can select carpet in several colors and textures. He also has a choice of a dozen colors of upholstery in two textures of crushed velvet. Other colors and textures can be ordered by catalogue. A standard carriage will cost nearly $4,000, with another $1,000 in accessories such as clock, speedometer, four-wheel brakes, thermopane windows, and extra lights. A new carriage will last from ten years to a lifetime, depending on its use and care.[19]

The Amish, in essence, have refused to concede the traditional form and color of the carriage but have accepted modern technology under the surface. Some changes were induced by legal regulations, while others sneaked in by default beneath the stalwart symbols of tradition. In this way the buggy is a metaphor of the larger process of social change in Amish society.

Thus, dialect, dress, horse, and carriage are symbols of integration and separation. They require daily rituals of Gelassenheit—of surrender to communal values. Unlike ceremonial symbols reserved for historical festivities, these concrete expressions of ethnicity shape everyday behavior in practical ways. They link members together in a common history and a common mission against worldliness. As means of defense, they draw the boundary lines between church and world. As badges of ethnicity, they announce Amish identity to insider and outsider alike. In many ways they are sacred symbols, which the Amish have guarded with care. Their public visibility conveniently masks a multitude of changes on the backstage of Amish life.

The Social Architecture
of Amish Society

Bigness ruins everything.
—Amish carpenter

SOCIAL BUILDING BLOCKS

Human interaction is shaped not only by cultural beliefs and symbols but also by patterns of social behavior. Societies, like buildings, have distinctive architectural styles. Like blocks of Legos, social relations can be arranged in many different ways. In some societies males dominate, in others females do, and in still others neither does. The organizational pattern of each society creates a distinctive social architecture.

Growing up in an Amish family with eighty first cousins nearby is quite different from living in a nuclear family with two cousins living a thousand miles apart. Child-rearing practices in Amish families, where both parents often work at home, differ radically from dual-career families whose children play in daycare. A society's architectural design shapes human behavior in profound ways. What features distinguish the social architecture of Amish society? What is the organizational shape of Gelassenheit?

Demographic factors—birth rates, mobility, marital status, and family size—are the building blocks of a society's social structure. Table 4.1 compares the demographic differences between the Amish and non-Amish population in Lancaster County. The Amish are more likely than their neighbors to marry, live in large households, terminate school early, and engage in farming. A striking feature of Amish society is the large proportion (52 percent)

TABLE 4.1
Demographic Characteristics of Lancaster County Amish and Non-Amish Populations (in percentages)

	Amish	Non-Amish
Sex		
Male	48	48
Female	52	52
Age		
Under 18 years	52	28
18–44 years	30	40
45–64 years	12	20
65 and over	6	12
Marital Status of Adults[a]		
Single	24	39
Married	76[b]	61
Education		
Eighth grade or less	100	23
High school attendance	—	17
High school graduate	—	37
More than high school	—	10
College diploma or more	—	13
Occupation		
Professional	—	27
Farming[c]	44	4
Household		
Single-person households	5	20
Mean Number of people per household	5.0	2.8
Mean Family Size (children and adults)	8.5	3.3

SOURCE: Settlement profile of 812 adults (eighteen years and older) described in Appendix A. 2000 U.S. Census summarized by the Lancaster County Planning Commission.

[a] 18 years and older.

[b] Among those 25 years and older, 95 percent are married.

[c] Males 25 to 65 years of age.

of people under eighteen years of age. With only 6 percent of its members over sixty-five, Amish life tilts toward child rearing. Schools, rather than retirement villages, dominate the social landscape.

The individualization of modern society, reflected in spiraling percentages of single people and single-parent homes, is largely absent from Amish society. Whatever the Amish do, they do together. Only 5 percent of Amish households are single-person units, compared to 20 percent for the county. Moreover, virtually all of the single-person households adjoin other Amish homes. Several households are often on the same property. Many double households include a small adjacent *Grossdaadi* house for the grandparents.

Five people live in the average Amish household—nearly double the county rate of 2.8 per household. The majority of Amish reside in a household with a half dozen other people or at least live adjacent to one. Moreover, additional members of the extended family live just across the road or beyond the next field.

AGE AND GENDER ROLES

Age and gender roles are essential building blocks in Amish society. The Amish identify four stages of childhood: babies, little children, scholars, and young people.[1] The term *little children* is used for children from the time they begin walking until they enter school. Children between the ages of six and fifteen are often called *scholars*. Young people from mid-teens to marriage explore their independence by joining informal youth groups called "gangs" that crisscross the settlement.

Social power increases with age. In a rural society where children follow the occupations of parents, the elderly provide valuable advice. Younger generations turn to them for wisdom in treating an earache, making pie dough, training a horse, predicting a frost, or designing a quilt. In a slowly changing society, the seasoned judgment of elders is esteemed, unlike fast-paced societies where children teach new technologies to their parents. The power of age also molds the life of the church, where the words of an older minister count more than those of a younger one. The chairman of the ordained leaders in the settlement is traditionally an older bishop with the longest tenure in that office. Wisdom accumulated by experience, rather than by professional or technical competence, is the root of power in Amish society.

Although power increases with age, gender distinctions produce inequality. In the realm of church, work, and community, the male voice carries greater influence. Age and gender create a patriarchy that gives older men the greatest clout and younger females the least. One mother said, "How people see women hasn't changed that much. We're still seen as second class. Of course, we really emphasize family life. And when you think about how much the children of divorce suffer—that's all such a mess. We emphasize family life. That's what is important to us, to have good family relations. But I don't think women are becoming more free in our community. That's how it seems to me."

Amish families are organized around traditional gender roles. Although in

Amish marriages, like others, various power equations emerge depending on the personalities of the partners, the husband is seen as the spiritual head of the home. He is responsible for its religious welfare and usually has the final word on matters related to the church and the outside world. Among farm families, husbands organize the farming operation and supervise the work of children in barns and fields. Many husbands assist their wives with gardening, lawn care, and child care, but others do little. Husbands rarely help with household work—washing, cooking, canning, sewing, mending, cleaning. The visible authority of the husband varies by household, but Amish society is primarily patriarchal and vests final authority for moral and social life in the male role.

THE ROLE OF WOMEN

The church teaches that, in the divine order of things, wives are expected to submit to their husband's authority. This theme is emphasized in the wedding vows.[2] A fifty-year-old woman noted, "I think maybe our wedding sermons today are easier on the woman's role in the home. I know a lot of women have felt put down in the wedding sermon. I know some of the preachers try harder these days to say kinder things about the woman's role in the home."

Entrusted with the responsibility of raising a large family, many Amish women are very efficient managers. Married women rarely have full-time jobs outside the home. In addition to providing child care, the wife normally oversees the garden, preserves food, cooks, cleans, washes, sews, and supervises yard work. An Amish woman's garden and flowers are her kingdom.[3] Many women mow their lawns with push mowers, without engines. Moreover, those who live on a farm often assist with barn chores—feeding calves, milking cows, and gathering eggs—as well as harvesting crops and vegetables. Others do clerical work or bookkeeping in their husband's shop. The work is hard and the hours long, but there is quiet satisfaction in nourishing thriving families, tending productive gardens, baking pies, sewing colorful quilts, and watching dozens of grandchildren find their place in the Amish world. One woman, who had baked fifty-six pies in preparation for the lunch following church at her home said, "It's no big deal because the children always help."

Mingled with the work are many pleasant moments of reprieve—a quilting party, a "frolic," a sale, a wedding, and, of course, perpetual visiting. In addition to the endless chores, one woman said, "we sing, laugh, smile, and go through mid-life crises. We are real. Some of us even believe in women's rights, anyhow if we know what they are."

Women vote in church business meetings and nominate men for ministerial duties. They do not, however, participate in the community's formal power structure. They cannot be ordained, nor do they serve as members of special committees. Virtually all Amish schoolteachers are single women, but they too are on the fringe of the formal leadership structure.[4]

One of the remarkable changes in gender relations is the growing number of women who own and operate businesses. About 15 percent of the hundreds of Amish businesses are operated by women. In some cases husbands work for their wives who are the owners. Gender influences shape business involvements. Women tend to operate food, craft, and quilt industries but not metal, woodworking, or construction firms. An attorney who works with both Old Order Mennonites and Amish noted that Amish women are much more involved in real estate transactions and much more likely to speak up at a real estate settlement.[5]

Without the prod of market forces, labor-saving devices have come more slowly in the kitchen than in the barn. The ban on electricity has, of course, eliminated many appliances from Amish homes. Even with ample help from children, it is a challenge to manage a household of eight or more people without electric mixers, blenders, dishwashers, microwave ovens, and clothes dryers. Increasingly, washing machines and sewing machines are powered by air pressure as are mixers, beaters, and blenders. The kitchens and bathrooms in newer Amish homes have a modern appearance, with lovely state-of-the-art cabinetry. Contemporary-looking gas stoves and refrigerators have eliminated old wood cookstoves and iceboxes, although kerosene space heaters are still widely used. Permanent-press fabrics, disposable diapers, cake mixes, and cleaning detergents have lightened household work in many ways. Nevertheless, some Amish women think the acceptance of labor-saving devices has favored the men. One young woman described the tilted balance of power this way:

> The joke among us women is that the men make the rules so that's why more modern things are permitted in the barn than in the house. The women have no say in the rules. Actually, I think the main reason is the

Using horses to pull a modern hay baler, a family works together to harvest
a new crop of hay.

men make the living and we don't make a living in the house. So you
have to go along with what they need out there. You know, if the public
health laws call for it, you have to have it. In the house you don't. Even
my Dad says that he thinks the Amish women get the brunt of it all
around. They have so many children and are expected to help out with
the milking. Some help for two hours with the milking from beginning
to end and they have five little children. That's all right if a man helps
them in the house and puts the children to bed, but a lot of them don't.
I don't think it's fair that we have the push mowers to mow the lawns
with. It is hard work on some of these lawns. We keep saying that if the
men would mow the lawns there would be engines on them, and I am
sure there would be. Years ago they used to mow the hay fields with an
old horse mower, but now they have engines on the field mowers so it
goes easier for the horses, but they don't care about the women.

Another woman declared that the church accepted gasoline-powered weed
trimmers "because the men needed to trim their fence posts, which left the

women feeling, at last, we may need to fight for our rights!" These statements show the growing sensitivity of some women to gender roles. Amish women are not liberated by modern standards, but many find fulfillment in durable, defined roles within their extended families. They know who they are and what is expected of them. One husband said: "A wife is not a servant; she is queen and the husband is the king."

Marriage in Amish society accents not romance but the importance of a loving, durable partnership. Many Amish couples experience a partnership in their marriage that was typical of preindustrial, rural life before the rise of factory work. One woman described the joy of a good partnership as she drove the horses pulling the hay baler while her husband stacked the bales on a wagon in the face of an impending storm: "The machinery all worked, and the green hay smelled so good, and the horses felt brisk, and we were in a hurry. It's a wonderful feeling at a time like that. We two, the four horses, and the baler all working harmoniously together, with the wind grabbing at our clothes and manes, as if to say, it's helping us along."[6]

Several Amish women offered the following recipe on "How to Preserve a Husband" from the back of a cookbook they had printed for distribution.

> First use care and find one not too young, but one that is tender and a healthy growth. Make your selection carefully and let it be final. Otherwise, they will not keep. Like wine, they improve with age. Do not pickle or put in hot water. This will make them sour.
> Prepare as follows:
> Sweeten with smiles according to the variety. The sour, bitter kind are improved by a pinch of salt of common sense. Spice with patience. Wrap well in a mantle of charity. Preserve over a good fire of steady devotion. Serve with peaches and cream. The poorest varieties may be improved by this process and will keep for years in any climate.[7]

As largely self-employed people, Amish women, ironically, have greater control over their work and daily affairs than do many other women who hold full-time clerical and nonprofessional jobs. Unfettered by the pressure to succeed in a career, Amish women devote their energies to family living. While their work is hard, it is *their* work, and it brings as much satisfaction as a professional career, if not more. Amish women view professional women working away from home and children as a distortion of God's created order that can only lead to divorce, unruly children, and family disruption. Their role models are other Amish women who have managed their families well. Happiness, after all, depends on one's values and social point of reference. All things considered, within their context Amish women express high levels of social and personal satisfaction. Indeed, women in modern society, often burdened by conflicting role expectations and professional pressures to excel, may experience greater anxiety over their roles than many Amish women.

FAMILY TIES

When Amish leaders tally up the size of their churches, they count families, not individuals.[8] The family, the keystone of Amish society, is large in both size and influence. Most Amish youth marry between the ages of nineteen and twenty-five, on a Tuesday or Thursday in November, as the harvest season comes to a close. Marriage is highly esteemed, and raising a family is the professional career of Amish adults. Nine out of ten adults are married.

Marriage vows are rarely broken. An Amish woman explained, "I don't

Many Amish babies are born at home and welcomed by siblings.

think us Amish should allow divorce. I think you need to work things out. That's how we're taught. We're taught over and over, when you decide to marry, you will spend the rest of your life with this person. You need to work it out." There are, of course, some de facto divorces, and in rare cases couples may live apart, but divorce is taboo. People who initiate divorce are automatically excommunicated. If a husband divorces his wife and leaves the community, she can remain within the church but cannot remarry until he dies.

Believing that large families are a blessing from God, couples yield to the laws of nature and produce sizeable families.[9] Although the church informally frowns on birth control, some couples do use artificial and natural means to regulate the arrival of newborns in one way or another. Despite such attempts, Amish culture continues to value large families. One young mother, after giving birth to four children, said with a measure of satisfaction, "Well, I'm half done now." Including parents and children, the average family has 8.5 members, compared to the county norm of 3.3. By age forty-five, the typical Amish woman has given birth to 7.1 children, whereas her neighbors average 2.8. Death and disease reduce the number, yielding families that average 6.5 children. Slightly over 10 percent of Amish families have ten or more children. By the turn of the twenty-first century, about 1,100 new babies were arriving in the Lancaster settlement every year.

While Amish children are numerous, the cost of their upbringing is relatively low. There are no swimming pool memberships, tennis lessons, stereos, computer games, summer camps, sports cars, college tuition, or designer clothes to buy. Children assume daily chores by five or six years of age, and their responsibilities in the barn and house grow rapidly. They are seen not as economic burdens but as blessings from the Lord and as new members who will contribute their share to the family economy. Even with the growth of businesses, the labor provided by children is an economic asset to the community.

The power of the family extends beyond sheer numbers. The family's scope and influence dwarfs that of the modern nuclear family. Amish life is spent in the context of the family. In contemporary families social functions from birth to death, from eating to leisure, often leave the home. In contrast, Amish activities are anchored at home. Children are usually born there. They play at home and walk to school. By age fourteen, children work full-time in the home, shop, or farm. They are taught by their extended family, not

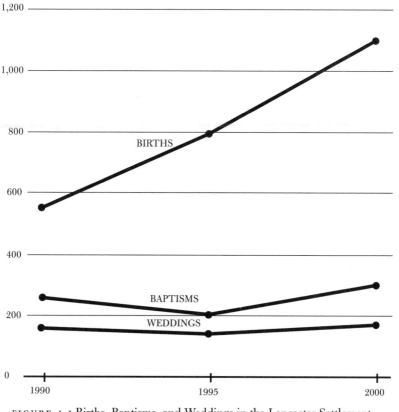

FIGURE 4.1 Births, Baptisms, and Weddings in the Lancaster Settlement, 1990–2000. *Source: The Diary*

by television, babysitters, popular magazines, or daycare teachers. Young couples are married at home. Church services rotate from home to home. Most meals are eaten at home. Adults work at home or nearby. Plentiful recreational activities, such as swimming, sledding, skating, softball, volleyball, and corner ball, centered near home, have no admission fees.

Social events, singings, "Sisters Days," quilting parties, and work "frolics" are staged in homes. Occasionally, men will slip away for a day of deep sea fishing or several days of hunting, but the majority of Amish recreation is close to home and nature. In the past, vacations to "get away from home" were rare, but increasingly many couples take "trips" of several weeks to other settlements. Others will take shorter trips to historical sites, the zoo, or a flower show. A few older couples vacation in Florida for several winter months at Pinecraft, a small Amish village that attracts retirees from many

settlements.[10] Out-of-state travel by van, train, or bus (but not air) often includes visiting in other settlements.

Despite increased traveling, home remains the site for many activities. Although the Amish do buy groceries and commercial products, much of their
food is homegrown, and much clothing is homemade. Even table games are
homemade. Instead of eating at a pizza shop, they will more likely make pizza
at home. Men's hair is cut at home. Time and money spent on shopping trips
are thus minuscule compared to the American norm. There are no visits to
the health spa, pet parlor, hairdresser, car wash, or sports stadium, and thus
there is more time for "home work" and "home play." Although the Amish
use modern medicines, they are more likely to rely on home remedies, natural foods, and herbs; and they only visit a doctor as a last resort. Retirement
occurs at home. Funerals are held at home, and the deceased are buried in
nearby cemeteries. All of these centripetal forces pull the Amish homeward
most of the time. Staying home is not a dreaded experience of isolation; it
means being immersed in the chatter, work, and play of the extended family.

Despite their commitment to home, recent trends are pulling some activities away. Less food and clothing and fewer toys and products are made at
home. More commercial games and toys are bought. More couples are taking
extended trips away from home. Nevertheless, by contemporary standards
most of the dramas of Amish life are staged at home or very nearby. Very few
life-cycle functions have left their homes, and in this regard the Amish stand
apart from the modern world.

In contrast to the mobility of contemporary families, Amish families are
tied to a geographical area and anchored in a large extended family. Many
people live on or within several miles of their childhood homestead. Others
may live as far as fifteen miles away. After a new family settles down in a
residence, it typically remains there for life. Thus geographical and family
roots run very deep. A mother of six children explained that all of them live
within Lancaster County and that she delights in visiting her thirty-six grandchildren at least once a month. Those living on the other side of her house,
of course, she sees every day. With families averaging nearly seven children,
it is not unusual for a couple to have forty-five grandchildren. A typical child
will have two dozen aunts and uncles and as many as eighty first cousins.
Although some of these relatives are scattered on the settlement's fringe,
many live within a few miles of home. To be Amish is to have a niche, a

A modern kitchen in a contemporary Amish home. A gas refrigerator chills food and gas-pressured lamps provide light.

secure place in a thick web of family ties. Embroidered or painted rosters of extended family names hang on the walls of every Amish home—a constant reminder of the individual's notch in the family tree.

THE CHURCH DISTRICT

The Amish families who live near each other form a church district or congregation—the primary social unit beyond the family. In the Lancaster settlement the number of households per church district ranges from twenty to fifty, with an average of thirty-four. With many double households, the average district has about twenty major family units. Some 80 adults and 90 youth under nineteen years of age give the typical district a total of 170 people.[11] Church services are held in homes, and as congregations grow, they divide.

A district's geographical size varies with the density of the Amish population. On the edge of the settlement, church districts stretch twelve miles from side to side, but in the settlement's hub they shrink dramatically. Families in small geographic districts, often within a half-mile of each other, are able to walk to services. In recent years the physical size of church districts has shrunk because more people have gone into nonfarm occupations, which has reduced the spread of land required for a district.

Roads and streams form the boundaries of most church districts. Like members of a traditional parish, the Amish participate in the church district that encircles their home. The members of a district worship together every other week. Sometimes they attend the services of adjoining districts on the "off Sunday" of their congregation. Residents of one district, however, cannot become members of another one unless they move into its territory. Because there are no church buildings, the homes of members become the gathering sites not only for worship but also for socializing.

The church district is the social and ceremonial unit of the Amish world. Self-contained and autonomous, dozens of congregations are linked together by a network of ordained leaders and extended families. Baptisms, weddings, excommunications, and funerals take place within the district. Fellowship meals after worship and other activities bring members of the district together. Members visit, worship, and work together in a dense ethnic network. In short, the church district is family, factory, church, club, and precinct all bundled into a neighborhood parish.

Districts ordain their own leaders and, on the recommendation of their bishop, have the power to excommunicate members. Errant members must confess major sins publicly before other members. Local congregations, under the leadership of their bishop, vary in their interpretation of religious regulations. Some districts permit power lawn mowers and others do not. Some allow fancier furniture than others. Decisions to aid other districts financially and to participate in community-wide Amish programs are made by the local district. Congregational votes are taken on recommendations of the bishop. John Hostetler has aptly called this system a "patriarchal democracy."[12] Although each member has a vote, it is usually a vote to accept or reject the bishop's recommendation.

Because families live so close together, many members of a district are often related. Throughout the settlement six surnames—Stoltzfus, King, Fisher, Beiler, Esh, and Lapp—account for over 70 percent of the households. The rank order of surnames is displayed in Table 4.2. Kinship networks are dense both within and between church districts, and there are

TABLE 4.2
Rank Order of Household Surnames

Name	Households	Percentage
Stoltzfus[a]	1,424	25.7
King	681	12.3
Fisher	587	10.6
Beiler	517	9.3
Esh[b]	397	7.2
Lapp	314	5.7
Zook	285	5.1
Glick	203	3.7
20 names[c]	1,076	19.4
14 names[d]	54	1.0
TOTAL	5,538	100.0

SOURCE: Address Book of the Lancaster County Amish (1998).
NOTE: Includes households in settlements that originated from the Lancaster County settlement.
[a] Eighty-three of these households spell their name "Stoltzfoos."
[b] Forty-six of these households spell their name "Esch." Technically, these are two different families.
[c] Representing from eleven to seventy-two households.
[d] Representing ten or fewer households.

many repetitious names. For example, there are 115 Samuel Stoltzfuses, 115 Mary Stoltzfuses, 56 Mary Kings, 52 John Kings, and so on in the Lancaster settlement. One rural mail carrier had to distinguish among sixty Stoltzfus families. Moreover, he had three Amos E. Stoltzfuses and three Elam S. Stoltzfuses on the same route!

The frequency of similar names has led to many nicknames based on physical traits, personal habits, or an unusual incident related to the person. The nicknames tend to follow patriarchal lines across several generations. "Cookie Abner" derives from a teenage eating incident, and "See more Levi" has very large eyes. "Pud Reuben" was a heavyset man who was nicknamed "Pud." His children became Pud's Aaron, or Pud's Sally. Families sometimes develop nicknames—"the Squeakies," "the Piggys" (who live near Piggy's Pond), "the Mo-boys," "the Izzies," "the Jackies," and "the Butchers" to name a few of hundreds. One woman said, "I'm a Bootah. That goes way back to my great-grandparents. When they got their marriage license, the clerk wasn't too bright, and she wrote their names 'Bootah' (butter) instead of Beiler. So ever since we've been the Bootahs. I think our children will be Squeakies because the nicknames usually follow the man's line, but they don't always pass from one generation to the next."

LEADERSHIP ROLES

The leadership team in each district typically consists of a bishop, two or three ministers, and a deacon.[13] The leaders are viewed as servants of both God and the congregation. In fact, their German titles translate literally as 'servant.'[14] A bishop serves as the spiritual head and typically presides over two districts.[15] One district is the bishop's "home" congregation. Congregations meet every other week, and thus their bishop is able to attend each of their regular meetings. The bishop officiates at baptisms, weddings, communions, funerals, and members' meetings. As spiritual head of the leadership team, he interprets and enforces church regulations. If disobedience or conflict arises, he is responsible to resolve it. Family and church networks are often entangled in controversies of one sort or another that require delicate diplomacy.

The bishop is responsible for recommending excommunication or, as the case may be, the reinstatement of penitent members. While considerable authority is vested in the office of bishop, final decisions to excommunicate or reinstate members require a congregational vote. Diverse personalities among the bishops lead to diverse interpretations of rules. Some leaders are "open-minded," whereas others take firm doctrinaire positions. Some are stern, and others are loving and gentle. The bishop is the incarnate symbol of church authority. One member remarked that every time she sees a policeman, he "reminds me of a bishop." She added, however, that her bishop is a kind person, more concerned about the inner spiritual life of people than about outward regulations.

If the office of bishop is vacated by death or illness, a nearby bishop is given temporary oversight of the congregation. Eventually one of the ministers from the two congregations is ordained bishop by the biblical custom of "casting lots." The ordination of a bishop may be delayed several years if the eligible ministers are too young or inexperienced. A senior bishop explained that he prefers to ordain bishops who have demonstrated their ability to raise a family dedicated to the church. Plans to ordain a bishop are approved by the local congregation as well as by the settlement-wide Bishops' Meeting.

The minister, or preacher, fills the second leadership role in the local district. A congregation usually has two and sometimes three preachers, depending on their age and health. One of them serves as the lead minister, working closely with the bishop to give spiritual direction to the congregation. In addition to general leadership, ministers preach long sermons without the aid of notes. Without professional credentials or special training, ministers are selected from within the congregation and serve unpaid for life. They earn their own living by farming, carpentry, or other related occupations, including business.

Each congregation has a deacon whose public duties are limited to reading Scripture and prayers in worship services. He supervises an "alms fund" and attends to the material needs of families. The deacon assists with baptism and communion and carries responsibility for reproving wayward members. At the request of the bishop, the deacon, often accompanied by a minister, visits members who have violated church regulations. The outcome of the visit is reported to the bishop, who then takes appropriate action. The deacon also carries messages of excommunication or reinstatement to members from the bishop. One bishop called this aspect of the deacon's role "the dirty work."

The deacon also represents the congregation when young couples plan to marry. The groom brings a church letter of "good standing" from his deacon to the deacon of the bride's congregation, who then meets with her to verify the plans for matrimony. The bride's deacon then announces, or "publishes," the date of the wedding in the local congregation. The deacon does not arrange marriages, but he does symbolize the church's supervision of them. The bishop, ministers, and deacon function as an informal leadership team that guides and coordinates the activities of the local district.

THE MOBILE SANCTUARY

The rotation of worship services from home to home shapes Amish identity and forms the bedrock of their social organization. This distinctive feature has bolstered the strength of their community. While the Old Order Amish share some cultural traits with other Plain people in the region, the Amish are set apart because they are *not* "meetinghouse" people. Their mobile "sanctuary" distinguishes them from Old Order Mennonites, who worship in meetinghouses. The Amish view a permanent church building as a symbol of worldliness, a view that goes back to the Anabaptist rejection of cathedrals in Europe.

At about the time of the Civil War, some Amish were tempted to use church buildings. Beginning in 1862 a series of national Ministers' Meetings grappled with, among other things, lightning rods, insurance, photographs, and holding worship services in meetinghouses.[16] Few Lancaster bishops participated in these meetings because they feared that liberal changes in the Midwest would drift eastward and stir up controversy at home. Their fears were not in vain.

Progressive-minded members in two districts of eastern Lancaster County began pressing for changes. The internal strife forced a stalemate that delayed the observance of communion in one congregation for seven years (1870–77). The discord came to a head in the late fall of 1876 when preacher Gideon Stoltzfus in the lower Pequea district was "silenced" from preaching by his bishop. He was charged with fellowshipping with liberal Amish in the Midwest. Eventually, about two-thirds of his district, some seventy-five progressive members, left the Old Order Amish and formed what later became a Mennonite congregation. Within several years, the progressives fulfilled the Old Order's worst fears by building a meetinghouse.

A few miles to the east and a few months later, in the spring of 1877, a similar division erupted in the Conestoga district, leaving only eight families with the Old Order Amish. And as the sages predicted, the progressives in that area also erected a meetinghouse by 1882.[17] These ruptures in two Lancaster districts within six months stunned the small Amish community, which at that time contained only six districts and less than five hundred members.

Thus 1877 marks a pivotal point in the Amish saga—a landmark that still casts a shadow over Amish consciousness. From that juncture to the present, the Old Order Amish have seen what happens when a progressive group drifts off and builds a meetinghouse. Eventually they hold Sunday school, and soon they drop the German dialect. In time they accept cars and electricity, and before long they wear fancy clothes and attend high school. The 1877 division serves as a timely reminder of the long-term consequences when a progressive group becomes enchanted by such worldly things as meetinghouses.[18]

Worshiping in homes is a prudent way of limiting the size of Amish congregations. The physical size of houses controls the numerical size of church districts. This practice serves two important roles: it keeps the organizational structure of the settlement simple, and it guarantees that each individual has a social home in a small congregation. So while the Amish sanctuary floats, the individual is securely anchored in a strong social network. People are known by first names. Birthdays are remembered, and illness is public knowledge. In contrast, Moderns often float anonymously in and out of permanent sanctuaries. The mobile Amish sanctuary affirms the centrality of the family by keeping religious functions tied to the home and integrated with family life. This is a radical departure from modern religion with its specialized services in sanctuaries cut off from the other sectors of life.

A mobile meetinghouse not only assures individuals of a secure niche in a small social unit but also enhances informal social control. Close ties in family networks place informal checks on social behavior. The mobile sanctuary assures that, on the average, members will visit the home of every family once a year. These annual visits also serve as subtle inspection tours that stymie the proliferation of worldly furnishings in Amish homes. The visits shore up social cohesion and solidarity. How many people in contemporary congregations have toured the homes of *all* of their fellow members in the past year?

The mobile sanctuary protests the "cathedrals" of modern Christendom, which the Amish view as ostentatious displays of pride that point, not heavenward, but earthward to the congregation's social prestige. The financial resources used by many congregations for buildings, steeples, organs, and pastors are used by the Amish for mutual aid. Expansion, fueled by biological growth, is not dependent on evangelistic programs and state-of-the-art facilities that compete with other churches. The Amish are baffled as to why Moderns build opulent homes but do not worship in them and then construct expensive sanctuaries for once-a-week gatherings. Although Amish homes are not luxurious, they are heavily used for worship, work, eating, and socializing.

The decision to reject the meetinghouse has profound theological and sociological implications. Moving to a meetinghouse separates church and home, religion and life. It cuts a congregation's ties to a specific geographic area and breaks up the intimate bonds of face-to-face relations. The use of a meetinghouse encourages the growth of large congregations where individuals easily become lost in the crowd. Finally, a meetinghouse becomes an abstract symbol, so that church becomes a place, rather than the living embodiment of a people; a location for worship, rather than the incarnation of religious practice.[19] The mobile sanctuary, while not a public symbol, is deeply etched in Amish consciousness. Small, local, informal, lowly, and unpretentious, it is the structural embodiment of Gelassenheit—a major clue to the growth and well-being of Amish society.

A FLAT STRUCTURE

One of the striking aspects of Amish society is the absence of bureaucracy. The organizational structure is loose and fuzzy. Kitchens, shops, and barns provide office space for informal committees. There are no headquarters, professionals, executive directors, or organizational charts. Apart from schoolteachers, there are no paid church employees, let alone professional ones. The nebulous structure confounds outsiders. Public officials are not always sure who to contact to ascertain Amish opinions and policies. The vitality of Amish culture is remarkable, despite the lack of consultants, corporate offices, strategic plans, and elaborate flow charts. Amish society is linked together by a web of interpersonal ties that stretches across the community. How is unity possible with dozens of loosely coupled congregations?

The solution to this riddle lies in the fairly flat leadership structure. Each bishop typically serves two districts. The eighty adults in each district are only one step away from the top of the church hierarchy. The flat, two-tier structure links grassroots members directly to the citadel of power and has several benefits. Each bishop personally knows the members of his districts and in this way monitors the pulse of the community. Members feel a close tie to the central decision-making structure because their bishop attends the fall and spring Bishops' Meetings and can provide feedback on the discussion. The bishop, in turn, understands the larger concerns of his fellow bishops across the settlement. Thus he can personally explain churchwide regulations to his members. With about 160 adult members in his two districts, he knows his people well and is able to monitor social change on a first-name basis.

A seniority system based on age and tenure undergirds the power structure of the bishops. A young minister described the decision-making process among the bishops: "The oldest ones have priority. It tends to point to the oldest one. If they want a final decision, they say to him, 'Let's hear your decision.'" If health permits, the senior bishop presides over the Bishops' Meeting, as well as various Ministers' Meetings a few weeks later. The diplomatic skills of this highly esteemed elder statesman are crucial for upholding harmony. A minister described the seniority system: "Many bishops go to the oldest bishop to ask for his advice on a certain issue. And he will not hesitate to give his opinion, based on Scripture. Then he will conclude and say, 'Don't do it that way just because I told you, go home and work with your church.' So it is not a dictatorship by any means; it works on a priority basis and a *submitting* basis" (emphasis added).

Twice each year, some seventy-five bishops across the settlement confer on problems and discuss changes that might imperil the welfare of the church. Four regional Ministers' Meetings, involving bishops, ministers, and deacons, follow on the heels of the Bishops' Meeting each fall and spring. These regional meetings of ordained leaders, numbering over one hundred men, meet in a home, barn, or cabinet shop. The bishops report on issues from their Bishops' Meeting and solicit the ministers' support. Other concerns or special problems are also handled. The leaders' meetings play a significant role in maintaining cohesion and harmony across the settlement.

Historically, the hub of the settlement was around the village of Intercourse, but with the southward expansion the geographical and ideological center has shifted toward Georgetown. The number of districts grew from 11 in 1920 to 131 by 2000, stretching the organizational patterns. The leadership structure was revised in three ways to fit the prolific growth. First, the span of each bishop's control remained the same. In pyramid fashion, growing organizations often add rungs in their hierarchy as well as widen the control of top managers. The Amish have resisted this pattern. Instead of adding more congregations to each bishopric, they increased the number of bishops as districts multiplied. Keeping two districts per bishop and allowing all bishops to participate in the Bishops' Meeting prevented the development of new levels of authority. The flat architecture enhances social control as well as the church's ability to monitor social change.

Multiplying the number of bishops, however, led to other problems. With eighteen districts in the 1940s, nine bishops could easily meet and conduct their business informally. As the number of bishops increased, leadership became consolidated in an informal "executive committee" of senior bishops. The wisdom of this small group carries compelling authority in the Bishops' Meeting. Membership in this senior caucus of bishops is based on age and tenure rather than on election or appointment. Members of this inner circle

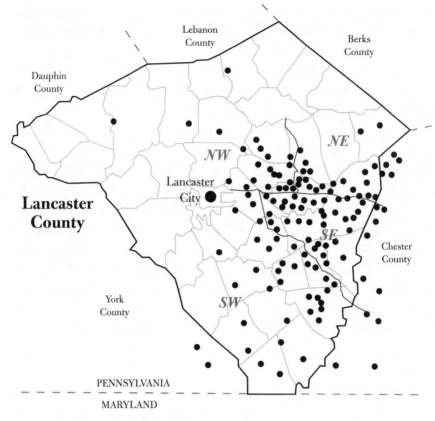

FIGURE 4.2 Distribution of Church Districts in the Lancaster Settlement and
Boundaries of Four Regional Ministers' Meetings

do not directly supervise other bishops, for even these senior members have
their own districts. Without the benefit of professional consultants or middle
managers, all the bishops serve, in their words, as "watchmen on the walls
of Zion," looking out for the church's welfare.

The growing number of districts precipitated a third change in organizational structure. By 1975 the community had expanded to fifty-two districts.
It was difficult to find a meeting place to accommodate the large group of
ordained leaders, which by then consisted of some two hundred bishops,
ministers, and deacons. Conducting business was hampered without a loud-
speaker system and formal parliamentary procedures. Thus, in April 1975,

the leaders were divided into north and south subgroups along Route 340, an east and west road through the heart of the settlement.[20] Facing relentless expansion, the settlement was divided again in 1993 into four quadrants, as shown in Figure 4.2. Bishops from the entire settlement continue to meet twice a year, followed by meetings of the ordained leaders in each respective quadrant. Many members credit the leaders' meeting as a key factor that enabled the settlement to avoid schism and maintain a semblance of unity despite enormous change in recent years.

NETWORKS OF SOCIAL CAPITAL

No formal committees report to the Amish bishops. Over the years, as lay members have formed committees for special projects, they have often consulted with ordained leaders as a gesture of goodwill. In general, the ministers and bishops, guardians of tradition, are reluctant to initiate or endorse new ventures or serve on committees. The formal power structure, slanted toward tradition, reacts to social changes but rarely exercises a leadership role in establishing new programs. Although the bishops' body has steered clear of formalized procedures, several networks have emerged to address special needs. In each case, interested laymen, sometimes with, and other times without, the blessing of the bishops, have coordinated activities that require resources beyond the scope of local districts. These networks illustrate how social capital is mobilized to address special needs across the settlement.

1. *Amish Aid Society.* Community barn raisings have been a longtime public symbol of mutual aid among the Amish. An informal plan pays for replacement materials and property destroyed by a fire or storm. Begun in 1875, the Amish Aid Society seeks to spread the costs of disaster across the community. Property owners who join the plan are assessed a fluctuating amount per $1,000 of property valuation. It is "assessment by need after the fire," said one member. A committee monitors the plan, and each church district has a director who records property assessments and collects the "fire tax." When the central treasury becomes depleted, the committee asks the director in each district to collect a new assessment. Collections vary by the frequency of fires but average about one a year. This modest system of fire and storm insurance operates without paid personnel, underwriters, agents,

offices, computers, lawsuits, or profits. Its sole purpose is to provide a network of support for members. Manual labor for cleanup and rebuilding is freely given by members whenever disaster strikes.[21]

2. *Old Order Book Society.* In 1937, in response to the consolidation of public schools, a group of laymen organized a School Committee, which sought to have Amish children excused from public school after the eighth grade. Eventually Amish schools were built and administered by local Amish school boards. The School Committee evolved into a statewide organization known as the Old Order Book Society, which coordinates Amish schools today. The society maintains a liaison with state education officials and provides guidelines for the administration of one-room Amish schools. Representatives from different settlements in Pennsylvania attend the society's annual meeting.[22]

3. *Amish Liability Aid.* In the 1960s, Amish businessmen began purchasing commercial liability insurance to protect themselves from lawsuits. The church had a longstanding opposition to worldly insurance programs, which use the force of law and undermine mutual aid. To resolve the dilemma of providing protection against lawsuits without using commercial insurance, Amish Liability Aid was established in 1965. Within a decade, the plan had nearly a thousand members.[23] According to one member, this plan "protects you from others when there's an accident and you're not protected yourself." Participation is voluntary, and members of the plan make a small annual contribution that fluctuates with the level of need across the settlement.

4. *National Steering Committee.* In the early 1960s, some Amish youth served as conscientious objectors in hospitals as an alternative to military service. These young men frequently became worldly, sometimes married non-Amish nurses, and often did not return home. And when they did, they found it difficult to fit into their rural communities. In an effort to solve this problem, Amish leaders across the nation met in Indiana in 1966. This meeting gave birth to a National Steering Committee, which became a broker of sorts between the Amish community and government officials.

Initially focused on alternative service, more recently the committee has mediated legal disputes between the government and the Amish on Social Security, hard hats, unemployment insurance, Worker's Compensation, 401(k) savings plans, and many other matters. In the role of a meek lobbyist, the committee chairman stays abreast of legislation that might impinge on Amish

TABLE 4.3
Social Networks and Committees by Date of Origin and Function[a]

Date of Origin	Name	Function
1875	Amish Aid Society	Fire and storm aid
1913	Amish Book Committee	Book publishing
1957	Old Order Book Society[b]	Coordination of schools
1965	Amish Liability Aid	Liability assistance
1966	National Steering Committee	Government liaison
1969	Amish Church Aid	Medical assistance
1969	Disaster Aid[c]	Disaster assistance
1979	Pequea Bruderschaft Library[d]	Historical resources
1992	Product Liability Aid	Liability assistance
1998	Helping Hand	Financial loans
1998	People's Helpers	Social support
1998	Safety Committee	Farm/shop safety

[a] Dates of origin are approximate. Many committees developed over several years.
[b] Began in 1937 as the School Committee.
[c] Serves as a subcommittee of Mennonite Disaster Service.
[d] Incorporated in 1984.

life. He also provides feedback to legislators who want Amish reactions to pending legislation. The National Steering Committee has three members, directors in various states, and a network of local representatives. An annual national meeting reviews the work of the committee, whose chairman lives in the Lancaster settlement.[24]

The committee functions as a self-perpetuating body outside the formal structure of the church. Individual bishops support the committee and often attend some of the meetings. In terms of size, structure, procedures, and written guidelines, the committee reflects the greatest imprint of bureaucracy of any organization to date. Despite this bureaucratic stamp, the committee operates from a home office with volunteer labor.

5. *Church Aid.* Caught between the rising costs of hospitalization and their reluctance to accept Medicare, some Amish families began buying medical insurance in the late 1960s. Fearing that commercial insurance would undercut the community's reliance on spontaneous mutual aid, the Amish have always frowned on commercial policies. Rising hospital costs threatened to bring a fuller embrace of commercial insurance and to undercut traditional mutual aid. Thus, a group of Amishmen initiated Amish Church Aid—an informal community-based version of hospital insurance. The program began in January 1969, and within four years 1,450 members from thirty-six districts were involved in the program.[25] Amish families may join Church

Aid only if the ordained leaders in their district support the plan. About 75 percent of the districts participate. Some districts do not subscribe because of its similarity to commercial insurance. Nonparticipants with large medical bills are usually assisted by alms funds from their own district as well as from adjoining ones. Members who participate in Church Aid make a monthly contribution and receive help with medical bills that exceed a deductible of several thousand dollars. Church Aid guidelines make it clear that members involved in motor vehicle accidents in which they are the driver will not be reimbursed for medical expenses.[26] The plan will also not assist with organ transplants or expenses at cancer clinics in Mexico.

6. *Disaster Aid.* The Lancaster Amish have been longtime participants in disaster relief projects organized by Mennonite Disaster Service. In 1969 they formed an Amish Disaster Committee to coordinate responses to Hurricane Camille in Florida. This committee eventually became a subcommittee of Mennonite Disaster Service and provides volunteers to assist in cleanup and rebuilding projects following natural disasters—tornadoes, hurricanes, and floods—outside the Amish community.

7. *Bruderschaft Library.* Following the example of some other Amish communities, the Lancaster Amish organized a historical library in May 1979. The project blossomed, and in August 1984 the Pequea Bruderschaft Library was incorporated northeast of the village of Intercourse. Established by a board of seven directors, the historical library exists "to assist members of the Amish Church and others in learning about past historic beliefs and practices of the Amish Church."[27] A new building was constructed in 1990, south of Gordonville. Several part-time librarians maintain the collection and aid researchers and curious tourists.[28]

8. *Product Liability Aid.* With more and more Amish operating businesses, product liability issues began to create concerns in the late 1980s. On the one hand, dealers selling Amish products in other states wanted proof of product liability insurance. The bishops, on the other hand, were not eager for businesses to rely on "worldly insurances that could prove harmful to the Old Order Amish way of life."[29] Finally, in 1992 the Product Liability Aid program was established to help members with large liability claims for one of their products. A five-member board of directors and an advisory board of ordained officials gives oversight to the plan, which solicits funds to help

shop owners, contractors, bakers, farmers, and others who face liability problems related to their products.

9. *Helping Hand.* This informal network provides loans to Amish people who are purchasing property or setting up a business. Begun in the Midwest, the network was established in the Lancaster settlement in 1998. This network provides connections between the wealthy and the needy.

10. *People's Helpers.* This mental health network that formed in 1998 was described by one participant as "a group of our people nationwide who do counseling." Although this informal network of caregivers began in another state, Amish from the Lancaster settlement who are interested in mental illness and depression actively participate. The group provides informal support to families who have members struggling with mental illness and refers friends to professional counselors and medical personnel.

11. *Safety Committee.* In response to accidents on farms and in shops, a Safety Committee formed in 1998 to encourage both safety training and compliance with government safety standards. "It helped us know what to do in case of an accident or fatality," said one member.

These eleven informal networks link resources with special needs across the community.[30] For the most part, committee leaders work with ordained leaders to build ties of understanding and gain their support. No central board or administrator appoints or oversees these special interest clusters. The networks mobilize social capital resources to serve community-wide needs. Each committee arose spontaneously to meet special needs beyond the capacity of local districts. While some of these committees show traces of bureaucracy, they are mostly informal, flat, small, and obedient to tradition. Although their loose structure would create nightmares for modern bureaucrats, they have served the Amish community well.

A health-related organization that is not formally operated by the Amish merits special mention: the Clinic for Special Children. Established in 1990 by a physician, Dr. Holmes Morton, it serves Old Order Amish, Old Order Mennonites, and other families who suffer from a high incidence of genetic diseases such as glutaric aciduria and maple syrup urine disease. It provides infant testing programs as well as diagnostic and medical services for children with inherited metabolic disorders. The clinic addresses a major need and has provided excellent service to the community. The Amish have expressed their gratitude for Dr. Morton's work by generously supporting annual benefit auctions for the clinic.[31]

ARCHITECTURAL SUMMARY

The social architecture of Amish society is small, compact, local, informal, and homogeneous—what sociologists sometimes call a *Gemeinschaft.* These features dramatically diverge from the design of postindustrial societies. Amish social structure embodies Gelassenheit and bolsters the groups' defensive strategy against worldliness. A brief overview of the distinctive features concludes our architectural tour of Amish society.

1. *Small.* From egos to organizational units, Gelassenheit prefers small-scale things. The Amish realize that larger things bring specialization, hierarchy, and elite subgroups that remove average people from power. Meeting in homes for worship limits the size of congregations. Ironically, this commitment to small-scale units makes individuals "big" psychologically in that they are known intimately by a small, stable group. It is impossible to get lost in the crowd in an Amish congregation. The security provided by a small congregation lessens the pressure for individuals to "make it on their own." Small farms are preferable to large ones. Small schools provide a personalized education. Large craft and manufacturing operations are frowned upon because big operators garner attention to themselves, establish a threatening power base, and insult the egalitarian community with excessive wealth.

An Amish businessman explained:

> My people look at a large business as a sign of greed. We're not supposed to engage in large businesses, and I'm right at the borderline now and maybe too large for Amish standards. The Old Order Amish don't like large exposed volume. You don't drive down the road and see big Harvestore silos sitting on Amish farms, you don't see one of those big 1,000-foot chicken houses. I can easily tell you which are the Mennonite farms. They'll feed 200 head of cattle, have 50,000 chickens, and milk 120 cows. They're a notch completely ahead of us. . . . My business is just at the point right now where it's beyond where the Old Order Amish people think it should be. It's just too large.

Another businessman expressed the fear of large organizations: "Our discipline thrives with a small group. Once you get into that big superstructure,

Volleyball is a favorite activity at family gatherings.

it seems to gather momentum and you can't stop it." Describing a growing Amish organization that the bishops curbed, he said: "It became self-serving, like a pyramid. Suppose we get a rotten egg leading it sometime? He can do more damage, and wreck in one year what we built up in twenty years. That's why the bishops curbed it." The Amish do not read the scientific literature that analyzes the impact of size on social life, but they realize that in the long run the modern impulse for large-scale things could debilitate their community.

2. *Compact.* The Amish have resisted the modern tendency to specialize and separate social functions. Unlike many forms of religion in modern society, Amish faith is not partitioned off from other activities. Work, play, child rearing, education, and worship, for the most part, are neither highly specialized nor separated from one another. The same circle of people interacting in family, neighborhood, church, and work blends these functions together in a compact network of social ties. Members of these overlapping circles share common values. Social relations are multiplex, meaning an actor relates to another person in many different functions: as a relative, neighbor, co-

worker, and church member. The dense webs of social interaction minimize privacy. Gossip, ridicule, and small talk become informal means of social control as networks crisscross, so that as one member observed, "Everybody knows everything about everyone else." Indeed, in the words of another member, "The Amish grapevine is faster than the Internet."

If modernity separates through specialization and mobility, it is not surprising to hear Amish pleas for social integration—for "togetherness," "unity," and a "common mind." On one occasion, the bishops admonished teenagers to stay home more on weekends and urged parents to have morning worship with their families as "a good way of staying together." A young woman explained why the church frowns on central heating systems: "A space heater in the kitchen keeps the family together. Heating all the rooms would lead to everyone going off to their own rooms." Another member described the compact structure of Amish society this way: "What is more Scriptural than the closely-knit Christian community, living together, working together, worshiping together, with its own church and own schools? Here the members know each other, work with and care for each other, every day of the week."[32]

3. *Local.* Amish life is staged in a local arena. Largely cut off from mass communication, rapid transit, geographical mobility, and the World Wide Web, Amish life revolves around the immediate neighborhood. Businesspeople are somewhat conversant about national affairs, but the dominant orientation is local, not cosmopolitan. Things close by are known, understood, and esteemed. Typical phrases in Amish writings—"home rule," "home community," "local home standards"—anchor the entire social system in the local church district. The local base of Amish interaction is poignantly described in an Amish view of education: "The one-room, one-teacher, community school near the child's home is the best possible type of elementary school. Here the boys and girls of a local community grow up and become neighbors among each other."[33]

4. *Informal.* With few contractual and formal relationships, Amish life is fused by informal ties anchored in family networks, common traditions, uniform symbols, and a shared mistrust of the outside world. The informality of Amish society expresses itself in many ways. Social interaction is conducted on a first-name basis without titles. Oral communication takes precedence over written. Few written records are kept of the meetings of ordained leaders. Organizational procedures are dictated by oral tradition, not policy

Burials take place in local family cemeteries marked with equal-size tombstones.
The small stones in the foreground mark the graves of children.

manuals and flow charts. Although each bishop wields considerable influence, the congregations across the settlement are loosely coupled together by
family networks rather than formal policies.

5. *Homogeneous.* The conventional marks of social class—education, income, and occupation—have less impact in Amish society. Ending school
at eighth grade homogenizes educational achievement; and in the past, the
traditional vocation of farming leveled the occupational structure. Some
Amish own several farms and display discreet traces of wealth in their choice
of farm equipment and animals. In recent years, business owners and artisans
have emerged as new occupational groupings. Similar occupational pursuits
in bygone years minimized financial differences, but that is beginning to
change with the rise of Amish businesses. Today farms are typically valued
at over $500,000, and it is not uncommon for an Amish business to have
annual sales exceeding $2 million. The recent changes seriously threaten the
historic patterns of equality.

The financial resources of farm and shop owners often exceed that of shop
workers, who toil for hourly wages. High land values and productive businesses are disturbing the egalitarian nature of Amish society. One member,

describing a certain rural road, said: "Three Amish millionaires live up there, but they don't drive around in Cadillacs, own a summer home at the bay, or have a yacht." Although wealth in Amish society is not displayed conspicuously, the recent changes have generated a social class of entrepreneurs with considerable money. Despite growing inequality, there is at least an attempt to maintain common symbols of faith and ethnicity on the surface. A well-to-do businessman and farm laborer dress alike, drive a horse to church, and will be buried in identical Amish-made coffins.

On the whole, the structure of Amish society is relatively flat, compared to the hierarchical class structure of postindustrial societies. There are few examples of extreme wealth and virtually no poverty in Amish society. In all of these ways, Amish architecture displays an elegant simplicity—small, compact, local, informal, and homogeneous—a simplicity that embodies Gelassenheit and partially explains the riddle of Amish survival.

Rites of Redemption
and Purification

Shunning works a little bit like an electric fence around a pasture.
—former Amishman

RITUAL: THE MUSIC OF INTERACTION

Social life balances on a tripod of culture, structure, and ritual. In order to survive, societies must develop cultural blueprints—collective guidelines that translate values and beliefs into expectations for social behavior. The social architecture, the organizational structure of a society, reflects the values in its cultural blueprint. However, culture and structure are lifeless forms until they are energized by social interaction. Chapters 3 and 4 examined the cultural blueprint and the social architecture, respectively, of Amish society. This chapter explores the patterns of social interaction and the religious rituals that energize and reaffirm the moral order of Amish life.

Religious rituals fuse culture and structure into social music. Without ritual, a group's culture and structure are static—like an orchestra frozen on stage. For example, culture exists in the minds of the musicians; the players understand the musical notations and they know how to play their instruments. Structure is present on the stage as well. Arranged carefully in their proper sections, the musicians face the conductor. But there is no ritual, no interaction, no music until the conductor's baton signals the start of the performance—the ritualized interaction. Cultural knowledge and social architecture suddenly blend into music. In a similar fashion, the rituals of interaction combine culture and structure into a social symphony in Amish life.

Social interaction in American society is organized by rituals ranging from handshakes and greetings to graduations and funerals. Religious rites rejuvenate the moral order of a group and place its members in contact with divine power. Amish rituals are not hollow. From common meals to singing, from silent prayer to excommunication, the rites are filled with redemptive meanings. As sacred rituals, they retell holy stories, recharge group solidarity, and usher individuals into divine presence.

The rituals of Amish life have two striking features: their oral character and their predictable formulas. The orality of Amish culture stands in contrast to the written documents of modern life. Collective memory is a powerful organizer and transmitter of Amish values. Hymns do not have musical notations, and neither sermons nor church rules are written down. The tradition is embodied in the people and their stories. This gives the ethos of the community an organic character that is informal, nonrational, and flexible.[1]

On the other hand, the ritual sequence of events is fairly firm. From weddings to funerals, from baptisms to ordinations, the ritual pattern is fixed. Individuals cannot tinker with ritual recipes. In fact, the protocol for Amish weddings is so clear that a wedding rehearsal is not required. There is one way to be baptized, one way to be married, and one way to be buried—the Amish way. The rigidity of the ritual eliminates any individual choice and makes the ceremonial life of the community highly predictable.[2]

ORDNUNG: THE GRAMMAR OF ORDER

The Amish blueprint for expected behavior, called the *Ordnung,* regulates private, public, and ceremonial life. Ordnung does not translate easily into English. Sometimes rendered 'ordinance' or 'discipline,' the Ordnung is an ordering of the whole way of life—a code of conduct that the church maintains by tradition rather than by systematic rules.[3] A member noted: "The order is not written down. The people just know it, that's all." Rather than a packet of rules to memorize, the Ordnung is the "understood" set of expectations for behavior. In the same way that the rules of grammar are learned by children, so the Ordnung, the grammar of order, is absorbed by Amish youth. The Ordnung evolved gradually over the decades as the church sought to strike a balance between tradition and change. Interpretation of the Ordnung varies somewhat from congregation to congregation.

A young minister describes the Ordnung as an "understanding." He explained: "Having one *understanding*, getting together and discussing things and admonishing according to that *understanding* and punishing according to the *understanding*, getting principles built up on an even basis, you know, can be beneficial" (emphasis added). In some areas of life, the Ordnung is very explicit; for example, it prescribes that a woman's hair should be parted in the center and that a man's hair should be combed with bangs. Other facets of life, left to individual discretion within limits, include food preferences, job choice, style of house, place of residence, and hobbies. The Ordnung contains both prescriptions—you ought to wear a wide-brimmed hat—and proscriptions—you should not own a television.

Children learn the Ordnung from birth by observing adults and hearing them talk. Ordnung becomes the taken-for-granted reality—"the way things are" in the child's mind. In the same way that non-Amish children learn that women, rather than men, wear lipstick and shave their legs, so Amish children learn the ways of the Ordnung. To the outsider, the Ordnung appears as a maze of legalistic rules. But to the child growing up in the world of the Ordnung, wearing an Amish hat or apron wherever one goes is just the normal thing to do. It is the way things are supposed to be, the way God intended them.

The Ordnung defines certain things as simply outside the Amish world. Asked whether an Amish person could be a real estate agent, a member replied: "Well, it's just unheard of, a child wouldn't even think of it." All in all, the Ordnung represents the traditional interpretations—the rules, regulations, and standards—of what it means to be Amish. Although children are taught to follow the Ordnung from birth, it is not until baptism that they make a personal vow to uphold it forever.[4]

Core understandings of the Ordnung regarding education, divorce, cars, and so forth are fairly stable and need little verbal reinforcement. One woman said, "We're not supposed to wear makeup, but it's something the bishops don't need to mention. I don't even think they know about makeup. They wouldn't really know how to talk about it." The outer edges of Ordnung evolve, however, as the church faces new issues. Some technological innovations, such as calculators, are permitted by default; but others, such as embryo transplants in dairy cows, are strictly forbidden. Other issues, such as installing phones in Amish shops, may fester for many years. When a new practice such as eating in restaurants or using the Internet becomes "an is-

Two Amish teens rollerblade in front of their home. The Ordnung regulates dress,
technology, and the decor of homes.

sue," it is discussed by the ordained leaders, and if a consensus develops, it
becomes grafted into the Ordnung.

The Amish are reluctant to change their mind after a practice becomes
ingrained into the Ordnung. Rather than overturn old practices, they often
develop ingenious ways to bypass them. For example, freezers are not permitted in Amish homes because they would bring other electrical appliances,
but members are permitted to own one in the home of a non-Amish neighbor.
Because changing the Ordnung is difficult, the Amish are slow to outlaw
things at first sight. If seen as harmless, a new practice—for example, the use
of barbecue grills or trampolines—will drift into use with little ruckus.

Adherence to the Ordnung varies among families and church districts.
Some bishops are more lenient than others in their enforcement of it. If a
member conforms to the symbolic markers of the Ordnung, there is considerable "breathing space" in which to maneuver and still appear Amish. The
Ordnung is enforced with leniency under special circumstances. A retarded
child may be permitted to have a bicycle, which is usually off-limits, or a
family may be permitted to use electricity in their home to operate medical
equipment for an invalid. Although self-propelled riding equipment such as

a riding lawn mower is forbidden, electric wheel chairs are widely used by the disabled.

Examples of Practices Prescribed by the Ordnung:
color and style of clothing
hat styles for men
order of the worship service
kneeling for prayer in worship
marriage within the church
use of horses for fieldwork
use of Pennsylvania German
steel wheels on machinery

Examples of Practices Prohibited by the Ordnung:
air transportation
central heating in homes
divorce
electricity from public power lines
entering military service
filing a lawsuit
jewelry, including wedding rings and wrist watches
joining worldly (public) organizations
owning computers, televisions, radios
owning and operating an automobile
pipeline milking equipment
using tractors for fieldwork
wall-to-wall carpeting

A maze of rules to the outsider, the Ordnung feels like stuffy legalism even to some Amish, but for most of them it is a sacred order that unites the church and separates it from worldly society. In the words of one minister, "A *respected* Ordnung generates peace, love, contentment, equality, and unity. . . . It creates a desire for togetherness and fellowship. It binds marriages, it strengthens family ties, to live together, to work together, to worship together, and to commune secluded from the world."[5]

All things considered, there are several levels of piety in the moral order of Amish society:

1. Acceptable behavior—so widely practiced that it's never discussed;

2. Esteemed behavior—expected of ordained leaders and their spouses, but not of laymembers;

3. Frowned upon behavior—discouraged by the church but not a test of membership;

4. Forbidden behavior—proscribed by the Ordnung and a test of membership.

A fifth category involves behavior that is so immoral—for example, murder—and is so clearly wrong that it is not even included in the Ordnung. Indeed, in a sixth category are ambiguous practices that are acceptable in some districts but not in others. These levels of piety vary somewhat across the settlement from plainer to higher districts. The exact guidelines change over the years as the normative order flexes with new issues and new leaders.

Following the Ordnung—wearing proper clothing, plowing with horses, shunning publicity, avoiding worldly pleasures, and singing the hymns of the *Ausbund*—is a sacred ritual that symbolizes faithful obedience to the vows of baptism, the order of the community, and the will of God. Abandoning self and bending to the collective wisdom provide divine blessing and the promise of eternal life.

BAPTISM: THE PERMANENT VOW

Small children accept and practice the Ordnung as they receive it from their parents. Before they are baptized, Amish youth are under the care of their parents, and the church has no official jurisdiction over them. Some Amish teenagers conform to the Ordnung and others do not. Some rebel or "sow wild oats" during *rumspringa*—the "running around" years that begin at age sixteen. During this ambiguous stage, when they are neither in nor out of the church, teenagers face the most important decision of their lives: Will I join the church? It is not a trivial matter. Those who kneel for baptism must submit to the Ordnung for the rest of their lives. If their obedience to the church falters, they will be ostracized forever. Young adults who decline baptism eventually drift away from the community. However, they will not be shunned, because they have not made a baptismal pledge. As good Anabaptists, the church takes the importance and integrity of adult baptism very seriously.

Romantic ties may add an incentive for church membership, for Amish ministers only marry church members. "We have no weddings for someone who is not a member of the church. It's as simple as that," said one young husband. For many young people, the rite of baptism is the natural climax of a process of socialization that funnels them toward the church. For others, it is a difficult choice. Some leave home and flirt with the world, while others flirt with it behind their parents' backs. But in the end, nine out of ten youths promise to embrace their birthright community for life. A young married husband described the tug of romance, land, family, and community that pulls young people toward baptism:

> Most of the young sowing wild oats are just out there to put on a show. It's just something that kind of comes and goes. If they have well-established roots, most of them kind of have their mind set on a particular girl. There is something that really draws them back. . . . Like I say, the close family ties are the thing that really draws you back. I still think it [Amish life] is a better lifestyle, I really think so. If you grow up with it, there really is something here that just kind of draws. If you do a lot of this running around and going on, it kind of makes you feel foolish after awhile.

The typical age of baptism ranges from sixteen to the early twenties. Sixty percent join the church before they are twenty-one. Girls often join at a younger age than boys. Instruction classes during the five months preceding the ceremony place the stark implications of baptism before the candidates. During the first half hour of church services over the summer months, the novices meet with the ministers for instruction. The ministers and bishop review the eighteen articles of the Dordrecht Confession of Faith and emphasize selected aspects of the Ordnung.[6] On the Saturday before the baptism, there is a special wrap-up session when candidates are given their last chance to turn back. Hostetler notes that "great emphasis is placed upon the difficulty of walking in the straight and narrow way. The applicants are told that it is better not to make a vow than to make a vow and later break it."[7] Young men are reminded that they are consenting to serve as leaders if ever called by the church.

The baptismal rite follows two sermons during a regular Sunday morning service.[8] After the final instruction class, the ministers will say, "Go take your

The young owner of this carriage will need to get rid of his stereo speakers
and other frills before he is baptized.

seats with bowed heads." The candidates sit in a bent posture, with a hand
over the face, signaling their willingness to submit—to give themselves under
the authority of the church. The deacon provides a small pail of water and a
cup. The bishop tells the candidates to go on their knees "before the Most
High and Almighty God and His church if you still think this is the right

thing to do to obtain your salvation." The candidates are then asked three questions:

1. Can you *renounce* the devil, the world, and your own flesh and blood?
2. Can you commit yourself to Christ and His church, and to abide by it and therein to live and to die?
3. And in all the order (Ordnung) of the church, according to the word of the Lord, to be *obedient* and *submissive* to it and to help therein? (emphasis added)[9]

The congregation stands for prayer while the applicants remain kneeling. Then the bishop lays his hands on the head of the first applicant. The deacon pours water into the bishop's cupped hands and it drips over the candidate's head. The bishop then extends his hand to each member as he or she rises and says, "May the Lord God, complete the good work which he has begun in you and strengthen and comfort you to a blessed end through Jesus Christ. Amen." The bishop's wife greets the young women with a "holy kiss," and the bishop likewise greets the men and wishes them peace. In a concluding word, the bishop admonishes the congregation to be obedient and invites other ministers to give a testimony of affirmation. The ritual of baptism places the new members into full fellowship, with all the rights and responsibilities of adult membership.[10]

WORSHIP: A PLAIN LITURGY

The worship service dramatically reenacts the Amish moral order. Social structure and beliefs coalesce in a sacred ritual that embodies the core meanings of Amish culture. The worship service imprints the "understandings" of the Ordnung in the collective consciousness. This redemptive ritual reminds members who they are as it ushers them into divine presence. With few props and scripts, the drama of worship reaffirms the symbolic universe of Amish culture.

Each district holds services every other Sunday in the home of a member.[11] Services begin early, with some members arriving by 8:00 A.M. Members either drive by horse and buggy or walk to the service. The prelude for the day is played out on the keyboard of country roads as the rhythmic clip-clop of hoofbeats converge on the meeting site. The three-hour service culminates in a light noon meal, followed by informal visiting throughout the afternoon. The local congregation swells in size as some friends and family from other districts join the service. Unlike some contemporary congregations where attendance is sporadic, everyone shows up and packs into several rooms of a member's home, a basement, or a shop. It is not unusual for two hundred adults and children to squeeze into a house. Partitions between rooms are opened. Backless benches and folding chairs face the preacher in a central area. Benches, songbooks, and eating utensils are transported from home to home in a special wagon.

The service is organized around unison singing and two sermons. The main sermon lasts about an hour. Illustrations are taken from the Bible, nature, and local events. Preachers follow a published lectionary of New Testament scriptures for the year, which appears in Appendix E. Sermons often include references to accounts of suffering in the *Martyrs Mirror.* Preachers remind members that they are pilgrims and strangers traveling in a different direction than the outside world. Obedience and humility are key themes in the service. Ministers urge members to obey the commandments of the Scripture, the vows of baptism, and those in authority over them. After reading the Scripture, the deacon may also admonish members to be obedient to the Lord. The following is the traditional order of the Sunday morning service:

fellowship upon arrival
silence in worship areas
congregational singing (40 minutes)
ministers meet in a separate room
opening sermon (25–30 minutes)
silent kneeling prayer
scripture reading by deacon (members standing)
main sermon (50–70 minutes)
affirmations from other ministers and elders
kneeling prayer is read from a prayer book
benediction (members standing)
closing hymn
Members' Meeting, as necessary
fellowship meal
visiting and fellowship[12]

The Amish have no altar, organ, offering, church school, ushers, professional pastors, printed liturgy, pulpit, cross, candles, steeples, robes, flowers, choirs, or handbells. Contemporary props of worship are completely absent. Plain people gather in a plain house and worship in simplicity. A traditional, unwritten "liturgy" regulates each moment of the service. The ceremony symbolizes the core values of Amish society.

Following the last hymn, a brief Members' Meeting may be held to discuss mutual aid, to discipline a member, or to announce plans for district activities. A light lunch with a traditional menu follows the service.[13] The modest meal has the character of a fellowship gathering rather than a large feast. In the afternoon visiting cliques emerge around age and gender, but for the most part, the day is a common experience. From beginning to end, the worship symbolizes waiting, unity, and humility; it is a ritualistic reenactment of Gelassenheit.

Gender, age, and leadership roles shape the worship in several ways. Men and women enter the house by separate doors and sit in separate areas. Women do not lead any aspect of the worship, but after the service they prepare and serve the meal. They eat at separate tables from the men and are responsible for cleaning up. Age characteristics are pronounced in the ordering of social behavior. The eldest members enter the house and worship areas first, followed by others in roughly descending age. Seating in the worship areas is dictated by age and gender, with spaces designated for older and younger members.

One enters the worship area as a man or woman, not as a family member or an individual. One is accountable to the church, expected to behave and dress according to the patterns for a particular role—young woman, older man, and minister. By dividing families in the seating area, the church symbolizes its authority not only over the individual but over the family as well.

Leadership status is also visible. The ministers take their seats in the "ministers' row." The adult men shake hands with the ministers outside as they assemble or as they find seats in the house. Women may shake hands with the ministers in the kitchen or as they enter the worship area. The handshake, often without words, is an act of deference to the ministers' authority and a reaffirmation of good standing in the fellowship.

As the young unmarried men enter the house, the older men, who are already seated, take off their hats. The young men walk by the ministers' row and shake their hands in an act of deference as well. As the first song begins, the ministers take off their hats in one sweeping action. On the first word of the third line of the first song, the ordained leaders take their hats and walk to another room in the house to counsel together and select the preacher of the morning. After meeting for thirty minutes, they return during the last verse of the second hymn, hanging their hats on the wall which signals that the worship is about to begin. Ordained men are the only ones who stand or speak in the service. Afterward, they sit at the table that is served first.

The cultural values embedded in the ritual structure stun modern consciousness. The entire service creates a radically different world—a world of waiting. There are no traces of rushing. The day of worship stretches from 8:00 a.m. to about 3:00 p.m. The extremely slow tempo of singing ushers in a different temporal order. One song may stretch over twenty minutes. In a rising and falling chant, each word expands into a miniature verse in itself. The congregation sings from the *Ausbund*—a hymnal with only printed words.[14] Many of the *Ausbund* hymns were written by persecuted Anabaptists in the sixteenth century. The ancient tunes, learned by memory, are sung in chant-like unison without any rhythm. The slow and methodic chant-like cadence reflects a sixteenth-century medieval world in image and mood.

A song leader sits among the congregation. In a spirit of humility, he is selected on the spot. A member described the selection process: "You'll see men whispering, 'You do it, you do it,' until someone finally goes ahead and does it." The leader sings the first syllable of each line and then the congregation joins in the second one.

The lengthy service is conducted without coffee breaks, worship aids, or special music. Very young children sleep, wander among the aisles, or occasionally munch crackers. Four- and five-year-olds sit patiently on backless benches and on the laps of their parents. The service trains children in the quiet discipline of waiting. It is a lesson in Gelassenheit—waiting and yielding to time, parents, community, and God.

The grammar of the worship incorporates humility and submission. It would be considered pretentious for a minister to prepare a written sermon or even bring a polished outline. Ministers do not know who will preach the morning sermon until they meet while the congregation sings the first hymn. If a visiting minister is present, he will likely be asked to preach. The preacher is chosen by a consensus of the ordained leaders while the congregation is singing. The spontaneous selection preempts any pretensions of pride. As he begins his sermon a few minutes later, the preacher reminds the congregation that he is a servant of God ministering to them in his "weakness."

The rite of humility is described by one member: "The one who has the main sermon will often begin by saying, 'I'm not qualified to preach, but I preach because God called me to preach. I wish that someone else, a visiting minister, or someone who would be more capable of delivering the sermon, would preach but because that's not the case, *I will give myself up* to be used by God to preach the sermon today'" (emphasis added). The member continued: "I never cease to be amazed how they can get up and preach for a whole hour without referring to notes or their closed Bible." In a ritual enactment of humility that downplays individualism, preachers and audience rarely look directly at one another. By yielding in humility to others and giving himself up in front of the congregation, the preacher reenacts the essence of Gelassenheit.

The congregation kneels twice in prayer. The first prayer, a silent one, follows the opening sermon and lasts several minutes. The entire congregation waits on God quietly, in humility, on their knees on a hard floor. The Amish believe that it would be preposterous for someone to offer a spontaneous prayer. It is better to wait together in silence. The congregation kneels a second time near the end of the service as the deacon reads a traditional prayer.

Symbols of collective integration unite the ritual. Singing in unison prevents the showy display that accompanies solos, choirs, and musical performances. A praise song, the "Lob Lied," is the second hymn in every service just before the sermon.[15] Thus, on a given Sunday morning, all the congregations holding services across the settlement are singing the same song at roughly the same time, an experience one member described as giving a beautiful feeling of unity among the churches. From the elderly bishop to the youngest child, kneeling together in prayer and singing in unison create a shared sense of humility. Children are not shuttled off to church school, and adults are not given a chance to select a stimulating adult class. The common worship does not cater to special-interest or age groups. The specialization of modern life is simply not present. There is little individual expression in the service. One does not choose a special pew. Seating patterns are determined by age and sex, and one simply follows in line and fills in each bench. Ministers and a few elders give brief affirmations to the main sermon—in essence, endorsements of it. For the most part, the service is a common experience for old and young alike.

Simplicity pervades the service, from backless benches to bare walls and black vests. The uniform dress code prevents ostentatious display. Members dress in full conformity with the Ordnung. Some young men may sport styled hair to show off their last months of independence before joining the church, but they also kneel in humility. Members dress appropriately for their age and sex because this is the sacred moment of the religious week when even the careless are careful to follow the Ordnung. The outward uniformity signals spiritual unity as the community gathers in the presence of God.

Fitting some two hundred people into several large rooms or the basement of a house forces a physical closeness. Chairs and benches are packed tightly together. A young minister replayed the surprised reaction of visitors to the kneeling: "They said, 'Everyone squats, bangs, crashes, and suddenly goes down, and where's the kneeling pads?' We don't have them, you know, and it's nothing to us because it's our tradition." Though viewed as confining by Moderns, the physical closeness symbolizes the unity of the tight-knit community, close to one another and close to God, in worship. For some, of course, the worship becomes an empty Sunday protocol. But for most, it is a redemptive heartbeat that reaffirms the community's moral order twenty-six times a year.

The continuity of Amish worship over the decades is striking. A description of an Amish service written more than a century ago is virtually identical to the format today.[16] Members born at the turn of the twentieth century report few changes across the decades. "It might be a little shorter and the singing might be a little faster! The sermons are very similar. There has been very little change in the Scripture that is quoted. Each minister is different, but, as a whole, it's the same meaning expressed in different words." Indeed, the speed of the singing signals the extent of assimilation into the larger culture. High districts sing faster.[17] As the geographical size of some districts shrank in the 1990s, their services began earlier because people had less distance to travel. Compared to other spheres of Amish life, the patterns of worship have remained largely unchanged.

Hymn books and benches arranged in an Amish basement await a worship service.

Sunday is a holy day and many things are sacralized. Work, unless required for the care of animals, is forbidden as is the use of money or any purchase. Carriages are used to attend church services; cars may be hired only if there is an emergency. Coats with hooks and eyes and dresses fastened with pins are worn to Sunday service. Even smoking is discouraged among the few men who do. One minister said, "Those who smoke should leave their tobacco at home. Who would think of carrying a loaf of bread to church and eating a slice of it in front of others?"

COMMUNION: A UNIFYING EXPERIENCE

Communion and the ordination of leaders are ritual high points that underscore the lowly values of Gelassenheit. The fall and spring communion services are rites of intensification. They revitalize personal commitment and fortify group cohesion within each district and throughout the settlement. A traditional sequence of events prepares the way for each fall and spring communion service: the Bishops' Meeting, a congregational Counsel Meeting, the Ministers' Meeting, and finally holy communion.

An all-day meeting of the bishops in September and March addresses controversial issues stirring in the community. Contentious issues, such as using voice mail, playing baseball in local leagues, playing golf, using computers, using harvesters, and troublesome youth, are discussed. If a consensus among the bishops emerges, it becomes embedded into the "understanding" of the Ordnung.

Following the Bishops' Meeting, a "preparatory," or Counsel Meeting is held in local districts in conjunction with the regular worship service. This service of self-examination is held two weeks before communion. The sermon of the morning creates an emotional buildup to the counsel service, when members are asked to affirm the Ordnung, indicate peace with God, and express a desire to partake of communion. Sometimes the counsel service is a tense time when sin and worldliness are purged from the community. A member said: "Twice yearly, you know, they have their Bishops' Meeting, and then they come back to the church and announce what's up, you might say. Then the church, everybody, is given a voice to say 'yes or no.' And you can say, 'No, I'm not agreed,' but you'd better have good documentation, and that's the way it should be."

The counsel sermon is often two and a half hours long, signaling the meeting's importance. Children and nonmembers usually are not present. The sermon traces the Old Testament story from Genesis to the conquest of the Promised Land. The pivotal moment is the defeat of Joshua's army by the people of Ai. Amish ministers stress that hidden plunder had to be confessed and given up before Joshua's army could proceed to victory. The sermon then turns to the New Testament and shows how the golden thread of the Bible leads to Christ. Ministers plead with the congregation to destroy the "old leaven" so the body can be healthy and grow. They stress that hidden sins of pride and disobedience, if not confessed, will, like the hidden sins of Israel at Ai, lead to the church's defeat.

Much of the counsel sermon and admonitions emphasize positive examples of how to live. The bishop also presents the church's position on issues that are "making trouble at the time," or things that "the bishops are not allowing yet."[18] The dress code is reaffirmed, and questionable social practices—cell phones, credit cards, the Internet—are discouraged. "We are asked to work against these troubles," a young minister explained, "and clean ourselves of them, and then we expect a testimony from each member to see if he is in agreement with that counseling." A member explained the procedure: "Two of the ministers go around, one with the men and one with the women, and they go around and ask each one, 'Are you agreed?' and everyone says, 'I'm agreed.' And you'd better be, too! Or have some grounds for it, which is right. This is done in front of the entire congregation." If they disagree, members are asked to come to a front bench and explain their position.

If a serious impasse cannot be resolved, communion may be postponed until the congregation is "at peace"—meaning that all members concur with the Ordnung. The Counsel Meeting is a critical moment for purging sins of selfishness, pride, self-will—any moral decay that might erode the common life. The Counsel Meeting is a special moment when the moral order, the Ordnung, is reaffirmed and the collective will prevails. It is especially moving if a repentant offender rejoins the fellowship. If harmony emerges in the Counsel Meeting, communion follows in two weeks. The results of the local Counsel Meetings are reported at the respective Ministers' Meetings in the settlement. A day of fasting normally occurs between the Counsel Meeting and communion.

Although somber in mood, the communion service is a celebration of unity within the body. The observance of communion begins about 8:00 A.M. and continues until 4:00 P.M. without a formal break. During the lunch hour, people quietly leave the main worship area in small clusters to eat in an adjoining room. The service peaks as the minister retells the suffering of Christ and the congregation shares the bread and wine. Some ministers pace their sermons so that the passion story occurs about 3:00 P.M., to coincide with the supposed moment of Christ's death.

The bishop breaks bread to each member. The congregation drinks grape wine from a single cup that is passed around to commemorate the suffering and death of Jesus Christ. The sacrifice and bitter suffering of Christ are emphasized and held up as models for members. When speaking of the wine and bread, the bishop stresses the importance of individual members being crushed like a grain of wheat and pressed like a small berry to make a single drink. A bishop explained: "If one grain remains unbroken and whole, it can have no part in the whole . . . if one single berry remains whole, it has no share in the whole . . . and no fellowship with the rest."[19] These metaphors legitimize the importance of individuals yielding their wills for the welfare of the larger body.

The service culminates in footwashing, as the congregation sings. Segregated by sex and arranged in pairs, members dip, wash, and dry each other's feet. Several tubs of warm water and towels are placed throughout the rooms. Symbolizing extreme humility, the washer stoops rather than kneels to wash the foot of a brother or sister. One bishop reminds his members that they are "stooping to the needs of their brother." The ritual of humility concludes with a "holy kiss" and an exchange of blessing between the two partners. At the end of the footwashing, alms are handed to the deacon for the poor fund, the only offering ever taken in an Amish service. Having affirmed the moral order, the purified community is rejuvenated for another six months of life together.

ORDINATION: DIVINE LOTTERY

The ordination of leaders is the emotional high point in the ritual life of the community. The customary practice of leadership selection mirrors Amish values and stands in sharp contrast to the selection of professional pastors.[20] Only married men who are members of the local church district are eligible for ministerial office. The personal lifestyle of candidates is valued far above training or competence. There is no pay, training, or career path associated with the role of minister. It is considered haughty and arrogant to aspire for the office. Ministers are called by the congregation in a biblical procedure known as "the casting of lots," in which they yield to the mysteries of divine selection. The term of office is for life. If a vacancy arises because of illness, death, or the formation of a new church district, a unanimous congregational vote is required to proceed.

The ordination service is typically held at the end of a communion service, often on a weekday. Male and female members proceed to a room in the house and whisper the name of a candidate to the deacon, who passes it on to the bishop. Men who receive three or more votes are placed in the lot. Typically, about a half dozen men receive enough votes. At the last instruction class before baptism, young men pledge to serve as leaders if called upon by the church. Thus, personal reasons for being excused from the lot are unacceptable. Those in the lot are asked if they are "in harmony with the

Members of a church district gather at a home for a worship service.

ordinances of the church and the articles of faith." If they answer yes, they kneel for prayer, asking God to show which one he has chosen.[21]

The lot "falls" on the new minister without warning. A slip of paper bearing a Bible verse is placed in a song book. The book is randomly mixed with other song books, equaling the number of candidates. Seated around a table, each candidate selects a book. The bishop in charge says: "Lord of all generations, show us which one you have chosen among these brethren." The presiding bishop then opens each book, one by one, looking for the fateful paper that says the lot "falls on the man as the Lord decrees."[22] The service is packed with tears and emotion. Like a bolt of lightning, the lot strikes the new minister's family with the stunning realization that he is about to assume a high and heavy calling for the rest of his life.

In the spirit of Gelassenheit, the "winner" receives neither applause nor congratulations. Rather, tears, silence, sympathy, and quiet words of support are extended to the new leader and his family, who must now bear the heavy burden of servanthood for the rest of their lives as they give themselves up to the church. This is the holiest of moments in Amish life because in a mere second, Almighty God reaches down from the highest heavens and selects a shepherd for the flock.

The simple ritual, based on biblical precedent, is an astute mechanism for leadership selection.[23] Once again, personal desires are surrendered to the common welfare. The leader and his family yield to the community by "giving themselves up" for the larger cause. No perks, prestige, financial gain, career goals, or personal objectives drive the selection or accrue to the officeholder. In fact, just the opposite. Members of the congregation quietly speculate what the newly ordained couple will have to give up as they more fully "give themselves under" the authority of the church. In addition to wearing plainer clothing, they may have to put away some borderline items— fancy curtains or machinery—to better comply with the Ordnung and exemplify faithful behavior for the rest of the flock.

Core values of Amish culture are reaffirmed in the ritual, for only local, untrained men are acceptable candidates. The congregation can nominate the brightest and best who have lived among them for many years. Although it would be haughty to seek ordination, some individuals may privately hope for the office or at least enjoy the rewards of respect if ordained. The permanency of the choice underscores the durability of commitment and community. The entire ritual is a cogent reminder that leadership rests on the bedrock of Gelassenheit.

Unlike many Protestant denominations, the Amish rarely have a leadership crisis. Although to the outsider the simple ritual may resemble a divine lottery, it has profound social consequences. The abrupt "falling of the lot" prevents "campaigning" beforehand. All members may nominate candidates, but in the final analysis the leader is "chosen by the decree of the Lord." In a critical moment that will shape its life for years, the community *also* yields because it must accept "the shepherd that the Lord selects." Being selected by divine choice is quite different from being invited to serve a congregation with a sixty-to-forty vote. The minister may not be the first choice of some members, but his authority comes by divine mandate unequaled by charisma, seminary training, or theological degrees. Members who are unhappy with the choice can quarrel with God, not a faulty political process or a power play by a search committee. Furthermore, only God fires Amish ministers. It is, in short, an ingenious solution to leadership selection that in a plain and simple manner confers stability, authority, and unity to community life.

CONFESSION: AMISH THERAPY

Communion is a sacred rite that revitalizes the moral order, but it is not enough to preserve the Ordnung. The Amish, like other people, forget, rebel, and, for a variety of reasons, stray into deviance. Formal social controls swing into action when informal ones fail. Rituals of confession help to punish deviance and reunite backsliders into full fellowship. Confessions diminish self-will by reminding members of the supreme value of submission. A few deviants may play the confessional role with little remorse, but most confessions are cathartic moments when the power of the corporate body unites with divine presence to purge the cancerous growth of individualism.[24]

In general, transgressions against the moral order are redeemed by two types of confessions: free will or requested. Free-will, or "open and willing" confessions are initiated by the offender. By contrast, requested confessions are initiated by church leaders to deal with deviant members. Depending on the circumstances and severity of the issue, the confession may take four forms: private, sitting, kneeling, and kneeling followed by a six-week ban.

In a free-will confession, a member may feel guilty for having a fault (*fehla*). The guilt might arise from various violations of the Ordnung—having some banned technology, inadvertently riding with someone under the ban, premarital sexual relations, cheating in a business transaction, or flying in an airplane. The person goes to the deacon or minister and confesses the fault. In some cases the deacon may offer loving counsel and close the issue in private. In other cases a public form of confession may be required. Free-will confessions involve few complications because the wayward person is cooperative and penitent.

The process becomes more strained when violators do not take the initiative. Through personal observation or reports of members, ordained leaders become aware of a transgression. A member may have used a tractor in the field, installed a silo unloader, joined a township planning commission, filed a lawsuit, attended a dance, participated in a non-Amish Bible study group, or installed a computer in their business.

Following the procedures for dealing with an offending person outlined in Matthew 18, the bishop typically asks the deacon and a minister to visit the wayward member. If the offense is a minor matter that has drawn little attention in the church, and if the member displays an attitude of contrition, the issue may be dropped at this stage. Minor issues solved in the privacy of barns and homes do not require public confession. The errant member simply acknowledges the fault and promises to stop the insulting behavior or to "put away" the offensive item. The deacon reports the outcome of the private confession to the bishop.

Serious matters that draw public attention require public confessions. The offender will be asked to make a confession at a Members' Meeting before the entire congregation. Depending on circumstances, it may be a sitting, kneeling, or kneeling and ban confession, representing levels two, three, and four respectively. Confessions are handled in a Members' Meeting, known as the sitting church or *sitz gma,* which follows a Sunday worship service. Children, nonmembers, and visitors are excused. The frequency of Members' Meetings varies according to the press of issues in each district.

In the case of a sitting confession, the bishop explains what happened, and the member remains seated wherever he or she is and then says, "I want to confess that I have failed. I want to make peace and continue in patience with God and the church and in the future to take better care." For a kneeling confession, the bishop invites the wayward member to come forward and kneel near the ministers in the midst of the congregation. The bishop asks the person several questions about the offense and if they are willing to stop it. The person may be sobbing with remorse. Defendants may also be given time to explain their side of the story. After answering the questions, the person leaves the area and the bishop explains a possible punishment.

If the hearing does not produce new information, the bishop presents the congregation with a punishment proposed by the ministers earlier in the morning. Members are asked if they agree with the proposed sanction. A member said: "The congregation usually agrees with the bishop's layout, except if they know things that the ministers don't, then they may have to re-counsel the whole thing again." A vote (*der Rat*) is taken by asking each member if they support the proposed punishment. Sometimes there will be disagreement or discussion at this point, but generally the congregation affirms the action proposed by the bishop. The unanimous consent of the congregation is sought before the individual returns to hear the verdict. The

A Lancaster bishop testifies before a government committee.

confessor is then invited back to the meeting and asked: "Are you willing to take on the discipline of the church?" Depending on the circumstances, the person is then reinstated or informed that a six-week ban will be enacted.

The most severe form of punishment (level four) is a six-week ban.[25] This, in effect, is a temporary excommunication. If penitent, the offender is eventually restored to full fellowship. Offenders come to the three church services during the six-week period and meet with the ministers for admonition during the congregational singing. The offender enters the service after everyone else has been seated and sits near the ministers in the center. As a sign of remorse, he or she sits bent over with a hand over the face during the service. The offender leaves immediately after the worship service without shaking hands or participating in the meal and fellowship. The six-week exile allows them time to reflect on the seriousness of their transgression and to taste the stigma of shunning. Other members often visit them during this time to show their love and support.

At the end of the ban, offenders are invited to make a kneeling confession in a Members' Meeting. They are also asked two questions: Do you believe the punishment was deserved? Do you believe your sins have been forgiven through the blood of Jesus Christ? Those who confess their sin and promise to "work with the church" are reinstated into it. The bishop offers offenders the hand of fellowship, pulls them up from their knees, and gives them a kiss of peace. In the case of women, the bishop's wife gives the kiss. The meeting concludes with some fitting words of comfort.[26] Many times this is a beautiful moment of catharsis and healing in the life of the church.

For the "headstrong" who will not submit or confess to the church, the six-week probation leads to full excommunication. Errant members are invited to come to church. "If they don't come," explains a member, "then the church, you might say, subpoenas them; they must be there in two weeks, and if they don't come then they lose their membership." This places the burden of responsibility on the offender.

In each situation there is considerable freedom to improvise. Ministers try hard to "work with the church" and mediate conflicts in peaceful ways. There is, however, a firm resolve to seek solutions that will maintain harmony and save the integrity of the Ordnung as well as the authority of leaders. The entire process hinges on an attitude of submission—of Gelassenheit. Individuals who display an attitude of contrition are quickly forgiven and reinstated into the fellowship.

The obstinate who challenge the authority of leaders will feel the harsh judgment of the church. A petty, tit-for-tat syndrome, fueled by envy, sometimes sours the confessional process. In one case, a member pressed for action against a bishop's son who was attending films and flaunting a car. In due time, the bishop sought his revenge by threatening to excommunicate the member for installing a telephone in his barn. In general, senior bishops counsel younger bishops and ministers to "work with their people," to try to persuade them to cooperate through gentle discussion.

The ritual of confession is filled with humility and healing as well as shame. A member sketched the sequence after young church members attended a wild party hosted by Amish youth who had not joined the church:

> They go before the church and they must make a confession depending on the severity of what happened, and they may even lose their membership. They hardly ever refuse to make a confession. Can you picture

this, after the church service, after these long sermons, we have a song, and then all the nonmembers go out quiet as a mouse, and can you imagine yourself, a young boy or girl, and you have to get off your seat and walk up and sit right in front of the ministers, and you're supposed to talk so that the whole church hears you and you get questioned about this thing. Can you imagine not *giving up?* [emphasis added]. That's pretty impressive, it gets pretty strong.

The social pressure to confess is strong, but some confessions also become moments of healing that unite the congregation. A young couple, married for several years, asked the church to exclude them for six weeks because they felt guilty about their premarital behavior. A member described the experience: "They asked to be expelled, and so there was this six-week period of repentance. When they were reinstated as members it was such a sensational thing, and everybody felt that this couple really wanted to expose themselves and let the church know that they were sorry for what they had done and wanted to lead a better life. Everybody felt so good about it. It was really a healthy thing for the church. It was really a good feeling."

Confession in front of the gathered body ritualizes an individual's subordination to the group. It strikes at the heart of individualism and heralds the virtues of Gelassenheit. In its cathartic value, it bears a rough resemblance to modern psychotherapy, but it is less expensive and much more humiliating. In contrast to psychotherapy, most Amish confessions are initiated by the call of the church, not the individual. The ritual of Amish confession, one of the costs of community, has been largely untouched by modernity. A minister emphatically claimed that "not a thing has changed" in the confessional procedure over the years.

EXPULSION: PURGING THE WAYWARD

Corporations are not afraid to dismiss insubordinate employees, but contemporary churches, in the name of tolerance and love, are reluctant to dismiss deviant members. When confession fails, excommunication is the final recourse among the Amish. If baptism is the front door to Amish life, excommunication is the exit. The back door, however, is not slammed quickly. It can only be closed by the unanimous vote of a congregation after efforts to win back the deviant have failed. The German word *Bann* means 'excommunication."[27] The English word *ban* is also used. From the internal perspective of Amish culture, the ban is designed to purify the body and redeem the backslider. The separation unites the community against sin, purges deviance, and reaffirms the moral order. In the same way that punishing criminals reaffirms the legal code of modern society, expelling sinners clarifies and rejuvenates the Amish Ordnung.

If persons refuse to come before the church to confess their sins, they will face excommunication. A congregational vote (*der Rat*) is taken to endorse a proposed expulsion. Hoping for the best, members may ask the deacon and minister to make a final visit with the offending member and plead for his or her return. If stubbornness persists, the congregation will eventually vote to excommunicate.

A final rite concludes the series of sad events. The deacon and a minister visit the wayward person and inform him or her of the church's action. Following an old Benedictine formula, the elders repeat the following verse: "To deliver such an one unto Satan for the destruction of the flesh, that the spirit may be saved in the day of the Lord Jesus." This quote from Luther's German translation of 1 Corinthians 5:5 terminates the membership.[28] If the member refuses to come to the door, the verse is repeated aloud outside the house.

Although expulsion sounds harsh to Moderns, who value tolerance, the Amish demonstrate considerable patience and leniency. A young farmer is given six months, until the next communion service, to remove the rubber tires from his tractor. A businessman using a computer is allowed to complete a major eight-month project before he must "put it away." A family that buys an "English" house outfitted with electricity has a year of grace before the wiring must be torn out. In the case of adultery, divorce, or purchase of an automobile, excommunication is virtually automatic unless the deviant confesses the wrong. In most cases, ordained leaders display considerable patience as they work with their members and "try to win them back."

If all else fails, the back door to the Amish house will close. An old bishop was fond of saying: "The ban is like the last dose of medicine that you can give to a sinner. It either works for life or death." Leaders believe that errant members bring excommunication upon themselves by their stubbornness. But the back door always remains open a crack. Expelled members are always welcome to come back and will be reinstated if they are willing to kneel and confess their error. One man, excommunicated for dishonest business practices, decided to repent and confess his faults after nearly a year of exile. Others occasionally rejoin the church after many years. A senior bishop, in explaining the ban, emphasized the importance of love: "If love is lost, God's lost too. God is love, doesn't the Bible tell us God is love? And I sometimes think that love is worth more than fighting about this and that. You lose friendship through it."

The doctrinal statement of the Amish emphasizes the importance of maintaining the church's purity. "An offensive member and open sinner [must] be excluded from the church, rebuked before all and purged out as a leaven and thus remain until his amendment, as an example and warning to others and also that the church may be kept pure from such 'spots' and blemishes."[29] Although the theological intent of excommunication is to purge sin from the body, its social consequence is maintenance of the Ordnung. The ban is the ultimate form of social control. When mavericks sidestep the Ordnung or "jump the fence too far," they are disowned to preserve the integrity of the moral order. Order, authority, and identity take precedence over tolerance. These practices may seem harsh to modern sensitivities, but even Moderns, who cherish tolerance, are ready to imprison criminals and expel dissidents, political traitors, illegal aliens, and insubordinate employees.

MEIDUNG: SOCIAL QUARANTINE

A unique feature of Amish excommunication is the practice of *Meidung,* often called "shunning." As a reminder of the seriousness of their infractions, expelled people are shamed in ceremonial ways. Contrary to popular opinion, members can talk with persons who are under the ban, but certain forms of interaction are taboo. "Compared to other church disciplines, ours has teeth in it," said one member. *Meidung,* the "teeth" of Amish discipline, is designed to bring the wayward back and to preserve the moral boundaries of the community.

Disagreements about the practice of *Meidung* helped to trigger the Amish separation from other Anabaptists in 1693. It has remained a distinguishing feature of Amish life. An Amish bishop explained: "In the *Martyrs Mirror,* you read that if there's a ban and no shunning, it's like a house without doors or a church without walls where the people can just walk in and out as they please." The application of shunning varies in Amish settlements, but in principle, it remains a cornerstone of Amish polity.[30]

The Dordrecht Confession of Faith includes an article on shunning that spells out its theological justification:

If anyone whether it be through a wicked life or perverse doctrine is . . . expelled from the church he must also according to the doctrine of Christ and his apostles, be shunned and avoided by all the members of the church (particularly by those to whom his misdeeds are known), whether it be in eating or drinking, or other such like social matters. In short that we are to have nothing to do with him; so that we may not become defiled by intercourse with him and partakers of his sins, but that he may be *made ashamed,* be affected in his mind, convinced in his conscience and thereby induced to amend his ways.[31] (emphasis added)

A statement by the Lancaster bishops calls for shunning members "if they behave in a way that is offensive, irritating, disobedient or carnal, so that they may be caused to turn back, or till they come out of their disobedience."[32]

Shunning is a ritual of shaming that is used in public occasions and face-to-face interaction to remind the ostracized that they are outside the moral order. Shunning does not reflect personal animosity, but rather it is a ritual means of shaming the wayward and reminding everyone of the boundaries of membership. Conversation is not forbidden, but members may not shake hands or accept anything directly from the offender. However, members are encouraged to help, assist, and visit people under the ban.

Thus, shunning is an asymmetrical, one-way relationship. Members can help offenders, but offenders may not have the dignity of aiding a member. A grandmother who is a member may not accept her baby grandson directly from the hands of her shunned daughter. A check or a Christmas gift should not be accepted directly from a shunned person. Gifts, money, or payments from an offender, following the ritual formula, are placed on a table or counter and picked up by a member in a separate transaction. Members cannot accept a ride in the car of someone under the ban. Members of a volunteer fire company should not ride on a fire truck driven by a former member. Said one member about to face *Meidung,* "You suddenly lose all your security, and you become a goat, like a piece of dirt."

The symbolic shaming also takes place during meals at weddings and funerals if shunned persons are present. The practice makes some family gatherings awkward. The banned person may attend but will likely be served at a separate table or at the end of a table covered with a separate tablecloth. In one case, an adult male who was shunned was excluded from the plans for his father's funeral. Soon afterward, he decided to make amends with the church and return to the fold. A woman who persisted in attending a non-Amish Bible study was placed under the ban. Although continuing to live with her Amish husband, she eats at a separate table and abstains from sexual relations. Parents must shun adult children who are excommunicated. Brothers and sisters are required to shun each other.[33] Members who do not practice shunning will jeopardize their own standing in the church.

The application of shunning varies widely from family to family. Many times it is relaxed in private homes but tightened in public settings if other church members are present, attesting to its ritual character and ceremonial role in the community. Many families treat family members under the ban with love and care in the privacy of their homes. Despite its theological purposes, shunning is a painful process. One woman said, "I'm not responsible for being born into a church that practices shunning. I have an uncle and aunt and cousins in the ban, and it may separate us on the social level, but it could never sever the cord of love." Another person, whose parents are shunned, said, "Most people learn to live with it and not make a big deal of it. But it's always there casting a shadow over all the relationships with people that are Amish."

Excommunicated people are shunned until they repent. Upon confessing their sins, they are fully restored to membership in the church. But for unrepentant people, shunning becomes a lifetime quarantine. Amish-born people who never join the church are not shunned. Only those who break their baptismal vow by leaving the church or falling into disobedience are ostracized. Shunning places a moral stigma on the expelled because as "blemished" ones they have broken their baptismal vows and have turned their back on the church and God.

Meidung also clarifies an important principle in Amish life that is hard for Moderns to grasp. The church holds higher authority than the family. Individuals are accountable first to the church and then to their families. Only the church can divorce members. Only the church can separate families, because its authority reigns over all other spheres of life. Whereas in modern life the ranking of moral authority is individual, family, church; the order is turned upside down in Amish life. The threat of shunning is a powerful deterrent to disobedience in a community where everyone is linked by family ties.

The possibility of *Meidung* cautions those who would mock the church, scorn its Ordnung, or spurn the counsel of ordained leaders. To be shamed for life is no small matter when it means separation from family, friends, and neighbors. *Meidung* is a potent tool for social control. "It has holding power," an Amish minister said. A former Amishman, shunned for more than fifty years because he joined a liberal church, said: "Shunning works a little bit like an electric fence around a pasture with a pretty good fence charger on it." When asked about the ability of the church to hold its members, one person said: "That's easy to answer, it's the Meidung. If it weren't for shunning, many of our people would leave for more progressive churches where they could have electricity and cars."[34]

Shunning is the cornerstone of social control in Amish society. Baptism, communion, and confession are redemptive means to encourage compliance with the Ordnung. When those modes fail, the *Meidung* is there—a silent deterrent that encourages those who think about breaking their baptismal vows to think twice! Indeed, it is one of the secrets of the riddle of Amish survival.

Two cornerstones of Amish faith and practice give it credibility. Young adults clearly have a choice regarding church membership. In this way the church maintains the integrity of adult baptism. Second, those who are excommunicated are always welcome to return upon confession of their transgression. Sins that are confessed before God and the community are forgiven and as much as possible forgotten. These two features—the integrity of adult choice and full restoration of the wayward—lend credibility to the Amish story.

Amish rites of redemption and purification have stood the test of time and show few, if any, traces of erosion. They symbolize, rehearse, and communicate the essence of Amish culture. Kneeling for the rites of baptism, prayer, ordination, footwashing, and confession portrays the humble stance of Gelassenheit. The Amish have refused to yield their sacred rituals to modern individualism, with its easy tolerance of any behavior. Such a concession would surely erode their moral order. Their attempts to preserve order may seem legalistic and harsh at first blush, yet the personnel policies that shape the ethos of corporate and government bureaucracies are hardly less restrictive. The regulatory mindset is not unique to the Amish; they have simply applied it to the moral bedrock that undergirds their entire way of life.

Auctions, Frolics, and Gangs

Barn raisings are for us what the World Series is for the non-Amish.
—*Amish farmer*

SPONTANEOUS CARING AND SHARING

The rites of redemption in Amish society are enmeshed in a network of social activities that knit the community together. Spontaneous visiting and informal gatherings create solidarity and generate social capital across the settlement. Somewhat like its financial equivalent, social capital provides a collective pool of resources that contribute to the well-being of the community and benefit individual members.[1] The cultural values and social structures of Amish society generate many resources that bolster the common good. An Amishman described it this way: "There's much caring and sharing in times of need, helping together to raise barns and in funeral and wedding arrangements, to plant and harvest crops if a farmer is laid up. . . . Much of this caring is done at a moment's notice, when the neighbors see the crops need to be tended."[2]

The traditional Amish barn raising provides a good example of how cultural and social capital are mobilized for a special need. When a barn goes up in flames, everyone in the Amish community knows exactly what will happen in the next three days, without consulting a book or looking at a Web site. Neighbors will immediately drop their work and help with the cleanup while the debris still smolders. On the next day, a hundred or more people will arrive and raise a new barn in a matter of hours. All the labor is donated. The recovery effort automatically swings into action without lengthy discussions with insurance adjustors, lawyers, and contractors. It happens spontaneously because the barn-raising habit is so tightly woven into the texture of Amish life. Everyone freely donates their time because their house or shop may be next. This simple but powerful tradition is embedded in the cultural capital—the values of mutual obligation, duty, and trust that are simply taken for granted in Amish society.

A barn raising is perhaps the most dramatic example of how the pool of social capital is mobilized in Amish society. Social capital resources include strong networks of face-to-face relationships, extended family, and long-standing traditions and rituals that support them. Both cultural values and social structures provide the raw materials, so to speak, to mobilize the resources to raise a barn as shown in Figure 6.1. Many social activities in the Amish life cycle generate and expend social capital from birth to death for the well-being of the community. And many of the decisions the elders have made over the years, decisions that may appear silly to outsiders, were in fact attempts to preserve the social capital that energizes the life of the community.

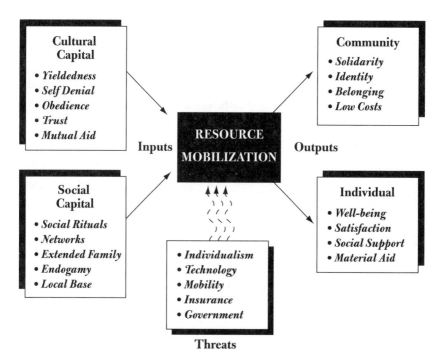

FIGURE 6.1 Cultural and Social Capital Resources

CHILDHOOD

Strong social networks make it easier to generate and store social capital. An Amish child is born into a dense network of extended family relations that will surround and support her for the rest of her life. This web of siblings, cousins, aunts, and uncles—as many as a hundred or more people who are directly related to the child—provide a ready-made system of support that is already in place when the infant arrives. The newborn child does not need to develop support groups or join interest groups because an entire system awaits its arrival. The child inherits these social supports at birth and later reproduces them as an adult.

Most Amish children are born at home under the supervision of a trained non-Amish midwife. Sometimes the first child is born at a hospital, but later children typically greet the world at home. A birthing is a family affair. Increasingly, fathers attend the delivery and siblings excitedly await the arrival in an adjoining room. A physician who cares for Amish patients noted that whenever a newborn arrives, one or two adult women suddenly appear in the household. These mothers, older sisters, or aunts are experienced: they know the secrets—the wisdom of the culture. Instead of reading books on birthing, they tap the wisdom, the cultural capital afloat in the networks around them. And as children grow up, there is ample help to raise them. A young mother with two children explained that whenever she needs a babysitter, "I can just drop them off at one of my two sisters and three cousins that live within a half-mile of here."

Unlike children who are socialized to become independent and successful in a competitive world, the Amish child is taught meekness, humility, and obedience. The child must master these virtues of Gelassenheit in order to prepare for a successful Amish life. Child-rearing practices, school curriculum, and apprenticeship in home and shop immerse children in Amish values and prepare them for adulthood. Most basic of all, the child learns to be obedient to authority—whether embodied in parents, teachers, or leaders. Such obedience is the key to shaping members who will support the habits and sentiments that generate community.

RUNNING AROUND

Amish youth anticipate their sixteenth birthday with great excitement. This is the moment when they can join a youth group and begin running around (*rumspringa*) with their friends on weekends. *Rumspringa* continues until they are married, typically at between nineteen and twenty-two years of age.[3] During this liminal period they are betwixt and between the authority of their parents and the thumb of the church because they are not baptized. Some are baptized a year or so before they marry and others shortly before marriage. The friendships and networks that develop during *rumspringa* form a lifelong web of social ties across the community.

About twenty-seven youth groups, called "gangs," ranging in size from fifty to a hundred and fifty members, crisscross the Lancaster settlement. By the age of ten, an Amish child will be able to name some of the groups— Bluebirds, Canaries, Pine Cones, Drifters, Shotguns, Rockys, and Quakers—and even describe some of their activities. Youth are free to join the gang of their choice. Young people from the same church district or family may join different groups. The gangs become the primary social world for teens before they marry, but the groups vary considerably in their conformity to traditional Amish values.

Some groups are fairly docile, but others engage in boisterous behavior that occasionally makes newspaper headlines. The reputation of the various gangs signals how Plain or rebellious a young person likely will be. The groups engage in various recreational and social activities—volleyball, swimming, ice skating, roller skating, singing, picnics, parties, and dances. For many of these activities, the more rowdy boys "dress around," that is, shed their sectarian garb. Hatless, wearing styled hair and store-bought jackets, they may "pass" as typical youth in a bar or movie theater. Young men in some groups will have fancy reflective tape on their buggies and perhaps a hidden radio or CD player inside.

Sunday afternoon and evening is the traditional time for youth gatherings. Members of Plainer gangs will typically stay home on a Saturday night unless they are dating. The faster gangs, by contrast, may sponsor a "band hop," attend movies, or play cards on a Saturday night. Members of the more rambunctious groups drive cars and sponsor dances, called "band hops," featuring Amish bands with electric guitars and kegs of beer. Wilder parties often

involve the use and abuse of alcohol. In one case, alcohol abuse was so consistent and flagrant that public officials wrote to church leaders asking for
help to curb it.[4] Youth are occasionally arrested for driving cars and buggies
under the influence of alcohol.

Unlike the more sensational gangs, many groups uphold traditional Amish
values—driving horses and carriages, and drinking sodas or hot chocolate.
The Plainer groups focus more on group games and outdoor activities. While
the faster gangs are more peer oriented, the Plainer ones are more adult-
centered, with parents participating in some of their activities.[5] After two
nationally publicized drug arrests in 1998, some parents established several
fairly Plain youth groups that have strict standards forbidding worldly clothing, cars, alcohol, and drugs. The gatherings of these gangs end earlier in
the evening and have more parental involvement.

The hundred or so members of a gang will gather at a member's farmstead
on a Sunday afternoon to play volleyball or softball before a sumptuous supper prepared by some of the parents. Following the supper, their caravan of
buggies will travel to another home for a singing that begins about 7:30 P.M.
and continues until 10:00 P.M., followed by socializing indoors and out until
midnight or later.

A dating relationship may begin when a fellow offers to take a young
woman home in his buggy. Depending on how far they must travel, some
lads may not return home until early dawn. One parent noted, "The groups
are intermingled throughout the settlement so that some girl-hunting lads
may travel twenty-five to thirty miles to win the lady of his choice. Some do
it pony express style, using two horses."[6] Youth often date several persons
before finding their lifelong partner.

The cohort of twelve to twenty youth that join a gang in a particular year
are known as a "Buddy Bunch." These subgroups within the gang sometimes
have their own name. The primary peer groups for teens, Buddy Bunches
often continue meeting throughout their lives. Within the Buddy Bunch, a
teen will often have a "sidekick," a best friend with whom to share secrets.
Interaction with the Buddy Bunch slows somewhat when a couple begins
serious dating, but sidekicks and Buddy Bunch members will often join the
church at the same time and remain friends for life.

In some ways the struggles of Amish families are similar to contemporary

A Buddy Bunch chats together before a Sunday evening singing.

ones. Parents worry about which groups their teens will join because they know that one group may invite temptation, whereas another will reinforce parental teaching. Youth inclined to rebel will deliberately join a more rowdy gang, and those with a docile heart will seek more conservative peers. But even most of the fellows who succumb to cars, alcohol, and movies eventually put away their foolishness and return to the fold prior to marriage. To enjoy the delights of the world as long as possible, some young men will delay baptism until the fall when they are married. In actuality, their decision to join the church is usually made in the late spring because candidates must attend instruction classes over the summer.

One elder thinks the crisscrossing youth groups help to unify the settlement by creating a web of extended family ties that binds the whole community together beyond local districts. In any event, the social ties that form in the *rumspringa* years lay a foundation for long-term networks of solidarity and support.

WEDDINGS

Weddings are held on Tuesdays and Thursdays in November at the end of the harvest season. As many as a dozen weddings may be held on the same day, and 180 may take place across the settlement in a wedding season. An individual may receive invitations to four or five weddings on the same day. The daylong affairs are held at the home of the bride and often involve 300 to 400 guests.[7]

The guests begin arriving at 7:00 A.M., and some may linger until midnight. The wedding ceremony is part of a three-and-a-half-hour service similar to Sunday worship. The service itself is a sober and plain event with no candles, flowers, veils, rings, tuxedos, or special music. Two couples who accompany the bride and groom constitute the wedding party. The festivities begin after the formal service. A hot lunch is eaten in several shifts, and a smaller meal is served again in the evening. Visiting, games, and singing fill the afternoon and evening hours until the last guests depart.

To orchestrate such a large gathering in a private home or shop without a catering service requires an enormous outpouring of free labor. The bride's mother and family take the lead role in planning, but they often have someone else coordinate the events of the day itself. Neighbors in the local church district provide food and help to prepare the property and assist in various roles throughout the day—as cooks, ushers, waiters, dishwashers, table setters, and hostlers to care for the horses. This generous outpouring of goodwill celebrates one of the happiest moments in Amish life. An older couple, returning from a bankruptcy hearing for a business they sold, belatedly joined the afternoon singing and festivities of a wedding. Struck by the contrast, they marveled, "How good we have it! The outside world has no idea what they're missing."

The newlyweds typically spend their first night at the bride's home and help to clean up the house the next day. Traditionally, the bride and groom live with their parents for several months until they set up their household in the spring when farm families typically move. Instead of a honeymoon, the bride and groom spend weekends with different relatives throughout the winter. During these visits the couples receive their wedding gifts and cement their relationships with the new members of their extended family. With the wedding behind them, they are now considered adults and expected to fully

A dating couple in their open courting buggy.

participate in the life of the community. In the summer following the wedding, the groom's parents hold an *infare,* a celebration to thank the bride's family and all the friends and neighbors who helped with the wedding—a way of replenishing the goodwill—the social capital—in the Amish reservoir.

HOLIDAYS AND VISITING

The Amish observe a different cultural calendar. Although they do not formally celebrate public holidays—Washington's Birthday, Martin Luther King Day, Memorial Day, Fourth of July, or Labor Day—they do recognize Thanksgiving and New Year's Day. They also observe sacred days that stretch back to their roots in Switzerland. In addition to Easter and Christmas, they celebrate Good Friday, Easter Monday, Pentecost Monday (Whit Monday), and a second day of Christmas on 26 December. Good Friday in the spring and St. Michael's Day in the fall are days of fasting and prayer to prepare for holy communion.

Second Christmas, Easter Monday, Pentecost Monday, and Ascension Day are festive times for visiting and relaxing. Amish businesses close on these days, and people typically dress up as they visit with friends, families, or Buddy Groups. Youth groups will plan special outings with volleyball and a meal with their "supper crowd." Some groups may plan a van or bus trip to another settlement in Pennsylvania on one of these holidays. Fishing is a favorite activity on Ascension Day, which comes on a Thursday, forty days after Easter. One Amish person described Ascension Day this way: "The day is for visiting and starts early for young and old alike. Uncles, cousins, and families congregate. Youth groups plan outings—softball and volleyball. Charter buses take youth and married folks to other communities 150 miles away to visit, relax, and ponder the philosophies of Amish life. With about 22,000 Amish here in Lancaster, about half of them are on the move. . . . If 11,000 folks move about in six per buggy that's 1,800 horses clip clopping down the roads, so drive carefully those of you driving Detroit and imported vehicles. We appreciate it."[8]

Visiting is the national sport of Amish society. It is the social glue that bonds the community together through informal ties of trust and respect. Much of the visiting occurs spontaneously when family and friends drop in unannounced for a visit. Other visiting takes place in dozens of informal gatherings, reunions, quilting parties, frolics, and picnics. Still other visiting occurs in more formal settings, after church meals, at weddings, and funerals. Some older folks complain that some young married couples are even getting together in their "off Sunday" for brunch instead of worshiping in an adjoining district or spending a worshipful day at home. Unlike more modern forms of one-on-one visiting, Amish visiting is virtually always collective, with five or six persons, if not a dozen, in a circle.

To the casual observer, visiting may appear as a waste of time, but in fact it is an important means of renewing the networks of social capital throughout the community. These relationships, rejuvenated through visiting, strengthen the informal bonds that link the community together in joy and suffering. Interpersonal relationships in Amish society are enmeshed in a concrete social context. Unlike the context-free relationships of cyberspace, Amish people interact with others in a high-context culture. They know more than just the other person's name and e-mail address. They know the *full* social context surrounding the person—their parents and grandparents, their church district and ministers, their occupation and hobbies, their stature within the community—as well as their temperament. These are deeply embedded, highly contextualized relationships that are quite different from the multitude of transitory ties in modern society and cyberspace. Relationships in Amish society are full-bodied, high-context, durable connections that stretch over a lifetime.[9]

FROLICS AND FUN

Unlike modern societies that segregate work and play, the Amish often blend them together. Banter and humor abound as work crews clean up after a flood. Staging a wedding for 350 guests involves a lot of hard work as well as fun. The growth of the settlement has expanded options for social involvements. "We have many more social activities today," said one woman. "We used to have a more quiet pace of life, but now there's so many activities. We don't go and play tennis, but we have many more visiting activities."

A great deal of visiting happens with frolics—typically one-day gatherings that blend work and fellowship in a variety of activities. Twenty-five people might come together to help finish and clean a new house or prepare a school and play yard for a new school year. Depending on the task, men and women may attend the frolic together or the women may go alone. Some activities fall along gender lines. A quilting party or Christmas cookie bake is for the women. Traditional farm life made it easy to participate in frolics. More recently, with more people involved in business and milking larger herds, schedules are less pliable. One frolic coordinator complained, "Today some people don't arrive until the morning coffee break, and then they have to leave at 3:00 P.M. to begin their milking."

A unique family tradition is "Sisters Day." The sisters in a family, which might include five or six women, may meet monthly for fellowship and work in one of their homes. Sometimes they preserve vegetables, quilt, bake, or clean. "Oftentimes," said one woman, "we take our sewing and just talk while the children play." Some sisters sew comforters that are distributed to refugees in other countries through the Mennonite Central Committee.

Buddy Groups, extending from running-around days, often continue meeting through adulthood as well. The women may get together once a month for a small frolic or a quilting party much like a Sisters Day. Several times throughout the year the couples may gather for a picnic, a Christmas singing, or to sing for older folks who are homebound. One leader complained that the women are always "going away too much. They're just not home enough."

If the women are going away too much, the men are just as guilty. Especially in the late winter and early spring, men can often be found at auctions. A favorite place to visit with friends and neighbors, the farm auction also mingles work and play. One might have to wait all day to bid on a corn binder or drill press to get a "good buy." Yet throughout the day of waiting, there is incessant visiting, fellowship, food, the excitement of endless bidding, and the auctioneer's sing-song call. Amish and Old Order Mennonite youth, on opposing teams, often play corner ball in barnyards before cheering crowds of youth and adults. The longstanding auction tradition, the English equivalent of a parade or fair, provides fun and fellowship in the context of making a living.

Clusters of men often go hunting and deep sea fishing together. In addition to local small game hunting, many go deer hunting for several days in central or northern Pennsylvania. In fact, it has become popular for some groups to buy an old farmhouse upstate and convert it into a hunting lodge. Fishing in the Chesapeake Bay as well as deep sea fishing are also favorite sports. A few Amish men were tempted by golf in the 1990s, but that ended with a decree against the sport in 1997.

A lunch break during a quilting frolic.

In recent years many more couples are taking trips for a week or two out of state. Two or three couples will hire a van and driver to visit Amish settlements, national parks, or historic sites in other states. Whether fishing, frolicking, or traveling out of state, the Amish are always doing it in groups, visiting and chatting as they go. The visiting mingles moments of work and play. Some of the elders frown on the growing number of trips to faraway places and worry that they eventually will lead to costly vacations and worldly entanglements away from watchful eyes.

CIRCLES OF SUPPORT

A variety of informal support groups have emerged in recent years that revolve around special interests. Some of these are based in Lancaster County; others stretch across the nation. They range from annual gatherings of occupational clusters to support groups for medical concerns. Still others are chatty letters that circulate within a "circle" of family and special friends.

As more Amish moved into nonfarm occupations in the last quarter of the twentieth century, special occupational groupings also emerged. These Amish versions of professional associations, often called "reunions," are a favorite time to meet old friends from across the country. They also provide opportunities to share expertise and knowledge about tools, products, and markets—to expand the pool of social capital related to quilting or cabinetry. Since 1981 Amish woodworkers from across the country have gathered for a get-together. Several hundred woodworkers gather to reminisce and to share the latest developments in cabinetry, millwork, and furniture making. The harness makers, machine shop operators, wooden shed builders, and quilters have similar reunions as well. A harness makers' get-together attracted some 525 people who devoured six hundred halves of chicken, eleven gallons of baked beans, eighteen dozen dinner rolls, sixty pies, and forty gallons of drink. "It got pretty hectic," said the coordinator, "but we had a lot of fun."[10]

Other gatherings focus on medical concerns. Beginning in 1963 in Ohio, individuals with various disabilities began to gather for support in what became known as the "Annual Handicap Gathering." The reunion rotates around the country and includes some one hundred participants from Lancaster County with cerebral palsy, polio, blindness, dwarfness, multiple sclerosis, and deafness among other disabilities. The gathering provides emotional support as well as information about sources of medical care and equipment. Some Lancaster Amish also participate in the People's Helpers, an informal network of people assisting persons afflicted with mental illness and depression.

Another form of support for individuals with special interests or needs is the old-fashioned circle letter, where each participant adds their letter to a packet of letters that circulate within a circle of friends. Letter writing is not a lost art among the Amish. Without easy access to telephones or e-mail, the circle letter provides an important source of information and affirmation for persons with similar afflictions. Examples of "circles" include couples without children, persons who have had open heart surgery, parents of children killed in accidents, individuals with a special illness (e.g., muscular dystrophy). Circle letters also rotate among persons with similar circumstances—ministers ordained in the same fall or spring, parents of twins, parents of all boys or all girls, to name but a few examples. In addition, circle letters rotate among relatives or members of Buddy Bunches who have moved away. The many circle letters help to bond the community together.

A more public form of bonding occurs among readers who follow the endless stories of local scribes who write for *Die Botschaft* and *The Budget*, Amish weekly newspapers, and for *The Diary*, a monthly magazine. Accounts of local happenings—church services, accidents, visiting, harvesting, travel, medical problems, and much more—are shared in these publications for Amish audiences across the country. The reunions, circle letters, and newspapers not only disburse information, they also build solidarity and confirm identity in the Amish community.

MUTUAL AID

Mutual aid runs deep in the Amish soul. Church membership carries responsibility to care for the material and social needs of fellow members. An Amish farmer in another state summarized the assumptions about mutual responsibility this way: "When I am plowing in the spring, I can often see five or six other teams in nearby fields, and I know if I was sick they would all be here plowing my field."[11] When disaster strikes in the form of illness, flood, or fire, the community rallies quickly to help the family in need.

The barn raising after a fire is the classic symbol of mutual aid. In a matter of eight hours, more than a hundred men will erect a new barn, and dozens of women will prepare the food that sustains them. Under the quiet directions of a wise foreman, the complicated task flows smoothly, seemingly almost without effort.

An Amishman described it this way:

> There isn't a crane poking its long boom skyward, hook dangling. There are no white-hatted foremen dashing about with squawking radios. Now watch as, just for the last 500 years, a forty-six foot long line of straw hatted men, facing east, bend down. Forty-six feet of rear ends face westward, with all hands on the top timber of the assembled frame. All are ready to push it skyward. The moment is dramatic, everyone is quiet as several late comers rush up the barn hill to help. Reuben says, "Take her up"—not a holler, but a positive command—in a voice filled with experience. With some minor grunts the ponderous frame moves up, hands outstretched.[12]

The observer also noted that over the years a few things have been added—porta-potties, colorful coolers of drink, and battery-operated hand drills, for example.

Describing the clamor as dozens of men gather around a wagon loaded with coffee, hot chocolate, and cookies, one participant said, "There's a lot of visiting going on here. There are cousins, and friends from other settlements here who haven't seen each other for years." By 4:00 P.M. the structure is secure and most of the tin roof and siding is finished. The barn raising not only addresses a member's material need but also symbolizes the enormous collective resources of the community. Said one Amishman, "Barn raisings are for us what the World Series is for the non-Amish."

Although the barn raising is the traditional symbol of mutual care, many other forms of mutual aid flourish, as well. As many Amish moved into nonfarm jobs and as the community has interacted more closely with the outside world, new patterns of aid have emerged. Because of their belief that members of the church should be accountable to and responsible for each other, leaders have strongly discouraged commercial insurance, which would undercut aid within the community and drain away the precious social capital.

A variety of informal aid programs have developed within the church to assist with special needs related to fire, storm, health care, liability, and product liability. Although some of these programs require an annual premium, most of them gather special collections within the community as major needs

The community gathers and quickly erects a new barn after a fire.

arise. For example, a collection may be taken to assist a farmer faced with excessive liability charges for selling spoiled milk or a family faced with an overwhelming medical bill. Adjoining church districts also help each other as needs arise. As noted in Chapter 4, the remarkable feature of all these aid programs is their spontaneous response to need without bureaucratic red tape, formal offices, or paid employees. Unlike commercial forms of insurance, transaction costs and administrative overhead are virtually nil.

Auctions have also been used in recent years to help members with special needs. Known as "benefit auctions," these sales of crafts, quilts, food, and barbecued chicken help families with excessive medical bills or a paraplegic injured in an accident. An annual benefit auction supports the Clinic for Special Children that provides medical care for Amish and Old Order Mennonite children. From frolics to benefit auctions, the community surrounds its members with care and in the process rejuvenates its pool of goodwill. In so doing, it distinguishes itself from the broader society, where needy individuals often have to haggle with lawyers and insurance providers to solve their problems.

HELPING OUTSIDERS

The spirit of caring and sharing does not stop at the borders of Amish society. Although the Amish have historically emphasized separation from the world and shunned worldly involvements, they also extend a helping hand to those beyond their fold. By supporting local fire companies, benefit auctions, the Mennonite Central Committee, Mennonite Disaster Service, and Christian Aid Ministries, Amish care extends beyond the confines of their ethnic community.

Although the Amish typically frown on civic involvement, they have readily joined local fire companies. Indeed, in some communities as many as 75 percent of the members of local firefighters are Amish. In some townships they may own the bulk of the farms and homes protected by the fire companies. Although they don't drive the fire trucks, they do drop their work at a beeper's notice and scramble to fight the fires.

Many of the fire companies have benefit auctions, sometimes called "Mud Sales" because thousands of people walking on soggy fields in March can quickly turn grass into mud. The Amish donate merchandise and labor for these sales, which attract thousands of outsiders. Many people drive from eastern seaboard cities to bid on quilts, buy some shoofly pie, and witness the Amish in action. Proceeds from such a sale may generate several hundred thousand dollars. The Amish also support disaster relief auctions sponsored by the Mennonite Central Committee to aid international refugees. In addition, they support an auction for the Light House, a local rehabilitation center, and the Haiti Benefit auction for the needy of Haiti. Quilts, lovely furniture, crafts, construction materials, and farm equipment are among the many valuable items the Amish donate to these auctions as well as their labor.

As members of the larger Anabaptist family, the Amish also aid international relief and service projects organized by the Mennonite Central Committee, an international agency with headquarters in Akron, north of the city of Lancaster. One year some 1,200 Amish, in a four-day period, participated in a meat canning project for refugees in Bosnia. A mobile canner moves from area to area, utilizing local labor and donated beef. Sometimes the Amish purchase the beef and then provide the labor for canning it. "We could just buy the meat and send it there," said one bishop, "but there's much more satisfaction in helping to do something directly."

Some Amish women piece comforters or sew other clothing that is donated to the Mennonite Central Committee for distribution to refugees. Many church districts send volunteers to sort and pack clothing at the Mennonite Central Committee's warehouse in Akron. In a typical year 2,000 members from 125 church districts volunteer thousands of hours at the warehouse quilting, preparing health kits, and packing clothing to be shipped abroad for victims of disaster.

The Amish have also been active participants in Mennonite Disaster Service, a national agency that responds in Red Cross fashion to disasters in the wake of hurricanes, tornadoes, and floods. Amish crews travel by van and bus to work sites, where they clean up debris and rebuild homes for a day or week at a time.

The Amish have assisted with cleanup and reconstruction related to Hurricane Camille in 1969 and Hugo in 1989, as well as tornadoes that struck in Alabama in 1974 and Somerset, Pennsylvania, in 1998. They also contribute to "hay drives" and "corn drives" in which hay and corn are donated to drought-stricken farmers in other parts of the country or world. In addition they donate heifers to a "Heifer Relief Sale," whose proceeds benefit refugees around the world.

In all of these ways, the Amish extend a hand of friendship and care beyond their ethnic borders, and in the process, they are replenishing their own pool of social capital. For whether it is preparing for auctions, quilting for relief, packing clothes for the needy, or building homes for the homeless, they are doing it *together*—chattering away, telling stories, building community. This pattern of civic service and philanthropy is much different from the lone volunteer who extends a hand on a civic project or the philanthropist who writes a check in isolation. As they serve the needy, the Amish also build community.

PASSING ON

Members draw their final check from their social capital account at death, as the community surrounds the bereaved with care. A funeral director observed that the Amish accept death in graceful ways.[13] With the elderly living at home, the gradual loss of health prepares family members for the final passage. The community springs into action at word of a death. Family and friends in the local church district assume barn and household chores, freeing the immediate family. Well-established funeral rituals unburden the family from facing worrisome choices. Three couples are appointed to extend invitations and supervise funeral arrangements—food preparation, seating arrangements for three to four hundred people, and the coordination of a large number of horses and carriages.[14]

A non-Amish undertaker moves the body to a funeral home for embalming. The body—without cosmetic enhancements—returns to the home in a simple hardwood coffin within five to six hours. Family members of the same sex dress the body in white garments that symbolize the final passage into a new and better life beyond. Women often are garbed in the white cape and apron worn at their wedding.

Friends and relatives visit the family and view the body in a room on the first floor of the home during two days prior to the funeral. Said one person, "People come and visit together—it's almost a social affair." They stay awhile and visit, with as many as one hundred in a room. Meanwhile, community members dig the grave by hand in a nearby family cemetery as others oversee the daily chores of the bereaved. Several hundred guests attend the funeral in a barn or home, typically on the morning of the third day after the death. During the simple hour-and-a-half-long service, ministers read hymns and Scripture, offer prayers, and preach a sermon. Singing and eulogies are missing, and there are no flowers, burial tents, or sculpted monuments.

The hearse, a large black carriage pulled by horses, leads a long proces-

Community solidarity is expressed at death as a funeral procession follows a hearse.

sion of carriages to the burial ground on the edge of a farm. A brief viewing and a graveside service mark the return of dust to dust. Pallbearers lower the coffin and shovel soil into the grave as the bishop reads a hymn. A small tombstone, the size of all the rest, marks the place of the deceased in the eternal community. Following the burial, friends and family members return to the home for a meal prepared by members of the local congregation. One widower, recounting the funeral meal for his wife with tears of appreciation, repeatedly asked, "Where else could you ever get support like that?"

A bereaved woman signals her mourning for a close relative by wearing a black dress in public settings for as long as a year. This symbol reminds and invites the community to respond with thoughtful care. Families who have lost a loved one will typically receive Sunday afternoon visits from friends for several months. A painful separation laced with grief, death is received in the spirit of Gelassenheit—as the ultimate surrender to God's higher ways. Surrounded by family and friends, and comforted by predictable rituals filled with religious meaning, the separation is humane by many standards. The tears flow, but the sobs are restrained as people submit quietly to the rhythms of divine purpose. From cradle to grave, the mysteries of life and death unfold in the context of loving families and supportive ritual.

This sampler of the rhythms of Amish society demonstrates the many ways in which cultural capital and social capital are mobilized to assist individuals and bolster the common good. Longstanding Amish traditions and the organizational structure of their community provide powerful means for mobilizing collective resources for the common good. Indeed, one way to interpret Amish history and its related puzzles is to see it as an ongoing struggle to preserve social capital. Ample resources of cultural and social capital have enabled the Amish to prosper many ways—from financial to social and emotional well-being. The solidarity and identity of their community results in part from their success in thwarting four challenges that threatened to diminish social capital and weaken their community: modern education, technology, nonfarm occupations, and government intrusion. The Amish struggled with all four of these challenges in the last half of the twentieth century—challenges that we explore in the following chapters.

7

Passing on the Faith

Too much worldly wisdom is poison for the soul.
—*Amish minister*

THE RIDDLE OF EDUCATION

Groups facing cultural extinction must indoctrinate their offspring if they want to preserve their unique social heritage. Socialization of the very young is a potent form of social control. As cultural values slip into a child's mind, they become personal values—embedded in conscience and laced with emotion. Socialization legitimated by religion is more powerful than law in directing and motivating personal behavior. Concerned that the dominant culture will demolish their traditional values, the Amish carefully guide their children.

The Amish believe that the Bible commissions parents to instruct their children in religious matters as well as in Amish ways. For example, day care centers, nursery schools, and kindergartens are not permitted because children are to be taught by their parents. Child rearing is an informal process where children learn the ways of their culture through interaction, observation, and modeling. Unlike modern youth, Amish children have little exposure to diverse ideas and cultural perspectives beyond their family and ethnic community.

Given their fears of the outside world and their convictions about parental instruction, it is surprising that the Amish sent their children to public schools for more than a century. However, the peaceful coexistence was shattered in the mid-twentieth century when a bitter clash erupted between the

Amish and state officials that resulted in dozens of arrests and imprisonment. What disrupted the century-long peace?

The rise of the Amish school system chronicles a fascinating dialogue between the Amish and the forces of progress. The Amish were willing to negotiate on some issues, but on the education of their children they refused to budge. Many parents paid for their stubbornness with imprisonment. Why were these gentle people willing to sit behind bars? Why did they resort to courts, petitions, and politics to preserve humility? Those intriguing questions thread their way throughout the story.

The voices of progress trumpeting the virtues of education were not about to be insulted by a motley group of peasant farmers. Through a variety of legal actions, the Amish were subpoenaed back to the bargaining table again and again.[1] Finally, in 1972, the United States Supreme Court ruled in their favor, stating that "there can be no assumption that today's majority is 'right' and the Amish and others are 'wrong.' A way of life that is odd or even erratic but interferes with no rights or interests of others is not to be condemned because it is different."[2] But that is getting ahead of our story.

THE LITTLE RED SCHOOLHOUSE

"We're not opposed to education," said one Amishman. "We're just against education higher than our heads. I mean education that we don't need." Indeed, for many years Amish youth were educated in public schools alongside their non-Amish neighbors.[3] When one-room public schools were established in Pennsylvania in 1844, the eldest son of an esteemed Amish bishop was a member of a school board.[4] The enforcement of compulsory attendance laws in 1895 stirred some criticism, but for the most part, the Amish supported public education in one-room schools.[5] Even in the twentieth century, Amish children attended public elementary schools, and their fathers frequently served as board members. In fact, in some schools Amish children held the majority. Policies and curriculum reflected local sentiment. Teachers affirmed the rural culture, often their own, and complied with local requests. In rural Pennsylvania, children typically attended school about four months of the year. Providing a practical education in basic skills, local public schools were ensconced in a rural context that dovetailed smoothly with Amish culture. All of that was about to change as state officials, in the name of progress, decontextualized education.

Amish children at the blackboard in a one-room public school ca. 1950.

The changes began in 1925, when the state legislature lengthened the school year. Eventually it raised the age of compulsory attendance, enforced attendance, and encouraged the consolidation of large schools. At first the Amish took the changes in stride. But when they realized that the forces of modernity would pull schools away from local control, away from their rural roots, the Amish began to resist.

Rumors of a new consolidated school agitated a heavily populated Amish township in 1925. A candidate for public office declared his opposition to consolidated schools and promised not to close any of the one-room buildings.[6] Fears of consolidation were not illusions. The state was already paying school districts $200 each time they closed a one-room school. Indeed, over a twenty-year period (1919–39), 120 one-room schools were abandoned in Lancaster County alone.

Mushrooming interest in education prompted an Amishman to write four articles debunking "excessive" education in a county newspaper in 1931. In a rare public outcry, he contended that a common elementary education was enough for an agricultural people. "Among all the Amish people in Lancaster County," he said, "you couldn't find one who ever took any high school, college or vocational school education. Yet I don't believe there's a class of people in the entire world that lead a happier life than do our people on the average. For pity's sake, don't raise the school age for farm children . . . for if they don't do farm work while they're young they seldom care for it when they're older." Complaining of rising school taxes, he asserted, "I am in favor of public schools, but I am not in favor of hiring teachers at twice the salaries that farmers are making to teach our girls to wash dishes and to dance." He then described a young, educated female acquaintance who unfortunately could not boil an egg even though she was "a bright scholar, a good dancer, busy attending parties, in fact very busy equipping herself to be modern flapper with lots of pep." Concluding that experience is a better teacher than higher education, he said, "Brother, if you want an educated modern wife, I wish you lots of wealth and patience and hope the Lord will have mercy upon your soul."[7]

THE TUMULT OF 1937

The farmer's fear of encroaching education was an omen of a confrontation that came to a head in 1937. A plan to abandon ten one-room schools in one sweep and replace them with a consolidated elementary building sparked the controversy. Induced by a federal grant, officials in East Lampeter Township, home of many Amish, began building the new school despite local objection. Incensed that the plans would place their children on school buses and in large classrooms with strange teachers, a coalition of citizens, largely Amish, organized themselves. Without the blessing of the church but with the help of Philadelphia lawyers, they obtained a court order in April 1937 to halt construction. The two-month delay was soon overturned by a higher court. Construction resumed, and the "newfangled" school opened in the fall of 1937. Some Amish children attended a one-room school that was still open, but others hid at home.[8]

In a surprising display of stubbornness, attorneys for the Amish renewed their fight in court. After meeting with Amish parents, Governor George H. Earle declared that he would reopen the ten one-room schools. The local school board balked, and the matter was tossed back and forth in a game of political ping pong for another nine months. The issue was finally settled when the U.S. Court of Appeals blessed the new school. In a conciliatory gesture, public officials maintained a one-room school for the Amish, but it only accommodated a few of them. The highly publicized dispute divided the larger community as well as the Amish themselves.[9] Such aggressive use of the law was rare, if not unprecedented, in Amish history.

In the midst of the East Lampeter dispute, a more ominous cloud loomed over Amish country.[10] School codes required attendance until age sixteen, but farmhands and domestic workers could drop out at fourteen. Hoping to bolster public education, legislators wanted to stretch the school term from eight to nine months and raise attendance age for farm youth to age fifteen. Such talk, on top of the recent strife, frightened Amish leaders. Raising the compulsory age to fifteen years for farmhands and extending the school year would deprive farmers of valuable help. Moreover, Amish youth would be bused to a large consolidated high school for a year until they were fifteen.

Frightened by the rumors, eight Amish bishops, representing all sixteen districts, petitioned a state legislator in March 1937 to "oppose all legislation" extending the school year and raising the age of compulsory attendance. The proponents of progressive education were not intimidated, however, by a few barefoot farmers. In July 1937, as the Amish began their wheat harvest, state legislators raised the compulsory attendance age for rural youth to fifteen and lengthened the school term to nine months. This action mobilized the Amish in a massive protest that would dwarf the ongoing dispute in East Lampeter Township. After finishing their harvest and watching the completion of the consolidated building, the bishops met in September to chart their course. Sure that the revised school code would "lead our children away from the faith," they asked someone in each church district to tap local sentiment. Most of the members supported making a plea to state officials if it could be done in a "gentle way." The opinion of a small minority was articulated by preacher Jacob Zook: "Better leave our fingers off; the Amish have stirred up enough stink for the present."

Most of the Amish, however, wanted action. With tacit support from the bishops, sixteen delegates, preachers, and laymen met on 14 September 1937. They organized themselves and began a two-year struggle that would take them to legislative halls and the governor's office. Calling themselves the Delegation for Common Sense Schooling, they hammered out a bargaining position with two key features. First, they would not send their children into the nurture and teaching of the world until they were grown. Second, they would send their children to public schools on four conditions: an eight-month school year, exemption after eighth grade, one-room schoolhouses, and teaching children the truth. After polishing a formal petition, the delegates launched a plan to gather sympathetic signatures and agreed "not to go to law, nor court, nor hire a lawyer."

Armed with a thousand copies of their petition, the Amish canvassed for signatures in numerous townships among members and nonmembers. Public opinion split in response to the Amish plea. To haggle over one additional year of schooling seemed petty to many, but others applauded the Amish. In any event, the Plain folk were able to garner more than three thousand signatures of support, which they pasted into a 130-foot scroll. Moreover, prominent businessmen from several communities rallied in support of the Amish with their own petition.

Bearing their signed petition, Amish representatives visited Governor Earle. Surprised by the public outcry, he stalled by asking Attorney General James H. Thompson to investigate whether the new school law violated religious freedom. Shifting their tactics in the Thanksgiving season, the Amish tried some rural diplomacy on the governor. They presented him with a basket holding a dressed turkey, a gallon of cider, and an ear of corn—symbolic first fruits of the field, flock, and orchard—hoping he would reciprocate with leniency.

Despite their Thanksgiving offering, the Amish soon realized that their only recourse was to petition the General Assembly of Pennsylvania. So the Delegation for Common Sense Schooling wrote a new petition, "To Our Men of Authority," hoping to persuade state legislators to change the statewide law. They pleaded again to have Amish children exempt from schooling after the eighth grade regardless of their age. "We do not wish to withdraw from the common public schools," they concluded, but "at the same time we cannot hand our children over to where they will be led away from us." The delegation also sent a pamphlet explaining their goals to Amish churches and promised that they would defend themselves "with the word of God rather than . . . with the services of a lawyer."[11]

THE POLITICAL STRUGGLE

In December 1937 three events shrouded the traditional gaiety of the Amish wedding season. First, the consolidated East Lampeter school had opened its doors despite Amish protests. Second, their Thanksgiving offering, formal petitions, personal meetings with state officials, and pleading letters had not exempted Amish fourteen-year-olds from school. Many, in fact, were hiding at home. Third, the Amish learned that Moderns cherished education and would not cater to rural peasants. Amishman Aaron King, living on the settlement's eastern fringe, was jailed for refusing to send his fourteen-year-old daughter to high school. King was convicted after a federal district court turned down his appeal in December 1937.[12]

The Christmas present that the Delegation for Common Sense Schooling had hoped to receive in exchange for their Thanksgiving offering had not arrived. Instead, they faced a frightening question: Would they be willing to sit in prison for the sake of their children? The new year opened on a bleak note. Attorney General Thompson declared that religious freedom and the rights of conscience could not obstruct the enforcement of law. In a blunt assessment of their bargaining clout, the Amish school committee concluded in January 1938 that "we got nothing."

Writing a letter to Attorney General Thompson the next day, Stephen F. Stoltzfus, the head of the Amish delegation, said that his impatient delegates wanted "to take a stand, but I tried to cool them down and got them persuaded to just keep quiet and see what we get." He ended by saying: "If we get nothing from our men in authority, we must do something ourselves. Why can't the Board of Public Instruction show us leniency and exempt our children when they have a fair education for farm and domestic work? If we educate them for businessmen, doctors, or lawyers, they will make no farmers." Hoping to avoid a public confrontation, the attorney general urged the Amish not "to do something drastic such as take a stand, as you call it." Citing the rumors and publicity that would surely come if they "took a stand," he admonished them to have "patience as taught in the Bible."

By the late spring of 1938, Amish patience was dwindling. They discussed setting up private schools and decided to consult state officials. Public officials discouraged such schools and urged the Amish to bring their plea to the legislative assembly. The Amish proceeded on both fronts. They laid plans to open two private schools and to approach the State General Assembly. So in the midst of the July wheat harvest, the Amish were once again drafting a petition. After receiving the bishops' blessing, 500 copies were sent to legislators and other public officials. Included with the petition was an amendment to the school code prepared for the Amish by the attorney general's staff to allow fourteen-year-olds to obtain work permits. Thus, in May 1939 state legislators passed a measure permitting fourteen-year-olds to quit school for farm and domestic work. But by then the Amish had already opened their first two private schools—on nearly the same day that the ten one-room schools were sold on public auction.[13]

After two years of strenuous effort, the Amish had reached only one of their goals—work permits for fourteen-year-olds who had completed eighth grade. Accordingly, fifty-four permits were granted to Amish youth in the fall of 1939. The two-year battle had not achieved much, but it brought a gift in disguise. The struggle had forced the Amish to hone and clarify their educational philosophy for the first time. In the midst of intense bargaining, they had developed strong convictions about the nature of Amish education that would guide them in future battles for the minds of their children.

Some outsiders were dismayed by the Amish. Ralph T. Jefferson, an "educated" state representative from Philadelphia, wrote to the Amish and declared that "education is the greatest gateway to knowledge." Displaying gross ignorance of Amish culture, he urged them to "turn on your radio, the water, the light, the heat, the gas, the electric, and turn your mind again to the electric churn, milker, sweepers, irons, and washers" as evidence of the fruits of education. Such counsel to the Amish was a superb example of the folly of higher ignorance!

Ironically, World War II gave the pacifist Amish a brief reprieve. The demand for farm products and the national preoccupation with the war put domestic politics on hold. In May 1943 new legislation gave local school boards more flexibility to issue work permits. The war also stalled construction of new Amish schools for another decade. Apart from minor skirmishes in local school districts, the battle for the minds of Amish youth was eclipsed by the war, and leniency prevailed.

IMPRISONMENT

The educational peace of the war years vanished in 1949. With the war behind them, educators and politicians across the country were more convinced than ever that public education was the key to keeping the world safe for freedom and democracy. In April 1949 new legislation raised the compulsory school age to sixteen, unless children were excused for farm or domestic work. A hidden clause gave the state superintendent of public instruction new power over work permits. The new law also required districts to bus students to high schools in neighboring townships if the district did not have a high school of its own. This sudden turn of events incited a bitter dispute between the Amish and public officials. Hundreds of Amish parents were arrested, and many were jailed until a compromise was struck in the fall of 1955.

Brandishing the new regulations, the state superintendent restricted work permits to "dire financial circumstances." The permits had to be approved not only by local and county educators but also by the superintendent himself. As a final gesture of his determination to enlighten Amish citizens, he threatened to withdraw state subsidies from school districts that overlooked the new regulations.

These actions only crystallized the Amish resolve. At least two dozen Amish fathers were arrested in the fall of 1949 for refusing to send their fourteen-year-old children to school.[14] Two fathers appealed the conviction, but a court decision upheld the Amish arrests by ruling that religious sects were not immune from compliance with reasonable educational duties.[15] Provided with such legal ammunition, the Pennsylvania Department of Public Instruction opened a vigorous campaign to keep Amish youth in school.[16]

Meeting in February 1950, Amish bishops issued a fifteen-point statement, once again reiterating their traditional opposition to education beyond eight grades and fourteen years of age. Unlike earlier statements, this one was not addressed to legislators and did not plead for leniency. It merely spelled out their position and implied that this time they would "take a stand." They would follow their conscience, and like Anabaptist martyrs of old, they were willing to suffer the consequences. One thing was certain in this round of negotiations—they would sit behind bars before acquiescing to educational progress.[17]

The bishops' statement fell on deaf ears. In the fall of 1950, 98 percent of the work applications from Lancaster County were rejected by the Department of Public Instruction.[18] Realizing that the state's threat to withdraw financial subsidies was not a bluff, local school districts began arresting Amish fathers who refused to send fourteen-year-olds to school. Within a three-day period in September 1950, thirty-six fathers were prosecuted. Refusing to pay fines because, they argued, they were innocent, many spent several days in jail until they were bailed out by non-Amish sympathizers.[19] Front-page newspaper photos showed Amish entering the Lancaster County Prison. Bold headlines declared: "Dozens Go to Jail," "Twenty Amish Violators Prosecuted," and "Two Ministers Among Nineteen Sent to Jail."

Some fathers are released from prison during the school crisis of the 1950s.

The arrests and jailing continued intermittently for five years. In Leacock Township alone, more than 125 parents were arrested, some of them five to seven times. One Amish father, arrested seven times, appealed his conviction as a test case in February 1954. Once again, a higher court sustained the conviction. This spurred a new round of arrests in the fall of 1954.[20] The five-year confrontation was bitter. Public opinion split. Amish members of local school boards as well as some other members resigned. Still, many officials were annoyed that the obstinate Amish were making such a ruckus over one year of schooling.

In order to keep their fifteen-year-olds out of public high school, some Amish parents made them repeat eighth grade. Others held their children back from first grade so that they would be fifteen by the time they completed eighth grade. Still others decided to take a stand and suffer arrest and brief imprisonment. One township developed an "eighth-grade-plus" program so that Amish students did not have to go to public high school.

Not all Amish were willing to sit in jail. One Amishman recalled his experience as a fourteen-year-old after his father had taken him out of school: "We were in the field one day, and the constable came and served Dad some papers. I had three days to appear in school. The next morning Pop said, 'You are going to school. I have neighbors all around me, and I am not going to sit in jail. I just can't.' He was looked down on by some. After repeating eighth grade again, I read a hundred books, everything from classic literature to a series of biographies of the leaders of our country. And the irony of it was that when we had to take our high school entrance tests, I had the highest mark in the whole county."

THE VOCATIONAL COMPROMISE

Was there no escape from this bitter battle between modernity and tradition? After his adamant stand on work permits, the state superintendent could hardly renege on his policy. But he was also tired of the rancorous public opinion that scorned his interpretation. Finally, he conceded that "something might be able to be worked out within the law for both." For their part, the Amish had chosen martyrdom over political action, and they were not about to lose face. As the arrests continued in the fall of 1953, the Amish bishops endorsed a proposal that promised to save face for everyone involved.

The Amish position congealed in December 1953, when the bishops and the Amish School Committee approved a proposal for a vocational training program for children who had completed eighth grade in a public school. The proposed solution appeased both parties. On the one hand, the state could say that Amish fourteen-year-olds were indeed in school; and on the other hand, the Amish were able to control the educational context and curriculum. After several delays and rounds of discussion, an agreement on the compromise was finally reached in 1955. With the blessing of the state, the

TABLE 7.1
Turning Points in the Amish School Controversy

East Lampeter consolidation dispute	March 1937–May 1938
Bishops protest pending legislation	March 1937
School Committee[a] organizes	September 1937
School Committee protests legislation	1937–1941
Two Amish schools open	November 1938
Coexistence during war years	1942–1948
Enforcement and imprisonment	1949–1955
Bishops' eighteen-point statement	1950
Vocational school compromise	1955
Amish schools increase	1955–1975
U.S. Supreme Court decision	1972

[a] Sometimes called the School Delegation, this group evolved into the Old Order Book Society in 1957 and currently coordinates Amish schools.

six-year struggle ended when the Amish opened their first vocational school in January 1956 in an Amish home.[21]

Under the vocational program, an Amish teacher held classes three hours per week for a dozen or so fourteen-year-olds in an Amish home. The youth recorded their work activities and studied English, math, spelling, and vocational subjects. Attendance records were submitted to the state. But in essence the children were under the guidance of their parents for most of the week, an astonishing victory for the Amish.[22] It was a victory that Lancaster County School Superintendent Arthur Mylin called "ridiculous." Nevertheless, the vocational school arrangement continues today.

The inauguration of the vocational program silenced debate on high school attendance, but it camouflaged a more serious issue stalking the Amish—the consolidation of public elementary schools. Elementary consolidation was gaining momentum by the mid-1950s. The Amish refused to send their children to the consolidated schools or, in some townships, to new junior high schools.[23] They had always resisted busing children to faraway classrooms with strange teachers and children, but it was the use of television in public elementary schools that incensed them, according to one Amishman. Beleaguered by political fights and imprisonment, the Amish decided to withdraw from the bargaining table once and for all and build their own schools. Thus, over the years, the Amish of Lancaster County have built and operated some 160 one-room elementary schools.

THE FEAR OF EDUCATION

Back to our riddle: Why did the Amish, in the words of preacher Jacob Zook, make such a "big stink" about education? Why were these gentle people willing to be arrested, fined, and imprisoned? What provoked them to hire attorneys, lobby legislators, solicit signatures, and circulate petitions? A scrutiny of the statements they wrote during the struggle reveals their objections to modern education. In short, they did not want to lose control of education, to have it pulled out of their rural cultural context. For religious endorsement, they appealed to the Bible, the teachings of Christ, the examples of the apostles, the witness of Anabaptist martyrs, their Amish forebears, tradition, and conscience as well as religious liberty granted by the Constitution.

Numerous themes echoed throughout their litany of protest:[24]

(1) *Location.* The Amish wanted a local school, preferably one within walking distance. They did not want their children bused away.

(2) *Size.* They objected to large consolidated schools where pupils were sorted into separate rooms and assigned different teachers each year. The Amish repeatedly pled for the one-room school, which had served them so well in the past.

(3) *Control.* They believed that schools should be under the local community's control. According to their interpretation of the Bible, parents were responsible for nurturing and training their children.

(4) *Length.* While they supported local one-room elementary education, the Amish felt that children belonged at home after the elementary grades. Parents also campaigned for a shorter (eight-month) school year so that children could help with spring planting.

(5) *Teachers.* They wanted teachers who were trustworthy and also sympathetic to Amish values and rural ways. The Amish refused, in their words, to just "hand their children over" to professional educators.

(6) *Curriculum.* They argued that high schools lauded "worldly wisdom," a phrase they borrowed from the *Martyrs Mirror.* Worldly wisdom clashed with "wisdom from above." A favorite scripture stated clearly that the wisdom of man was foolishness in the eyes of God (1 Cor. 1:18–28). Fur-

thermore, knowledge "puffeth up" and makes one proud (1 Cor. 8:1). Citing still another scripture, the Amish insisted that worldly philosophy would spoil their children (Col. 2:8). Evolution, science, and sex education in the public school curriculum symbolized the vanity of worldly wisdom.

(7) *Mode.* Although they use textbooks in their own schools today, the Amish have always stressed the limits of "book learning." They repeatedly argued for practical training guided by example and experience. They stressed learning manual skills, for they believed that they should earn their bread by the sweat of their brow. Book learning, they feared, would lead their youth away from manual work. They wanted an Amish equivalent of internships and apprenticeships supervised by parents.

(8) *Peers.* Too much association with worldly friends, they feared, would corrupt their youth and lead to marriage and other forms of "unequal yoking" with outsiders.

(9) *Consequences.* The paramount fear lurking beneath all the concerns was that modern education would lead Amish youth away from farm and faith and would undermine the church. The wisdom of the world, said Amish sages, "makes you restless, wanting to leap and jump and not knowing where you will land." In the final analysis, they knew that modern education would deplete their cultural and social capital and, in the long run, ruin the church.

Religious reasons undergirded Amish objections to consolidated modern education. But could not these spiritual explanations be brushed aside for economic ones? Were not children essential to the maintenance of a labor-intensive farm economy? Both religious and economic factors partially explain the stubborn Amish resistance to modern education; however, a deeper reading of the bargaining sessions provides some additional clues to why these gentle people resorted to political action in order to preserve humility.

SOLVING THE RIDDLE

An Amish leader provided hints to the deeper reason for rejecting progressive education when he described Amish opposition to high school: "With us, our religion is *inseparable* with a day's work, a night's rest, a meal, or any other practice; therefore, our education can much less be *separated* from our religious practices."[25] An Amish farmer said: "They tell me that in college you have to *pull everything apart,* analyze it and try to build it up from a scientific standpoint. That runs counter to what we've been taught on mother's knee" (emphasis added). Although few articulated it as eloquently as these people, the Amish realized that the consolidated high school, designed to homogenize different cultures, would also destroy them. Indeed, a major purpose of public education is to integrate diverse students into a common national culture.

The engineering logic of specialization and efficiency—so successful in producing radios and Model T Fords on the assembly line—was being applied to education, resulting in large educational factories for hundreds of students. Having rejected the Model T, the Amish also feared the new model of education. They intuitively grasped that modern schools would immerse their youth in mainstream culture. Such an education, outside an Amish context, would divorce Amish youth from their ethnic past. Despite their eighth-grade education, Amish parents realized that progressive education would fracture their traditional culture. Today dozens of one-room Amish schools, woven into Amish culture, stand as the antithesis of modern, specialized education.

An embodiment of modernity, the consolidated school was a Great Separator. High school education would separate children from their parents, their traditions, and their values. Education would become decontextualized—separated from the daily setting of Amish life. The Amish world, tied together by religious threads of meaning, would be divided into component parts: academic disciplines, courses, classes, grades, and multiple teachers. Even religion would be studied, analyzed, and eventually separated from family, history, and daily life. It would become just another subject for critical analysis. Professional specialists—educated in worldly universities and separated from the Amish in time, culture, and training—would be entrusted with nurturing their precious children. Such experts would encourage Amish youth to maximize their potential by pursuing more education to "liberate" themselves from the shackles of parochialism. By stirring aspirations and raising occupational hopes, the experts would steer Amish youth away from farm and family or would certainly encourage restlessness if they did decide to stay at home.

Passing from teacher to teacher and from subject to subject in an educational assembly line, Amish students would encounter bewildering ideas that would challenge their folk wisdom. The same teacher would not trace a child's performance in several subjects or have the delight of seeing a student mature over several years. Moreover, Amish parents would be severed from the curriculum, policies, and authorities that would indoctrinate their youth. Abstract textbooks, written by distant specialists, would encourage intellectual pursuits that surely would turn manual labor into drudgery. Most importantly, public schools would plunge Amish youth into social settings teeming with non-Amish. High school friendships with outsiders would make it easier to leave the church in later years. Finally, high school would separate Amish children from humility. In an environment that champions individuality, they would become self-confident, arrogant, and proud. Academic competition would foster individual achievement and independence, which in turn would diminish Gelassenheit and sever dependency on the ethnic community.

In sum, the high school, a merchant of modernity, would sell young Amish a new set of values that would pull them from their past. The intellectual climate—rational thought, critical thinking, scientific methods, symbolic abstractions—would breed impatience with the slow pace of Amish life and erode the authority of Amish tradition. Amish youth would learn to scrutinize their culture with an analytic coolness that would threaten the bishops' power. In all of these ways, high schools would cultivate a friendship with modernity and encourage youth to leave their birthright church. The Amish did not define the threat in such rational ways, but they understood its menace.

The goals of Amish education differ drastically from the agenda of contemporary education. Amish schools are designed to prepare Amish youth for successful careers in Amish life, not in mainstream society. By all accounts, Amish schools meet their objectives well. Amish schools create cultural and social capital by controlling the flow of ideas and social interaction. The schools build upon ethnic ties and stifle relationships with outsiders— all of which increases dependence on the church. The boycott of high school obstructs the path leading to marriage with outsiders, preparation for professional careers, and participation in civic life.

Abstract and analytical modes of thought are simply not encouraged in Amish schools. The teachers propagate ideas and values that undergird the ethnic social system. Overlapping networks of like-minded others within the small school insulate the child from rival explanations of reality and help to

School children practice for a parents' day program. Colorful chalk artwork is on the blackboard. The teacher is on the far right, her assistant is on the left.

keep Amish ideology intact. The schools are an important link in the process of socialization that reproduces the values and structures of Amish society.

To Moderns, this is indeed a provincial education that restricts consciousness—and so it is. But in a society where an expanded consciousness is not the highest virtue, Amish schools have ably passed on the traditions of faith to new generations. Indeed, they are one of the prime reasons for the growth and vitality of Amish life. These islands of provincialism may not stretch Amish consciousness, but they do provide secure and safe settings for the emotional and social development of children. And that is the solution to our riddle. In order to protect the meek ways of Gelassenheit, these normally gentle people had to bargain aggressively with imperialistic forces that sought to enlighten them with a worldly education, an education that in time might have destroyed them.

AMISH SCHOOLS TODAY

Today, with few exceptions, children in the Lancaster settlement attend one-room private schools staffed by Amish teachers.[26] In some cases, the

Amish bought one-room schoolhouses when the public townships discarded them. Most recently, they have built their own schools. However, the twenty-year transition to Amish schools (1955–75) provoked some internal debate. Some Amish parents wanted to send their children to public elementary schools to give them more opportunities to interact with outsiders. However, the interest of such parents in public education quickly waned upon the arrival of sex education, television, and the teaching of evolution. These developments prodded the rapid growth of Amish schools. In 1950 there were only three Amish schools, but by 1975 there were sixty-two.

Today more than 4,700 Amish pupils attend nearly 160 private schools in the Lancaster settlement, as shown in Figure 7.1.[27] On average, thirty-one students attend the one-room schools, which are typically built on the edge of an Amish farm. Throughout eight grades they learn spelling, English, German, mathematics, geography, and history. Although taught by Amish teachers, classes are conducted in English. Practical skills, applicable to everyday Amish life, are emphasized rather than abstract and analytic ones. Science is excluded from the curriculum.

The values of obedience, tradition, and humility eclipse rationality, competition, and diversity. Whereas modern high school students write analytical essays, conduct scientific experiments, and learn to think critically, Amish youth prepare for apprenticeships in farming, crafts, business, and manual trades—where experience counts more than a degree. Devotional exercises—Scripture reading, singing, and repeating the Lord's Prayer—are held each morning, but religion is not taught. To teach religion as an academic subject would objectify it and open the door for critical analysis. The Amish believe that formal religious training belongs in the domain of the family and church. They hope that religion permeates the school "all day long in our curriculum and in the playgrounds." This goal is accomplished "by not cheating in arithmetic, by teaching cleanliness and thrift in health, by saying what we mean in English, by learning to make an honest living from the soil in geography, and by teaching honesty, respect, sincerity, humbleness, and the golden rule on the playground."[28]

A one-room Amish school is a beehive of orderly activity as a teacher moves around the room teaching about thirty pupils in eight grades. Fresh cut flowers sit on the teacher's desk, colorful chalk art decorates a side of the blackboard, smiley stickers adorn pages of completed homework, seventeen

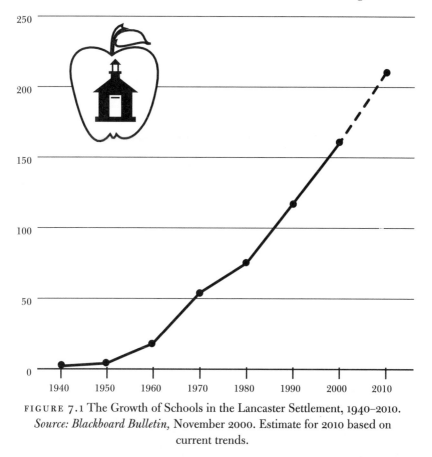

FIGURE 7.1 The Growth of Schools in the Lancaster Settlement, 1940–2010.
Source: Blackboard Bulletin, November 2000. Estimate for 2010 based on
current trends.

straw hats hang in a row on the back wall, and a paddle stands near the
teacher's desk. Some teachers work with two grades at a time. While some
students come forward to work on the blackboard or recite answers, others
quietly do their lessons or help each other. Hands are frequently in the air,
asking permission to sharpen pencils, clarify an assignment, or go to the
outhouse. Order prevails amidst the hum of activity, and students receive a
great deal of personal attention from the teacher as well as help from peers.
At recess a mother brings Popsicles to celebrate her daughter's birthday. A
middle-aged professional photographer seeing this sight for the first time was
moved to tears as he muttered quietly, "This is the way it should be compared to our modern commotion."

Amish schools lack the educational trappings taken for granted in public
schools—sports programs, dances, physical education, cafeterias, field trips,

clubs, bands, choruses, computers, guidance counselors, and principals. Even new Amish schools are copycat buildings—all constructed alike from an 1877 blueprint for a cost of about $35,000, which includes books and other supplies. Battery-operated clocks, gas lanterns, coal stoves, hand-pumped water, and outdoor toilets are the typical accessories in an Amish school. Many of the textbooks are produced by Amish publishers.[29] Recess breaks in the morning and afternoon provide "time-out" for recreation. Spelling bees and recitation by class groups are common. Children usually carry their lunches in colorful plastic lunch boxes. Since 1975 the Amish have also operated several "special schools" for students with various physical and learning disabilities.[30]

Amish parents control their schools. They elect a three- to five-member school board that oversees the school's operation. In some cases a board may administer up to three schools. The school board hires and fires teachers, maintains the building, and advises on curriculum. Other parents are involved with the school through visits, work "frolics," and special programs. The Amish support their own schools through two taxes collected by the treasurer of the board. Members pay a head tax to support the schools, and in addition, parents pay a fee for each pupil. On the average it costs about $400 per year to educate an Amish child, about one-twentieth of the $8,000 it costs to educate one in a local public school. Nevertheless, the Amish in Lancaster County also pay millions of dollars each year in real estate taxes to support public education. In contrast to some public schools, where parents are kept at arm's length by professional educators, Amish schools give parents free access to the curriculum, instruction, and administration. In all ways, the schools are locally owned and operated.

The teachers are typically single Amish women who were educated through the eighth grade in Amish schools. Teachers typically earn $40 to $50 per day, or about $8,000 per year. This is about one-sixth of the pay of their public school counterparts, not to mention their lack of benefits. They are not state certified but are selected on the basis of their natural interest in teaching, their academic ability, and their endorsement of esteemed Amish values— faith, sincerity, and willingness to learn from other teachers.[31] Whereas modern school administrators recruit teachers on the basis of degrees, certification, and professional skills, the Amish believe the foremost qualification is "good Christian character."[32] Ironically, these nonprofessional Amish teach-

Students enjoy the delights of community over lunch.

ers—free of the typical restrictions imposed by principals, professional organizations, and bureaucratic classroom policies—have great latitude to shape curriculum and policies according to their best judgment.

The Old Order Book Society provides guidelines for curriculum and administration to encourage uniformity across the schools.[33] Amish teachers must support church values, but in contrast to professional teachers, they have an astonishing amount of freedom to shape their instructional setting. Typically, teachers are on probation for the first three years until they have proven themselves.[34] Each year several countywide teachers' meetings provide opportunities to receive teaching tips from experienced teachers. In addition, an Amish teachers' magazine, the *Blackboard Bulletin,* is a helpful source of ideas and encouragement for teachers. In Amish schools, cultural integrity triumphs over specialized expertise.

What are the outcomes of Amish schools? Research evidence from other settlements suggests that, on the average, Amish students perform as well as other rural non-Amish students in basic quantitative skills, spelling, and word usage.[35] While Moderns ask whether Amish schools compare favorably with public ones, the more important question is how well an education prepares pupils for adulthood in their society. On that issue, Amish schools fare as well as if not better than many public schools. The vitality of Amish culture certifies the ability of its schools to prepare its pupils for a successful life in Amish society.

THE MELLOW YEARS

The social continuity in an Amish school is astonishing. In some instances, all the children in one family will have the same teacher for all eight grades. And unlike modern children, who may have as many as fifty different teachers by the time they graduate from high school, many Amish children have had only *one* teacher. Parents relate to one teacher, who over the years develops a keen understanding of the family's idiosyncracies. A teacher may relate to as few as ten families in a school year because several children come from the same family. Older children tutor younger ones. On the playground, like-minded Amish play together with cousins and neighbors, insulated from the contamination of outside culture. In the Amish school, sacred and secular, moral and academic, spiritual and intellectual, public and private spheres are not mixed together; they have never been separated.

Although some may occasionally take high school correspondence courses, Amish children rarely attend high school. Even Amish teachers are urged to prepare for teaching through self-education rather than correspondence courses. Young shop workers occasionally take short courses in specialized mechanics, but few Amish youth aspire to go to high school. Describing high school, a minister said: "There's no longing for it, no call for it. It's rarely mentioned. I don't know of anybody who would want to go." For the occasional youth who does attend high school or college, separation from the church is painful if the youth is a member.

A professional social worker, excommunicated by the Amish church prior to her senior year in college, described trying to dissuade her bishop from excommunicating her: "He was a just and deeply caring person. I met him out in the field. I asked questions about education and sin and tried my best to make him understand that I wanted to continue both my education and my membership in the Amish community. He would not say that further education was a sin and he agonized in his efforts to explain why excommunication was necessary if I would not repent. Both of us were sensitive and hurt deeply; we cried unashamedly."[36]

The relationship between the Amish and public education officials mellowed after the Amish received the blessing of the U.S. Supreme Court in 1972. Some legislators share pending regulations with Amish leaders for reaction and counsel. In some cases, informal agreements spell out mutual expectations. Amish schools, for instance, are typically heated by coal stoves in the classroom because they rarely have basements. Building basements for the sole purpose of housing furnaces would have been quite costly. However, state fire regulations prohibit furnaces in open classrooms. After several discussions, state officials agreed to overlook the furnace requirements. In addition to heating systems, a variety of other issues have been quietly solved behind the scenes with state officials over the years in favor of the Amish— water testing, teacher certification, attendance reports, immunization, Worker's Compensation, and unemployment benefits among others.[37]

In the mid-1980s new regulations called for schools to be state certified. This was a rather perfunctory process for the Amish. According to an Amish spokesman, state officials agreed to honor past informal agreements and not impose new regulations if the Amish, in turn, would agree not to obstruct the pending legislation. Free to set their own standards, the Amish designed and printed their own certification forms. A few descriptive facts on each school are reported on the certification form, which is sent to the state each year. Schools are required to be open 180 days a year. "For many things," an Amish spokesman said, "it is better if we don't even ask state officials because it just puts them on the spot." The bitter struggles of early years have been replaced with benign neglect and mutual respect.

All things considered, the Amish have held the upper hand in the thirty-six-year dispute that finally ended with the U.S. Supreme Court decision in 1972. Following that decisive judgment, the Old Order Amish Steering Committee "fully accepted and approved" the Supreme Court's ruling, leaving no doubt about the hierarchy of judicial authority in Amish minds.[38] The only issue they had to concede was a longer (180-day) school year. Even so, with fewer holidays and shorter vacations, Amish schools are able to end early to honor spring planting. Thus, on all the key issues—location, size, control, compulsory age, and curriculum—Amish convictions held sway.

SOWING AND REAPING WILD OATS

In March 1989, President George Bush and drug czar William Bennett visited Lancaster County to promote a national campaign against illegal drugs. After making a speech at a local high school, the president's entourage met with Amish and Old Order Mennonite leaders in an Old Order school.[39] Meeting with Old Order leaders in a simple classroom without television cameras, the president said, "We came here to salute you" because the national drug problem is "hopefully nonexistent" in communities like yours.[40] He was wrong.

According to one Amishman, a few Amish youth had begun dabbling with drugs in the 1970s. The problem hit the national press in the summer of 1998 when two Amish boys were arrested for dealing cocaine with the Pagans motorcycle gang. The sensational story prompted a feeding frenzy by the national media as news of the story spread.[41] Television, newspapers, and news magazines from around the world covered the story, almost with glee, at the discovery of sin among the Amish. Parents and elders were embarrassed by the stigma and the media attention. Some of them were quick to note that although the two lads had been raised Amish, they were not members of the church and thus were "really not Amish." The two men were eventually sentenced to twelve months in prison with immediate work release privileges, a sentence that some Amish considered far too lenient.

The whole event was a sobering wake-up call for the church and for many Amish teens as well. Indeed, the crop of baptismal candidates hit an all-time high in the fall of 1998, when more than four hundred entered the church. Concerned parents, in cooperation with the FBI, helped to arrange a series of informal meetings in the Amish community to tell Amish parents and teens about the dangers of drugs. The sad episode reminded church leaders that the evils of the world were not always found in faraway places but were sometimes lurking behind their own barns.

The arrested youth and their drug-using friends are a small minority within the Amish community, but they pose a perplexing riddle. Why do the Amish, who fought so hard for the right to teach their children, permit rebellious teens to flirt with the world? And why do some youth, educated in the ways of obedience, turn to mischief just a few years later? Rowdy youth are an embarrassment to church leaders and a stigma in the larger commu-

An unbaptized Amish youth dressed in contemporary clothing adjusts the
sunroof on his car.

nity. The rebellious antics, often called "sowing wild oats," have become a
rite of passage for some youth during *rumspringa,* the "running around"
years that begin at age sixteen. In some cases, the mischief is carefully hidden
from parents; but in other instances, church rules are openly mocked. Sometimes Amish parents, themselves constrained by the rules of the church, may
vicariously participate in their offspring's misconduct. Although all Amish
youth join a gang and "run around" before marriage, the majority of them
enjoy their freedom in fairly traditional and quiet ways.[42]

Rumspringa is an awkward moment in Amish life—a liminal stage when
youth are neither in the church nor out of it. They are truly betwixt and
between; no longer under the control of their parents, yet still free from the
church. Although socialized in an Amish environment, they have not taken
their baptismal vow. Amish leaders, chagrined by the worldly behavior of
some teens, point out that they are helpless to control the problem because
the youth are unbaptized. They attribute this slippage in the social system to
poor parental guidance and lax enforcement.

To both insider and outsider, the rowdiness appears, at first glance, as a
tatter on the quilt of Amish culture. There is, however, a compelling socio-

logical explanation for this persistent tradition. Most of the rowdy youth eventually settle down to become humble Amish adults. There are exceptions, but for the most part the youth that flirt with the world eventually return to the church. Flirting with the world serves as a form of social immunization. Teenage mischief provides a minimal dosage of worldliness that strengthens resistance in adulthood. Indeed, this apparent quirk in Amish culture has a redeeming function in the social system that may partially explain its persistence.

A fling with worldliness gives Amish youth the impression that they have a choice regarding church membership. The open space before baptism underscores the perception that they are free to leave the Amish if they choose. The evidence, however, suggests that the perceived choice is partially an illusion. Amish youth have been thoroughly immersed in a total ethnic world with its own language, symbols, and worldview. Moreover, all of their significant friendships are within the Amish community. To leave the Amish fold would mean severing cherished friendships and family ties, although if unbaptized, they would not be shunned. Rejecting their birthright culture would thrust them into an entirely different world—a foreign world and a foreign culture. Even on escapades to faraway cities, Amish youth travel together. These portable peer groups insulate even the would-be rebels from the terror of a solitary encounter with the larger world.

In many ways, Amish youth do not have a real choice because their upbringing and all the social forces around them funnel them toward church membership. This is likely why more than 90 percent of them do, in fact, embrace Amish ways. A few youth do not join the church, and they appear to fare quite well as they move into mainstream society. But for the majority who do join, the illusion of a choice serves a critical function in adult life. Thinking they had a choice, adults are more likely to comply with the demands of the Ordnung later in life. Members might reason this way: After all, because I chose to be baptized and vowed on my knees to support the church with the full knowledge of its requirements, I should now be willing as an adult to obey the demands of the Ordnung.

Without the perception of choice—the opportunity to sow wild oats— adult members might be less willing to comply with church rules, and in the long run this would weaken the community's ability to exercise social control. Many rowdy youth are "reaped" later by the church in the form of obedient adults who willingly comply with the Ordnung because they believe they had a choice. Thus, the wild oats tradition yields a rich harvest for the church—a cornerstone in the group's ability to develop compliant adults. And that may be the reason that parents who were willing to suffer imprisonment for the sake of their youths' education are also willing to let them flirt with the world.

CHAPTER

8

The Riddles of Technology

We've had trouble with phones for twenty-five years.
—Amish deacon

THE BREACH OF 1910

Some stereotypes of Amish life imply that they reject technology and live in a nineteenth-century cocoon. Such images are false. The Amish adopt technology selectively, hoping that the tools they use will build community rather than harm it. In short, they prefer technology that preserves social capital, rather than depletes it.

The positive marks of Amish identity—horse, buggy, dress—have their negative counterparts in cars, computers, and televisions. Wary of the impact of certain forms of technology, the Amish have categorically rejected things like televisions and video cameras. In other cases, they have made a distinction between ownership and use. For example, they have been willing to negotiate selective *use* of telephones, electricity, cars, and other types of technology. The bargaining sessions, stretching over the decades, have produced what appear today as perplexing riddles. This chapter and the following one explore some of these puzzles. Solving them requires a brief historical excursion into the breach of 1910—a turning point in the Amish saga that sets the stage for many of the riddles.

The roots of the 1910 schism go back to the early 1890s. An Amish minister, Moses Hartz Sr., had a son by the same name who became a traveling agent for a milling company. Finding Amish ways too restrictive, the son stopped attending services and, among other things, began wearing pockets on the outside of his coat—a convenience forbidden by the Amish. In April

1895, without the unanimous consent of his congregation, the presiding Amish bishop excommunicated Moses Jr. and placed him under the ban. As an Amish minister, Moses Sr. was expected to uphold church rules. Caught between church and family, he balked and refused to shun his son. After futile efforts by the church to change the father's mind, he was "silenced" as a minister and, along with his wife, was placed under the ban.[1]

Eventually the Hartzes were received into a progressive Amish-Mennonite congregation, following a "kneeling" confession. Upon hearing of their confession, Amish leaders called a special meeting and decided to lift the ban. However, a minister who had missed the special meeting was perturbed by the decision. He promptly contacted other Amish leaders and persuaded them to renew the ban. The Amish leaders eventually reversed their decision, and the Hartzes were once again shunned. They remained in social exile for the rest of their lives.[2] This action in the late 1890s marked the enforcement of "strict shunning" on members who left the Amish to join similar but more progressive Anabaptist churches. The episode triggered intense debate on the practice of shunning, a discussion that smoldered for twenty-five years, until the bishops reaffirmed the practice in a special statement in 1921.[3]

The Hartz incident, however, is only a prelude to the real story. The controversy was still brewing in 1909 when electricity and telephones were making their debut. Some disenchanted families had already been dabbling with progressive changes, but the strict enforcement of shunning galvanized their dissent. In the fall of 1909, about thirty-five families, disturbed by the Hartz incident, began holding separate services every three or four weeks for singing and Bible reading. The group petitioned the bishops for a more lenient use of the ban and announced their intention to withdraw if the request was not granted.[4] Meeting on 12 October 1909, the Amish bishops denied their request. The splinter group, composed of some eighty-five people, represented about one-fifth of the membership in the settlement at the time. The new group held its first worship service in February 1910 and ordained two ministers in April 1911.[5]

The progressive faction was eventually dubbed the Peachey church, for it was assisted by two ministers named Peachey from an Amish congregation in central Pennsylvania.[6] In contrast to the mild separation of 1877, the breach of 1910 stirred strong emotional feelings. Even some seventy-five years later, an Amish minister dismissed the dissenting group as "just a bunch of hotheads." Although it followed some Amish practices, the Peachey church adopted new technology more readily than the Old Order Amish. Soon the renegades began using telephones, tractors, and electric lights. They permitted cars by 1928, and by 1930 they were worshiping in a church. In 1950 the Peachey church became affiliated with a larger national body, the Beachy Amish Church. Today six congregations are affiliated with the Beachy Amish Church in Lancaster County.[7] They conduct their worship services in English, hold Sunday school, drive cars, and use electricity. The men wear an abbreviated beard, and members dress in Plain garb, although not as Plain as that of the Old Order Amish.

An intriguing aspect of this historical milestone is the contrasting interpretations used by the two factions to explain the schism. Most printed interpretations were written by those on the progressive side, Beachy Amish or Mennonites. These accounts attribute the 1910 split to the strict shunning of the Hartzes.[8] An Old Order Amish document verifies that shunning was central in the dispute.[9] However, as often happens in oral history, various explanations evolve over time. It is striking that Amish leaders, even seventy-five years later, insisted that telephones and the use of electricity were key issues, or "handles," in the 1910 cleavage. While acknowledging that shunning was an issue, the Old Order Amish contend that technological changes were the key irritants. Other members suggest that although the telephone may not have been the catalytic factor, the Peachey church began to use telephones at about the same time that the Old Order Amish forbade them. Regardless of the historical facts, the important thing is that the Amish still perceive the telephone as a symbol of the breach of 1910. The division cast a long shadow on the phone and shaped the Amish view of it for many decades.[10]

THE TELEPHONE RIDDLE

The use of telephones has been a contentious issue among the Amish for many years.[11] To this day, phones are forbidden in their homes. Why would the telephone—that indispensable modern mouthpiece—be stigmatized as worldly? Why would God frown on a phone?

Invented in 1876, the telephone gradually entered American homes after the turn of the century. But even as late as 1940, only half of Pennsylvania farmers had one.[12] Rejecting it early in the century, the Amish have gradually, in the words of one member, "allowed it to creep in and now everybody uses them—well, at least 99 percent!" The phone saga provides a fascinating example of the Amish ordeal with modernity.

Surprisingly, a number of Amish purchased phones as they appeared in rural areas in the first decade of the century. Some early phones were home-made concoctions of lines strung between neighboring homes. An Amish historian estimates that "around 1908 the bishops decided that the phone should be put away and those involved in it just dropped it and tore the lines out."[13]

Amish leaders are not entirely sure why the bishops banned the phone, except that they made gossip too easy, were too handy, and were too worldly. Apart from the tag "worldly," no religious injunctions are cited against the phone. However, its *use* was never banned. The Amish have readily used a neighbor's phone for emergencies and have borrowed phones in nearby garages or shops for many years. The taboo against installing phones in houses, however, has held firm since the Ordnung forbade it around 1910.

A complicating factor in the phone decision was the formation of the Peachey church. An Amish minister explained: "A group of people got a bit rebellious and they started to get telephones and this dragged along until 1909." An Amishman who was thirteen at the time said: "The phone was one of the issues [in the division]."[14] Whether phones helped to provoke the division or whether the dissidents installed them soon after they left the Old Order is unclear. What is certain is that the bishops rejected phones about the time that the progressive Peachey church left the Amish fold. And, among other things, some Peachey church members installed phones, which was reason enough for the Amish to permanently outlaw them. When asked about the prohibition, an Amish leader said: "It's something that's left over from 1909." Regardless of the sequence of events, the liberals had adopted the phone, and thus the Old Orders could not accept it again without a severe loss of face. Permitting phones would be a de facto endorsement of the insurgents. In essence, the Peachey church functioned as a negative reference group—a model of worldliness that the Amish hoped to avoid.

To explain the phone taboo solely as an intergroup face-saving ploy overlooks its deeper social meanings, however. The phone is a tool of modernity in both symbolic and substantive ways. It threatened to tie the Amish to the outside world and to erode social capital within. In the words of one analyst: "The telephone was a major means of alleviating the isolation of country life."[15] Lacking automobiles, good roads, electricity, radios, mass media, and regular postal service, many rural areas were insulated from urban influences. The telephone line was the first visible link to the larger industrial world—a real and symbolic tie that mocked the Amish belief in separation from the world. Phones literally tied a house to the outside world and permitted strangers to enter a home at the sound of a ring. Moreover, the telephone was the first form of communication technology available to the Amish—an entirely different order of technology from plows, planters, and other types of productive tools. Thus, in the context of an isolated, rural people, bombarded with new inventions, it was not a thoughtless reflex to dub the phone a "worldly object."

In a mobile cellular society, the phone connects people continents away, but for the Amish, bonded through face-to-face interaction, the phone posed a threat to internal communication. A phone decontextualizes conversation. It extracts talk from a specific social context where both speakers can observe symbolic codes. Friends can discuss intimate matters on the phone, but such conversations lack the rich nuances of body language, facial expression, and eye contact. In contrast to the spontaneity of face-to-face conversation, phone talk is more formal, abstract, distant, and mechanical. Phone talk conveys disembodied "half messages," stripped of the symbolic codes of dress and gesture so critical to Amish communication. Young children find telephone conversations baffling because they require greater abstraction than face-to-face chatter. One can only imagine the other speaker's location, appearance, and context. And one is never sure if the other person is mocking, winking, or, worse yet, doing things to relieve boredom, while giving the impression of listening. In all ways, phone conversations are "half messages" devoid of body language and contextual symbols.

Phone talk is segmented, rational, and impersonal—an idiom of the mechanical language of modernity in form, tone, and structure. Amish who are unfamiliar with phones speak with awkward pauses and uncertain sentences when they call a nurse or physician.[16] Phone conversations reflect distant, secondary relationships in several ways. The old adage "It's easier to say 'no' on the phone than in person" reflects the greater social distance and lower accountability of phone conversations.

In Amish society, face-to-face talk and spontaneous visiting are the chief forms of social interaction. They generate social capital. The Amish share death, birth, and wedding announcements as well as everyday news through personal visits. Telephoning reduces visiting. If one can phone, why visit? Although quicker and handier, the phone threatened to erode the core of Amish culture: face-to-face conversations. Thus, the restrictions on phones help to preserve separation from the outside world as well as social capital within.

THE TELEPHONE SHANTY

The ban on phones created problems in times of emergency. In the mid-1930s, several families approached church leaders and requested permission to share a phone. According to oral tradition, they argued that "in case of a fire or something, or an emergency, if someone needs a doctor, there's no telephone nearby." They pleaded with the ministers to have a "community phone." "It was tolerated," said an Amish leader, "and that was the beginning of the community phone."

After 1940, community phones gradually appeared. Telephone shanties—which often resemble outhouses in size and appearance—are typically found at the end of lanes or beside barns and sheds. Several families share the phone and its expenses. With an unlisted number, the phone is primarily used for outgoing calls to make appointments and conduct farm business. Loud call bells that amplify the ring are prohibited in some districts to restrict incoming calls. Community phones in public shanties were widely accepted by 1980. But the growing use of phones was not easy. "We had a good bit of trouble with these telephones," said a bishop. Other members worried that the phone would split the church.

In the mind of one Amish grandmother, telephones were still "on probation" in 1986. Nevertheless, many Amish were calling one another. Friends or business associates scheduled routine times when they were "handy" to receive calls, and "appointments" were often made in advance. The principle of separation from the world was expressed by using unlisted numbers.

The Amish give various reasons for permitting community phones: (1) the lack of nearby non-Amish neighbors in densely populated Amish areas, (2) the embarrassment of farmers dragging barn dirt and smells into non-Amish homes, (3) the need to make appointments with doctors, (4) the need

A businessman places a call in the phone shanty adjacent to his shop.

of farmers to call veterinarians and feed dealers,[17] (5) the need of businessmen to order supplies, and (6) the need to contact family members living in
other settlements or on the outer edge of the Lancaster community.

Over the years convenience, economic necessity, and a sprawling settlement have created ingenious arrangements that brought phones within easy
reach. Although still forbidden in homes, telephones are widely used today.
Church districts vary on the placement of phones in shops and barns. Dis-

tricts in the conservative southern end have a stricter policy on phones. But in the heart of the settlement, with shops galore, telephones abound. Many farmers have a private phone in the barn, tobacco shed, or chicken house, usually tucked away from public view. Lacking a radio, some farmers routinely call the national weather service for forecasts every morning.

The strongest pressure for phones comes from business owners. Some bishops permit phones inside shops, but many require adjacent telephone shanties. Sometimes the caller can literally reach through a window to use the phone. By the turn of the twenty-first century, many entrepreneurs were printing phone numbers on their business cards and brochures, an unheard of practice only a few years earlier. A successful businessman who uses a state-of-the-art electronic cash register explained why he does not have a telephone: "The bishop said that he'd really rather that I didn't have one if it's just for the sake of convenience, unless I have to. So I use a neighbor's answering service since [a phone] isn't really necessary and since the bishop is on top of the list of the people that I respect."

A growing number of families have private phones outside their homes. An Amish family living in a double house rents a phone from their "English" neighbors on the other side. Many people have a phone in a shanty adjacent to their home, shop, or barn. Two single sisters living in a small village installed one in their small horse barn. One person said her uncle has a hidden one in his home, and "his father would turn in his grave if he saw it." Although the phone remains outside the home, many families now have one on their property. Indeed, in the words of one Amishman, "Community phones are history."

By the turn of the twenty-first century, heated discussions focused on the use of answering machines, voice mail, fax machines, and cell phones as well as the installation of phones in offices. Although church elders frowned on answering machines because these required electricity, they were lenient with voice mail provided by the phone company. The church discourages cell phones, but many contractors use them to coordinate mobile work crews on several jobs. In fact, one person said, "Cell phones are springing up everywhere." The church has steadfastly maintained its taboo on phones in private homes, but that line is difficult to enforce with the portability of cell phones, which makes them especially troublesome.

THE TELEPHONE BARGAIN

Apart from the historic forces that shaped the interdiction against phones, present-day explanations for banning them from homes hinge on two issues: separation and community integration. The Amish believe that a home phone separates but that a community phone integrates. When asked why the Amish are afraid of the phone, one member said: "If you have a phone in the house and you have growing children, as they get older, why then you're going to have one child who wants one up in her bedroom and the other one who wants an extension in her bedroom and it just goes on and on and it *separates* the whole family" (emphasis added). A grandfather explained: "If you have a place of business and need a phone, it must be *separate* from the building, and if it's on the farm it must be *separate* from the house. It should be *shared* with the public so that others can use it. It's just not allowed in the house, where would it stop? We stress keeping things small and keeping the family *together*" (emphasis added).

Some men contend that with phones in homes women would "waste a lot of time in endless chatter." A businessman described the practice as a buffer against interruptions: "If we had a telephone up there in the shop, I would just be bothered all the time. I just don't want any up there. It needs to be separate from the building." Said one mother, "A phone in the house would just be a nuisance."

The Amish do not consider the phone a moral evil that will lead to eternal damnation. Their question is "If we 'give in' on the phone, what will be next?" They have a good grasp of the social consequences of the phone for family life—gossip, individuation (multiple phones), and continual interruptions. A ringing phone would spoil the natural flow of family rhythms. The Amish worry that phones would pull families apart by encouraging attendance at meetings, scheduling appointments, and spending less time together. Phones not only permit unwanted visitors to intrude into the privacy of a home at any moment, but they also impose a technological structure on the natural flow of face-to-face interaction.

The phone deal that the Amish negotiated is an ingenious arrangement. They have agreed to exclude it from homes, while allowing limited use for commercial purposes. The bargain incorporates key understandings in the fine print: (1) It upholds the historic taboo and thus keeps faith with tradition. They can say, "As always, we don't approve of home phones." (2) It saves face with the splinter group of 1910 by demonstrating that the Amish have not drifted into the worldliness of the liberal churches. (3) It preserves the natural rhythms of face-to-face interaction in home and family. (4) It encourages cooperation through the use of community phones. (5) It permits the development of small industries that are critical for the economic viability of the Amish community. (6) It symbolizes key Amish values—separation from the world, establishing limits, shunning convenience, preserving family solidarity, and respecting past wisdom. (7) It controls technology. These understandings keep the phone at a distance and limit its use. The Amish are its master rather than its servant.

The phone story is an intriguing parable of human interaction with technology—a demonstration that technology can serve the community without dominating it. The inconvenience of walking to an outside phone or taking messages from an answering service is a daily reminder that membership in an ethnic community exacts a price—a reminder that things that are too handy and too convenient may lead to sloth and pride. The phone agreement is a way to uphold tradition and absorb change, to appease the traditionalists as well as the entrepreneurs who need phones for economic survival. It is a deal that allows the Amish to have their cake and eat it too—preserving tradition while bending to economic pressures.

THE RIDDLE OF ELECTRICITY

Electricity is conspicuously absent from Amish homesteads. Newer Amish homes with contemporary decor have pleasant kitchens and modern bathrooms. But electrical appliances—microwaves, air conditioners, hair dryers, dishwashers, toasters, mixers, blenders, can openers, electric knives, TVs, VCRs, CD players, and computers—are missing. Bottled gas is used to heat water and to operate modern stoves and refrigerators. Homes, barns, and shops are lit with gas-pressured lanterns hung from ceilings, mounted on walls, or built on mobile cabinets that hold pressurized tanks of gas.

The Amish use electricity in several ways. Flashing red lights on the back of buggies warn approaching traffic. Electric fences keep cattle in pastures. The milk in bulk tanks is stirred by electric motors. Battery-operated alarm clocks buzz before dawn. The elderly read by small, battery-operated lamps. Electric welding machines abound on Amish farms. Carpentry crews use electric power saws at construction sites. Battery-operated tools fill many shops. The solution to this baffling maze of electrical use is found in tradition, intergroup relations, economic pressure, and conscious decisions to avoid worldly entrapments. A brief overview of electrical usage in the larger society sets the stage for the Amish story.

The Edison Electric Company began operations in Lancaster City in 1886. Arc lights soon illuminated streets, and some six thousand incandescent bulbs were eventually burning in homes and businesses. From 1890 to 1900, hotels and businesses used electric motors for power, and soon electric trolley cars were replacing horse-drawn "buses."[18] But for the most part, electricity stayed within city limits in these early years. In the first two decades of the twentieth century, power lines gradually crept into the countryside along major roads. Some outlying towns began operating their own power plants, but many rural areas still relied on kerosene lamps. In 1924, only 10 percent of non-Amish farms had current for lights and appliances. By 1930, there were 10,000 private electric plants on farms, but most Pennsylvania farmers still milked by lantern light.[19]

Several types of electrical services had emerged by the 1930s. First, cities and boroughs had independent generating plants. Second, many farms and businesses in rural areas operated small Delco or Genco electrical plants. These private plants provided homeowners with electricity from batteries charged by a generator powered by a gasoline engine. Third, farms along main roads began hooking up to public power lines as they gradually became available. Finally, many remote areas remained in the dark. By 1946, however, 80 percent of the non-Amish farmers were using electricity.

COPING WITH ELECTRICITY

Although the Amish hedged on using electricity from public utility lines, they had been using batteries for many years. Batteries were used to start gasoline engines that powered washing machines, water pumps, and feed grinders. Flashlights were also acceptable. Batteries were self-contained and unconnected to the outside world. They were handy but not "too handy," and they posed no threat to the Amish community. However, the church soon began to frown when light bulbs were hooked to batteries.

With a gasoline engine for power, Amishman Isaac Glick rigged up a generator with an electric light in about 1910.[20] He used the light to check the fertility of eggs in his hatchery business. The church, without a firm policy on electricity, did not censure Glick's light. Several years later, Glick's sons used batteries to hook up a light in their barn. One son stated: "The church 'got wind of it' and Father was brought to task in a church counsel meeting. After that, Daddy didn't want us to use the light." However, other Amish farmers were lighting their horse stables with bulbs connected to batteries without incurring the church's wrath. Thus, prior to World War I, the Amish attitude toward electricity was still in flux.

The menacing shadow of the 1910 division hovered over the Amish once again as they coped with the use of electricity. Indeed, the split in 1910 made it easier for the Amish to address the issue because the progressive Peachey church welcomed electrical innovations. Its members installed small Delco plants and generated their own electricity for lights and motors. An Amish minister described the electrical taboo: "An order was established that was not changed until the bulk milk tanks came in the late 1960s. The Peachey church had it [electricity], and that just about ruled it out for us." Once again, like the telephone decision, the readiness of the liberal group to welcome electrical lights helped the Amish say no.[21]

As the Peachey church accepted electricity, the Old Order position began to gel. Three incidents in about 1919 hardened the Amish policy. A tinsmith known as "Tinker" Dan Beiler ran some of his power tools with a gasoline engine. An inventive Amishman, he rigged up a light bulb whose brilliance flickered with the speed of his generator. Community folks—Amish and non-Amish alike—often stopped by to see the contraption. One person noted: "He didn't really need the light for his tinsmith business. He was a tinkerer, and he liked to tinker with the light." Ben Beiler, an influential Amish bishop, was not amused. He did not mind if "Tinker" Dan tinkered with his tin, but tinkering with a light bulb was taking things too far. The bishop's "no" was firm. Unwilling to yield, "Tinker" Dan soon packed up his light and moved to Virginia.

At about the same time, Ike Stoltzfus, who lived a few miles down the road, bought a Genco electric plant for his greenhouse business. An electric water pump provided a steady supply of water for his vegetable plants. According to one account, Bishop Beiler "just clamped down on him without taking it up with the church. Ike didn't know it was wrong, but the bishop, in his mind, thinks this member here was always kicking over the traces and his attitude isn't too good toward the church and we just can't tolerate this. So they gave Ike several weeks to get rid of it." And he did.

Another member, Mike Stoltzfus, used electrical power tools for repairs in his carriage shop. According to one informant, Bishop Beiler said, "'This may not be.' He was just not going to have any of this stupidity." So Mike got rid of his electric tools. A former member said Bishop Beiler "was very influential on this electric question, in setting the direction, definitely. With another bishop it might have gone a different direction. It probably would have." In any event, the Amish taboo on electricity solidified.

The Peachey church's use of electricity and Bishop Beiler's influence were not the only factors involved. Electricity provided a direct connection to the outside world, and to practical-minded rural people, electricity was mysterious. Where did it come from? Where would it lead? The fear was articulated by an Amish farmer: "It seems to me that after people get everything hooked up to electricity, then it will all go on fire and the end of the world's going to come." For a people trying to remain separate from an evil world, it made little sense to literally tie one's house to the larger world and to fall prey to dependency on outside power.

Fearing an unholy alliance with an evil world, steering a careful course away from the Peachey group, and bearing the imprint of a strict bishop, the electric taboo became inscribed in the Ordnung by 1920. One member recalled: "The church worked against it when electric first came and set a tradition, and it just stayed a tradition up to today." The tradition that crystallized about 1920 permitted the continued use of electricity from 12-volt batteries. Higher voltage electricity, tapped from public power lines or generated privately by a Delco plant, was forbidden. Electric light bulbs were taboo as well. As before, batteries could be used to start motors and power flashlights. So in essence, the decision was not a new decree; it was merely an attempt to uphold customary practice, to set a limit, until the Amish could see where the new electrical trends might lead. The distinction, however, between 12-volt direct current (DC) stored in batteries and 110-volt alternating current (AC) pulled from public lines became a critical difference over the years as standard electrical equipment became dependent on 110-volt current.[22]

Reflecting on the church's decision to limit the use of electricity, a member said: "Electric would lead to worldliness. What would come along with electric? All the things that we don't need. With our diesel engines today we have more control of things. If you have an electric line coming in, then you'd want a full line of appliances on it. The Amish are human too, you know." Another person noted: "It's not so much the electric that we're against, it's all the things that come with it—all the modern conveniences, television, computers. If we get electric lights, then where will we stop? The wheel [of change] would really start spinning then." "Electric is just not allowed," said one member, "because it's too worldly. Air power is better because it's privately owned." And according to one bishop, using electricity would simply mean "hooking up with the world too much."

In 1920, Bishop Beiler had no inkling of the avalanche of electrical appliances that would sweep across society in the following years. The taboo on

Diesel engines are used to operate air and hydraulic pumps to power equipment on Amish farms and businesses.

110-volt electricity conveniently preempted debate over each new gadget and eliminated them from Amish life. Banning electricity was an effective means of keeping the world at bay—literally and symbolically.

THE GENERATOR DEAL

Amish farm equipment changed rapidly in the 1960s as horse-drawn machinery became more difficult to buy. To replace worn-out equipment, Amish machine shops began converting tractor-drawn machinery to horse-drawn in a backward technological step. Electric welders, an important tool in this process, were also used to repair broken machinery. Portable electric generators, powered by gasoline engines, could produce the powerful electricity needed for welders. Amish farmers and mechanics gradually began using portable generators and welders, clearly breaking the 12-volt tradition. Given the compelling need to adapt farm machinery for use by horses, the bishops looked the other way. But the mechanics who began using electric generators for welders were tempted to use them in other ways as well.

Testing the rules of the church, some farmers began plugging home freezers and other electrical motors into their generators. Some even hung light bulbs in their barns. Worried about where this trend might lead, ordained leaders condemned the generator in a special series of ministers' meetings in the early 1960s, with one exception—it could still be used to operate electric welders to repair farm machinery. Asked about the use of generators for welders, a farmer said: "Our bishops are sometimes pretty hard pressed. They don't know where to draw the line. Now the welder's a piece of machinery that was allowed. They said it is something that we can have, it is almost necessary to keep our equipment running and that sort of thing." Allowing generators to be used for electric welders enabled Amish farmers to convert tractor-drawn equipment for use by horses. It was better to permit selective use of generators than to lose the horse altogether.

THE MILK TANK BARGAIN

The electricity issue returned again in 1968. To improve sanitation and reduce hauling costs, milk companies began requiring dairy farmers to store and chill milk in large stainless steel tanks instead of in old-fashioned milk cans. Bulk storage tanks, powered by electricity, could hold a ton or more of milk. Amish farmers had already been chilling their milk in cans in mechanical coolers powered by diesel engines, but the bulk tank edict placed church leaders in a quandary. The dairy industry was booming in the 1960s. Amish herds with a dozen cows were doubled and sometimes even tripled. Milk prices were good. The diversified farming of the past was giving way to specialized farming. Amish farmers were using mechanical milkers, and the monthly milk check was becoming the prime source of income for many families.

In 1968 Amish farmers received a series of letters spelling out the stark ultimatum: install bulk tanks or lose the market for your milk. The tanks required electricity. Amish leaders were caught in a dilemma. If they banned the tanks, many members might lose their prime source of income: some would be forced to quit farming altogether, and others would sell their milk for cheese and take a financial loss. Rejecting the bulk tank might encourage young farmers to leave the church or force them to take factory jobs, placing the family farm in jeopardy.

An Amish farmer summarized the impasse: "The milk companies said we had to get bulk tanks or lose our milk market. Milk was our most important income and so we tried to keep it. The bishops had a hard line to draw so that farmers could make a living off the family farm, but yet not get too big and go in debt or go for government financing. We didn't want electric or to have to tap into public lines." If the bishops took a hard line on bulk tanks, they might annoy enough members to trigger a new division—something they surely did not want two years after the schism of 1966. And yet the bishops could not capitulate to modernity by overturning tradition and using public power lines. They could not rescind their recent taboo on electric generators. If they did, history and the Lord himself would never forgive them; moreover, how would they ever control the use of electricity with all its complications?

Although the milk companies pressed the issue, they also needed milk from Amish farmers and thus were willing to negotiate. In a series of three delicate meetings, a settlement was chiseled out between the stewards of tradition and the agents of modernity. Five senior bishops and four milk inspectors negotiated the deal in an Amish farmhouse. The senior milk inspector, who spoke the Amish dialect, called the meeting. He said in retrospect: "We had a long battle with them, but we didn't want to lose them."

The milk inspectors and the moral inspectors dickered over a variety of issues. First, how would the tanks be powered? That was easy. The Amish were already using small diesel engines to operate mechanical coolers to chill their milk in cans. The refrigeration units on the bulk tanks could also be operated by a diesel engine. Running the diesel twice a day would power the vacuum milking machines as well as run the refrigeration unit. This was acceptable to the milk inspectors as long as the diesel engine was outside the milk house. Second, the milk inspectors insisted that the milk be stirred by an agitator five minutes per hour to prevent cream from rising to the top, inviting bacterial growth. Additionally, the inspectors demanded that the agitator be operated by an automatic switch, which placed the negotiators at loggerheads.

There were two problems for the Amish. First, the word *automatic* sounded too modern, too convenient, too fast—downright worldly. Second, an automatic agitator required 110-volt electricity. Small generators could be installed on the diesel motors to provide 110-volt current for the agitator; however, the generator had been restricted to welders just a few years earlier, and it would require swallowing a great deal of pride to erase a decision so

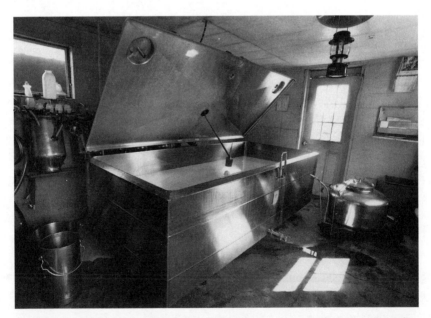

A 12-volt motor stirs the milk in this bulk tank, but lanterns illuminate the milk house and cow stable. The mobile "sputnick," lower right, is used to bring the milk from the cows to the bulk tank.

recently engraved in the Ordnung. Moreover, having a generator in every Amish diesel shed would open the door to other temptations. Ingenious farmers might start plugging a host of other gadgets into their generators— fans, cow clippers, radios, televisions.

The milk inspectors would not budge on the automatic agitator. Nor would the Amish on the use of generators. Was there no escape from this dilemma—no way to prevent an economic disaster and also maintain faith with tradition? Could the agitator be powered by a special 12-volt motor rigged up to a battery? The Amish reluctantly agreed. They could live with the automatic starter, but only if it was powered by a 12-volt battery. And so a deal was forged. The bishops would accept bulk tanks if their refrigeration units were powered by diesel engines. They also agreed to automatic agitators run by a 12-volt battery, recharged by *small* generators.

There was one more snag. The milk companies planned to haul the milk in large tank trucks every other day. Thus, they would collect Amish milk on every other Sunday. In the past, the Amish never shipped their milk on "the Lord's Day." An automatic electric starter was one thing, but shipping milk on Sunday was an unthinkable profanity. The Amish "no" was adamant! It was the milk companies' turn to concede, and concede they did. When asked if the milk companies considered dropping the Amish because of Sunday pickups, the head inspector said: "We never took it that far because we needed the milk. When you need it, you can't bargain too much. You can bargain, but you can't put too much pressure on." So at great inconvenience, plus the cost of overtime pay and extra miles, bulk tank trucks arrive at Amish farms on Saturday, or very early Monday morning.

The tank deal of 1969 was an ingenious settlement for the Amish as well as for the milk inspectors. The family farm could survive without using 110-volt electricity from public power lines. Moreover the Lord's Day would not be tarnished with Sunday milk pickups. Both religious tradition and economic vitality had been preserved. A few bishops were unhappy with the modern trend, but most Amish farmers quickly installed bulk tanks, stabilized their economic base, and thus preserved the family farm. The basic arrangement continues today. Small generators, run by diesel, recharge 12-volt batteries, which power the bulk tank agitators on the tanks.

Despite these efforts to stay on the farm, land was becoming scarce and expensive. So in the 1970s some Amish began working off the farm. Carpentry was a traditional and safe choice, but carpentry crews also needed power tools for commercial work. Reluctantly, portable generators were permitted so that mobile carpentry crews could operate electric tools at construction sites. In addition, carpenters working at construction sites with electricity were allowed to tap into public lines. On the farm, however, the generator did create new temptations. One farmer said: "If you got in a pinch, it might be necessary to use electric to clip cows or debeak chickens, as long as no one happened to be watching." Other farmers found it convenient to "get in a pinch" in other ways. Some ran their hay elevators and other small motors with 110-volt current from the generators until "the bishops really tightened up on these devious uses of the generator," according to one young farmer. In cases of special need, the regulation is relaxed. For example, a family with an asthmatic child needed 110-volt electricity for an oxygen pump, and they were happily granted the use of a generator.

CURRENT UNDERSTANDINGS

The present "understanding" of the Ordnung on electrical usage is five-fold. First, 110-volt current from public utility lines is forbidden, as always. Second, battery-supplied 12-volt current is acceptable for a variety of uses: fence chargers, cow trainers, agitators for bulk tanks, calculators, adding machines, reading lights for the elderly, hand-held drills and small motors to operate equipment in shops. Third, generators are permitted for welders, bulk tanks, and the electrical tools needed by mobile construction crews. Generators may also be used to recharge batteries for a variety of uses. Fourth, 110-volt current for uses other than welders and carpentry tools is forbidden. In several cases computers, appliances, and motors using 110-volt alternating current that were operated directly from generators had to be "put away." Fifth, inverters are widely used. They gradually came into use in the 1980s and 1990s, but that interesting story requires a telling of its own.

The inverter became available in the late 1970s. This small electrical gadget—the size of a car battery—could convert, or invert, 12-volt current into "homemade" 110-volt current. The trail of electricity thus goes from diesel to generator, to 12-volt battery, to inverter, and finally to a typical 110-volt appliance, bulb, or motor.

This fascinating circumvention symbolizes the delicate tension between tradition and modernity. A 12-volt battery provides the electricity for the inverter, which is certainly within the spirit of the 1920 taboo. Yet the inverter, in turn, produces "homemade" 110-volt current, which can run electronic equipment—cash registers, soldering guns, digital scales, calculators, copy machines, typewriters, and other small gadgets. The inverter brings temptations because toasters, TVs, CD players, computers, and light bulbs can also be plugged in. But because the inverter depends on a 12-volt battery, it severely limits the number and size of appliances that can be attached, and the battery must be periodically recharged. In Amish culture such limits are welcomed. Inverters are primarily permitted in shops and businesses, not homes.

Asked what the difference is between electricity coming directly from the generator or coming from an inverter via a battery, an Amish businessman replied: "It's more acceptable from a battery, but it does the same thing in the end. A generator produces electricity, pure electricity, and really, I guess an inverter after the battery also produces electricity but it is in a different sense, in a different form. If we were to allow generators across the board, then we would have our own electricity right off and then everything, everything, deep freezers, lights, and the whole bit."

Inverters are widely used by businesses, but the use varies somewhat by church district and the disposition of the local bishop. On this issue, there is a good deal of polite looking the other way. If inverters are used to operate computers, televisions, and popcorn poppers, they will challenge the limits and may have to be "put away." For the moment, at least, they remain an ingenious bargain that permits electric cash registers in retail stores while respecting Amish tradition. Such cultural compromises perplex those who appreciate neither the importance of tradition nor the fragile base of a peaceful community.

The distinction between direct current stored in 12-volt batteries and 110-volt alternating current tapped from public utility lines sounds absurd to Moderns. When the Amish church distinguished between batteries and higher voltage electricity in 1920, they were merely drawing a safe line. The long-term implications of their distinction were unknown, but in the wisdom of their ignorance, the ban on high-voltage current became a useful way of regulating social change. To a young Amish farmer, it makes sense to draw the line at 12-volt direct current: "You are really limited, you know, with 12-volt direct current. You can't go and put in a television or something like that

TABLE 8.1
Telephone and Electrical Guidelines

Forbidden		
Computer	110-volt public electricity	Telephone in home
Electric light[a]	Radio	Video player
110-volt appliance	Tape recorder	
Ambiguous		
Cell phone	Fax machine	Word processor
Acceptable		
Beeper[b]	Electric generator[c]	Inverter[e]
Calculator	Electric welder	Photocopy machine
Digital scales	External telephone[d]	12-volt motor
Electric cash register	Flashlight	12-volt reading light
Electric fence	Hearing aid	Voice mail

NOTE: Patterns of use vary by church district.
[a] Lights are often permitted for paint rooms and other special purposes in shops.
[b] For fire company and emergency medical use.
[c] Generator use is restricted to welders and battery rechargers.
[d] Telephones must be outside homes and shops in most districts.
[e] Inverters convert 12-volt to 110-volt for cash registers and copy machines, etc.

because you don't have enough current, unless you hook up dozens and dozens of batteries. If you have alternating current, your 110, there is no limit to what you can do. You can get yourself a hair dryer, if you want to. You really don't have anything to keep you from doing it, either. Because if you can have a coffeepot, who says you can't have a hair dryer?" So over the years, limiting electrical use to 12-volt current became a practical way of arresting and controlling social change.

As in many other issues, the Amish make a firm distinction between *use* and *ownership*. Amish farmers renting a farm from a non-Amish neighbor are permitted to use electric lights in the barn and house. However, the wiring is torn out if Amish purchase the property. A quilt shop owner renting from a non-Amish neighbor may have lights in a showroom. An Amish family buying an English home has a year to tear out the electrical wiring. One Amishman, hopeful that the church would eventually accept the wider use of electricity, placed conduits throughout his newly constructed house. But so far his hopes have been in vain.

AMISH ELECTRICITY

As small industries sprang up in the 1970s, they required heavy power tools in order to be competitive. Diesel engines could operate large drill presses and saws from their power shaft but not lathes, jig saws, grinders, and metal punches. The church doggedly forbade the use of electricity from public utility lines, so Amish mechanics explored other alternatives. They discovered that electrical motors on shop equipment could be replaced with hydraulic or air motors. Hydraulic and air pumps, powered by a diesel engine, could then force oil or air under high pressure through hoses to power the motors on grinders, drills, and saws. The use of hydraulic and air pressure was quickly dubbed "Amish electricity."

An Amish shop owner chortled: "We can do anything with air and hydraulic that you can do with electricity—except operate electronic equipment." Today state-of-the-art saws, grinders, lathes, drills, sanders, and metal presses, powered by air or hydraulic pressure, stand in Amish shops. Once again, tradition triumphed. This new technology allowed the Amish to modernize while retaining their historic ban of public power lines and 110-volt current. Today Amish businesses have all the power they need to operate modern equipment and remain competitive. As long as televisions and computers cannot run on air pressure, air and hydraulic is a safer option than the

This large machine, powered by hydraulic pressure, bends and cuts sheets of metal. The mobile gas-pressured light, on the left, helps to illuminate this welding shop.

inverter. Many families also use "Amish electricity" to power water pumps, small machinery, washing machines, sewing machines, and food processors. Indeed, hydraulic water pumps have rapidly replaced windmills on many farms. An unwritten understanding of Amish culture says: "If you can do it with air or oil, you may do it." "Amish electricity" has enhanced economic growth, ethnic identity, and symbolic separation from mass society. This remarkable deal simultaneously preserves tradition and permits progress.

HOME FREEZERS

The advent of home freezers in the 1950s offered a better way to preserve garden produce for large Amish families. But freezers required electricity. A few freezers, in fact, were operated by electricity from on-site generators in the early 1960s. However, leaders feared that allowing freezers in homes would make it too easy to plug televisions, radios, and all sorts of appliances into electrical outlets. Thus, the freezer was banned in 1966, not because the Amish view it as evil, but because other worldly devices would have likely followed it into Amish homes.

However, most Amish families do have access to a freezer. Many rent small storage freezers located in fruit markets or stores. Other families own a freezer in a non-Amish neighbor's garage or basement. The Amish family may contribute to the electrical costs or barter services or garden produce in exchange for the neighbor's hospitality. At first glance, the practice of keeping freezers at nearby non-Amish homes appears hypocritical. However, rather than two-faced deviance, this arrangement is but another compromise. It permits the use of a modern appliance to preserve food, which supports self-sufficiency, the extended family, and labor in a family context. At the same time, the arrangement bars other electrical gadgets from entering Amish homes. The freezer riddle keeps technology at a distance while still using it to preserve the family garden and self-sufficiency.

ELECTRICAL WISDOM

The compromises emerging from Amish history point to several conclusions: (1) The taboo on electricity was a literal way of separating from the world and maintaining self-sufficiency—an independence that is still preserved today. For instance, the Amish are less threatened by power shortages caused by storm, disaster, or war. (2) The taboo on electricity also created a

Electric cash registers are powered by inverters. Gas lanterns light this retail store.

symbolic separation from the world, a daily reminder that "we are different." (3) The rejection of electricity provides a symbolic bonding that unites the community internally. (4) The Amish policy on electricity implies that community wisdom, not individual fancy, must govern its use. In other words, individuals cannot be trusted with such powerful technology. (5) The 1920 rejection of high-voltage electricity conveniently slowed social change by eliminating new electrical appliances and machinery that appeared in the twentieth century. (6) By avoiding rancorous debate over each new technological item, the Amish were able to preserve communal harmony. Apart from the bulk tank and the welder, the big decision on electricity preempted a host of small debates over hair dryers, shavers, coffeepots, and so forth. (7) The proscription against electricity effectively quarantined the Amish from outside electronic media—radios, televisions, record players, CD players, and computers. Curtailing such external influences is crucial for the preservation of Amish values. (8) The concessions on electricity have been driven primarily by economic concerns. Although it benefits the whole community, the use of air and hydraulic power has facilitated the work of men more than that of women. (9) Sacrificing electrical conveniences is a daily reminder that individual desires must yield to larger community goals.

Inside the Amish world, the riddles of technology make sense. Permitting selective use of the telephone and electricity in some settings and not in others is simply a commonsense solution to everyday problems posed by industrialization. Using air and hydraulic pressure to power modern shops while forbidding 110-volt electricity is a reasonable way to encourage economic growth within certain limits.

As we have seen, the Amish are certainly not opposed to technology. They simply use it selectively. They are more likely to accept new technology for productive purposes, "for making a living," as they would say, than for consumption and communication. They are adamant in not using media technology to consume the values and images of mass society. That line is nonnegotiable. Clearly, they want to build community and preserve social capital, so they employ technology cautiously, ever wary of its potential to tatter the social fabric. And one thing is certain: although the Amish may not enjoy all the conveniences of modern life, they try to control technology and anticipate its long-term consequences.

Harnessing the Power of Progress

The first thing people do when they leave the Amish church is get a car.
—*Amish leader*

SCOOTERS, TRAINS, AND CARS

A funny thing happened in the summer of 2000. Outsiders who for many years had been snickering at the Amish riding on old-fashioned scooters fell in love with scooters themselves. The Amish had their turn to laugh as a scooter craze spread across the country, prompting sales of several million scooters.[1] Because both bicycles and automobiles are banned, Amish children and adults for many years have used scooters for local travel—a compromise between walking and riding. The larger world was finally catching up with Old Order ways!

The Amish readily use public transportation—trains, buses, and boats, but not airplanes. Already in the nineteenth century, before the arrival of motor vehicles, they used trains to travel to other Amish settlements. When commercial air travel developed in the middle of the twentieth century, it was simply considered unnecessary. Moreover, airports were located in large urban areas. The few Amish who go to Europe travel by ship rather than by plane. The Amish had been using public transportation since the mid-nineteenth century, so the big challenge for them was how to respond to private transportation in the form of a car.

In the Amish mind, the car epitomizes worldliness. Car ownership is one of the few violations of the Ordnung that triggers automatic expulsion. "Well, anybody that gets a car just isn't Amish, that's all," said an Amishwoman.

Describing early attitudes toward cars, an Amishman said: "Our leaders never looked at them." Other members widely agree that the car "didn't make no issue among us." Yet today the Amish ride in cars and often hire them on a daily basis. How can they conscientiously embrace a double standard— forbidding ownership while permitting use? That question lurks beneath the riddle of the car.

On 14 February 1900, a battery-operated car appeared on the streets of Lancaster for the first time.[2] Four years later a six-year-old Amish boy, accompanying his father to Lancaster to sell vegetables, saw nine cars in one day. In those days, cars were a rich man's hobby. The National Automobile Company organized itself in 1907 in Lancaster and advertised motoring as "the king of sports and the queen of amusements."[3] For the Amish, who disdained both sports and amusements, such slogans turned the car into a profane symbol. They viewed the early ones as worldly toys for the wealthy.

Henry Ford's Model T, first produced in 1908, popularized the car for the masses after 1914. Although only 7 percent of Pennsylvania farmers had a car in 1914, 72 percent of them were driving the "devil's machine" by 1921.[4] Progressive Mennonites, along with the rest of the world, were buying new cars. An Amish leader remembers that Mennonite boys drove their cars to fairs, farm shows, and other worldly amusements. On the other hand, the liberal Peachey church, which had splintered off from the Amish in 1910 and had few qualms about using electricity, telephones, or tractors, was not seduced by the car until 1928. The Amish resolve held firm over the years; they were not about to stray after their Mennonite cousins or their wayward stepchildren.

Some practical considerations made it easy for the Amish to avoid using cars. Between 1900 and 1910 in Lancaster County, 150 miles of electric trolley lines were strung from Lancaster City to outlying towns. The Amish rode the trolleys to town for shopping. Public trains were also used for long-distance trips to Midwestern Amish settlements. Furthermore, early cars were impractical. They were often in the garage more than on the road. Over the winter they were jacked up on blocks, because the muddy roads were impassable. As late as 1930, only 22 percent of Pennsylvania farmers lived by a paved road, which gave credence to the 1931 gubernatorial campaign, "Take the farmers out of the mud."[5]

THE CAR TABOO

The Amish taboo on car *ownership* intensified by about 1915 as cars became more widely accepted in the larger society.[6] *Use* of the car, however, varied by church district in the early years. Some Amish declared they would never "crawl into a car," and they never did. Others rode with neighbors. Some bishops permitted traveling with a non-Amish neighbor but forbade hiring a car or driver. Other districts made a distinction between pleasure and business use, but that line was often fuzzy. In 1928 two farmers, stuck with a broken corn planter in the midst of planting, hired a trucker to haul a new planter from a dealer some fifty miles away. The farmers went along for the ride. Gossip soon spread about the "unnecessary trip," and the culprits had to confess their sin in church. Other Amish, however, used the services of a neighbor's car regularly for business trips.

There is little evidence of the Amish owning cars, but some did drive on the sly. Around 1915, an Amishman "practiced" driving his hired man's Model T Ford behind the barn. Unfamiliar with the steering, he lost control and drove over the front shafts of his own buggy, smashing them to bits. In the 1930s, an Amishman employed by a feed mill drove a pickup truck to make deliveries for the mill. But as one bishop noted: "Before 1930, we hardly rode in cars. We had no businesses, we could drive to all the Amish places by horse. The community was all close together."

The Amish fear of the car was not a naive one, for the car revolutionized rural life. By 1933, a presidential commission concluded that no other invention with such far-reaching importance diffused so quickly through the national culture, transforming even habits of thought and language.[7] Another historian contended that no other mechanical invention in history influenced the rural farmer more than the car.[8] Leaving no phase of rural life untouched, it facilitated interchange with urban life and widened the social horizon of farm families. Its arrival was cheered by many as an enormous boost to the farmer's success.[9] In the eyes of the Amish, however, the car endangered their ethnic community. A thief in disguise, it threatened to steal social capital.

The very name of this new invention, *automobile,* offering self-propelled and automatic mobility, spelled trouble for the Amish. It freed individuals to travel autonomously, independently—whenever and wherever they pleased. For Americans frustrated by the end of the western frontier, the new promise of unlimited mobility was a great antidote. Auto travel symbolized the spirit of American individualism and independence—freeing people from train and trolley schedules, breaking the confines of geography, and smashing the provincialism of rural life. Liberated from geography, an individual could travel and explore at will. However, for a traditional people who preferred manual and stationary things, automatic mobility was a menace. Automatic things signaled a loss of control, and mobility would fragment local communities bonded together by the constraints of horse-drawn transportation.

Furthermore, the car would make it difficult to remain separate from the industrial world. Manufactured and distributed in the city, the car brought "city slickers" out to secluded rural areas on pleasure-seeking excursions. The car was also a separator. Individuals could now drive away from home— far away. Youth could drive away to urban worlds of vice. Adults could drive away for business. The car would surely pull the local community apart. For a people concerned about staying together, the last thing they wanted to do was to turn the keys of cars over to individuals. A personalized version of mass transit, the car was perfect for a complicated, individuated, mobile society. But for a stable, simple, local people who cherished their close-knit community and sought separation from the world, the car was a peril.

The car threatened to separate the community in other ways as well. If only wealthy members could afford it, the car would produce inequality. Proud individuals would use the car to show off their status, power, and wealth—all of which would mock the spirit of Gelassenheit. Cars would speed things up dramatically and disrupt the slow pace of Amish rhythms. Drivers would be out of control, mobile, independent, and free floating. The car contradicted the very core of Amish life. It was the symbol of modernity par excellence, for it entailed individualism, freedom, acceleration, mobility, and autonomy. Indeed, it was a modern brainchild, pieced together on a mechanical, rational, and highly specialized assembly line. In all of these ways, the car posed a primary threat to Amish life.

There was little hesitation in the Amish "no" to car ownership. Yet the car brought many advantages. So over time, the Amish agreed to some concessions. They would ride in cars but only for emergencies and in special circumstances. They would not own them, for then things would surely get out of control. This firm line between *use* and *ownership*—or, as the Amish sometimes say, between use and abuse—often strikes Moderns as outright hypocrisy. But from the Amish perspective, it is a practical solution that keeps the car at bay, controls its negative side effects, but nevertheless uses it in ways that reap economic benefit and build community life.[10]

AMISH TAXIS

The use of motor vehicles by the Amish has liberalized over the decades. "Use of the car," said one grandfather, "is something that the church has slipped on." A bishop pointed to the collapse of the trolley system and poor rural bus service as reasons for the increasing use of cars. Distinctions were made between business and pleasure, need and luxury, emergency and convenience. But in all these concessions the taboo on ownership held firm. The Amish use of cars expanded in the mid-twentieth century with the opening of a daughter colony in Lebanon County, some thirty miles northwest of Lancaster. After this expansion, hiring drivers became more widely accepted by the church.

A van load of Amish people visiting Lancaster from another settlement prepare
to return home in a "taxi."

The first regular taxi service for Amish came into existence in the early
1950s, when a non-Amish neighbor began earning a living "hauling" Amish
friends to funerals, sales, family gatherings, distant settlements, and hospitals. Some adults even hired drivers on Sunday for questionable pleasure
trips. In the mid-1950s, church leaders, fearing things would get out of hand,
agreed to ban the hiring of drivers on Sunday except for emergencies. Present
policy still prohibits hiring drivers on Sunday except in special circumstances, such as visiting family members in the hospital. Many bishops even
frown on accepting free rides on Sunday. The horse and buggy—core symbols of Amish identity—must at least be hitched up on the sacred day of
worship. This ritualistic abstention from cars on Sunday reaffirms the Amish
moral order and the sacred significance of the carriage.

The Ordnung specifies that members may not own or operate a motor
vehicle, hold a driver's license, or lend money to someone to purchase a car.
Drivers may be hired when necessary. The definition of "necessity" is, of
course, a slippery one. Members sometimes accuse one another of hiring
drivers for unnecessary trips. Many businessmen have standing agreements
with drivers who provide transportation on a daily basis.

Today Amish taxis, operated by non-Amish neighbors and members of other Plain churches, transport Amish to auctions, job sites, funerals, weddings, and family gatherings. Many of these taxi arrangements developed over the years as acts of neighborly kindness. Dozens of taxi operations function as full-time and part-time businesses. Indeed, according to one Amish woman, "We jest among ourselves that if we continue to prosper, half of North America will soon be Amish and the rest will be taxi drivers."

In 1977 the Pennsylvania Public Utilities Commission (PUC) cracked down on non-Amish taxi owners who were charging fees for their services without holding a common carrier license. An abrupt crackdown on five drivers at an Amish funeral angered both the Amish and non-Amish. Responding to pressure from bus companies who could not compete with the informal taxis, a PUC spokesman justified the enforcement: "We've seen this thing grow like a cancer. At least a hundred people must be doing this illegally and we are going to try and cut it out. It's a thorn in our side."[11] After fourteen months of hearings and negotiations, the PUC agreed to issue taxi permits to about forty drivers who transported the Amish. The special permits allow the drivers to charge fees for their service as long as they only transport people whose beliefs and religious convictions prevent them from owning or operating a vehicle.[12]

Amish concessions to car *use* were prompted by several factors: the collapse of the rural trolley system, the birth of Amish settlements in other counties, Amish expansion in Lancaster County, and the rapid growth of Amish businesses. Carpentry crews need transportation to construction sites, cabinet makers sometimes travel to nearby states to install "Amish kitchens," and manufacturing establishments must find ways to transport their products.

Many Amish businesses have a non-Amish employee who provides a car or truck for company use. The employee owns the vehicle, and the proprietor pays mileage. The employee may be an unbaptized son of the owner or, more frequently, a member of another Plain group that permits automobiles. The mileage rate pays for the vehicle's initial cost and maintenance and perhaps a marginal profit. Amish businessmen often have agreements with other non-Amish neighbors or commercial truckers to transport their products. In some cases, business owners have made "sweetheart" loans to employees, enabling them to purchase vehicles for company use. Most bishops have forbidden such "under the table" deals that amount to de facto ownership.

THE AUTOMOBILE AGREEMENT

The solution to the car riddle lies in the fine print of the public agreement negotiated with modernity. In brief, the Amish vehicle policy prohibits holding a driver's license as well as owning, driving, and financing a vehicle. With the exception of Sundays and obvious frivolities, hiring drivers and riding in vehicles is permitted. A fascinating settlement, the bargain balances the tug of traditional values with the press of economic survival and convenience. The compromise controls the detrimental effects of the car, yet allows access to it for business and building community.

The agreement acknowledges that car ownership cannot be entrusted to the individual. If ownership were permitted, the church would lose control of the car. Ownership would intensify the pace and complexity of Amish life. Parents and youth alike would spend more time away from home at meetings and worldly amusements. Car ownership, in the long run, would not only erode the social base of the small face-to-face community, but it would also destroy the local church district—the cornerstone of social organization. The limitations of horse travel hold the local community together; uncontrolled access to cars would fragment and scatter it. The car, in short, would drain social capital out of the social system.

Hiring a taxi is inconvenient: arrangements must be made, and drivers paid. Amish taxis provide transportation, but not automatic mobility. One yields to the schedule, itinerary, fees, and mood of the driver. One Amishman explained: "When we need a driver, we call the ones who are less expensive or who we enjoy riding with. Oftentimes we must call as many as a half a dozen before we can find one who is not busy. When we want to go on a long trip, there are quite a few things to consider, such as: Does he drive carefully; does he gladly go where we want to go; does he allow us to give our small children something to eat such as pretzels or crackers to keep them quiet during the long drive; is he a pleasant, courteous driver who charges a decent fee."[13]

In forging the car deal, the Amish gave up autonomy and independence, but some benefits come with the compromise. By permitting the use of cars, they are able to travel to distant places and conduct business in a kind of door-to-door limousine service without the typical costs of purchase and maintenance and without driving fatigue. In this way, the Amish have re-

English drivers wait while an Amish construction crew pumps gas in their trucks before traveling to a construction site.

tained the virtues of simplicity as well as the convenience of modernity. It is a way of using modern technology without being enslaved by it or allowing it to destroy community. The use of motor vehicles has become essential for the fiscal survival of Amish industries. Moreover, it also links families and friends living in other counties and states.

Traveling by van also fosters community; it builds social capital. As with other things, the Amish do it together. Traveling in groups not only reduces costs but also builds community. Van loads of Amish are, in essence, portable subcommunities, keeping the Amish world alive on daily jaunts to work and on visits to relatives in far-flung settlements. They are traveling at high speeds but traveling with like-minded others in the context of community.

Controlled use of the car is a way of keeping faith with tradition while giving just enough freedom to maneuver in the larger society. The Amish believe that by turning the use of cars over to individuals, they would quicken the pace of their life, erase geographical limits, weaken social control, deplete their social capital, and eventually ruin their community. The rejection of self-propelled mobility encourages people to work near home, which helps to hold the family together. Thus the Amish took the car, the charm of modernity, on their own terms and struck a deal that enabled them to use it to enhance their community. It is a cultural compromise that baffles Moderns who miss its fine print.

THE SOD PACKERS

Tractors are standard equipment on Amish farms today, but they remain at the barn and rarely go out to the fields. Horses and mules pull plows and other machinery across the fertile soil. Why would anyone purchase a tractor and then keep it at the barn? How did the tractor riddle emerge?

Banning the car was an easy decision for the Amish. The tractor, however, was a different story. Tractors support agriculture. They enhance productivity, ease work, increase efficiency, and speed up planting and harvest. An attractive product from the merchants of progress, tractors could not be easily scuttled like the car. Tractors tantalized and enticed Amish farmers in the 1920s, 1940s, and again in the 1960s. Although there is little evidence that members of the church drove cars, they were indeed driving tractors, not only near their barns, but in their fields as well. But that is getting ahead of our story.

By the late 1880s large steam engines operated threshing machines on many Lancaster County farms. Small gasoline engines were widely used by the turn of the twentieth century to saw wood, grind feed, pump water, and power washing machines. Like their neighbors, the Amish owned and operated steam and gasoline engines and used horses to pull machinery in their fields.

In 1906, the International Harvester Company built a single-cylinder tractor, and by 1910, a non-Amish farmer on the eastern edge of Lancaster County had purchased one of the clumsy contraptions.[14] Boasting the power of twenty horses, some of the early tractors weighed as much as six tons. Due to labor shortages and the demands of World War I, all-purpose tractors were not available until the mid-1920s. The first tractors were awkward monstrosities, ill-suited for the modest farms of eastern Pennsylvania. Their wide steel wheels packed the soil, and they were difficult to maneuver in small fields. But, surprisingly, some Amish began using them.

In the early 1920s, there were probably a dozen or more Amish farmers experimenting with these sod packers in their fields.[15] According to oral tradition, Moses King took his newly purchased tractor out in the field and began harrowing. The dealer who had sold the tractor forgot to explain how to stop it, so King simply drove it in circles until it ran out of gas. On several occasions, tractors were overturned by inexperienced Amish drivers. In about 1920, Ike Zook was using a noisy tractor to plow. His neighbor, Deacon Jonas Beiler, irked by the clanging noise, thought the contraption was ridiculous. So according to oral tradition, Deacon Beiler tied his horses to a post, walked across the road, and told Zook: "Now you have to get rid of this stupid thing, I'm offended by it." Beiler was not only the deacon of Zook's congregation, but he was also the brother of stern Bishop Ben Beiler. Zook was soon "called on the carpet" and asked to confess before the church. But liking his tractor more than the church, Zook left the Amish for the Peachey church, which permitted tractors without any qualms.

About the same time, two ministers visiting Amish settlements in the Midwest discovered that tractors were not being used there, even on large Amish farms. Upon their return, the ministers concluded that if sod packers were not needed on big farms in the Midwest, they certainly were not necessary in Lancaster County. However, the tractor experiment continued until 1923, when tractors were finally banned from Amish fields.

THE TRACTOR RECALL

Several factors tightened the Amish tractor policy. First, the wayward Peachey church permitted tractors in the field, a sure sign of decadence. Second, the early tractors were quite expensive and impractical. Horses were clearly advantageous. Although horses required feeding, they were easier to turn in the field, cheaper to buy, and did not pack the soil. Moreover, they provided free fertilizer. Third, in the first two decades of the twentieth century, Amish leaders had already blessed a host of new farm equipment—mechanical manure spreaders, hay loaders, tobacco planters, and silos. In fact, the Amish were often the first ones in a community to buy the new inventions as they came on the market.[16] Was not the use of tractors going just a bit too far? Fourth, Bishop Ben Beiler believed that the tractor seemed dangerously close to the car, which was already taboo. A nephew remembers the bishop saying he was afraid "that the tractor would lead to the car." The early tractors did not have rubber tires, but they were self-propelled, mobile units—suspiciously similar to the car. Given all of these concerns, tractors were recalled from Amish fields in about 1923.

Discussions about tractors quieted down in the late 1920s. During the Depression, horse feed was cheap, and tractors were too expensive for farmers anyway. But by the late 1930s and early 1940s, general purpose tractors on rubber tires were available. They were handy for cultivating crops even in small fields. Such tractors were appearing on virtually every non-Amish farm in the early 1940s. In a single decade (1940–50), the number of workhorses in Lancaster was cut in half.

Several Amish farmers were lured by these improved tractors for fieldwork. Clearly superior to horses, the new tractors were lighter, cheaper, and more versatile. The bishops could no longer condemn them as impractical. But in the judgment of the older bishops, the 1923 distinction between barn and field was a wise line, and they stood firm. So once again, in the early 1940s, tractors were recalled from Amish fields. Young farmers were soon on their knees in front of the church promising to "put their tractors away" and vowing to stay in touch with nature, tradition, community, and God.

The issue was not entirely settled, however. In the late 1950s and early 1960s, a wide array of new tractor-drawn machinery was being manufactured. The new equipment—hay mowers, hay crushers, grain combines, hay balers, and corn harvesters—required a powerful engine and was heavy for horses to pull. Horse-drawn machinery was becoming scarce as non-Amish farmers shifted to tractors. So the tractor became tempting once again. Trying to strike a balance between tradition and efficiency, some Amish mechanics built a power unit that soon claimed the nickname "Amish tractor."

The power unit consisted of a gasoline engine on a four-wheel cart that could power various implements. It functioned, in essence, as a homemade tractor. The power unit was pulled, of course, by the symbolic horses, for as one farmer said in jest, "We need the horses to steer it." Moreover, the ingenious young farmers were staying within a senior bishop's rule of thumb: "If you can pull it with horses, you can have it." But the old sage probably never imagined that horses would someday pull such modern, powerful, and shiny machines—forage harvesters, combines, and haybines. Even younger bishops were sure that the power unit was only a step away from a tractor. Furthermore, the mocking laughter of Mennonite neighbors was embarrassing.

The bishops were not fooled by the new contraption, and they held to the old line: no tractors in the field. The line has remained taut ever since.

THE TRACTOR RIDDLE

Why did the church not outlaw tractors completely? Why permit this worldly contraption to sit around the barn? Why play with temptation? When asked that question, a bishop said: "I don't know. I can't answer that. I still think if we don't want to go with the world altogether, why we better use horses instead of going along with the modern way." Although using a tractor in the field simply feels "too worldly" to this bishop, there were good reasons for drawing the line that way in the 1920s.

Gasoline engines were widely used on Amish farms by World War I. Feed silos, thirty feet high, jutted up by Amish barns. Hefty power was needed to blow chopped silage to the top of the silos in order to fill them. The gasoline engine and the steam engine were used for such high-power demands around the barn—grinding, threshing, and blowing silage. Several Amishmen owned steam-powered threshing rigs and harvested wheat on neighboring farms. In fact, Bishop Beiler's own brother had a steam engine for his threshing rig. To outlaw tractors around the barn would have been a step backward, one that surely would have ignited a political ruckus in the church. In essence, limiting tractors to the barn amounted to freezing history on the farm, drawing a line that simply conformed to customary practice. Such a policy allowed the silage to blow and the wheat to be threshed so that things could go on much as they had before.

The ban on field tractors and other self-propelled equipment that crystallized in about 1923 remains firm today. The fear that tractors would lead to cars is the most frequently cited reason for not using them in the field. Amishmen tell numerous stories of progressive churches in other localities that permitted tractors in the field. "Before you know it, they put rubber tires on the tractors, and the next thing they are driving them to town for groceries. And as the next generation grows up, they can't understand the difference between using a tractor for trips to town and a car. And so they get a car."[17]

If tractors had been manufactured before cars, might the Amish be driving them in their fields today? Possibly. But there are other compelling reasons for banning tractors from the fields as well. They displace farm workers. In contrast to Moderns, who seek to save labor at every turn, the Amish have

A tractor provides power to blow green corn to the top of a silo. Tractor wheels and farm wagon wheels are steel; hand-pulled wagons and carts may have rubber wheels.

always welcomed work as the heartbeat of their community. The church was anchored on the farm where work, like a magnet, pulled everyone together. A tractor might save labor, but in Amish eyes that spelled trouble. With more and more labor-saving gadgets, there might not be enough work to go around for all the children. Leisure, the devil's workshop, would run rampant. Worse yet, the loss of home work would lead to factory work and unwanted ties to the outside world. So in these ways, a labor-saving device like a tractor could threaten not only the family but the church itself.

The use of the tractor conspired against community in other ways as well. In the first two decades of the twentieth century, local farmers, Amish and non-Amish alike, worked closely together in large crews, especially at planting and harvest times. It was hard manual work. But it was good work— communal work—as the community pitted itself against the forces of nature. Self-propelled tractors would not only enable individuals to work fast and independently, but they would also destroy the neighborhood work crews that in bygone days had joined together to harvest crops. The tractor was a great labor saver but also a sure way to lose social capital and the joy of collective work.

Insisting on horses and mules in the field was also a way of perpetuating a horse subculture. Family members would continue to learn about the care and feeding of horses. Related occupations such as blacksmiths and harness makers would survive to support the horse culture—an essential infrastructure if the Amish were to keep the horse and buggy on the road. With only a driving horse in the barn, the entire horse culture as well as its supporting industries might collapse. Thus, keeping horses in the field helped indirectly to keep them on the road.[18]

The line drawn between barn power and field power in 1923 appears today as a perplexing riddle, but it was a sensible compromise. With tractor power at the barn, silos could be filled, grain ground, and wheat threshed as always, thus avoiding an economic setback and a political brawl. Furthermore, the bargain provided some breathing space, a time-out to observe the consequences of the new contraptions more carefully. The arrangement has served the Amish well over time. As new power needs developed around the barn, the tractor was handy and helpful.[19] Today modern steel-wheeled tractors power large feed grinders, spin ventilating fans, run manure pumps, blow silage, operate hydraulic systems, and power irrigation pumps on Amish farms. They power all sorts of equipment from their power takeoff shaft, belt pulley, or hydraulic system. Tractors are also used to pull stumps out of fence rows and milk trucks out of snowdrifts. Thus, while horses protect Amish identity in the field, tractors at the barn help to boost agricultural productivity.

There are some restrictions, however, even around the barn. Steel wheels are mandatory. Pneumatic tires, initially associated with the car, came to symbolize freedom and mobility—and hence worldliness. Thus, over the years the Amish have rejected pneumatic tires on farm equipment, fearing they might lead to the car. Hard rubber tires and pneumatic tires are permitted on small hand-held items such as wheelbarrows, tricycles, wagons, and feed carts. However, the steel-wheel restriction applies to all machinery pulled by horses—wagons, corn pickers, balers, and so forth.

A front-end forklift on a tractor to hoist heavy items up to a second floor is acceptable as a necessity. However, a front-end manure loader, which would lessen the work of family members, is off-limits. In some church districts,

TABLE 9.1
General Patterns of Farm Equipment Use

Acceptable Modern Equipment		
Automated chicken houses[a]	Forklifts	Hay rakes
Bulk milk tanks	Hay balers	Mechanical milkers
Corn pickers	Hay crimpers	Silage blowers
Corn planters	Hay elevators	TMR feed mixers
Feed grinders	Hay mowers	Tractors at the barn
Amish-Manufactured or -Modified Equipment		
Bale wrappers	Grain bins	Hydraulic systems
Cattle feeders	Harrows	Manure spreaders
Corn binders	Harvestore silos (Blue)	Plows
Corn planters	Hay rakes	Sprayers
Engines on implements	Hay tedders	Steel wheels on implements
Forage cutter/blowers	Hay turners	Wagons
Unacceptable Farm Equipment		
Barn cleaners	Front-end manure loaders	Rubber tires
Combines	Haybines	Self-propelled implements
Forage harvesters[b]	Milk pipelines	Silo unloaders

NOTE: Patterns of use vary by church district.
[a] Air and hydraulic power operate feeding and egg gathering equipment.
[b] Forage harvesters were a contentious issue in 2000.

small Caterpillar-like tractors push and load manure inside barns. In other districts, they are forbidden. Many businesses use small forklifts to load and unload goods. For safety reasons and because of pressure from shop owners in the 1990s, the church permitted hard rubber on the wheels of forklifts.

Preventing tractors from replacing horses in the field marked a major turning point in Amish history. It maintained the pace of the past and offered daily evidence that the Amish had not capitulated to modernity. The tractor would not *separate* them from the soil, their past, their identity, or their families. Thus, by the mid-twentieth century, the horse in the field had become a cogent symbol of Amish identity—a symbolism underscored by nearby Old Order Mennonites who used steel-wheeled tractors in their fields.

MECHANIZED HORSE FARMING

Today horses and mules pull modern farm implements in Amish fields. This unusual union of tradition and modernity jelled in the mid-1960s. Before the 1950s, the Amish used traditional horse-drawn equipment to harvest their crops. Grain binders and grass mowers, for example, were powered by their own "ground-driven" wheels.

Numerous factors converged in the 1950s to create strong pressures for change. Farming became more specialized as dairy farms took the lead. Farmers who began with eight cows in the 1930s expanded their herds to twenty-four or even thirty-six. The use of commercial fertilizer and alfalfa produced three to four crops of hay per year. Like other farmers, the Amish had traditionally stored hay loose in their barns. The expanding dairy herds and larger hay crops created storage problems. Farmers had to either limit their herds, build larger barns, or find new ways to store their hay.

The engineers of progress had been tinkering with a solution. Hay balers, pulled by tractors through the field, were able to pack loose hay into tight rectangular bales that were easy to haul and stack in the barn. The tightly compressed bales alleviated the storage problem. After World War II, hay balers became popular among American farmers. Some non-Amish farmers began baling hay for the Amish in the early 1950s. And by 1955, several Amish farmers had purchased their own hay balers. Pulled by horses, the balers were powered by a gasoline engine installed at the factory. It seemed like an innocent turn of events, but it was a revolution of sorts, for it was the first widespread use of gasoline engines in Amish fields.[20] Surprisingly, church leaders said little about it. Economic forces propelling the dairy industry as well as the hay storage problem had forced the bishops' hand. Besides, the baler conformed to the old bishop's favorite dictum: "If you can pull it with horses, you can have it."

Amish oral historians report that the hay baler stirred little agitation in the church. One leader reflected: "It surprised me that the baler slipped through." By 1960 the baler had slipped onto many Amish farms, and when the bishops drew up a list of taboo equipment in the early 1960s, it was conspicuously missing.[21] Shunning the baler would have been foolish for both political and financial reasons. Some limits, however, were placed on the baler. Labor-saving bale throwers, which automatically tossed bales onto wagons behind the baler, were forbidden. And steel wheels, of course, were placed on the balers.

Other issues incubating in the early 1960s also brought change and controversy. Manufacturers of farm equipment were producing large, heavy machinery designed for powerful tractors. New horse-drawn machinery was becoming scarce, so the Amish began buying old-fashioned used machinery in other parts of the country. But this pool started to shrink. Commercial fertilizers, hybrid seed, and improved methods of cultivation produced bumper crops that were difficult to harvest with antiquated equipment.

With horse-drawn machinery scarce, some bold farmers, knowing the baler had slipped into use and feeling the pressure for increased productivity, began using modern corn harvesters and wheat combines. In the past, the Amish had used "ground-driven" binders pulled by horses to cut their corn and wheat. The new corn harvesters chopped green corn in the field and blew it into a trailing wagon. The silage was then hauled to the barn and blown into silos for storage. The corn harvester was a boon to the dairy farmer because chopped corn silage was a prime source of feed. The combine was a modern threshing machine that cut and threshed wheat in the field in one operation.

Meeting in 1960, the Amish bishops singled out the harvester and the combine as two inventions they would not tolerate. Several factors likely explain the ban. First, the modern harvesters and combines on nearby non-Amish farms were self-propelled.[22] The horse-pulled corn harvesters and wheat combines, already slipping into use on some Amish farms, might eventually lead to self-propelled units. Second, the lenient bishops had already "looked the other way" when the hay baler slipped in. Why, they reasoned, let another labor-saving device slip through? They had to draw the line somewhere in order to govern the expansionist impulses of farmers. Unlike the baler, the corn harvester did not improve storage. It just saved labor and time, and that was no excuse for tolerance. Third, as dairy operations flourished, wheat and tobacco were in decline.[23] The combines used for harvesting wheat were not critical for the survival of dairy farmers. The few acres of wheat farmed by the Amish could still be cut with old-fashioned, ground-driven binders and threshed at the barn in traditional ways. Although the bishops would tolerate the hay baler, the economic and political pressures were not strong enough to persuade them to endorse corn harvesters and combines.

FARM MACHINERY PUZZLES

A new development in the fall of 1960 sealed the fate of the modern corn harvester for at least several decades. An inventive Amish farmer mounted a gasoline engine on a corn binder designed to be pulled and powered by a

A state-of-the-art round baler is pulled by horses. A large engine mounted on the baler provides power. The rubber tires are permitted because the baler is jointly owned with a non-Amish neighbor.

tractor. Using the gasoline engine to cut the corn, he could pull the tractor binder with his horses. Until this time, old-fashioned ground-driven binders were used to cut green corn for silage. The inventive farmer explained: "We put engines on the corn binders because there weren't enough ground-driven binders around anymore and to keep away from the combines and harvesters." Amish mechanics soon began making replacement parts for the binders, which were no longer manufactured. It was a watershed in the evolution of Amish technology: the Amish could now move beyond simple ground-driven machinery. By mounting engines on equipment designed for tractors, they could increase productivity, use modern equipment, eliminate the need for large self-propelled models, and still keep horses and mules plodding across their fields. Rather than being dominated by modern farm technology, the Amish had redesigned it to fit their moral order.

Using engines to power field equipment was another bargain that delicately balanced a variety of factors; it (1) kept the modern harvester off Amish fields, (2) retained the symbolic horse, (3) provided plenty of work for farm hands, (4) permitted silage harvesting to continue according to tradition, (5) eliminated the difficulty of buying scarce ground-driven binders, (6) created new jobs for Amish mechanics who manufactured replacement parts, (7) provided extra power to cut the larger varieties of hybrid crops, (8) enabled dairy farmers to remain financially competitive, and (9) opened a way for the bishops to escape from their political quandary.

The bishops negotiated a deal that has lasted for more than four decades. In essence, they said: "You may use modern farm equipment powered by gasoline engines as long as you pull it with horses, but you may not use self-propelled equipment." The farmer who mounted the first engine on the corn binder described the technological watershed innocently: "I just mounted it [the engine] on to see if it would work. There was no meeting with the ministers and bishops. It didn't make no ruckus." But it was a historic compromise that cleared the way for gasoline engines to be installed on other farm equipment—the hay crimper (1960), corn picker (1965), grass mower (1966), and eventually the roto beater, round baler, and sprayer.

The riddle of pulling modern implements with horses is indeed a compromise between modernity and tradition, a way of keeping the horse in the field and the family on the farm while tapping new power sources to harvest robust crops and increase productivity.

THE BREACH OF 1966

The increased mechanization was welcomed by most farmers, but for some it was too little too late. Their impatience set the stage for the division of 1966. Despite two world wars, the Depression, and rapid social change, things had been relatively quiet among the Amish since the cleavage of 1910. They had struggled with a variety of changes, none of which had induced a schism. The serenity broke in the late 1950s. Pennsylvania farmers were rapidly adopting mechanized field equipment, modern milking machines, and barn cleaners. Banks encouraged Amish farmers to enlarge their operations, and dairy herds were expanding.

Joining the tide of mechanization, Amish farmers in several districts began using haybines, wheat combines, and corn harvesters to harvest their crops. Others installed mechanical barn cleaners to clean manure from their barns. A few enterprising farmers even hooked electric generators to their diesel engines to make 110-volt electricity for light bulbs, home freezers, and appliances.

In 1960, the bishops met and identified six worldly items—combines, forage harvesters, barn cleaners, power units ("Amish tractors"), electric generators, and deep freezers—that they wanted "put away" before they got completely out of hand. Outlawing these items, which had been slipping onto Amish farms, was easier said than done. A number of bishops had difficulty enforcing the decrees, and others were reluctant to act because some of their members had been using the items for several years. The bishops agreed to permit generators to be used for welders, but they would not budge on the other issues.

In the fall of 1962, twenty bishops assembled and agreed once again to prohibit these worldly items. In December 1962, a special all-day meeting of 140 ordained ministers, deacons, and bishops was called to discuss the volatile issues. The bishops gave persuasive talks on the need to "hold the line" on the six items and urged the ministers to help "clean them out." Most of the ordained men supported the eradication effort, but leaders in several districts, obviously hedging, gave qualified responses to the bishops' requests. The hesitant ministers were in a quandary—caught between the requests of senior bishops and the enormous consequences back home if they forced their members to get rid of the six conveniences.[24] Another special Ministers' Meeting in July 1964 also failed to resolve the impasse.

Consequently, during the spring and summer of 1966, about one hundred families severed ties with the Old Order Amish and began worshiping separately. These New Order Amish formed two church districts and by 1967 added a third.[25] They accepted the controversial items and also used tractors in their fields and electricity in their homes. Abandoning another Amish marker, some New Orders placed rubber tires on their tractors and used them not only in the fields but also on the road for errands and shopping. Disagreements over the use of tobacco, cars, and other conveniences eventually fragmented the New Order group, leaving only one viable district by 2000.

Forklifts are widely used in shops to move products. Hard rubber tires are permitted to ease turning on concrete floors. This shop produces steel garbage containers.

MORE TEMPTATIONS

The social fabric of the Old Order Amish has not been rent since 1966—an amazing feat in the face of much subsequent change. Ridding themselves of the progressives in 1966 fortified the Amish taboo on combines, harvesters, barn cleaners, power units, electric generators, and deep freezers. These items remain forbidden by the Ordnung, except that generators may now be used for welders, bulk tanks, and recharging batteries.

Why would barn cleaners appear on the bishops' taboo list? As the dairy herds expanded in the 1950s, barn cleaners became popular. Small paddles, pulled by motor-driven chains, cleaned the manure from gutters in dairy barns and saved an enormous amount of hand labor. The barn cleaners troubled the bishops in three ways: they required electricity, they would leave Amish boys idle, and they were a license for expansion. Farmers who had already doubled their herds from twelve to twenty-four cows would soon be expanding their herds again if they could clean their gutters so easily. Forbidding barn cleaners was a way of braking the burgeoning dairy business. Consequently, the cleaners were banned.

In the 1970s and 1980s, high milk prices and easy credit tempted Amish farmers once again. To the dismay of some leaders, many herds were doubled, with up to forty-eight cows—still a modest number in contrast to the hundred-cow herds of their non-Amish neighbors. Because no one enjoys the sloppy work of cleaning up after four dozen cows, farmers devised two detours around the bishops' taboo on mechanical cleaners. Some cleaned their barns by scraping the manure through the gutters with a cable paddle pulled by a mule. Others installed liquid manure pits by digging "basements" beneath the barns at considerable expense. These liquid manure pits hold the slop as it drains out of the gutters by gravity. The manure is then pumped from the pit into a tank spreader, which scatters it over the fields.

Reflecting on the barn cleaner taboo in light of twenty-five years of history, an Amish minister said that the leaders "made a big mistake with the barn cleaner. They should have never tried to stop it, because these pits and stuff are so expensive." Although they were unwilling to renege on their 1960 decree, leaders did permit Amish farmers to devise alternative ways to clean their barns. These new barn-cleaning methods pay respect to traditional au-

TABLE 9.2
Selected Technological Adaptions by Approximate Date of Use

1930s	Washing machines with gasoline motors	1970s	Modern kitchens
1940s	Chain saws	1980s	Battery-powered tools
	Hiring cars and trucks[a]		Electric cash registers
1950s	Electric tools at construction sites		Electric inverters
	Engines on farm machinery		Forklifts
	Mechanical milking machines		Telephones for shops
	Hay balers		Weed cutters
	Household gas appliances	1990s	Agbags (silage)
1960s	Air and hydraulic power		Air-powered household appliances
	Bulk milk tanks		Beepers
	Community telephones		Hard rubber tires on forklifts
	Flashing lights on buggies		Laser cutters[b]
	Manufacturing equipment		Plasma cutters[b]
1970s	Calculators		Round balers and bale wrappers
	Generators for welders		Voice mail
	Modern bathrooms		Word processors

NOTE: Many of these changes occurred over one or two decades. Dates indicate the approximate time of widespread use. Patterns of use and dates of adoption vary by church district.

[a] Hiring vehicles began in the 1920s but became more widespread after 1950.

[b] Electric laser and plasma cutters are used to cut steel for manufacturing.

thority and, at the same time, ease the burden of work that accompanies a larger herd. It is a gentleman's stand-off. The farmers have respected the letter of the law by not installing mechanical cleaners, and the bishops have respected the dirty work of farming by not clamping down on the new methods, which pay polite deference to tradition.

In order to limit herd size, church leaders added other restrictions for dairy farmers. Amish farmers had been using mechanical milking machines for many years, but they carried the milk to the milk house in buckets. In the 1960s and 1970s many non-Amish farmers replaced their milk buckets with glass pipe lines. Pumped through the pipe lines, the milk flowed directly from the cow stable to an adjacent milk house, thus eliminating the need for buckets. By outlawing these popular pipe lines, church leaders hoped to stifle expansion and preserve work for Amish boys. Furthermore, shiny glass pipes in Amish barns seemed a bit too modern. They looked worldly and certainly seemed out of character with Amish modesty. Today Amish farmers either carry their milk in buckets or transport it in a small wagon-sized tank from the cow stable to the milk house.

Two developments in the 1990s prompted new controversies. Some farmers experimented with large round balers. Instead of creating rectangular bales, the new balers rolled the hay into large bales that could be stored out-side or wrapped in plastic to make haylage. Pulled by horses, these state-of-the-art round balers stirred debate in the church but were gradually accepted in some districts. Another issue surfaced in the summer of 2000, when several farmers took the bold step of replacing their corn binders with modern forage harvesters, pulled by horses. This move created intense controversy because harvesters had been banned in 1966. Ironically, scarce labor was one of the reasons that made the harvesters tempting. Farmers had difficulty finding help because Amish boys were landing well-paying jobs in shops and construction. In any event, the bishops who remembered the earlier ban on harvesters were very annoyed.

The bishops' rejection in the early 1960s of the six items, with the exception of the household freezer, is seen by thoughtful elders as a sincere attempt to arrest social change, limit the size of farm operations, and keep the family on the farm. Describing those pivotal decisions, a farmer said: "I can't give enough credit to our leaders for keeping us back from large equipment, tractors, combines, and harvesters. They stressed not having big equipment and said that if we allow big equipment we'll go in debt and need more land to pay if off and it will break up the family farm."

The division of 1966 became a benchmark in Amish history. It was a time when key understandings became inscribed in the Ordnung. Horses would stay in the field. Plodding symbols of Amish identity, they would set the pace of things and curb expansionist tendencies. Self-propelled harvesters, combines, and haybines were outlawed, probably forever. Modern farm machinery—mowers, balers, sprayers, corn pickers, all powered by engines—would be tolerated if pulled by horses. And so the Amish farmers who baffle Moderns by pulling state-of-the-art balers through the fields with mules are not ridiculous. They are simply yielding to a reasonable compromise with modernity, an agreement that respects tradition, curtails expansion, provides labor, protects ethnic identity, and permits just enough technology for economic growth. It has become a good bargain—one that harnesses the power of progress in creative and positive ways for the welfare of the community.

The Transformation of Amish Work

We're not just backwoods dirt farmers anymore.
—Amish shop owner

THE LEGACY OF THE SOIL

In the later part of the twentieth century, the Amish experienced two trans-formations that had the potential to destroy or bolster their destiny. Sweeping changes in the broader society forced them to grapple with two simple, but profound questions: Who will educate our children? How will we earn a living? Over the years, the answers would determine their fate. Public school consolidation and scarce farmland placed these questions on the bargaining table. The Amish would have preferred the serenity of the past, but the forces of progress were relentless. As we have seen, schooling was nonnegotiable. They refused to relinquish the education of their children. The question of work, however, was different.

At first, the Amish refused to bargain, but gradually they agreed to deal. Ironically, they had refused to budge on public education for fear that it would lead them off the farm. Yet a few years later, a bleak economic scenario led them to hedge on their commitment to farming. Why were they willing to abandon the soil after plowing it for almost three hundred years? What factors led to this historic agreement, which could bring their cultural demise?[1]

The Amish have always been a people of the land. Ever since persecution in Europe pushed them to rural isolation, they have been tillers of the soil— and good ones.[2] The land has nurtured their common life. They have been stewards of the soil—plowing, harrowing, fertilizing, and cultivating it. The springtime fragrance of freshly plowed ground energizes them. They pulverize soil in their fist to test its level of moisture. Whereas all soil looks like dirt to city folks, the Amish have an eye for good soil. The rich limestone soil of Lancaster County, like a magnetic force, holds their community together and ties them to their history. They have tenaciously clung to the soil and have purchased more of it whenever possible.

"Agriculture," according to one leader, "is a religious tenet, a branch of Christian duty." The divine injunction to Adam in Genesis "to till the ground from which he came" provides a religious mandate for farming.[3] The Amish believe that the Bible instructs them to earn their living by the sweat of their brow. Tilling it ushers them into the presence of God. "I don't know what will happen if we get away from the soil," a young farmer said. "I can see where it's not a very good thing. You get away from working with the soil and you get away from nature and then you are getting away from the Lord's handiwork."

Another member argues that the Amish were unable to establish a stable life in North America until they began farming the rich soils of Lancaster County, where they could "live together, worship together, and work together."[4] A businessman explained that "good soil makes a strong church" but worries that a paradox lies below the soil's surface. "The best soil," he said, "holds the best people and makes them a faster people and they become prosperous and the prosperity is not good for the church and so it gets you coming in the back door." He believes that the vitality of the Amish community depends on the quality of the local soil. But he fears that the prosperity germinating in the land will, in the long run, ruin the church with luxury.

An Amish woman who left a farm said, "Leaving it means leaving part of my soul. When you've tilled the soil for generations, the feel of it can never be left behind." Describing her former garden, she said, "On each side were wooded areas. The soil was very good, with a sand-like substance. The garden grew veggies, watermelons, and grapes to perfection. And how I loved it!"

Although the Amish delight in working in it, the soil is not an end in itself; it is the seedbed for Amish families. A persistent theme, extolled by virtually all Amish elders, praises the farm as the best place to raise a family. Even the owners of booming Amish industries repeat the litany of praise for the family farm. Despite satisfaction in their thriving enterprises, businessmen worry about the fate of their grandchildren, growing up away from the farm. Farms provided a habitat for raising sturdy families. Parents and children worked together. Daily chores taught children personal responsibility and the virtue of hard work. Parents were always nearby—directing, supervising, advising, or reprimanding. Pitted against the forces of nature, families forged a strong sense of identity and cohesion. Moreover, the demands of farmwork kept young people at home and limited interaction with the outside world. The family farm was the cradle of Amish socialization—a cradle that until recently held the core of their way of life.

A DEMOGRAPHIC SQUEEZE

Although farming has always been foremost, some Amish settlers had worked as millers, tanners, and brewers. A few Amish have always worked in traditional crafts, such as blacksmithing, carpentry, painting, watch repair, and furniture making.

Nonfarm work evolved gradually after the Depression of the 1930s. As cars gained widespread acceptance and horse travel declined, the Amish developed their own carriage and harness shops and began shoeing their own horses. Amish shops also began repairing horse-drawn machinery in mid-century as tractor farming gained in popularity among other farmers. A few small carpentry shops also developed in the 1950s. The third phase of nonfarm work evolved in the 1970s, when more sizeable cabinet and welding shops emerged.[5]

By the late 1960s and early 1970s, the Amish were caught in a demographic squeeze. Their population had doubled between 1940 and 1960. To accommodate their growth, they bought more farms in the center of the settlement and also began moving into southern Lancaster County.[6] In fact, one public official reported that between 1920 and 1940 the Amish bought every farm on public sale near the hub of their settlement except one, which was sold on a Sunday.[7] The pressure peaked in the late 1960s when eighty young couples started housekeeping in one year and only ten farms were sold on the open market.[8]

The Amish were not the only people desiring land. Lancaster County was the fastest growing metropolitan area in Pennsylvania between 1960 and 1970. Suburbs began nibbling away at prime farmland. The number of tourists jumped from some 1.5 million in 1963 to nearly 4 million a decade later.

Lancaster County was enticing new industry because of its dependable, anti-union labor force as well as its proximity to eastern metropolitan markets. Some thirty-six new industries entered the county between 1960 and 1970.[9] They, of course, needed land and attracted employees who needed housing.

All of these factors increased the squeeze on farmland. The cheap land of the Depression years had turned into gold. In 1940 the Amish were paying between $300 and $400 per acre for farmland.[10] By the early 1970s, farmland had escalated to $2,000 per acre, and it more than doubled again to $4,550 per acre by 1981, and again to $10,000 per acre by 2000.[11] The Amish found themselves in a serious quandary by the mid-1970s: How could they farm without land? At first blush, tourism, suburbs, and industrial expansion were the likely culprits, but that was only half the story. Even if development had frozen, the rapid growth of the Amish themselves would have forced the crisis. In short, there were simply too many babies for too few farms.

THE LUNCHPAIL THREAT

Without a high school diploma, the Amish could not pursue professional jobs. If they left the farm, their training held them to manual work. By 1960, some Amish were already working in shops, warehouses, and even factories. Higher wages made nonfarm work so attractive that a few even rented out their farms to take on "outside" jobs. Church leaders were alarmed. A bishop contended that "the lunchpail is the greatest threat to our way of life." Working in factories was not only frowned upon, it was in fact a test of church membership in the 1940s. In the school controversy of the late 1930s, the Amish repeatedly promised state legislators that they would keep their youth on the farm. Indeed, church members were excommunicated in that era if they worked in cities or nonfarm jobs.[12]

When some Amish began leaving the farm in the 1970s because of scarce land, a bishop worried: "Leave this one generation grow up off the farm, and their sons won't want to farm." In 1975 another bishop articulated his fears this way: "Past experiences have proven that it is not best for Amish people to leave the farm. If they get away from the farm they soon get away from the church, at least after the first generation."[13] The lunchpail threat intensified in the 1960s when mobile home factories were built on the edge of the Amish community to attract hardworking, anti-union Amish and Mennonite employees. By the early 1970s, more than one hundred Amishmen were car-

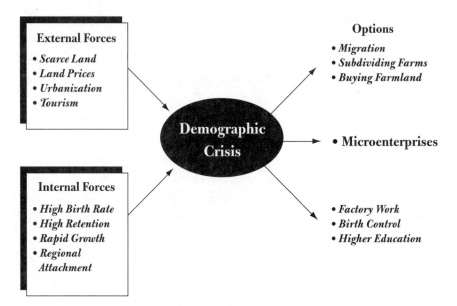

FIGURE 10.1 The Demographic Crisis in the Lancaster Settlement

rying their lunchpails to several nearby plants. But a few years later, an economic recession closed several of the trailer factories, to the quiet applause of Amish leaders.[14]

Why did the factory system, symbolized by the lunchpail, frighten Amish leaders? First, they believed that removing the father from the family during the day would weaken his influence. Without watching their father at work, Amish youth would lose a significant role model. Furthermore, fathers could not supervise children from a factory. Second, the factory might subvert the father's own values. Worldly values, conveyed by non-Amish employees, would undoubtedly tarnish even the most faithful member who spent five days a week in a foreign culture. Third, factory employment threatened community solidarity and social capital. Personnel policies, time cards, and production schedules would make it difficult to participate in community events such as funerals, weddings, barn raisings, and other mutual aid activities. Fourth, the fringe benefits of factory employment—health insurance, retirement funds, and life insurance—would undermine a community that thrived on mutual dependency. With such perks, who would need the support of the church?

The factory, in short, would fragment the family, deplete social capital, and eventually ruin the community. An elderly bishop summed up the dilemma: "It's best for a Christian to be on the farm. When they carry a lunchpail and go to a factory and some places it's not too good, men and women working together and so on. We'd rather have them on the farm but the land just doesn't reach around anymore."

Compared to the stormy school crisis of the 1950s, the occupational quandary of the 1970s was a quiet battle with little publicity or government meddling. But the long-term consequences of Amish work were just as important as schooling. Amish sages knew intuitively that factory work was dangerous. Even some experts predicted that without agriculture, "it is doubtful the Old Order Amish could survive."[15] Nevertheless, the babies kept coming as the acres declined. Was there no escape from the dilemma? The U.S. Supreme Court would not bail the Amish out this time; they would have to find their own way out. Given the harsh facts on the bargaining table, the Amish—with great reluctance—decided to talk.

SIZING UP THE OPTIONS

Was there any middle ground between the stark choice of factory work or financial collapse? There were a variety of alternatives: birth control, migration out of the United States, migration to other regions of the county and state, subdivision of farms, and nonfarm work. Birth control was not a likely option. Although the church had no official position, artificial contraception was generally considered interference with God's will and the natural order. Despite those sentiments, some families use various forms of birth control; however, sizeable families of five to seven children remain highly esteemed. Migration to other countries was never discussed, but the other alternatives were thinkable.

In the midst of the school controversy in the early 1940s, new colonies were established in Lebanon County, some forty miles north of Lancaster, and in St. Mary's County, Maryland.[16] But for the next twenty-five years, Amish migration to other counties stalled. In the 1950s, the Amish began to sprawl southward in Lancaster County, but by 1980 land was becoming scarce there as well. Migration within the county provided only temporary relief from the demographic squeeze. In the mid-1960s, land pressures as well as internal unrest prompted some families to start new settlements in other counties of the state.[17] Land in the new areas could often be purchased for one-fourth its price at home, enabling a farmer to sell a Lancaster farm and buy three or four elsewhere. Nearly a dozen new settlements were spawned from Lancaster by 1980, as shown in Appendix D.

The outward migration abated in the early 1980s, but by then roughly 15 percent of the Lancaster settlement had moved to other counties of the state.[18] Outward migrations began again in the 1990s—this time to Kentucky, Indiana, Wisconsin, and elsewhere. Indeed, by 2000, some 10,000 descendants of Lancaster were living in twenty-eight other settlements. But the migrations still did not relieve the pressure of growth at home.

Subdividing farms provided a second solution. A farm of seventy acres, divided in half, could support two families. Larger farms were sometimes split into three sections. A new house and barn were often erected on each section. A subdivision was frequently accompanied by a shift to specialized farming—vegetable farming, game animals, dog breeding, chickens—that required less land so the family could still cling to the farm, or at least to a corner of it. Outward migration and the subdivision of farms kept families on the land and perpetuated their home-based culture. But these adjustments were not enough.

With the friendly options exhausted, the Amish were finally forced to negotiate. Unwilling to leave Lancaster County en masse, they began to search for nonfarm work. It was not a formal decision by any means, but by 1980 the signals were clear—the Amish would leave the farm rather than migrate. By the 1980s, they were pressuring township supervisors for commercial zoning in the hub of their settlement—a sure sign that they had decided to shift occupations instead of to flee.

PRESERVING HOME WORK

Although the Amish were willing to negotiate the type of work, they refused to budge on the conditions of employment. First, they wanted to work at home or as near to it as possible. Second, they wanted to control the nature and content of their work. Third, they insisted that the work, whenever possible, stay within their ethnic environment. Finally, the work had to remain within the moral order of Amish culture. For example, photography, television repair, jewelry shops, and hair dressing were unthinkable.

Rejecting the lure of factory jobs, the Amish reluctantly agreed to leave the farm if they could retain control of their work. Small shops based at home

TABLE 10.1
Primary Work of Adults (aged 25–65) by Gender (in percentages)

	Women (N = 276)	Men (N = 269)	Combined (N = 545)
Location of work			
At home	91	60	75
Within 1 mile	1	7	4
More than 1 mile	8	18	13
Mobile crew	0	15	8
Employer			
Self	92	70	81
Amish	2	23	13
Non-Amish	6	7	6
Ownership			
Owns a farm	1	39	21
Owns a business	6	30	19
Not an owner	93	31	60

SOURCE: Settlement Profile 2000 (Appendix A).

made a perfect compromise. The Amish would leave their plows behind, but they would not work in large industrial factories owned by outsiders. Instead they would create their own Amish mini-factories—small shops and cottage industries—and keep them nearby home.

Today, about two-thirds of the Amish have abandoned their plows, but some of their jobs support the farm economy.[19] Involvement in nonfarm jobs varies greatly among church districts. In the heart of the settlement, with scarce land and easy commercial access, nonfarm jobs climb beyond 90 percent in some districts. In more rural areas, on the southern fringe of the county, the majority of men are still farming.[20] The percentage of men involved in farming varies by age. About half of the mid-age men are farming, but only a third of those who are under thirty or over fifty years of age are tilling the soil. Nearly 85 percent of adult women consider homemaking their primary work, but many of them have secondary jobs related to crafts, quilts, produce markets, retail stores, or domestic work. About 15 percent find their primary employment in such roles.

The location of Amish work is cross tabulated by gender in Table 10.1. Perhaps the most striking fact is that although fewer Amishmen are plowing fields these days, 60 percent of them are still working at home. Among women the number working at home rises to 91 percent. About 15 percent of the men, but none of the women, travel with mobile construction crews.

Many people are working at or near home even though they are working in cottage industries and retail stores. Thus, despite the transformation, Amish work, for the most part, remains near home.

Even more striking in light of societal trends, married women still work at home. One Amishwoman was very blunt: "You shouldn't be in business if you're married." It is rare to find married women with children who hold a full-time job outside their homes. Many mothers have sideline jobs—such as quilting, baking, craft work, and sewing—but these are usually based at home. Many women are involved in the quilting industry, which often involves several operations at different locations as well as "middle women" who buy and sell quilts.[21] Women and children often tend small roadside stands on their property that sell produce, baked goods, and crafts to tourists and non-Amish neighbors. Some married women hold part-time jobs cooking in restaurants or tending market stands in urban areas several days a week. Increasingly, women are becoming involved in a variety of businesses. Indeed, 17 percent of the hundreds of Amish businesses are owned by women.[22]

Many single females hold a full-time job away from home. Young women who work before marriage and older single women are typically employed outside their home. One older woman harnesses her horse on Sunday morning to travel to church, but on Monday she walks to a small real estate office where she works as a receptionist. She operates the office computer, which in a split second can display real estate listings throughout the country. The more typical pattern is for single women to work as teachers, cooks in restaurants, domestics in motels, bakers in bakeshops, or salesclerks in Amish stores and market stands. Others clean the homes of their non-Amish neighbors.

Farmers often retire at a young age to allow a son to take over the farm. After retirement, a grandfather or grandmother may set up a small shop on the farm for supplemental income. Whenever possible, a father "gets out of the way" so a son can raise his family on the farm, until the process repeats itself in the next generation.

Perhaps even more important than location is the context of work. Amishmen who work away from home carry lunchpails, but not to factory jobs— 70 percent are self-employed, and 23 percent work for an Amish employer. Thus, more than 93 percent of the men work in an Amish environment, as shown in Table 10.1. "Where," asked an Amish businessman rhetorically, "is the best place for these Amish boys to work if they can't all farm? In a big

TABLE 10.2
Primary Work of Adult Men by Age (in percentages)

	Aged 21–30 (N = 107)	Aged 31–40 (N = 81)	Aged 41–50 (N = 67)	Aged 51–60 (N = 39)
Type of work				
Farming	34	53	52	31
Woodworking	22	12	10	23
Metal manufacturing	12	5	5	5
Trades	18	12	8	10
Construction	8	11	8	5
Other	6	7	17	26
Location				
Home	46	63	70	59
Away from home	54	37	30	41
Employer				
Self	48	78	84	60
Amish	41	20	15	24
Non-Amish	11	2	1	16
Ownership				
Owns farm	9	38	54	54
Owns business	18	28	40	36
Not an owner	73	34	6	10

SOURCE: Settlement Profile 2000 (Appendix A).

factory or tobacco warehouse in Lancaster City, or in a small shop with an Amish boss and other Amish employees?"

Those who are not self-employed or working for fellow Amish may be part of an Amish work crew employed by a Mennonite or other Plain-dressing employer. Still others, employed by non-Amish employers, typically work side-by-side with fellow Amish. The Amish rarely work outside of ethnic networks.[23] In the final analysis, although 40 percent of Amish married men work away from home, they usually toil in an ethnic cocoon, which defuses the lunchpail threat. A few work outside the cocoon, but the number is minuscule.[24] Even non-Amish employers are usually local people who are sympathetic to Amish values and willing to adjust to community concerns in exchange for conscientious work.

Given the crescendo of nonfarm jobs in recent years, it is surprising to find so few differences between age groups in Table 10.2. Men under age thirty are more likely to work away from home in nonfarm jobs and less likely to be self-employed than older men. Thus, while nonfarm jobs have increased dramatically in some church districts, the Amish have not relinquished control over the conditions of their work. They were willing to dicker with modernity over the type of work, but they were not about to negotiate its location, control, or ethnic setting.

THE BEST AND WORST OF TIMES

In some ways the turn of the twenty-first century brought the best of times and the worst of times. Tobacco prices were in the cellar, and milk prices hit the dump of a thirty-year low, strangling the income of farmers. Searching for new ways to squeeze an income out of their land, more farmers began raising vegetables, flowers, organically grown chickens, exotic wild animals, and puppies for pet stores. Others were experimenting with yogurt and cheese products. Near Quarryville, about two dozen Amish farmers formed a milk cooperative. They bought milk processing equipment from Israel with hopes of making kosher milk products—yogurt and cheese—for Orthodox Jews in New York City.

Meanwhile, businesses were pulsing with profits, enticing more and more farm boys to abandon their cows and plows. In the heart of the settlement, one observer counted ten dairy barns with empty stables. The Amish were still farming the land, but they had turned to their shops for their primary income. In another township, a farmer sold his cows and rented his land to a non-Amish farmer so he could build storage sheds. A non-Amish neighbor worried about these ominous trends that "might destroy the Amish way of life." The economic woes of farming made the good fortunes of business even more attractive to aspiring young lads. Farming required an enormous investment for land, animals, and equipment. It was simply easier, cheaper, and more profitable to set up a shop than to go into farming.

An ironic turn followed the sagging fortunes of farmers. The wealthier businessmen were beginning to amass enough capital to buy more farms. One business owner was pleased that he could buy a farm for each of his four daughters. Between 1984 and 1996 the Amish bought nearly 180 farms totaling some 15,000 acres. By the mid-1990s they were buying about 20 farms a year. At the turn of the century, they owned some 1,400 farms—about 40 percent of the farms in Lancaster County.[25]

And so in an ironic twist of fate, the Amish who had entered business because of dwindling acres were now able to buy more land with their newly earned dollars. But twenty new farms a year were hardly enough to turn the tide with 170 couples pledging wedding vows each fall. Nevertheless, Amish

For new sources of income, this farmer began building storage sheds and
rented land for a cellular telephone tower.

purchases helped the countywide effort to preserve farm land. Public officials
are quick to point out that the Amish are a powerful force for farmland preservation because they rarely sell their land for development.

Two agencies in Lancaster County actively seek to preserve farmland: the
Agricultural Preserve Board, a government agency; and Lancaster Farmland

Trust, a private agency. Reluctant to accept government funds, the Amish have been more willing to cooperate with the Trust because of its private status. The first Amish farm was preserved in 1990, and by 2000, the Trust held easements protecting forty-seven Amish farms. Although skittish about receiving $2,100 per acre in government funds from the Agriculture Preserve Board, three Amish farmers stepped across the line and preserved their farms in 2000. Others were reportedly filing applications with the Agricultural Preserve Board, signaling a new openness among a few Amish to accept government funds to save their land.[26] Thus, on top of their rising fortunes in business, the Amish are also holding a growing portion of Lancaster County soil.

BUSINESS ENTERPRISES

When asked what you cannot buy these days from an Amish shop, an old sage wryly remarked: "About the only thing we don't have is an undertaker." While not quite true, his quip symbolizes the mushrooming infrastructure of Amish-owned services. The Amish own shops that sell shoes, dry goods, furniture, hardware, and wholesale foods. Amishmen work as masons, plumbers, painters, and self-trained accountants. The explosion of nonagricultural jobs has ushered in a new era of Amish history. Instead of depending on outsiders for the bulk of their services, they have developed their own capacity to supply many of the services and products needed within their community.[27] A streak of modernity lies beneath this ethnic umbrella, for some functions that were previously done at home are now performed by a specialist, albeit an Amish one. This extensive web of shops built on networks of social capital provides jobs and financial revenues, and also creates a buffer zone with the larger culture.

Amish enterprises vary in size, location, and function. The three major types are small cottage industries, larger manufacturing establishments, and mobile work crews. Home-based operations, often located on farms, are housed in tobacco sheds, retrofitted farm buildings, or new facilities. Bakeshops, craft shops, machine shops, cabinet shops, hardware stores, health food shops, and flower shops are a few of the hundreds that are adjacent or annexed to a barn or house. Many home-based retail shops cater to tourists, Amish, and non-Amish neighbors alike. These shops, like the old mom-and-pop grocery stores of bygone America, are largely family operations. A sampler of the shops appears in Table 10.3.

TABLE 10.3
A Sampler of Amish-operated Shops and Businesses

Air pumps and systems	Furniture	Plumbing
Bakery	Greenhouses	Printing
Battery and electrical	Groceries	Quilts
Beekeeping supplies	Hardware	Retail stores
Bookstores	Hat manufacturing	Roadside stands
Butchering	Health foods	Roofing and spouting
Cabinetry	Horseshoeing	Sawmills
Carriage	Household appliances	Spray painting
Clock and watch repair	Hydraulic systems	Storage buildings
Construction	Lantern manufacturing	Storm windows and glass
Crafts	Leather and harness	Tin fabrication
Drygoods	Log house construction	Tombstone engraving
Engine repair	Machinery assembly	Toys
Fence installation	Machinery manufacturing	Tree trimming
Floor covering	Machinery repair	Upholstery
Foundry	Masonry	Vegetable plants

One young father, for example, operates a washing machine shop in an oversized garage on his farm. He buys used washing machines and replaces their electric motors with solid-state ignition gasoline engines from Japan. The refurbished washing machines are sold to Amish customers. A cabinet maker works with four of his sons making quality kitchen cabinets that are distributed out of the county. Several adults—an uncle, a cousin, or a sister— may assist the nuclear family as part- or full-time employees in the cottage industries. Children help or hinder the operation, as the case may be. These microenterprises, lodged at home, range in size from one to a half-dozen employees. One thing is certain: work in these settings is securely under the family's control. "What we're trying to do, really," said one proprietor, "is keep the family together."[28]

Larger shops or manufacturing concerns are established in newly erected buildings on the edge of a farm or on a plot with a house. Some manufacturing plants are beginning to locate in small industrial parks to avoid zoning hassles. This trend will likely lead work farther away from home. The size-able shops, with a dozen or so employees, function as established entities in the larger business community. On the other hand, blacksmith shops and welding shops that manufacture horse-drawn equipment cater primarily to the Amish. But the bulk of the new businesses, such as cabinet shops and hydraulic shops, serve both Amish and non-Amish customers alike. Many

An Amishwoman owns and operates this shop. She makes dried flower
arrangements that are shipped out of state. A horse barn is on the left.
Her adjacent home is not shown.

retail outlets—hardware, paint, furniture, and food stores—also sell to both
groups. Woodworking shops produce fine furniture as well as portable storage barns, doghouses, lawn furniture, and mailboxes, all of which are sold
across the eastern seaboard to non-Amish customers. Some businesses sell
their products to large national chains such as Wal-Mart and K-Mart.

The larger manufacturing shops are efficient and modern. At first glance,
hanging gas lanterns provide the only clue to their Amish ownership. Air and
hydraulic power operate modern machinery. Diesel engines power the air
and hydraulic pumps. Even burglar alarms are powered by air. One Amishman argued that air pressure is superior to electricity and that "some
shops have electric systems beat hand over fist. That's all there is to it. They
even have their doors rigged up to an alarm. You know, if someone breaks in
at night, they have air alarms all over the place that will blow a horn loud
enough to scare a thief half to death."

Mobile work crews are the third type of Amish enterprise. Amish construction crews travel to building sites in Lancaster County and other counties as well. Carpentry and construction work have always been acceptable
alternatives to farming. Today, woodworking of one sort or another scores

second only to farming as the most preferred occupation. Amish construction crews, using the latest power tools operated by portable electric generators or onsite electricity, engage in subcontract and general construction of both residential and commercial buildings. Trucks and vans provided by employees or regularly hired drivers transport Amish work crews on a daily basis. Amish cabinet shops produce high-quality furniture, which is distributed out of state.

As the Amish have struggled to keep their work at home and their families together, they have encountered another modern obstacle: zoning. Ironically, the zoning laws that once protected their farms from outside developers now prevent some of them from building shops on their own farms. The proliferation of cottage industries and small manufacturing operations, often built in agricultural zones, have caused some tension with public officials. In the 1980s and 1990s several townships negotiated with the Amish, hoping to adapt zoning codes that would control the size of on-farm businesses in rural areas. Under pressure from the Amish, one township amended its agricul-

Hundreds of gazebos are made by this and other woodworking shops. They are shipped out of state by tractor trailer trucks. The panels near the roof lines help to illuminate the interior of the shop, which has no electric lights.

tural zoning ordinance to permit home industries that did not exceed 2,500 square feet or employ more than four workers, including the owner. Another township has a limit of two nonfamily employees.[29] It was an interesting twist, because modern law and government were being used to enforce Amish values of small-scale operations and family involvement. Because of zoning restrictions and their booming size, some businesses are moving into industrial parks.

THE TEXTURE OF AMISH BUSINESS

Amish industries bear the imprint of Amish culture in several ways. They are typically small. Although there is not an exact cap on size, it is rare for them to have more than fifteen employees. Church leaders caution owners about the dangers that accompany large-scale operations—pride, worldliness, excessive power, publicity, and status. Many Amish industries have annual sales exceeding $1 million; the largest ones likely reach $8–$12 million. Discreet expansion is more acceptable than a large complex of buildings, which gives the appearance of too much success. Installing cabinets or building silos around the county is less conspicuous and thus more palatable than operating a large manufacturing complex on one site with a hundred employees. Stories are told of Amish business owners who, refusing to bend to the limits of size, became proud and eventually left the church or were excommunicated. Describing one of these casualties, a businessman said: "You just have to be careful not to get proud wings and spread them like Ike Smoker did. That just won't fit. You need to keep your humility and keep your head down under the covers."

Even the largest businesses employ primarily fellow Amish. The non-Amish employees are frequently members of other Plain churches with similar cultural values. Sometimes outsiders are hired for the use of their vehicles or for particular technical skills. One businessman regretted hiring a non-Amish employee who created problems with his Amish employees, and since then he has hired within the fold.

Table 10.3 lists typical Amish businesses. Products ranging from mushrooms to plastic toys can be bought in Amish stores. Hundreds of Amish-made products—from finely sculptured cornhusk dolls to clumsy manure spreaders—are available for sale. In general, the products and services fit with Amish values. Selling and repairing radios, for instance, would be off limits, as would car, computer, or video sales. Selling new chain saws and barbecue grills is acceptable because these are used by the Amish themselves. Farm equipment is sometimes manufactured by Amish shops in two versions—a steel-wheeled edition for the Amish and a rubber-tired one for their neighbors. The taboo on electricity makes it difficult to sell refrigerated or frozen food products. Various trades, crafts, woodworking, construction, and manufacturing jobs as well as retailing provide the majority of nonfarm jobs. Few Amish work in service or information roles that require formal education and extensive interaction with the outside world.

An inventive streak runs through Amish culture. A tinkering attitude, the taboo on electricity, and a bent for self-sufficiency have stimulated dozens of inventions. For example, a manufacturer developed a hay turner that flips hay upside down and speeds its drying time in the field.[30] Other inventions include a horse-drawn plow with a wheel-driven hydraulic pump that presses the blade into the soil; a frost-free outdoor watering trough for cattle that uses the earth's natural heat to prevent freezing in the winter; a high-pressure sprayer to clean buildings; a golf course cupper to drill holes on the green; and a machine that wraps large hay bales in plastic. An Amish shop developed and manufactures its own 12-volt Pequea battery. The list goes on and on.

One thing is clear: the feeble repair shops of yesteryear have been superseded by manufacturing facilities that enable the Amish to manufacture most of their horse-drawn equipment and to supply other products to non-Amish around the world. One snag worries a leading manufacturer. He fears that newer manufacturing equipment, increasingly dependent on computerized controls, may be difficult to convert to air and hydraulic power and thus may limit Amish productivity.

The bishops, who had stubbornly insisted on horse-drawn equipment in the early 1960s, inadvertently seeded a host of new jobs in the Amish shops that build and refabricate farm machinery. In the same manner, Amish clothing, horse and buggy transportation, and the rejection of electricity have fostered innumerable jobs that serve the special needs of Amish society. These new jobs have diminished the lure of working in modern factories. The technological riddles that baffle outsiders not only defer to tradition but also create a panoply of jobs for Amish families. Although many nonfarm jobs produce products for the larger society, agricultural support and ethnic specialty jobs still undergird the economy of Amish society.

BUSINESS SUCCESS

A remarkable thing had happened by the turn of the twenty-first century: barefoot Amish farmers had become successful businessmen. Even more astonishing, they had done it in one generation without the help of high school, let alone college, and without computers, electricity, or courses in accounting, marketing, and management. Moreover, their failure rate for new business starts was less than 5 percent compared to a national rate of 60 percent. How did these backwoods farmers manage to turn their plows into profits?

Within one generation Lancaster County had witnessed, in the words of one observer, "a mini-industrial revolution." The Amish were no longer selling homemade root beer, brooms, and dolls in roadside stands. The fledgling shops of the 1970s had abruptly come of age. One Amishman compared the old with the new this way: "[The old cabinet makers] would start with a pile of 1 × 12 white pine boards, a small gas powered table saw, a box of cigars and lots of muscle. Nowadays over twenty large shops produce 800 storage sheds and thirty gazebos a week."[31] This yields some 40,000 items a year in only one of many product lines. About fifty Amish cabinet shops each produce fifteen to a hundred new kitchens every year. No longer restricted to the corner of an old tobacco shed, the larger businesses occupy 20,000- to 30,000-square-foot areas in spanking new facilities.

The number of establishments offers another measure of success. On average there are about twelve businesses in each church district, totaling some 1,600 enterprises across the settlement.[32] Indeed, one in five adults (aged 25–65) owns a business. With more and more youth entering business, the number rises every year. In addition to their negligible failure rate, all signals suggest financial success. A bank official, knowledgeable of Amish finances, said, "The huge wealth created by Amish businesses in recent years is simply staggering." A credit officer concurred: "The wealth generated in the Amish community in the last ten years is just fantastic, it's phenomenal." According to one financial observer, the top ten Amish businesses likely have annual sales of $8–$12 million and most of those net 10 percent, or about $1 million in profit.[33] The bulk of Amish enterprises have lower annual sales, but gross receipts of a million are not unusual.

The credit record of the Amish in the local financial community is enviable. An attorney who works closely with them knows of no suits against

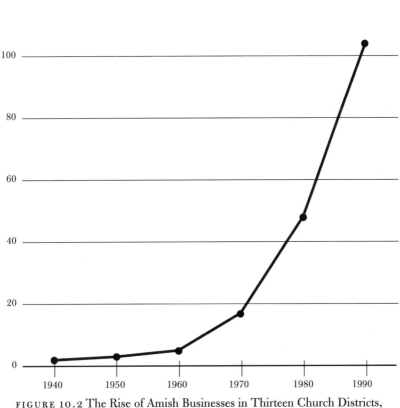

FIGURE 10.2 The Rise of Amish Businesses in Thirteen Church Districts, 1940–1990. *Source:* Amish Enterprise Profile (Appendix A).

them for bad debts. A credit officer who loans millions of dollars annually to the Amish has "never had to foreclose on a bad loan." Another banker said, "I never lost a dime lending to the Amish" in over fifteen years with a loan portfolio averaging $30 million.

What are the sources of the surprising success of these shops with humble beginnings that eschew electric power, computers, and trucks? The roots of success are both external and internal to Amish society.[34] External factors include a strong regional economy, positive public perceptions of Amish products, a sizeable tourist market, and cooperative public officials, as well as payroll exemptions for Social Security and Worker's Compensation.

Internal factors propelling the success include the pool of cultural and social capital in Amish society—a rural heritage of entrepreneurial values, a strong work ethic, religious values of austerity and simplicity, cultural taboos on education and certain forms of technology, family involvement, ethnic networks, small-scale operations, product uniqueness and quality, as well as an effective system of apprenticeship. All of these factors both within and beyond Amish society have bolstered their entrepreneurial success. Ample social capital was an important resource that enabled them to develop economic capital and achieve financial success.

The success has been aided by a supportive infrastructure both within and beyond the community. Within the community, a growing specialization of skills and shops provides the expertise to develop and operate sizeable enterprises. Numerous shops, for example, specialize in adapting modern equipment to hydraulic or air power. Beyond the local skill base, an infrastructure of external suppliers and dealers brings raw materials to Amish shops and distributes finished products across the country. Some of the national lumber companies send their best sales people and finest lumber to Amish country. Likewise a network of non-Amish dealers distribute products far and wide. An annual trade market brings hundreds of wholesale buyers from across the country to inspect hundreds of Amish products in one location. In reverse fashion, outside vendors bring samples of their latest equipment to the same site for Amish shop owners to inspect. The growing infrastructure has provided an important base for the booming growth of Amish business.

How will growing Amish businesses cope with the traditional limit on size and the restriction on using computers? One outside financial observer predicted that sizeable businesses may be sold off to outside buyers. Indeed, several large businesses have already been sold to outsiders. One successful owner reportedly sold his business for "millions" and bought a thousand acres of farmland in Indiana. He then sold some of the land back to other Amish families. In other cases, profits from selling off a business are invested in new enterprises within the community.

Two restraints imposed by Amish culture ironically play an important role as well. The taboo on higher education gives Amish men only two possible career tracks: farming or business. With professional careers off the screen, many of the brightest and best head into business. The would-be surgeons, lawyers, pilots, professors, and computer gurus end up creating their own businesses with enormous energy and ingenuity. Moreover, the Amish insistence on small-scale operations keeps businesses small and spreads entrepreneurship far and wide across the settlement. Instead of a few large factories, hundreds of people run businesses and enjoy the delights of entrepreneurship. And for those employees who are not at the throttle of the business, they are nevertheless close to the action and part of a small team effort. In different ways all of these factors have contributed to the profitability of Amish business.

THE FATE OF A RURAL PEOPLE

The occupational transformation underway in the Lancaster settlement is the most profound and consequential change since the arrival of the Amish in North America. Its long-term consequences will fundamentally alter a way of life that for more than two and a half centuries has been anchored in a rural, separatist culture. One social scientist has called the small cottage industries—not to mention the larger ones—a Trojan horse in Amish society.[35]

Human groups are resilient and dynamic, making it impossible to predict the long-term impact of this occupation swing. The Amish in particular are adept at creating new symbolic boundaries to protect their identity. How they will fare over the generations and what form their identity will take in the coming years is unclear, but one thing is certain: the transformation of work will change every aspect of their life. It is one thing for first-generation farmers to start successful businesses and abide by traditional cultural values; but it is quite something else to pass separatist values over several generations of entrepreneurs.

In some ways, nonfarm jobs have enhanced the vitality of community life. For example, they have increased the Amish population density. Single-dwelling houses on small lots have greatly reduced the geographical size of some church districts, which enhances face-to-face interaction. This reinforces the oral base and social ties of Amish culture as well as the practicality of horse-and-buggy travel because family and friends are nearby. With fellow Amish closer together, the dialect constantly reaffirms the sectarian worldview and provides a buffer against modern ways. In these ways the occupational changes have embellished community solidarity, replenished social capital, and fortified Amish identity.

Moreover, small-scale businesses and family-operated industries provide flexible work schedules that accommodate the community's predictable and unexpected needs. Requests to attend a half-dozen all-day weddings in November, welcomed with delight by an Amish proprietor, might annoy the human resource department of a mainstream corporation. Although they may seem numerous, the "community days" taken by Amish employees hardly exceed the sick days, personal days, and holiday time used by modern employees. Small Amish industries can more easily respond to community needs for volunteer help at frolics, barn raisings, or disasters than large corporate industries. Employees in Amish businesses forgo the perks of hospitalization and retirement benefits, which increases their dependence on the ethnic community.

In all of these ways, the new industries are truly Amish in character—designed to serve the needs of the community rather than those of the individual. And yet, paradoxically, the individual is also served rather well—with high levels of job satisfaction, a humane work environment, a high degree of control over production, and ethnic pride in the product. Alienation between employee and employer, typical of some contemporary work, is largely absent in the smaller shops.

Although the rise of Amish shops has stalled the lunchpail threat, the long-term consequences of this shift in the structure of Amish life are unknown. Small, home-based cottage industries promise few disruptions to traditional Amish values, even in the long run. However, the ramifications of the retailing and manufacturing businesses that exceed a half-dozen employees and boast multimillion-dollar sales are a different story. Amish leaders, including some proprietors, are uneasy about the debilitating social effects of these ventures. Dependence on daily wages and the press of production schedules in Amish factories may eventually create complications with community activities, even with sympathetic managers. An employee whose household budget depends on daily wages may find it difficult to forgo a whole day's wage to attend a wedding or frolic. Even Amish businessmen, under the stress of tight production schedules, may become reluctant to release employees for barn raisings or family reunions.

Amish manufacturing establishments and construction firms follow typical business routines with fixed hours and policies. Traditional farm work often requires sixteen-hour workdays during planting and harvest. Church leaders worry that the spare time afforded by an eight-hour workday will lead employees, especially youth, into questionable recreation. A major Amish retailer voiced his anxiety: "The thing that scares me the most is the seven-to-five syndrome with evenings free. Our people, not just the young ones, have too much leisure time, and money in their pockets. In the past we were always more or less tied within a small radius of home because there were always chores. I even thought that Pop raised some weeds for us to pull." Traditional Amish attitudes toward work and leisure will certainly change as the exodus from the farm continues.

Family size typically declines during industrialization because children, no longer needed for farm work, become an economic liability. A decline in family size would certainly temper Amish population growth. Although Amish families have shrunk a bit from their mid-twentieth-century size, they still average six or seven children. Children currently are involved in home-based industries, but all that could change over time.

Furthermore, even though young fathers are working within a mile of their families, they are nevertheless away from home. Despite a supportive ethnic system, some leaders worry that this will have a detrimental effect on child rearing. Children will no longer work with, or learn occupational skills from, their fathers; and mothers will carry a greater burden for child supervision. In a word, business involvements will surely change child-rearing practices.

Gender relations are under flux as well. As noted before, women own about 17 percent of the Amish businesses. In a patriarchal society this will induce some changes as women have more access to money, other resources, and the outside world. Women, in short, are gaining more power, and this will likely impact their broader influence within the community as well. Although some couples work together in their business ventures, many do not. In modern fashion, this eliminates the preindustrial type of partnerships that many Amish couples enjoyed on the farm. As more and more work leaves the home, work-based marital partnerships will dissolve. Women, for example, typically had joint legal ownership of farmland; but if a husband owns a business, his wife is rarely a joint owner.

The Pennsylvania German dialect will face greater contamination and decline as business involvements grow. Many business owners use English throughout the day as they interact with suppliers, consultants, sales people, dealers, and customers. More and more technical English words are seeping into the dialect. Children of business owners tend to learn English at an earlier age because of exposure to outsiders. Greater interaction with English

Sometimes called "The Wal-Mart" of Amish stores, this large retail store at three locations sells food in large sizes and damaged containers. Solar panels in the roof help to illuminate the interior.

speakers will obviously dilute the dialect over time and may shrink it to a sacred language, retained only for services on Sunday.

The COME IN, WE'RE OPEN signs on doors of Amish stores, the growing advertising used by some enterprises, and the daily contact with customers signal an openness and involvement with the outside world that is unprecedented in Amish history. Indeed Olshan notes that it is hard to imagine a more graphic denial of the claim to separation than the COME IN, WE'RE OPEN signs.[36] Never before have the Amish interacted so freely and so willingly with the larger society. Moreover, the commercial involvements are creating an economic dependence on outside markets that challenge longstanding principles of separation from the world. Will it be possible in the long run to have growing economic integration and still retain a semblance of social separation?

The greater interaction with the outside world will bring greater temptations related to technology. The Amish have carefully screened technology for its debilitating effects on community, but easy interaction with the larger world will make it more tempting to accept communicative technology—telephone, radio, television. As global commerce becomes increasingly dependent on the Internet, the use of computers will be a growing temptation. All of these factors will stretch, if not snap, traditional "understandings" of the Ordnung.

The rapid migration into business is not only transforming Amish values, but it is also creating a three-tiered society. The Amish have never advocated communitarian equality, and as one Amishman noted, "There have always been a few wealthy Amish." Nevertheless, the traditional farm economy placed everyone on equal social footing. All of that has changed. The ventures into commerce are producing a three-class society based on a triad of occupations: traditional farmers, business owners, and day laborers. The farmers have collateral wealth in their land but often meager cash in their hand. Farm families in general tend to be more conservative, reflecting the Plainer more traditional values. Day laborers in shops and farms have a steady cash flow but do not have significant wealth. Shop workers may earn $30,000 or more a year and enjoy a comfortable standard of living within the confines of Amish economy. The major business owners represent a new commercial class that heretofore has been unknown in Amish society. They bring the greatest challenge to traditional ways.

THE NEW COMMERCIAL CLASS

Despite an eighth-grade education, the members of the emerging commercial class are bright, astute managers. Some have taken special training in technical areas, such as hydraulics or fiberglass. Through self-motivation and experience, they have, within one generation, become proficient managers. Their stunning success in many ways validates the merits of their eighth-grade education. They understand the larger social system and interact easily with suppliers, business colleagues, customers, attorneys, and credit officers. They have learned basic management procedures and how to develop marketing strategies and calculate profit ratios. They walk a delicate tightrope between the boundaries of traditional Amish culture and the need to operate their business in a profitable manner. Reflecting on the electricity taboo, the young owner of a retail store said: "There is a whole new group of young shop owners who think some of the old traditional distinctions are foolish!" In the heat of a legal transaction, one business owner muttered to his attorney, "Business is business, and religion is religion," signaling a breech between the historical integration of faith and work in Amish life. Such thinking among this managerial class may destabilize Amish life in several ways.

First, managers, immersed in the daily logic of the business world, may become disenchanted with traditional Amish values. Will they, for instance, be satisfied on Sunday mornings with the slow cadence of Amish hymns and pleas for humility when their daily work intersects with the aggressive cut-throat world of commerce? How long will they pay polite deference to Ordnung rulings that obstruct rational planning and profits? One successful Amish entrepreneur was described by a banker as having "nine toes in the world and one toe in the church."

Second, this emergent class represents a new, informal power structure in Amish society. The financial achievements of this class earns it both respect and envy within Amish ranks. In some cases business owners have greater freedom to modernize their operations than farmers, because they are less constrained by longstanding rulings.[37] The fact that many ministers and some bishops are now business owners provides both understanding and leniency with business issues. Business knowledge and organizational savvy arm this new breed of Amish with a power base that, if organized, could pose a serious threat to the bishops' traditional clout.

Third, business owners often feel caught in the cross fire of traditional values and economic pressures. They know that aggressive promotion will enhance profits, yet church leaders criticize and even excommunicate them if they expand too fast. Commenting on a rapidly growing business, a cynical entrepreneur said, "Wait till they start making money, then the church will throw the Ordnung at them." One owner, under fire from church leaders for his booming business, voiced his frustration at being torn between business opportunity and small-scale values: "My own people look at my growth as a sign of greed—that I'm not satisfied to limit my volume. The volume bothers them. The Old Order Amish are supposed to be a people who do not engage in big business, and I'm right on the borderline right now. I'm a little over the line and maybe too large for Amish standards. My people think evil of me for being such a large businessman and I don't need any more aggravation right now." However, struggling with the delicate tensions, he continued: "Identity, having a people, is a very precious thing."

Business owners also find themselves in fiscal quandaries that force them to use the law to protect their own interests—a traditional taboo in Amish culture. The Amish use lawyers to draw up farm deeds, wills, and articles of incorporation and to transfer real estate. However, filing lawsuits is cause for excommunication. Following the suffering Jesus, in the spirit of nonresistance, the Amish traditionally have suffered injustice rather than resort to legal force.

Such humility defies normal business practice and makes Amish owners vulnerable to exploitation. "You know," said a businessman, "we are in a bind, being in business. When you deal with the business community you are at a distinct disadvantage, because there are those who would take advantage of you." Already the victims of shrewd debtors, entrepreneurs are asking their attorneys to write threatening letters and using legal means to recover unpaid debts, but they usually stop short of filing lawsuits. One Amishman, bilked by an out-of-state dealer for several gazebos, sent one of his drivers to pick them up under the cover of darkness and bring them home. Whether business owners will be able to retain nonresistant values in the midst of cutthroat competition is unknown.

Fourth, many of the new commercial class are doing well financially. "The old graybeards have no idea how much money is flowing around in this community," one banker noted. The more successful entrepreneurs earn several hundred thousand dollars a year.[38] One business owner paid $117,000 on personal taxes alone. In another example, a furniture shop owner earned $340,000 in profit in one year. Some construction foremen may make $65,000 a year, while their Amish boss makes upwards of $200,000. Meanwhile, however, many farmers and shop workers are only earning $35,000. Given modest Amish standards of living, such income levels generate considerable wealth.

Where does all the money go? Mostly into real estate, business expansion, community needs, loans within the community, mutual funds, and savings accounts.[39] Some of the newly rich are building expensive homes by Amish standards that cost upwards of $250,000. Historically the Amish have not invested in individual stocks, but in recent years hundreds of them have invested in mutual funds. One mutual fund manager noted that some of the "bigger business owners leave mutual funds because they want to be more aggressive with their investments. They are greedy and so they go to stockbrokers." However, not everyone is greedy. An employee of a very profitable

The office of a sizeable business. The word processor, calculator, and Rolodex symbolize the rational worldview of successful entrepreneurs.

Amish business said his boss would not build a new expensive house, "because he thinks it's not right with so many poor people in the world." However, the swelling wealth in a small circle may erode social equality over time.

Will Amish millionaires be content to drive horses and dress in Plain clothing over several generations? Inexperienced in coping with the inequalities of wealth, the church is uncertain how to respond to the new commercial class. In the past, modest profits from farming were reinvested in farming operations and used to help children establish their own farms. Revenues from Amish businesses were typically invested in real estate, used to buy new farms, or contributed to needs within the ethnic community, rather than invested in the stock market or devoured by conspicuous consumption. An Amishman in another settlement describes the Lancaster Amish as being "almost hyper about making money . . . some businesses are very successful and handling A LOT of cash and are RICH period. This affects the types of houses they build for themselves and for their children, where they travel, where they eat, and what they own."

Using outside standards of success, Amish businesses appear to be doing quite well. But success is not a favorite word among the Amish. Indeed, some elders worry that the pursuit of profit may be an ugly worm inside the rosy apple of Amish success. Bishops and businessmen alike fear that in the long run prosperity could ruin the church. Some church leaders believe prosperity is as dangerous as persecution. "Pride and prosperity," said one elder, "could do us in." Will the church be able to motivate the wealthy commercial class to use their resources for community enhancement rather than for self-indulgence?

The occupational bargain that the Amish struck in the 1980s when they left their plows for cottage industries has served them well for a generation. It kept their work within their control and allowed it to flourish in the context of family and community. However, it remains uncertain whether this was a good compromise or a worm that will eat their soul from within over time. Will the transformation of work undermine community stability and erode Amish identity? Furthermore, many of the regulatory concessions that the modern world has made for the Amish—for instance, in schooling and Social Security—were based on the premise that they were self-employed farmers. As they become successful entrepreneurs, legislative tolerance and leniency may also wane.

C H A P T E R

Managing Public Relations

There's more tourists than plow furrows, more flies than tourists.
—Amish farmer

THE PARADOX OF SEPARATION

Groups that hope to resist modernization must regulate the interaction of their members with the outside world. This chapter explores the ties and patterns of interaction between Amish society and the larger world. Although the church regulates the participation of individual members in the dominant society, there are also systemic bonds—contracts and patterns of economic exchange—that fuse the two social systems together.

The Amish have always emphasized separation from the world. This historic religious belief has taken an ironic twist in the throes of modernization, producing yet another riddle. The rejection of mass media, modern dress, higher education, and electricity has widened the gap between the Amish and the outside world. Yet at the same time the Amish are more entangled with the larger economic system than ever before. How is it that the cultural gap widened as the economic systems merged? Moreover, as Amish dependency on the larger society increased, a mutual dependency also emerged. Today they not only lean on the larger society, but it also leans on them. How did the larger society come to rely on the Amish?

As the Amish modernized their farming, created their own industries, and adopted more contemporary lifestyles, their dependency on the larger society increased. Farmers use the telephone to call veterinarians, to order fertilizer, and to check weather forecasts before making hay. Amish housewives cook with Teflon pans, buy butane gas for their stoves, use disposable diapers, clean with detergents, and buy permanent-press fabrics. Many households depend on income from the sale of quilts, produce, crafts, and baked goods to non-Amish. Amish business owners lean on commercial suppliers for raw materials, the latest machine technology, and the modern transportation system to deliver their products. Because they borrow from commercial banks, Amish fortunes fluctuate as interest rates rise and fall. When milk and tobacco prices dip, Amish profits fall. Business sales vacillate with the costs of transportation, raw materials, diesel fuel, and competing products. In all of these ways, the Amish are dependent on the larger society. Indeed, without these economic ties, Amish society in its present form would collapse.

The Amish also use the services of professionals—physicians, dentists, optometrists, accountants, lawyers, morticians—as well as those of banks, hospitals, and real estate agencies. They rely less on professionals than Moderns do, but they could barely function without the aid of such experts. Furthermore, the vitality of Amish society is indebted to the technological achievements of the scientific age. Antibiotics and other medicines have cut their infant mortality rate and increased the longevity of their elderly, both of which have contributed to their growth. Artificial insemination of dairy cows, hybrid seeds, chemical fertilizers, veterinary medicines, pesticides, and the careful management of flocks and herds have all boosted agricultural output. The use of the latest welding, fabricating, carpentry, and manufacturing equipment enables Amish businesses to compete successfully in the broader marketplace. In all of these areas, Amish success hinges on the services and advancements of the larger society. They do not live in a closed society; indeed, they are deeply entangled in the economic systems of American society.

Ironically, as the systemic links tightened, the cultural gap widened. Amish sages agree that the gulf between their life and that of their non-Amish neighbors is wider today than ever. With the rise of Amish schools in the 1960s, a new generation of Amish grew up without the influence of non-Amish teachers and non-Amish friends. An Amishman described the growing separation between the two cultures: "Oh yes, there's a stronger separation today, oh yes, oh certainly, and it's growing faster all the time." Over the years, the cultural distance between the two worlds has widened. As the worlds pulled apart, the economic ties tightened—all of which produced the puzzle of a separate people who are enmeshed in the modern economy. In short, cultural separation increased, and economic separation declined.

The Amish use banks and other professional services.

CIVIC AND SOCIAL INVOLVEMENT

The Amish have many friendly relationships with non-Amish neighbors. Businessmen deal with a variety of non-Amish clients, suppliers, and professionals on a daily basis. But the relationships, though pleasant and cordial, have limits. They rarely lead to romantic involvements, intimate sharing, or religious cooperation. The church's ability to regulate attire, control participation in public organizations, and maintain the dialect has reinforced Amish separation from the world.

Amish participation in outside organizations is selective, informal, and locally based. They usually do not hold public office or join civic organizations such as service clubs, country clubs, Boy Scouts, 4-H clubs, Little League softball teams, or the Red Cross. Membership in professional organizations is also restricted. Amish farmers are even discouraged from joining the Dairy Herd Improvement Association. Those who do join are careful not to have their achievements publicized. A few business owners are members of the Lancaster Chamber of Commerce, and a half-dozen or so are members of the Pennsylvania Dutch Convention and Visitors Bureau. As noted before, the Amish often join volunteer fire companies in many communities. Fire company benefit auctions are frequently staffed and supported by the Amish in a pleasant partnership with their neighbors.

Before World War I, an Amishman, in a rare instance, served as postmaster in a rural village.[1] However, holding public office is typically taboo because it involves an "unequal yoking" with the larger world. In the first half of the twentieth century, Amish fathers frequently served as board members of one-room public schools. Despite their avoidance of public office and political activity, the Amish are good neighbors who readily assist their non-Amish friends in time of disaster, fire, or illness. They support community benefit auctions, garage sales, and historical celebrations. In one case, an Amishman was appointed to a township planning commission, but such public involvement is rare. Occasionally, special township meetings are held to deal with issues involving the Amish—zoning hearings, road wear from horseshoes, immunization of children, and so forth. An increase in polio cases among the Amish in 1979 threatened a public epidemic, and an outbreak of measles posed a similar risk in 1988. In both instances, Amish leaders cooperated with health officials by encouraging mass immunization. In such ways, they seek to be good neighbors.

The Amish rarely participate in other civic affairs. Attendance at fairs, amusement parks, carnivals, dances, and the theater is prohibited for church members. However, some Amish youth indulge in these worldly activities before baptism. Occasionally adults, and more frequently youth, will travel to the beach or attend a professional baseball game, tennis tournament, or country music concert. In 1995 the church firmly denounced playing baseball for members; however, before baptism, some youth play on local baseball teams and even wear uniforms. In sum, Amish participation in community affairs tends to be local, selective, and informal. Moreover, they seek to avoid publicity and public confrontation at all costs.

USING THE LAW

The Amish want to be law-abiding citizens but are reluctant to use the legal system to protect their rights. Lawyers are readily used by the Amish to prepare wills, establish business partnerships, and handle real estate transactions, but using the law to protect one's personal or business rights contradicts the humble spirit of Gelassenheit. Filing a lawsuit is cause for excommunication. The Amish are taught to bear abuse and suffer insult rather than to fight injustice through legal means. But as more and more Amish move into business, use of the law becomes ever more tempting. In some instances, non-Amish customers have bilked Amish businessmen, knowing they would not likely sue. Using implicit threats, some Amish business owners have asked their attorneys to write letters to debtors asking for payment of delinquent bills. In other cases, under the advice of their attorneys, Amish have asked dubious clients to sign a "confessed judgement," which is then filed in the courthouse if products or services are not paid in full. The confessed judgment places a lien against the debtor's property. Asking a client to sign such a judgment is an implicit threat, but an Amish person will rarely execute such a note or testify at enforcement hearings.

In other situations, Amish businessmen have asked district magistrates to initiate bad debt collections. The Amish person is named as plaintiff, but this is not publicized. If defendants want to defend themselves at a public hearing, the Amish rarely appear but will ask their attorneys to resolve it in private. Careful not to file an actual lawsuit, some businessmen use the services of attorneys to resolve disputes quietly, out of the public limelight. The growing involvement in business will surely increase the tension between the gentleness of Gelassenheit and the brash realities of the marketplace.

GOVERNMENT TIES

The Amish are law-abiding citizens. Church leaders strongly encourage members to obey civil laws. Yet when civil law and religious conscience collide, the Amish are not afraid to "take a stand" and call on their members to "obey God rather than men." Although they support civil government, they always keep a healthy distance from it. Self-reliance, community autonomy, and the church's responsibility for the welfare of its members are persistent themes in Amish teaching that have made them wary of government.[2]

The Amish view of civil government is ambiguous. On the one hand, they believe the Bible teaches that government is ordained by God. On the other hand, the government epitomizes worldly culture, for it is the formal and legal apparatus of an unregenerate world. The European persecutors of the Amish were often government officials. Government embodies the force of law. When push comes to shove, governments engage in warfare and use capital punishment and raw coercion to impose their will. These methods violate the way of Jesus and the gentle spirit of Gelassenheit. Moreover, because the Amish church regulates much of the conduct of its members, it has little need for external control.

The Amish have a long history of caring for their own members and thus have little use for Medicaid, Medicare, public welfare programs, and other forms of public subsidy. Tapping into federal programs would, in the long run, erode the base of mutual aid and drain away precious social capital. Such an erosion would weaken the influence of the church. The Amish are adamantly opposed to government "handouts." Why, they ask, should they be forced to participate in government welfare programs such as Social Security and Medicare when they have cared for their own people for three centuries—long before such programs were ever envisioned by politicians?

Contrary to popular misconceptions, the Amish *do* pay their taxes. They believe the Bible teaches Christians to pay taxes and respect government. They pay state and federal income taxes, county taxes, sales taxes, real estate transfer taxes, and local school taxes. In fact, they pay school taxes twice—for Amish schools as well as public ones. Of course, they pay few gasoline taxes. The only taxes from which they are exempt are Social Security and Worker's Compensation.[3]

With the exception of serving on local school boards, the church has forbidden holding public office for several reasons. First, running for office is viewed as self-serving and arrogant, out of sync with the meek spirit of Gelassenheit. Second, holding government office means participating in the state, the most worldly of organizations—an embarrassing violation of the prin-

Voting is considered an individual matter in Amish society. Amish turnout is typically low.

ciple of separation from the world. Finally, a public official might need to use legal force to settle public disputes, violating the biblical admonition to not resist evil. In short, seeking, holding, and promoting political office simply contradicts a host of Amish values.

The Amish attitude toward voting is more tolerant. The church, surprisingly, leaves voting up to individual choice. Those who vote tend to be younger businessmen with an interest in community affairs. The Amish are more likely to cast a ballot in local elections than in national ones. In the 2000 presidential election, the chairman of the Lancaster County Republican Committee was urging the Amish to vote, knowing they would likely vote Republican. Interestingly, the Republican chairman was the great-grandson of an Amish leader involved in an Amish boycott of the East Lampeter School Consolidation in 1937, described in Chapter 7. Some forty years later, the offspring of this leader was hoping the Amish would help to carry Pennsylvania for George W. Bush.[4]

It is safe to assume that the Amish voting rate is much lower than the national average. One minister said that he stopped voting after he was ordained to the ministry. Indeed, the Amish National Steering Committee discouraged both voting and jury duty, concluding that "if we are concerned in this line, let us turn to God in prayer that HIS will be done."[5] While voting has been a matter of individual choice, serving on juries is strongly discouraged.

The Amish church strictly forbids participation in military service. In fact, entering military service brings excommunication. In the Amish view, Jesus' command to love one's enemies and not to resist evil are incompatible with being a soldier. The purposes and techniques of military service violate the very essence of Gelassenheit; obedience to biblical teaching must always transcend civil duty.

During World War II, many Amish conscientious objectors received agricultural deferments and continued to work on the family farm.[6] As the draft continued into the 1960s, some who were ineligible for farm deferments contributed two years of alternative service in public hospitals. However, working in a worldly, often urban environment created serious problems. Explained an Amish spokesman, "Many boys went with good intentions, but having so much idle time they became involved with amusements, with the nurses, or in other ways were led astray."[7] When their service was finished, many no longer wanted to come home, nor could they join the church if they had married a wife of a different faith. To alleviate this, the Amish negotiated an agreement with the Selective Service. Those ineligible for deferments at home could be assigned to farms under the supervision of the Amish National Steering Committee. In fact, it was this problem that led to the creation of the committee in 1966. The end of the draft in 1973 eliminated the problem of military service. Amish leaders continue to stay in contact with Selective Service officials in the hope that, if national conscription ever returns, they will once again be able to find alternative assignments. The church encourages young men to register with the Selective Service on their eighteenth birthday.

By the turn of the twenty-first century, the Amish National Steering Committee had become an important mediator between Amish interests and government concerns.[8] An informal network of directors from Amish-populated states gathers for an annual national meeting, and various states have their own statewide meeting of local representatives as well. An informal lobbying effort of sorts, the Steering Committee has grappled with many issues over the years—conscription, child labor, slow-moving vehicles, Social Security, IRA accounts, 401(k) plans, hard hat regulations, Worker's Compensation, and earned income credits, to name a few. The presence of the Steering Committee is also helpful to government officials at local, state, and national levels to ascertain Amish opinions on pending issues and legislation. The Steering Committee has become an important venue for negotiating traditionalist Amish convictions with the realities of the bureaucratic state. Because the chairman of the National Steering Committee has resided in Lancaster County since 1966, the Lancaster settlement has played a prominent role in coordinating discussions with government officials.

SOCIAL SECURITY

Although the Amish pay local, state, and federal taxes, they refuse to pay into Social Security or tap its benefits, which they view as an insurance program rather than a tax.[9] Indeed, when the federal program began in 1935, it was called Old Age and Survivors Insurance. The Amish have objected to public insurance programs for several reasons. First, they believe that the church should care for the welfare of its own members. The Amish record on this score is commendable. Widows, orphans, and the disabled are cared for by extended families and by the church. In cases of extreme difficulty, the needy are assisted by an alms fund. The elderly retire at home under the care of their children. Families often take turns caring for senile members and others requiring special support. Rather than institutionalizing dependent people, the Amish care for the needy through extended family networks. To turn these responsibilities over to the state would, in their mind, abdicate a fundamental religious duty—the care of one's brothers and sisters in the faith.

Second, insurance programs—especially life insurance plans—are viewed as gambling ventures that seek to plan and protect one's fortunes rather than yield them to the will of God. For example, the Amish usually will not buy annuities because they carry life insurance benefits. Insurance programs defy the stance of Gelassenheit—of waiting and submitting to divine destiny—because they guarantee a favorable financial outcome. Participation in such programs also entails economic involvement with, and reliance on, the world—a violation of the biblical injunction of separation. Finally, Amish involvement in public insurance programs would destroy dependency on the church and erode its centrality in the lives of members. Moreover, the mutual aid programs provided by the community—the networks of social capital— would be severely diminished.

The Amish plea for exemption from Social Security was voiced by an Amish spokesman in hearings before the Ways and Means Committee of the U.S. House of Representatives in 1983: "The Amish are only human and not as perfect as our non-Amish neighbors would take us to be, and not as near perfect as we would like to be, and we would not wish to be a burden to our government or men in authority or to be a hindrance to anyone. We desire no financial assistance from our state or federal government in any way. But again, we would humbly plea that we be allowed to take care of our own, in our own way, through alms and brotherly love as has always been our custom and has been sufficient to this day."[10]

When the Social Security program began, it created little problem for the Amish because the self-employed were exempt. The loophole closed in 1955 when the self-employed, including farmers, were required to participate.[11] The government, in the Amish view, had overstepped its bounds by forcing them to pay into, and receive benefits from, a federal insurance program. By May 1955, Amish representatives from across the nation, led by a Lancaster bishop, presented a petition asking for exemption to federal officials and members of Congress. The petition, signed by nearly fourteen thousand Old Order members, baffled Washington bureaucrats. This was the first time in the twenty-year history of Social Security that citizens were begging *not* to receive benefits. The Amish argued that if they began paying into the program it would be hard to keep their sons and daughters from collecting benefits, and in a generation or so they would be hooked on the system.

For the next several years, the Amish argued their case before congressional committees, but the legislators were hesitant to open the door for special exemptions, fearing it might dismantle the entire system. Finally, in 1958, the Internal Revenue Service (IRS) began filing liens on farm animals and other Amish assets in Ohio.[12] IRS enforcement varied by state and region. Frightened by the crackdown, some Amish farmers began making payments, but others still refused. In 1958 IRS agents in the Midwest began confiscating and selling Amish-owned horses. Such seizures continued intermittently. In 1961 agents seized three horses from an Amishman in western Pennsylvania while he was working in the field. By the time legislative relief arrived in 1965, there were an estimated 1,500 delinquent Amish accounts and 3,000 liens on Amish properties.[13] National publicity and public outcry on behalf of the Amish brought the issue to a stalemate.[14]

More than a dozen bills seeking to exempt the Amish from Social Security were sponsored by legislators from heavily populated Amish states in the early 1960s. A Social Security exemption was passed by Congress and signed into law by President Lyndon B. Johnson on 30 July 1965 as an appendage to the bill that established the national Medicare program. According to an Amish negotiator, Lancaster Bishop David Fisher told House Ways and Means Chairman Wilbur Mills that "we take care of our own people and if we start paying in, the next generation will collect and we don't want no government handouts." Mills replied, "There's nothing wrong with that." And, according to an observer, "Mills just hung an exemption rider on the Medicare bill and it sailed right through the Congress."

The exemption approved in 1965 applied only to the self-employed. A special IRS form (4029) was developed for religious groups that had convictions against Social Security. Today, within six months of their baptism, young Amish complete the exemption form, which is then signed by their bishop. After filing the exemption, they receive an "exemption number"—in essence, a Social Security number. Signers of the form agree to "waive all rights to any Social Security payment or benefit." Thus, the Amish receive no Social Security checks for welfare, retirement, disability, Medicaid, or Medicare.[15] Changes in the federal tax code in 1987 required wage earners to obtain a Social Security number for each dependent child over five years of age. The Amish objected to this and negotiated an agreement with the IRS to waive the requirement.

BOYCOTTING GOVERNMENT "HANDOUTS"

The Social Security exemption approved for the Amish in 1965 functioned smoothly for self-employed farmers and carpenters. However, it created complications as the Amish began moving into business. A variety of arrangements developed as the Amish coped with the self-employment restriction: (1) Amish who work for non-Amish employers have Social Security taxes deducted from their paychecks even though they will never receive Social Security payments. (2) Amish employers must pay the Social Security tax for their non-Amish employees. (3) Until 1988 Amish businesses paid Social Security premiums for their Amish employees even though they would never benefit from the program. "It's like paying for a dead horse," said a businessman. A retired Amish shop owner said: "I paid thousands of dollars for Social Security taxes for myself and my employees and won't get a penny of it back." (4) Some businesses organized themselves as legal partnerships so the employees—owners or partners in this case—were considered self-employed and exempt from Social Security payments, Worker's Compensation, and unemployment insurance. (5) In other cases, several Amishmen worked together as a carpentry crew but kept individual records and collected their pay separately to qualify for the self-employment exemption.

With business arrangements pressing the legal definition of self-employment and with more Amish moving into business, several legislators from heavily populated Amish areas sponsored bills in the United States Congress aimed at removing the self-employment restriction.[16] Finally, in 1988 the self-employment exemption was expanded by Congress to include Amish employees working for Amish employers, thus exempting both. However, non-Amish employers must continue to deduct Social Security taxes if they hire Amish employees.

Two other insurance related programs, Worker's Compensation and unemployment insurance, have also created problems for Amish employers. The Amish view these, like Social Security, as government insurance programs. Self-employed workers are exempt from Worker's Compensation and unemployment insurance. As employees of Amish school boards, Amish teachers were caught in a dilemma with these programs. In 1978 Pennsylvania legislators unanimously passed a bill exempting Amish teachers from Worker's Compensation. The IRS considers Amish teachers self-employed because they teach without direct supervision, thus freeing them from paying unemployment insurance. Several states—Pennsylvania, Kentucky, and Wisconsin—eventually exempted all Amish from Worker's Compensation because of their religious objections.

Over the years, numerous federal programs designed to stabilize the prices of agricultural products have regulated supply and demand. The Amish have typically avoided agricultural subsidy programs. For example, they refused to sell their cows in a federal buyout program in the 1990s and to accept payment to let farmland sit idle. They have historically opposed government "handouts," from Social Security to agricultural subsidies. This repudiation has baffled government bureaucrats.

Increasingly, a few Amish have participated in some programs underwritten with government subsidies—conservation programs, land preservation efforts, and Federal Home Administration (FHA) loans for farms. One minister accepted $17,000 to build a manure pit as part of a government effort to clean up the Chesapeake Bay. In the adjoining church district a lay member refused to accept a subsidy for his manure pit as a "matter of conscience." In 2000, several Amish families were conscientiously struggling with whether to accept $2,100 an acre in government funds to preserve their farmland.

The Amish boycott of Social Security and other government subsidies reflects two cherished ideals: community self-reliance and the religious conviction that church members are responsible for the economic welfare of their brothers and sisters.

THE *WITNESS* CONTROVERSY

In the spring of 1984, the Amish found themselves in a peculiar public relations quandary. They learned, to their astonishment, that Amish life would be depicted in a major Hollywood film, *Witness,* which Paramount Pictures planned to shoot in Lancaster County. The Pennsylvania Bureau of

Motion Picture and TV Development, eager for national publicity and tourist revenues, had solicited Paramount for an Amish picture.[17]

The story featured a Philadelphia detective (played by Harrison Ford), who finds refuge with an Amish family. Endangered by a criminal investigation, Ford lives with the Amish family and falls in love with an Amish widow (played by Kelly McGillis). The drama ends with a violent shoot-out on an Amish farm. The violence of a cop thriller, set in an idyllic Amish countryside, created a dramatic clash of images.

As the film was being shot in the early summer of 1984, the Amish began to protest for several reasons. First, they had always opposed television, movies, and photography. They resented being portrayed in a medium they abhorred. Second, they have typically shunned publicity, and a commercial film would project Amish images on screens around the world. Third, perhaps more than any other word, *Hollywood* symbolized worldliness in the Amish mind—a "den of iniquity" that distributes sin, sex, and violence to viewers around the world. Thus to have Hollywood, the symbol of moral vice, make a film about the Amish and catapult them into international fame was a triple insult. Finally, the Amish knew that they were being exploited commercially by the tourist industry. Writing in protest of the film to Pennsylvania's governor, an Amishwoman said: "We Amish feel we are serving as a tool to lure tourists to Lancaster County."

As the filming got under way, Amish bishops warned members not to cooperate with the Paramount production crews. "We can't stop them," said one Amishman, "but we don't have to help them. We don't want it. It doesn't belong here." In a conciliatory overture, director Peter Weir promised not to use Amish persons in the cast. However, the Amish soon discovered that Kelly McGillis had spent several days in disguise in an Amish home. Upon identification, she was asked to leave. This breach of trust added insult to injury. An irritated Amish grandmother said: "Now, that was an intrusion. I thought that was pretty bad. We wouldn't do that to them [the public] and they wouldn't want us to either. They'd hike us out the door faster than we ever came in." Although the Amish stayed aloof from the filming, they felt betrayed by some local officials who assisted Paramount Pictures. And as the Amish suspected, the monetary rewards were great. The filming alone pumped several million dollars into the local economy.

Unable to ignore the insult, three bishops and a lay leader took their pro-

Harrison Ford defends the Amish with fists during on-site filming of *Witness* in the Village of Intercourse. The Amish objected to this scene because Ford, dressed in ethnic garb, was fighting.

test to Lieutenant Governor William W. Scranton in Harrisburg. The delegation argued that the Amish had been mistreated because actors had been dressed as Amish and were engaged in physical fights and shown making nasty remarks. Said one leader: "If our principles were to fight, I feel we could go to court and get an injunction on the basis of misrepresenting the Amish, but this is not our way." Using the ultimate bargaining chip, one bishop remarked that the Amish "might have to move if they were not left alone."

After hearing their pleas, Lieutenant Governor Scranton promised to intervene. He arranged several meetings that produced an agreement with the secretary of commerce and the director of the Pennsylvania Bureau of Motion Picture and TV Development.[18] In brief, it stipulated that the state:

> Will not promote Pennsylvania Amish as subjects for feature films or television productions.
>
> Will not promote any script that uses the Amish and/or its culture as subject matter.
>
> Will refuse to deal with film companies that attempt to film the Amish without their consent.
>
> Will inform potential producers of the community's strong opposition to photographs and having its culture represented in any theatrical production.[19]

By the time the agreement was finalized, *Witness* was well on its way to the screen. The arrangement placated both parties. The state was pleased because no restrictions were placed on *Witness*, which would soon stir the curiosity of millions around the world. And though the state promised not to solicit film producers, the secretary of commerce admitted that "really, nothing would change if *Witness* were coming in tomorrow as a new production . . . other than making it clear that the Amish community does not wish to be intruded upon." The state commerce department, he noted, would again offer the same sort of support that it gives to other films.

"We were quite happy with the agreement," an Amish leader said. "We felt it was as far as the secretary of commerce could possibly go, legally." A bishop concluded: "We think we got what we asked for." Negotiating the agreement gave the Amish an opportunity to vent their frustration with the whole ordeal and to inform state officials that there were limits to Gelassenheit—they would not merely pray while being trampled upon by Hollywood greed. And while the state did not want to prohibit future Amish films, it surely did not want to provoke an Amish migration.

The local Pennsylvania Dutch Convention and Visitors' Bureau maintained a discreet distance from *Witness*. Although the bureau supported the agreement reached with the Amish, its representatives did not attend a highly publicized premiere of *Witness* in Lancaster City. After release of the film, however, bureau brochures began inviting tourists to Lancaster County, "as seen in the critically acclaimed movie *Witness*."[20] Meanwhile, *Witness* was doing well. It grossed $33.7 million at the box office in its first six weeks and even knocked another Paramount film, *Beverly Hills Cop*, out of the top slot. Things were also going well for tourism in Lancaster County. By the end of the first six-week run of *Witness*, tourism had climbed 13 percent, even before the summer rush.

PUPPY MILLS AND CHILD LABOR

Two issues that complicated Amish relations with the larger society at the turn of the twenty-first century were the so-called puppy mills and child labor laws. In fact, some observers felt these flashpoints were tarnishing public relations for the Amish community. Both issues, charged with emotion and stereotypical images, illustrate a clash of cultural values.

The "puppy mill" controversy began in 1993 when the *New York Times* published a story implicating some Amish farmers for violating health standards in the dog kennels where they raised puppies for pet shops.[21] The article pitted three Amish farmers, "who treated dogs like any other animals," against Humane Society officials who wanted better care. One Amishman charged that "the animal rights people are more concerned about dogs than their own children." By the turn of the twenty-first century, Lancaster County had about 230 licensed dog kennels for breeding purposes, many of which were Amish owned.[22] Amish farmers typically had twenty-five to fifty breeding dogs in licensed kennels that were inspected by the state department of agriculture.

The issue flared up again when several farmers in three different townships requested zoning approval to build more kennels in 2000. With milk and tobacco prices down, many farmers were searching for additional income. Public zoning hearings, generous newspaper publicity, and active opposition by the Lancaster Humane Society stirred lively debate.[23] One township received more than 120 emails and 55 faxes from "crazy people on a crusade," in the words of a zoning officer. Most of the protests came from outside Pennsylvania.

Some of the planned kennels were approved, and those that failed township codes were rejected. To Amish farmers, dogs—like cows or chickens— were simply another source of income. And as long as they met licensing and inspection standards, they saw no problem producing puppies just like they did calves or peeps. For animals' rights advocates, however, the so-called puppy mills mistreated dogs and produced an unnecessary surplus. One woman leaving a public hearing was so incensed that she doubted "that the Amish will go to heaven" if they continue raising dogs. Another person called the Amish farmers "killers." One member of the audience said, "You people disgust me and make me sick. I'm going outside and throwing up."[24] A few weeks later, irked by all the commotion, an Amishman wrote the editor of a local newspaper. "I'm surprised these folks come from so far away to mind our business. Seems to me someone needs something to do. Why not start some dog kennels?"[25]

The Amish were learning that making a living was no longer a simple matter of milking a few cows in the privacy of one's own barn. Now it involved zoning laws, publicity in faraway states, and Humane Society lawyers. In short, the heated discussions reflected a clash of modern and agrarian cultural values.

The Amish movement into business also brought other new complications. In 1996 U.S. Department of Labor investigators fined three Old Order saw mill operators in Pennsylvania for violating child labor laws. Fair labor laws prohibit children under age sixteen from operating power-driven manufacturing equipment and children under fourteen from working in any type of manufacturing facility.

The words *child labor* conjure up negative images of children working twelve-hour days in dangerous conditions in sweat shops, coal mines, and brothels. For the Amish, child labor means apprenticeship, family solidarity, and learning the basic values that form the foundation of their way of life. The arrests and fines frightened Amish leaders across the country. How would they train their children? What would they do without cheap labor?

The Amish system of apprenticeship involves youth in farm and business at an early age and especially after they complete eighth grade. Instead of attending trade school, vocational-technical school, or high school, Amish youth work on farms or serve apprenticeships in shops where they learn a variety of trades. Because child labor laws are not enforced on farms, the Amish were immune from them for many years. Concerned about the impact of enforcement on family, apprenticeship, and business, an Amish lobby effort swung into action under the coordination of the National Steering Committee. Amish representatives met with more than forty members of Congress to plead their case.

The child labor laws were designed to protect youth in the larger society from danger and exploitation in large manufacturing plants, not the needs of small family businesses providing an apprenticeship for their children. One Amish businessman complained about Department of Labor officials: "They're trying to tell me I can't have my own children working for me. My kids have been coming up here [to the shop] since they were two years old. This is part of our house. This is where we keep an eye on them."[26]

Even the *Wall Street Journal* joined the debate with an editorial by an Amish-raised woman who argued that America's "child spoiling culture— TV instead of work and encouraging youngsters to challenge parental discipline—contributes to the boredom and dissatisfaction that cause America's problems with juvenile violence." She noted that some of her most gratifying childhood memories involved work and urged the government "to stop causing stress for those who choose to raise their children close to the instincts of nature."[27]

Congressman Joseph R. Pitts, representative from Lancaster County, tried without success to persuade officials in the Department of Labor to respect the Amish concerns with light-handed enforcement. Eventually he scheduled a hearing with a subcommittee of the House of Representatives and introduced a bill that addressed Amish needs.[28] The legislation specified that fourteen-year-old youth in religious groups that forbid formal schooling beyond eighth grade could work in manufacturing plants if they were supervised by relatives or other members of the religious sect. The U.S. House of Representatives approved the legislation in March 1999, but the bill stalled in the Senate until it received a hearing in 2001.

In his testimony at the subcommittee hearing, the chairman of the Amish Steering Committee said that after eighth grade, Amish youth "learn by doing . . . we cannot tolerate idleness during these adolescent years, therefore we see a dire need that our youth learn a trade . . . we believe that forced idleness at this age is detrimental to our long-standing Amish way of raising our children and teaching them to become good productive citizens. Keeping young hands busy, keeps them out of mischief."[29] To Amish thinking, keeping children busy in meaningful work was central to their entire way of life.

THE IRONIES OF TOURISM

The rise of tourism in Lancaster County brought several ironic twists in Amish public relations.[30] The European forebears of the Amish were persecuted and exterminated because they dared to be different. Paradoxically, the Amish defiance of modern life has brought them not persecution but admiration and respect—enough to underwrite a massive tourist industry. The course of history has converted these descendants of despised heretics into esteemed objects of curiosity. Moreover, the world, which the Amish have tried so hard to keep at a distance, is now coming to them. Oddly enough, the more separate and unusual the Amish appear, the more attractive they become. And surprisingly, the tourism that appears to threaten their solitude may actually strengthen their cultural identity. Moreover, the tourism that nibbles away at farmland also tightens Amish ties to Lancaster by providing a ready market for crafts. And finally, the larger society, from which the Amish have sought independence, has now come to depend on them. These and other puzzles permeate the story of tourism.

Several national magazines featured stories on the Pennsylvania Germans in the late 1800s and early 1900s, but tourism in Lancaster County only began in earnest after the Great Depression. Interest in the Amish expanded in 1937 with the publication of an Amish tourist booklet and the East Lampeter school dispute, which received wide national press coverage.[31] An Amish farmer dates the mushrooming of tourism to the 1954 celebration of the 200th birthday of Intercourse, a village in the heart of the Amish settlement. "Mix together the word *Intercourse* with some Amish buggies," he said, "and you're bound to attract some tourists." In any event, by 1965 nearly 2 million tourists were trekking annually to Lancaster County to catch a glimpse of the Amish. Today, some 4 million tourists visit Lancaster County annually—about 180 visitors for each Amish person. The tourists spend over $1.2 billion and generate about $177 million in taxes alone each year. Certainly not all the visitors come to see the Amish, but even with conservative estimates, *each* Amish person generates about $30,000 in tourist revenues.[32]

The nearly six hundred members of the Pennsylvania Dutch Convention and Visitors' Bureau operate a variety of tourist sites throughout the county, including many attractions unrelated to the Amish. About a dozen Amish-owned businesses are also members of the bureau. The tourist industry cre-

Dozens of tour buses bring tourists to the village of Intercourse.

ates about 18,500 jobs, not to mention the thousands that produce crafts and products for the tourist market. Indeed, there are three tourist jobs for every farmer in the county.

The charm of the Plain people, especially the Amish, is the cultural magnet of tourism. The importance of the Amish for tourism is documented by several factors. The tourist sites are concentrated in the county's eastern part, near the Amish settlement. Tourist promotions—brochures, billboards, videos, and newspaper ads—highlight Amish images, especially the horse and buggy. The popularity of "Amish" tours, trinkets, food, and crafts underscores the primacy of Amish symbolism in the tourist industry. Without the Amish, Lancaster's tourism would likely not flourish, and if the Amish suddenly vanished, it would certainly decline. If the Amish lure half of the tourists, to use a conservative estimate, the Amish bring $600 million annually into the local economy as well as create thousands of non-Amish jobs. This hard economic fact gives the Amish a hefty bargaining chip whenever they negotiate with the larger world.

To relieve traffic congestion caused by tourism and growth, the Pennsylvania Department of Transportation proposed six routes for a limited access highway through Lancaster County in 1987. The most direct and least expensive route cut through prime farmland in the historic heart of the Amish settlement. Over one thousand Amish residents attended a public meeting to review the plans that, in the words of a county commissioner, "would kill the goose that laid the golden egg." The swirling controversy abated when Pennsylvania Governor Robert P. Casey declared, "We will not build a new highway in any corridor that will bisect the Amish farming community or cause major disruption to the Amish lifestyle."[33]

Whenever a distinctive culture becomes the focus of a tourist industry, special problems arise because the tourists and the "natives" have conflicting interests. Tourists hope to gain firsthand knowledge of the natives by talking to them. Visitors want to venture backstage and meet real Amish people in real Amish homes. The goal of the natives, in this case, is to avoid bothersome interruptions by people who treat them as museum objects or monkeys in a zoo. In many ways the tourist enterprise can be viewed as a social drama with both front-stage and backstage dimensions. Commercial tourist attractions provide a front-stage portrayal of Amish life that simulates a personal encounter by offering tours of refurbished Amish farms. Guided tours in the countryside are one attempt to go backstage. Busloads of tourists meander through the Amish countryside—the equivalent of a wild game preserve—ever on the lookout for a glimpse of genuine Amish life.

Tourist sites play several crucial roles in mediating the conflicting interests of tourists and natives. Tour organizations provide a buffer zone that protects the Amish from tourists. Tour guides and simulated attractions occupy the tourists' time and keep them a respectable distance from the Amish. Several million tourists roaming at will through the countryside would utterly disrupt Amish life. Tourist sites and guides provide structured restraints that permit Amish life to continue backstage in a normal fashion despite the presence of 4 million visitors. For the most part, tourists and their guides follow the established routes and stop at the designated spots on tourist maps. These helpful scripts and props organize the tourist experience into a predictable drama. The appearance of a real Amish person may temporarily disrupt things, but in general, the structured patterns of tourism—the sites and interpreters—provide a curtain that insulates and protects the Amish from an otherwise chaotic intrusion on their life.

Organized tourism also helps the tourists. Lost in a foreign culture with only a day or so of time, it is difficult to have a good experience without a guide. The front-stage operations offer tourists descriptive information and a succinct overview of Amish life that few Amish persons themselves could provide. Most tourist establishments provide an educational setting where questions can be asked without fear of embarrassment or insult. In these ways, the tourist enterprises bring natives and visitors close to each other but without the disruption of face-to-face encounters.

Tourist attractions, however, have two drawbacks. Discerning tourists realize that they are being duped—that the representations of Amish life projected in image and story are not authentic but are mere front-stage enactments. Thus, the backstage mystery lingers. What would it be like to walk inside a real Amish home and talk to a real Amish person? The Amish are also shortchanged. Commercial tourist enterprises are operated for profit by non-Amish entrepreneurs. A boon for the local economy, these enterprises bring jobs and profits to outsiders but not to the Amish. However, the financial equation began to change in the last two decades of the twentieth century.

In the 1980s the Amish and the tourists bypassed the tourist industry and quietly negotiated a new form of encounter—the native stand. Craft and produce stands operated by the Amish began sprouting up along country roads throughout the settlement. These miniature tourist sites, announcing "No Sunday Sales" and "No Photographs," are Amish owned and operated. They benefit both tourists and Amish alike. Tourists can peek behind the curtain and get a glimpse of backstage life. Under the guise of buying a product, they can talk with a real Amish person on Amish property. The tourist is treated to a close-up view of genuine Amish clothing and can buy authentic Amish foods and crafts. In exchange, the roadside stand enables the Amish to reap some financial benefits from tourism. As scarce farmland nudges more and more Amish off the farm, the tourist trade provides a new source of supplemental income.

The small native stands are a symbolic and literal middle ground—at the end of the lane—where tourist and Amish can safely interact at a polite distance. In these brief exchanges, the Amish are able to regulate the type and scope of interaction—effectively keeping tourists at arm's length. The stands also allow the Amish a firsthand look at the gaudy and frivolous dress of

An Amish roadside stand for tourists.

pleasure-seeking tourists. The proliferation of these native stands symbolizes yet another negotiated compromise between the Amish and modernity. The Amish have allowed the tourists to come one step closer to backstage Amish life, but the Amish are clearly in charge of this buffer zone—controlling its hours, personnel, location, and decor. In this sense, even the Amish roadside stand is a front-stage operation, and the tourists who had hoped to sneak backstage have been duped again.

THE IMPACT OF TOURISM

In many ways, tourism is a nuisance to the Amish. Cars and buses clog main roads, forcing some families to revise their weekly travel patterns during the peak of the tourist season. As many as fifty buses a day may stop at back road sites marked on tourist maps. Tourists who wish to photograph children sometimes bribe them. The clicking cameras, gawking strangers, and congested roadways are bothersome. One Amishman noted, "It's almost summer in the Pequea when: There's more tourists than plow furrows, more flies than tourists, more strawberries than flies, and more peas than pretty flowers."

Other aspects of tourism border on economic and cultural exploitation. The Amish realize that the bulk of tourist revenue fills the pockets of non-Amish entrepreneurs. "We are serving as a tool," said one Amishwoman, "to lure tourists to Lancaster County. Personally, I do not feel any resentment against tourists, but these tourist places are what's working against us. We are not living our peculiar way to attract attention. We merely want to live pure, Christian lives according to our religion and church standards and want to be left alone, like any human beings. We are opposed to having our souls marketed by having our sacred beliefs and traditions stolen from us and then distributed to tourists, and sometimes having them mocked." An Amish farmer added: "Some tourist places tell the most ridiculous stories about Amish craftsmanship, Amish dress, Amish cooking, and the Amish ways of life."[34] To see one's religious symbols—bonnet, buggy, beard—taken by outsiders and sold as plastic dolls, plastered on billboards, erected as statues, and fashioned into trinkets of all sorts is indeed a commercial assault on a religious culture. Insensitive entrepreneurs who snatch sacred symbols and convert them into profitable products exploit the Amish soul.

The Amish insulate themselves from tourism with negative images and humor. Some tourists, according to the Amish, are sincere, friendly, and courteous. But tourism, in general, symbolizes worldly pleasure in the Amish mind. Tourists kill time, seek entertainment, and waste money—all of which contradict basic Amish virtues. "The tourist attractions," said one minister, "have converted our Amish land into a leisure lust playground."[35] Others see tourism as a new form of persecution, a modern form of tribulation that must be endured with patience. "Tourism," suggested a minister, "is a test of our faith to see if we are as strong as our forefathers."

The Amish also use humor to defuse the tourism menace. Jokes about the stunts and foolish questions of tourists abound. Such humor keeps tourists at bay by trivializing their presence. By defining tourism in humorous ways, the Amish reduce its credibility and maintain social distance. Some Amish, of course, develop lasting friendships with tourists, but most Amish keep them at a healthy distance by converting them into a humorous reference group.

Although permanent relationships with tourists could erode Amish/non-Amish boundaries, tourists are relatively harmless; they eventually return home. Often bothersome, they are at least temporary. They bring fleeting moments of highly regulated interaction, staged in public settings, which hardly endanger Amish life. Indeed, prolonged relationships with non-Amish neighbors are more likely to lead Amish people astray.

Does tourism endanger Amish life? An Amish minister said: "We are caught in the jaws of tourism . . . and if the heat gets too hot we better get out . . . if it is our lot to move, we will."[36] Despite occasional threats and a dribble of migration, the evidence is to the contrary. The Amish community in Lancaster has remained and grown in spite of tourism. Indeed, tourism may inadvertently energize Amish life in several ways. An older Amish person noted that with the rise of tourism, "We are no longer looked down on," and an elder remarked: "We get loads of praise for our way of life." To many Amish, the fact that tourists come from around the world to learn of their ways reinforces their collective identity and values. Reluctant to admit pride, they take a quiet satisfaction in knowing that their culture is worthy of such respect. In this way, tourism bolsters Amish self-esteem.

At present, tourism underscores the cultural separation of the Amish. Tourists may be bothersome, but they do reinforce Amish separation from the world. Although the Amish complain of feeling "like monkeys in a zoo," the imagery does underscore the sharp difference between monkeys and visitors. In this way, tourism galvanizes the cultural gap between the two worlds and helps define Amish identity.

Tourism also creates expectations for Amish behavior. The symbolism on tourist billboards reinforces the boundaries of Amish culture even in the minds of the Amish themselves. Knowing that tourists come to see a people driving horses and living without electricity reinforces expectation for such behavior. Thus, Amish behavior, in part, fulfills the expectations created by tourism. Such external expectations likely fortify rather than weaken actual Amish practice. To discard the buggy, for instance, would not only break Amish tradition, but it would also shatter the expectations of the outside world.

In these ways, rather than endangering Amish culture, tourism may inadvertently fortify it. In any event, the economic value of the Amish as a tourist attraction has greatly enhanced their bargaining power with public officials.

Indeed, organized curiosity in the form of tourism may be their staunchest ally in legal confrontations with the state. There have been few public clashes with local officials since the mid-1960s, when tourism first thrust the Amish into the public spotlight. In fact, local, state, and federal officials have made striking concessions to the Amish, ranging from overlooking road damage from horseshoes, to the U.S. Supreme Court's endorsement of their schools.

A more sinister scenario may lurk beneath this happy ending, however. The rise of Amish-owned tourist shops could, over time, foster an unhealthy dependency if the Amish become parasites of tourism. This paradoxical situation might encourage them to maintain their unique lifestyle to attract tourism because it benefits the Amish community. At the turn of the twenty-first century, the hungry appetite of tourist markets for Amish trinkets, crafts, and quilts was luring more and more Amish into establishing their own retail shops. The Amish label on products commodified Amish images on the public culture market. For example, *Vogue* magazine, in a special section on Plain dress, featured images of Amish clothing.[37]

The once-despised heretics who sought separation from an evil world were now selling their own souls on the public market. With their own compliance, Amish images and symbols had become cultural commodities. Prosperity and worldly acclaim now threatened to erode the boundaries of separation that persecution had so clearly defined centuries ago.

Apart from its other rewards, tourist fame also provides the Amish with leverage as they bargain with the larger society. They occasionally threaten to migrate if things get too bad, and public officials worry about these muffled threats, for an evacuation would be catastrophic for tourism. Ironically, the outside world that years ago sought to banish Anabaptist heretics is now begging them to stay, which brings us full circle in the riddle of public relations. Like it or not, the Amish have become dependent on modern society for their survival. But it is not a one-way street, for Lancaster's image, identity, and economy also rest on the Amish in many ways. It is a symbiotic relationship, and for better or for worse, the county's dependency on the Amish has strengthened their hand at the bargaining table.

Regulating Social Change

We try to keep the brakes on social change, you know, a little bit.
—Amish craftsman

CHANGE AND ADAPTATION

Amish society is not a social museum; it is dynamic and evolving. Consider some of the household changes in the last fifty years. Amishwomen no longer wash clothes in hand-operated machines. They use washing machines powered by hydraulic pressure or gasoline engines. Gas refrigerators have replaced iceboxes, indoor flush toilets have replaced outdoor privies, hydraulic water pumps have replaced windmills, and gas water heaters have replaced the fire under wrought-iron kettles. Modern bathtubs have superseded old metal tubs. Kerosene lanterns have given way to gas lights. Wood-fired cookstoves have yielded to modern gas ranges. Hardwood floors and no-wax vinyl have replaced linoleum and rag carpets. Spray starch, detergents, paper towels, instant pudding, and instant coffee have eased household chores. Permanent-press fabrics have lifted the burden of incessant ironing. Although canning still predominates, some foods are preserved by freezing. Air-powered sewing machines are replacing treadle machines. Battery-powered mixers do the job of hand-operated egg beaters, and air-powered food processors have replaced hand grinders. The list goes on, but despite all these changes, wall-to-wall carpets, electric appliances, air conditioners, telephones, and electronic media have not entered Amish homes.

Things have changed outside the house as well. Many newer homes have attractive landscaping. In Amish shops, hand tools have given way to large air- or hydraulic-powered equipment, but the shops remain unhooked to public utility lines. Battery-powered drills and screwdrivers do the job of hand-turned tools. Amish farmers no longer milk their cows by hand but use modern vacuum milkers powered by diesel engines instead. Automatic-reset riding plows have replaced old-fashioned walk-behind plows. But horses still pull the new hydraulic plows. Modern hay balers towed by horses have superseded wheel-driven hay loaders. But the sophisticated balers, running on steel wheels, do not carry automatic bale loaders. Weeds and insects are sprayed by horse-drawn sprayers. Hybrid corn, grown with chemical fertilizer, is cut and picked by horse-drawn equipment.

An Amishman born in 1943 described the changes he witnessed in the last half of the twentieth century:

> You're halfway over the hill in the Pequea when you can tell your children and grandchildren about things you never had when you were their age. Never had sisters day, brothers day, etc. only work days, no fruit pizza, no cheese pizza, in fact no pizza at all. No bathrooms, no phone shanty, no church melody books. Our outside toilets then were smaller than today's phone shanty. No compressed air or hydraulic tools. No *Botschaft,* no *Diary,* no *Pathway Magazine.* No $100 scooters or rollerblades. No trampolines, no gang mowers, no outdoor grills. Balers and binders put hay bales and corn bundles on the ground. No Amish school board, teachers, or Amish schools in Leacock Township. No cheese dip or pretzel dip. In fact the only dip we knew was swimming in the Pequea Creek. No fire company sales, no benefit sales, no school sales. You never heard, "yeah right," or "have a good one." No hot air balloons, no seat belts.[1]

These examples and dozens of others illustrate the fact that Lancaster's Amish have changed dramatically in recent decades and that they have regulated the change within prescribed limits. They have avoided divisions within their church for nearly forty years despite the rapid change. Moreover, their growing population makes it ever more difficult to manage change in a uniform fashion. The riddle of social change is perplexing: Why do some aspects of Amish life change while others remain stuck in tradition? By what formula are some innovations accepted and others rejected?[2]

TABLE 12.1
Technological Restrictions by Approximate Date

1910	Telephone installation in homes	1966	Barn cleaners
1915	Automobile ownership		Home freezers
1919	Electricity from public utility lines	1970s	Milk pipelines
1923	Use of tractors for fieldwork		Silo unloaders
1940	Central heating in homes	1980s	Riding mowers
1950s	Power lawn mowers[a]	1986	Computers
1966	Grain combines and forage harvesters	1995	Internet
	Electric generators[b]	1996	Cell phones

NOTE: These are approximate dates because, in many cases, a decision developed over several years.
[a] Power lawn mowers are permitted in a few church districts.
[b] Generators may be used for welders and battery rechargers.

MOVING CULTURAL FENCES

The Amish view social change as a matter of moving cultural fences—holding to old boundaries and setting new ones. This dynamic process involves negotiating symbolic boundaries in the moral order. Church members who are moving too fast are "jumping the fence" and getting too involved with the outside world. Cultural fences mark the lines of separation between the two worlds. Coping with social change involves fortifying old fences as well as moving fences and building new ones. But regardless of whether they are old or new, cultural fences must remain if Amish ways are to persist.

No single principle or value regulates change in Amish society; it is a dynamic process, and the outcome is always uncertain. A variety of factors impinges on any decision to accept or reject a particular practice. Decisions to move symbolic boundaries always emerge out of the ebb and flow of a fluid social matrix. The factors shaping a particular decision vary greatly. With some seventy-five bishops, it is impossible to maintain uniform standards across the entire settlement. This diversity of practice, camouflaged by common symbols—horse, dress, lantern, dialect—increases as the settlement grows.

The acceptance of new products and the relaxation of old standards often occur by default. One Amishman said: "Well, change just kind of happens. Sometimes it is reviewed at a Ministers' Meeting but then it just kind of happens by itself." Leaders rarely plan or *initiate* social changes. The establishment of Amish schools is an example of intentional change. Yet even with that a consensus did not emerge for a decade. More typical are collective decisions to *resist* change. If a questionable practice—the use of computers or wall-to-wall carpet—begins to gain broad acceptance, the bishops may deliberately curtail it. Using biblical images, the bishops understand their role as "watchmen on the walls of Zion," responsible for guarding the flock. They are on the lookout for "little foxes" of worldliness that dig under the walls of Zion and undermine the welfare of the church. The bishops are not a source of innovation; instead, their duty is to inspect impending changes and resist the detrimental ones.

Change in Amish society typically comes, not from the top or the center of the social system, but from the periphery. It is often instigated by those living on the edge of the cultural system who try to stretch the boundaries. So called "fence jumpers" or "fence crowders," push against the traditional fences to test the limits. They experiment with new gadgets—a fax machine, a corn harvester, a mixer powered by air, a computer plugged into an inverter, or a Web site for their business. If someone complains and church leaders make a visit, the deviant may make a confession and "put away" the questionable item. Although Amish society has changed, it has also experienced painful steps backward when deviant practices were arrested and conveniences put away. Tractors have been recalled from the field. Bathrooms have been torn out on bishops' orders, only to be permitted two decades later. Rubber tires have been taken off machinery; electric wires and light bulbs have been ripped out. Computers have been sold and telephones disconnected.

The fence jumpers usually know what is likely to "pass inspection." If a new item—a calculator, disposable diapers, or a cash register—is adopted by others and no one complains too much, eventually the practice will creep into use by default. Leaders have to be careful to uproot deviant practices before they become too widely accepted and thus impossible to stop. The metaphors "walls of Zion" and "fence jumpers" suggest that the community has a clear understanding of Amish cultural boundaries. Many members explore the boundaries, "crowd the fence," or "test the waters" under a hundred watchful eyes.

A preacher described the importance of keeping the fences around "the Lord's vineyard" in good repair:

> The Savior warned against the little foxes that dig their way into the Lord's vineyard. I often think of the Lord's vineyard and compare it

with a good fence around the church of Christ, how it is like a good *Ordnung*. If the little foxes dig their way in and are not dealt with at once, or if they are allowed to remain, there is great danger that still more will come in. And finally, because they are allowed to remain and are not chased out, they grow bigger and become used to being there. . . . It is just the same with permitting little sins to go on till they are freely accepted as the customary thing and have taken a foothold. Wickedness takes the upper hand, and then, as the Savior says, the love of many becomes cold.[3]

The Amish are slow to make decisions regarding the adoption of new practices. They will act quickly if a technical development is obviously off limits—a video camera, for example. Borderline practices, such as artificial insemination of cows or the use of telephones, may be tolerated—put on probation—for several years to assess their long-term impact. Eventually a practice may grow by default, as it did with artificial insemination, or leaders may decide to forbid it. There is a delicate line of no return. It is one thing to ask a half-dozen people to "put away" their calculators but quite another thing to forbid calculators if dozens of members have used them for several years. Some probationary practices, for example the use of power lawn mowers, may continue for years within the district of a lenient bishop. Change sometimes speeds up or reverses with the ordination of a new bishop.

"When people are testing the lines," an Amish leader explained, "the leaders don't want to act too quick and harsh, so they just let it ride a little bit until they see what happens, or till they can get a picture of what might happen if they let it go. They clamp down if it's something that we don't need, that would disrupt the community, the closeness." The division of 1966 erupted when the bishops tried to eradicate several pieces of farm equipment that had been in use for ten years in several church districts. "The problem came," said one person, "when too many things were let go too many years." Questionable practices must be banned before they slip into widespread use. The fate of new products or practices is weighed cautiously, for once engraved in the Ordnung, taboos are difficult to change. A rash decision may appear foolish with hindsight and bring a painful loss of face a few years later.

Once drawn, lines become hard to erase. The Amish believe it is better to keep a few taboos consistently than to revise a host of them with each new

This new upscale home reflects increasing wealth among the Amish.
A horse barn is in the center, and a shop on the right.

whim of progress. Thus, it is easier to accept a new practice, never inscribed in the Ordnung, than to change an old taboo. It is difficult, for instance, to relax the taboo on power lawn mowers but relatively easy to accept new hand-held weed cutters powered by tiny gasoline engines. Side-by-side on an Amish lawn, the old-fashioned push mower and the modern weed cutter appear incongruous to the outsider. Although their functions are similar, the portable weed cutter can be accepted without embarrassment because it was never prohibited by the Ordnung.

Symbolic considerations are important in the change process. The popular adage of a senior bishop in the 1950s, "If you can pull it with horses, you can have it," is highly instructive. There are two levels of meaning in this statement. On the practical level, the old bishop understood that horses keep farming operations rather small. But in essence he was also saying, "You can use modern equipment in the field as long as you pull it with horses." All sorts of new farm equipment were permissible in the shadow of the horse, for the horse marked off the symbolic boundaries of Amish life. In the same way, the unwritten rule in Amish shops, "If you can do it with air or hydraulic [power], you can do it," creates cultural boundaries.

The verbal explanations given for accepting or rejecting new practices often mask the real reasons that are not stated. The labels "too worldly," "too modern," "too liberal," or "too handy," frequently cited as reasons for rejection, may hide underlying factors such as economic issues, gender roles, labor implications, or social capital questions related to social interaction or family integration. One businessman made the connection between the outward label of "worldly" and the underlying reasons for rejecting tractors:

> Our people will always come out with the statement in the Bible that says "be not conformed to this world." Any good Amishman will always say that the tractor's worldly, the automobile's worldly, the radio's worldly, and the telephone and electricity. But why? If we allowed tractors, we would be doing like the Mennonite people are doing, grabbing each other's farms up out there, mechanizing, and going to the bank and loaning $500,000, and later worrying about paying it off, putting three other guys out of business and sending them to town for work, away from their home. Do you follow? So we take the position, why do that? Let's put a guideline on our faith and say that it's [the tractor] not necessary; it's too worldly.

Technological advances rejected by the Amish are, surprisingly, not considered immoral, and few of them are forbidden by Scripture. Owning a car, using a tractor in the field, and flying in an airplane are not considered evils in and of themselves. The evil lies in where a new invention might lead. The Amish ask: What will come next? Will other changes be triggered by this one? How will a new practice affect the welfare of the community over the years? Describing the taboo on the telephone, a craftsman said: "If we allow the telephone, that would be just a start. People would say, 'Okay, now we'll push for this and then we'll push for that . . .' It would be a move forward that might get the wheel rolling a little faster than we can control it, if you know what I mean." A bishop reflected: "I might have a car and it wouldn't hurt any, but for the oncoming generation you oughta be willing to sacrifice for them." Such selective modernization, rather than being highly moralistic, is strikingly reflective, rational, and calculating—indeed, it is quite modern!

Finally, acceptable changes often have the appearance of compromise—

a willingness to edge toward progress, but not too far; a willingness to accept some new gadgets, but with limits. Indeed the compromises create the riddles—riding scooters (halfway between walking and riding a bicycle), using modern bathrooms without electricity, riding in cars but not driving them, using public transportation but not air travel, voting but not running for office, pulling modern machinery with horses, using permanent-press fabric for traditional garb, and working in Amish shops that permit some modernization but not too much. In each instance, social change is simply a matter of setting new fences—but setting fences nevertheless. All of these factors create a zigzag pattern of change that baffles outsiders.

The response to a new practice may follow several scenarios: (1) It may be terminated by the leaders in a local district. (2) If not extinguished at first, it may spread to several other districts. (3) A "friendly" change may gradually creep into practice by default in a large number of districts and eventually spread throughout the settlement. (4) A "hostile" change may become an "issue," provoking debate and controversy. The ordained leaders may then decide to overlook it and allow it to slip into practice. (5) The "issue" may come before the bishops' meeting, and if they agree to prohibit the practice, local congregations will be asked to support the taboo. (6) If the bishops cannot reach agreement, the issue may simmer for months or years and eventually find de facto acceptance, or it may trigger renewed debate and new attempts to forbid it.

An issue like the appropriate use of telephones has sparked controversy for decades. Playing baseball on local league teams, an issue for several years, was finally forbidden by the bishops in 1995. Maintaining old fences and setting new ones is a delicate process, for as one leader said, "If we're not tolerant, we'll have more splits, but too much tolerance can wreck the whole thing too."

CULTURAL REGULATORS

The mix of factors that determines the fate of a new cultural practice or product is always in flux. Decisions about symbolic boundaries emerge within a dynamic matrix of social forces. It is hopeless to search for a simple cultural formula to predict the destiny of a new practice. However, we can identify the regulators, the forces in the ever-changing cultural equation that may influence the outcome.

What are the regulators that govern social change in Amish life? A single factor will rarely be adequate to explain a particular outcome. Decisions to move cultural fences arise from the convergence of many social forces. The following propositions identify the cultural regulators that often influence the decision-making process.

1. *Economic impact.* Changes that produce economic benefits are more acceptable than those that do not. "Making a living" takes priority over pleasure, convenience, or leisure. Thus, a motor on a hay mower in the field is more acceptable than one on a lawn mower.

2. *Visibility.* Invisible changes are more acceptable than visible ones. Using fiberglass in the construction of buggies is easier to introduce than changing the external color of the carriage itself. Permanent-press fabrics, in old styles and colors, are more acceptable than completely changing styles. Working as a cook in the back kitchen of a restaurant is more acceptable than working as a waitress in public areas.

3. *Relationship to Ordnung.* Changes that overturn previous Ordnung rulings are more difficult than ones that are free from previous rules. Musi-

This booming machine shop grew beyond the appropriate limits of size
and was sold to a non-Amish owner.

cal instruments, consistently forbidden by the Ordnung, are less likely than calculators to be accepted. Power weed trimmers are more accepted than power mowers, which were forbidden in the past.

4. *Adaptability to Ordnung.* Changes that are adaptable to previous Ordnung rulings are more acceptable than those that are not. New tools that can be converted to hydraulic power or new farm machinery that can be pulled by horses are more acceptable than television, which cannot be grafted to the Ordnung in any conceivable way.

5. *Ties to sacred symbols.* Changes unrelated to key symbols of ethnic identity—horse, buggy, and dress—are more acceptable than ones that threaten sacred symbols. Using a modern forklift in a shop is more acceptable than using a tractor in the field, an obvious threat to horses. Jogging shoes and rollerblades are more acceptable than new hat styles because headgear for both men and women is a key identity symbol.

6. *Linkage to "worldly" symbols.* Changes linked to worldly symbols are less acceptable than those without such ties. Computers, with monitors similar to television screens, are rejected, whereas gas-fired barbecue grills are acceptable because they have no tie to a worldly object.

7. *Sacred ritual.* Changes unrelated to worship practices are more acceptable than those that threaten sacred ritual. Changing the Ordnung for nonfarm work is easier done than changing the ritual patterns of singing, baptism, and ordination. Old Order ritual changes very slowly.

8. *Limitations.* Changes with specified limits are more acceptable than open-ended ones. Hiring vehicles primarily for business on weekdays is more acceptable than hiring them any time for any purpose.

9. *Interaction with outsiders.* Changes that encourage regular interaction with outsiders are less acceptable than those that foster ethnic ties. Serving as a hostess in a public restaurant is less acceptable than working as a clerk in an Amish retail store. A business partnership involving outsiders is more questionable than one involving church members.

10. *External connections.* Changes that open avenues of influence to modern life are less acceptable than those that do not. Membership in public organizations and the use of mass media are less acceptable than subscriptions to ethnic newspapers and participation in church activities.

11. *Family solidarity.* Changes that threaten family integration are less acceptable than those that support the family unit. Forms of work and technol-

ogy that fragment family life are less acceptable than changes that strengthen family interaction. Bicycles are less acceptable than tricycles. Working away from home is less esteemed than working at home.

12. *Ostentatious display.* Decorative changes that attract attention are less acceptable than utilitarian ones. Landscaping a lawn is less acceptable than lovely kitchens. Fancy window drapes are less acceptable than modern bathtubs and commodes.

13. *Size.* Changes that enlarge the scale of things are less acceptable than those that reinforce small social units. High-volume business enterprises are less acceptable than small family-run businesses. One-room schools are welcomed over multi-room buildings, and forty-cow herds over larger ones.

14. *Individualism.* Changes that elevate and accentuate individuals are less acceptable than those that promote social equality. Higher education and public recognition are less acceptable than correspondence courses and informal affirmation of achievement.

15. *Social capital.* Changes that threaten to deplete social capital are less likely to be accepted than those that produce it. Amish schooling is more highly endorsed than public education. Throwing horseshoes at family reunions is more esteemed than playing golf on a public course.

None of these factors operate alone or in isolation. The question of playing golf involves not only family, leisure, and travel, but interaction with outsiders as well—an easy target for a taboo. The use of computers is contentious because it involves making a living, connecting to the outside world, and accessing communicative technology. Change becomes especially volatile in cases where both positive and negative forces intersect.

THE POLITICAL CONTEXT OF CHANGE

Apart from the cultural values that regulate the acceptance of a new practice, there are many political considerations. In some cases, internal political factors may play as important a role as cultural ones.

1. *Status of innovators.* The status of the innovators—the "fence jumpers"—within the Amish community plays a key role in determining the acceptability of a new practice. If insulated ice coolers in contemporary colors are used by respected church members at family picnics, they will likely spread rapidly throughout the community. However, when the innovators

occupy marginal positions on the fringe of Amish society, new practices are more likely to fail or to spread very slowly.

2. *Leadership.* The opinion and diplomatic style of the senior bishops regulate the acceptance of major changes that come to their attention. The influence of the ranking bishop and his senior colleagues is especially important. If elderly bishops have a strong aversion to a practice, its acceptance may need to await their death. Thus, the prevailing sentiment of the senior bishops is crucial in determining the reception of a new practice. The folklore surrounding the decision to accept weed trimmers shows the political influence of a senior bishop who apparently did not fully understand the issue under discussion at a Bishops' Meeting. During lunch, when he realized that his colleagues had been discussing weed trimmers, he reportedly said, "Oh, weed pigs—well, I have one and I think it's pretty nice." After lunch the issue was dropped, and power weed trimmers were here to stay, despite the taboo on power lawn mowers.

3. *Rate of change.* The Amish sometimes talk of how fast the wheel of change is spinning. "We are all moving," said one member. "Some are just moving faster than others, but we're really moving in Lancaster County." The rate of change within the community may also determine the acceptability of a particular item. The divisions of both 1910 and 1966 came at times of rapid change, and some practices may have been rejected then to simply slow the rate of change. In the early 1960s the ordained leaders placed taboos on six technological innovations after other ones, modern hay balers and gas appliances, had just been accepted. It was simply a case of how much change could be absorbed in a short period of time. Furthermore, restrictions on some of the six innovations were gradually relaxed over the years. Thus, the acceptability of a particular item may hinge on whether it comes during an era of rapid change, as well as on the number of other recently adopted practices.

4. *External pressure.* Legal and political pressure from the larger society has an obvious impact on moving Amish fences. Highway codes were responsible for adding electric lights, signals, red flashers, and large fluorescent triangles to Amish buggies. Dairy inspectors pressed for indoor toilets for sanitary reasons in the 1950s. In another instance, pressure from public health officials encouraged massive vaccinations following the outbreak of polio among the Amish in 1979. Zoning ordinances in some townships

have limited the size and location of Amish businesses. External constraints like these have produced some of the changes in Amish life.

5. *Cultural lag.* Cultural lag occurs in a society when the pace of technology races ahead of traditional beliefs—for example, if the ability to clone humans outpaces ethical guidelines. Although within their society the Amish have tried to control technology, they deliberately want to lag behind the larger world. By imposing limits on some practices, they maintain symbolic separation between their subculture and modern life. While change is necessary and acceptable, unrestricted change would erode the symbolic boundaries and close the gap with the outside world.

Thus, new practices are often accepted with limits to protect Amish identity and maintain symbolic separation. Permitting changes with restrictions signals that, true to their role, the Amish are still lagging behind modern society. A modern kitchen without a dishwasher, wallpaper without designs, a shop without a telephone, a silo without an unloader, and a hay baler without out a bale thrower are all ways of maintaining symbolic separation while still permitting change. Although the Amish are pleased to lag behind modern life, they have avoided the cultural lag that often plagues societies when technology leaps ahead of human values. By holding a tight rein on technology, the Amish have kept it subservient to community goals and thus have minimized cultural lag within their society.

AN INTERACTIVE MODEL OF SOCIAL CHANGE

The emergence of business enterprises in Amish society illustrates the interactive process of social change as shown in Figure 12.1. Amish culture contained both resources and restraints for the development of entrepreneurial activity. The resources and restraints, interacting together, often in opposition to each other, produced the hundreds of microenterprises described in Chapter 10. Their development, in turn, has acted back upon the traditional culture to produce a variety of cultural revisions.

The resources included both cultural and social capital—the values, norms, and customs, as well as the kinship networks across the settlement that were available to empower the work of prospective entrepreneurs.[4] These resources provided various forms of capital for underwriting the new commercial ventures. *Cultural resources* for entrepreneurship in the Amish community included frugality, a vigorous work ethic, and managerial skills

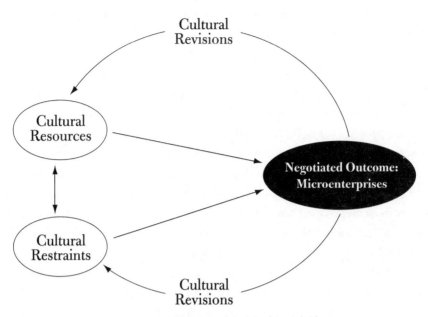

FIGURE 12.1 An Interactive Model of Social Change

forged on the farm. The social capital came in the form of strong kinship networks, large and stable family units, and an ample supply of cheap labor. A longstanding emphasis on practical education—especially apprenticeship—also facilitated the development of microenterprises. All of these resources floating in the ethnic reservoir provided cultural and social capital for the formation of Amish businesses.

However, not all the commodities in a cultural tradition are beneficial for entrepreneurial development. Indeed, many restraints in the Amish cultural warehouse impede entrepreneurial activity. These *cultural restraints,* stowed away in the heritage of the community, include historic values, norms, taboos, customs, and practices. The church's longstanding prohibitions against litigation, politics, individualism, commercial insurance, higher education, and involvements with the outside world all hinder the development of business. Moreover, restrictions on technology—motor vehicles, telephones, computers, and electricity—also levy constraints on entrepreneurs. The esteemed virtues of Gelassenheit—modesty and humility—as well as age-old taboos on pride, restrain advertising and promotional efforts. Many of these cultural constraints on entrepreneurship are at odds with other resources in the

Amish heritage that can empower business activity. Thus, the rise of micro-enterprises often involved delicate negotiations between the cultural resources and restraints of the ethnic community.[5]

Consequently, the emergence of microenterprises has produced *cultural revisions* in the traditional patterns of Amish life. Business involvements are reshaping old cultural values and social arrangements, and these changes will inextricably alter the face of Amish society in the years to come. The shops and stores that were developed because of certain deeply held Amish beliefs are now acting back upon—indeed, revising—the cultural values that gave rise to them in the first place. Signs of modernity—growing individualism, control, efficiency, rationality, mobility, and occupational specialization—are clearly more and more in evidence. The rise of microenterprises is, in short, transforming the traditional culture of Amish society.

POINTS OF TENSION

Social change is rarely simple or comfortable for any group, and the Amish are no exception. The pace of change in Amish society is typically slow, but the Lancaster settlement, sitting on the edge of the eastern megalopolis, is especially vulnerable to change. At the dawn of the twenty-first century, a variety of stress points emerged as the community struggled with rapid growth and change in the midst of an urbanizing region.

1. *North vs. south.* In the last decades of the twentieth century, tensions surfaced between the old historic center of the settlement and the newer, more conservative sector in southern Lancaster County. Some districts in the north had a more tolerant Ordnung, shaped by greater interaction with outsiders. The southern flank was more rural, plain, and traditional. All things considered, the more rural the setting, the plainer the church district. The north-south differences were driven not only by the external environment but by self-selection as well. Some families who wanted a plainer Ordnung moved south. The north-south tension, if not mediated carefully by the settlement-wide Bishops' Meetings, has the potential to divide the settlement.

2. *Farm vs. business.* A related but not identical point of tension surfaced in Ordnung differences for farm and shop. The rules for farming, developed over many decades, were more traditional and thus more difficult

to change. Because business enterprises have developed so recently, they faced fewer constraints in the Ordnung. The rules for business had to be created from scratch, and some farmers complained that the Ordnung for shops was too liberal, too flexible. Why should shop owners have so much freedom when farmers had faithfully followed the traditional restrictions for years? In response, the business owners asked why they should be restrained by old-fashioned rules designed for a barnyard when they were involved in manufacturing. Said one young shop worker, "Farmers and shop owners bicker like Democrats and Republicans." A young farm wife whose parents own a business said, "The farm and shop are two different worlds." The tension between these two worlds stretches across the entire settlement and is accented by the north-south cleavage.

   3. *Plain vs. fancy.* The foray into business created a new social class of entrepreneurs. Their resources, expertise, and lifestyle often challenge the traditional, Plain patterns of the past. Upscale homes, finer furnishings,

Gazebos, storage sheds, and playhouses produced in Amish shops are shipped across the country. The growth of shops has accelerated social change in Amish life.

longer trips, and greater use of technology set the commercial class apart from their more rural compatriots. The emergence of a wealthier class challenges communal values and authority as well as many traditional practices. Will the fast and fancy elite be willing to bend to the common order and use their wealth to support community life, or will they disrupt the entire system? That touchy question stalks the community.

The Amish have been a people of separation—embodied by dress, dialect, and social distance from the outside world. As we have seen, the social distance is shrinking in many ways. They are interacting more and more with outsiders on a daily basis. This growing contact dilutes the dialect, exposes them to technology, and erodes the traditional boundaries. Worried about these trends, some leaders argue for a Plainer, more separatist lifestyle.

These points of tension are propelled by two factors: occupational change and geographic location. The entry into business and the fact the Lancaster Amish community is encircled by an urban culture that is encroaching upon them at every turn have heightened the points of stress. In other words, some of the tensions would fade if the Amish were farming in secluded rural areas. But the Lancaster Amish are not. And the big question is whether church elders can mediate the tensions and hold the settlement together.

POSTMODERN CHALLENGES

If home is a fitting metaphor for preindustrial society and if the factory reflects the realities of the modern world, the theater, with its fleeting images of reality, perhaps best captures the postmodern ethos. In many ways the Amish are preindustrial people anchored at home. Their protest against progress has focused on the modern world with its cities, factories, and mechanical products—cameras, cars, tractors, and telephones. And as we have seen, the modern world with its mechanical ethos often decontextualized social life, yet the boundaries were rather clear. All of that has changed in the postmodern context, where lines and borders suddenly become quite fuzzy.

These developments raise new challenges for a separatist people. In the modern era, telephone lines could actually be seen. The tie with the outside world was clear. Telephones could easily be banned from the home and restricted to a community phone shanty. In recent years, with cordless and cellular phones, the old boundaries have suddenly evaporated. Cellular phones can easily be concealed and carried anywhere, oblivious to all borders. In the past, television was an easy target for the Old Orders to censure.[6] An agent of entertainment, television was easily banned by the church. However, computers are another story because they mix entertainment and business. The lines are becoming fuzzy, but the taboo on electricity nevertheless helps the Amish to hold computers at bay. However, the old lines were erased once again by battery-operated laptops that can be carried anywhere, mocking the old borders. Moreover, laptops can be easily tucked under a bed or hidden in a closet. Worse yet, they can be hooked up to the Internet and bring vile images and raunchy music into Amish barns and bedrooms.

Thus, the old taboos that forbade public electricity and sanctioned battery-operated gadgets face new challenges in a postmodern context. In short, the old rules of the Ordnung, designed for fixed lines and mechanical boundaries, are challenged by the amoebic web of worldwide telecommunications where everything blends into everything else. How will an Old Order people fare in a postmodern world? That, of course, is the new riddle emerging in Amishland.[7]

A BARGAINING UPDATE

The Amish encounter with modernity involved a process of negotiation—with give and take on all sides. On some issues, the Amish surrendered to the demands of modernity; at other times, the agents of change conceded to the Amish. And as we have seen, compromise was often the order of the day as bargains were negotiated between the stewards of tradition and the proponents of progress. In a few cases, the Amish refused to negotiate—to place certain things on the bargaining table. Thus, in broad strokes, four outcomes can be identified: concessions *by* the Amish, concessions *to* the Amish, compromises, and nonnegotiables.

The first outcome, concessions *by* the Amish, reveals aspects of their culture that have undergone modernization. Some concessions were *internally* induced changes that the Amish permitted by default—modern-looking homes, milking machines, washing machines, state-of-the-art tools, cash registers, and rollerblades. These changes enhance productivity, convenience, and comfort. Other changes came about because of *external* pressure—legal, political, economic—from the outside world. Examples include the acceptance of bulk milk tanks, lights and signals on buggies, zoning regulations, sanitary standards for breeding kennels, and school attendance through the eighth grade, to name but a few. Some concessions—indoor toilets, for example—were prompted by a desire for convenience as well as by ultimatums from milk inspectors. In any event, these adaptations represent areas in which the Amish have conceded to outside pressures for a variety of reasons. The following is a sample of the concessions made by the Amish:

> lights, signals, and reflectors on buggies
> bulk milk tanks
> farm management techniques
> large dairy herds
> artificial insemination of cows
> chemical fertilizers
> insecticides and pesticides
> nonfarm employment
> use of advertising in business
> power tools for manufacturing
> indoor bathroom facilities
> modern kitchen cabinetry
> contemporary house exteriors
> use of professional services (lawyers, physicians, etc.)
> modern medicine

Concessions *to* the Amish are found on the other side of the bargaining table. Here the agents of modernity made allowances for the Amish by lax enforcement, exemptions, or special legislation. In these instances, the Amish were able to achieve their cultural objectives. The Supreme Court endorsement of Amish schooling exemplifies the most dramatic concession. Other examples include the exemption from Social Security, the waiver of the hard hat regulation, and no Sunday milk pickups on Amish farms. Capitulations to the Amish include:

> alternative service for conscientious objectors
> waiver of school certification requirements
> waiver of school building requirements

This former tobacco shed, was converted to a gift shop for tourists. It tells the story of social change among the Amish of Lancaster County.

> waiver of minimum wage requirements for teachers
> Worker's Compensation exemption
> unemployment insurance exemption
> alteration of zoning regulations (by various townships)
> horse travel on public roads
> lax enforcement of child labor laws

A third outcome of the cultural bargaining sessions involves the riddles—the cultural compromises. These agreements reflect a mixture of tradition and modernity, for they typically involve some give-and-take on both sides. They symbolize a delicate balance between tradition and modernity. The distinction between the use and ownership of motor vehicles and the use of electric freezers in a neighbor's home reflect the delicate tension. The rise of Amish businesses, halfway between farm work and factory work, is a structural compromise. Some bargains—the vocational school, for example—rep-

resent an attempt to save face for both parties. The following sampler lists
some of the many cultural compromises:

> the vocational school
> selective use of telephones
> modern machinery towed by horses
> engines mounted on field equipment
> tractors used at barns and shops
> air and hydraulic power
> hiring of cars and vans
> modern gas appliances
> selective use of electricity
> electrical inverters
> nonfarm work based at home
> permanent-press fabric for traditional garb
> contemporary materials for carriage construction
> Amish-owned-and-operated businesses
> Amish-owned tourist stands

Finally, the nonnegotiables are traditional aspects of Amish life that have
remained largely untarnished by modernity. These staunch features of Amish
culture have never appeared on the bargaining table. They remain in their
traditional form despite the press of progress. Amish liturgy, ritual, and music, as well as the subordination of the individual to collective goals, remain
intact. Limiting education, using horses, and speaking the dialect are just a
few of the mainstays of Amish culture that have withstood the massive sweep
of history. Some of the nonnegotiable items include:

> small church districts
> worship in homes
> worship service format
> confession, excommunication, and shunning
> traditional authority structure
> lay ministers
> mutual aid
> limited education
> horse-drawn farm equipment

horse and carriage transportation
traditional styles of dress
Pennsylvania German dialect
traditional gender roles
large extended families
small social units

SOLVING THE BIG RIDDLE

We have explored the many ways in which the Amish have coped with modernity. These excursions have solved some of the smaller riddles and unraveled clues to the big one: How is a tradition-laden group thriving in the midst of modern life? Their dual strategy of *resistance* and *negotiation* has worked, for they have indeed flourished. What cultural secrets have enabled them to preserve their identity as a peculiar people for more than thirty decades? They have successfully blended numerous ingredients into their cultural recipe. One ingredient alone cannot explain their growth, and eliminat-

A snow couple faces an uncertain future.

ing a single factor would not spoil their good fortune. A variety of factors offer clues to solving the riddle of their success.[8]

1. *Reproduction.* Large families and strong retention have enabled the Amish to replenish their population and grow their community. Minimal use of birth control, the labor needs of farming, the use of modern medicine, and certain religious values have all contributed to sizeable families. Childhood socialization, private education, nonfarm work, and controlled interaction with the outside world have held young people within the ethnic community and encouraged its spiraling growth.

2. *Flexibility.* The Amish have been willing to negotiate. They have agreed to technological concessions that have reaped handsome financial rewards. While holding firm to some taboos, they have not allowed religious practices to stifle the economic growth of their community. Indeed, their flexibility has energized their fiscal and the cultural vitality.

3. *Gelassenheit.* Despite their flexibility, the Amish have insisted on the primacy of community concerns over individual rights. Excessive individualism, which would splinter the collective order, is simply not tolerated. In both childhood and adulthood, individuals remain subordinate to the moral order of the community.

4. *Ethnic organizations.* The rise of Amish schools and businesses has created a circle of ethnic institutions that surrounds people throughout their lives. Many interlocking networks shelter individuals from contaminating relationships with the larger world. This web of ethnic ties provides ample social capital and reconfirms Amish views through daily interaction.

5. *Social control.* Small-scale units, ethnic symbolism, traditional authority, and religious legitimacy enable the church to exercise pervasive social control. Behavior within the community as well as interaction with the outside world is regulated in harmony with cultural values. The ritual of confession and the practice of shunning are powerful forms of control that contribute to the vitality of the community.

6. *Small scale.* Small-scale units, from church districts to farms and from schools to businesses, have boosted Amish success. Small social units increase interaction, enhance social control, and encourage social equality. Moreover, they preserve the individual's identity and integration within the larger collective order.

7. *Managing technology.* Part of the Amish genius is the careful management of technology. They are neither enamored by it nor afraid to tame it. Able to perceive both its detrimental and its productive consequences, they have tried to selectively use technology in ways that complement and reinforce community goals and build social capital.

8. *Restricting consciousness.* By encouraging a practical education that ends with the eighth grade, the Amish are, in essence, restricting consciousness. Critical thinking that fosters independent thought and analysis would surely spur individualism and fragment the community. Filtering the flow of ideas and social ties with outsiders through private schooling has helped to preserve Amish society.

9. *Symbolizing core values.* Key symbols—horse, dress, carriage, and lantern—articulate core values of simplicity, humility, submission, and separation. These everyday symbols, used over and over again, become ubiquitous reminders of Amish realities. They objectify cultural boundaries and confer an ethnic identity on individual members. The preservation of these symbols has helped to fortify the community.

10. *Managing social change.* Amish survival pivots on the astute management of social change. It involves a delicate balance—allowing enough change to keep members content without destroying their core commitments. It requires selective cooperation with modernity without relinquishing cultural identity. The Amish have shown a remarkable ability to allow change while setting new symbolic boundaries to preserve the lines of separation from the world. Pulling out old stakes without planting new ones would quickly erode Amish identity.

Faced with dramatic changes in their social environment, the Amish have survived by carefully managing their cultural fences. While holding firmly to some ancient markers, they have permitted discreet change in the shadows. In other cases, they have moved old fences to keep up with the times. Moreover, they have also staked out new borders. Whether moving old fences or erecting new ones, the secret of their success lies in their insistence on keeping fences. They have discovered that good fences are imperative to preserving a people, so they move their fences rather than discard them.

Exploring Our Common Riddles

Having an identity as a people is a real plus, but it's not the
only way to heaven.
—*Amish leader*

HOMELESS MODERNS

The authors of a study of individualism and community in American society worry that "individualism may have grown cancerous . . . that it may be threatening the survival of freedom itself." Is there anything we can learn, they wonder, from the wisdom of more traditional societies?[1] We have been tapping the wisdom of a traditional society as we explored the riddle of Amish culture. What have we learned about the Amish, ourselves, and contemporary culture? Moreover, why are we attracted to a people that eschew many of the virtues that we applaud—diversity, inclusiveness, individualism, and consumerism? This is perhaps the most curious puzzle of all.

Exploring the Amish riddle raises questions about our own journey in the modern world. What is the price of progress? Do modern social arrangements enhance or diminish human well-being and satisfaction? One social analyst argues that modernity has left us "homeless," without a place in a coherent social order, as it dismantled the stable social structures that provided "homes" for people in preindustrial settings. Rapid social change, specialization, mobility, technology, and cultural pluralism have chipped away at our roots, at our identity, and at the very core of our lives, leaving our minds "homeless" as well.[2] Thus, modern youth must search for a self and a social home.

The Amish remind us that the modern story is a mixed one—a tale of both delight and despair. Beyond its dazzling technological achievements, modern life has freed us from the bondage of provincial ties, restricted opportunities, oppressive systems, and geographical limits. But human liberation has also been expensive. Although modern life has brought major strides in human rights and unprecedented possibilities for prosperity, it has also brought the blight of alienation—an evaporation of meaning.[3] The erosion of meaning and the loss of belonging have contributed to our "homelessness"—the bleaker side of modernity, which in so many other ways has liberated the human spirit.

The Amish have managed to preserve their social "home" despite the march of history. They have remained untouched by the blight of homelessness. Roots, meaning, and belonging remain intact in Amish life. Their Amish "home" looks nostalgically serene to us, but it remains entrenched in provincialism, sexism, and traditionalism. It is certainly not a modern home—or is it?

MODERN AMISH

The riddle of Amish culture raises intriguing questions about the meaning of modernity. What exactly does it mean to be modern—or postmodern for that matter? Are the Amish modern? Our first response to that question is surely "no." However, some scholars have argued that although the Amish do not appear modern at first glance, they act in modern ways. They have fashioned their lives in deliberate ways in the modern world as they have selectively picked the fruits of the industrial revolution. If the freedom to make choices is the trademark of modernity, then perhaps the Amish have indeed joined the modern world.[4] By deciding not to be modern—by bucking the sway of progress—they have ironically exercised choice and have acted quite modern.

The Amish have made self-conscious collective decisions to reject computers and accept calculators, to build their own schools, and to argue their convictions before congressional committees. They have controlled the conditions of their work, organized the equivalent of a political lobby group, and rejected car ownership.[5] In these and many other ways, they have taken charge of their destiny. They have made choices. In this sense they are modern and quite different from traditional peasants, who simply take whatever fate bestows. Some Amish decisions were guided by economic concerns; others were made to uphold religious values, bolster family solidarity, sharpen separation from the world, promote social equality, and preserve social capital.[6] In any event, the Amish as a group have made choices. They have decided just how modern they want to be.

This is not the whole story, however. When we shift from the collective to the individual level, things are quite different. An Amish individual has fewer choices than a modern one. Choices regarding dress, education, and transportation are dictated by group standards. Marriage is limited to other members of the church. Occupational choice is nil compared to the astonishing array of jobs in an information society. Amish society, as experienced by the individual, is quite restrictive—quite traditional. The restriction of individual freedom among the Amish is little different, however, than the restraints placed on individuals by sports teams, monastic orders, or military organizations in the broader society.

The Amish practice of adult baptism, in which individuals voluntarily decide to join the church, is indeed a rather modern idea. However, it is a choice that entails the decision to set aside personal rights and submit to the collective order of the church. It is not an entirely free choice because, as we have seen, Amish socialization funnels youth toward church membership. But the Amish have acted in modern ways by making self-conscious decisions to preserve their identity as a people—decisions that often restrict individual choice. To use the bargaining metaphor, Amish negotiators were unwilling to give up their collective identity in exchange for greater individual freedom.

Are there other ways to think about modernity? If to be modern means using the latest electronic technology, if it means ultraconvenience, if it means the embrace of scientific research, if it means the unfettered pursuit of individualism, if it means that joy comes in consumerism, and if it means that reality is found in glitzy entertainment, then the Amish have surely not joined the modern world.

If, however, being modern means controlling the conditions of one's work, if it means a delight in artisanship, if it means protecting the individual from the burden of choice, if it means taming the detrimental effects of technology, if it means safeguarding community identity, if it means caring for the unfortunate and the elderly, if it means guaranteeing the individual a secure identity, and if it means bestowing meaning to all of life, then perhaps the Amish have not only joined the modern world but are leading it.

NAGGING QUESTIONS

Nevertheless, we are bothered by some nagging questions. By what right do Amish parents limit the education of their children, restrict occupational choice, cap opportunities for personal achievement, stifle artistic expression, and prescribe rigid gender roles? Such controls squander human potential. Are not such restrictions downright oppressive and sexist by modern standards? Consider all the potential pilots, nurses, lawyers, artists, and social workers who are hauling manure and canning vegetables on Amish farms. Denying Amish youth educational opportunity makes a mockery of justice and human rights. Would it not be only fair, Moderns wonder, if Amish children were required to attend at least several years of public high school to taste the fruits of progress? Then they would be truly free to pursue professional careers or to return to Amish life. Such exposure would at least allow them to explore artistic and scientific careers as well as their own human potential.

The Amish are amused by such thinking, for they can flip the questions upside down. By what right, they ask, do modern parents push their children so rapidly through the turnstiles of modernity to face incessant choices and carry heavy emotional loads that they must shoulder all alone? By what right do Moderns deprive their youth of the psychological security and personal identity that come from membership in a lasting and durable group? The Amish would remind us that those who leave their Amish fold fare quite well in the modern world, for they have been taught the values of hard work, integrity, and frugality—values that serve them well in a variety of careers. Thus, the Amish contend that they are hardly depriving their youth—at least not any more than modern parents do. In fact, the Amish wonder, should not modern youth be required to live several years in a traditional community to experience the values of communal life firsthand? Then they could join the cultural system of their choice.

The provincialism of Amish culture irritates the modern penchant for diversity, inclusiveness, and pluralism. The cosmopolitan, well-rounded, well-traveled person is the charm of contemporary culture. The intolerance and rigidity of Amish life stifle the human spirit and nurture a myopic worldview. By what right, Moderns ask, can the Amish, in the name of Christianity, oppose the liberation of the human spirit and mind?

The Amish would likely agree that their culture is indeed local, parochial, and sectarian. But, they might ask, are Moderns as liberated as they proclaim to be? Blind adherence to some modern ideas results in its own form of bondage. An obsession with individualism precludes understanding and appreciating the benefits of collective endeavor. Addiction to consumerism leads to a hollow and shallow materialism. Rigid insistence on diversity can thwart the building of stable, disciplined communities. Intolerance for socialism, patriarchy, traditional authority, and religious views not only belittles the very notion of tolerance but also betrays a provincial mentality enslaved to modern values. The Amish might argue that they at least understand the modern world as well as or better than Moderns understand the Amish world, and hence they are *less* provincial. How many modern youth, the Amish might ask, are bilingual by the end of eighth grade? The Amish would contend that in the final analysis one must choose among ultimate values. Tolerance, diversity, and pluralism may have to yield if they threaten to spoil the greater values of a stable community and a secure personal identity.

Yet the conformity of Amish life nags us. Dutiful adherence to tradition— dressing alike, driving duplicate carriages, meekly following rules—cultivates a bland, even boring conformity. The recipe for success in Amish culture not only cultivates a herd mentality but also ridicules human dignity by promoting, even applauding, thoughtless ritualism. To modern ways of thinking, the Amish are puppets of their culture, controlled by the strings of their religious traditions.

The Amish would likely agree. Conformity does guide much of their conduct. They would simply remind Moderns that puppets abound outside Amish culture as well, that even in modern life individuals are puppets of their culture. Fashions of dress, consumer fads, leisure trends, housing and decorating styles—all driven by advertising—are thriving outside the Amish world. The preponderance of such conformity suggests that even modern individualists are controlled by the strings of social opinion. Moreover, the Amish might ask, which is more mindless, conformity to a religious tradition or conformity to mass advertising and popular fads? Under the pretense of free choice, Moderns bow to the Ordnung of contemporary fashion. From software packages to social etiquette, from music to dress, our preferences are also shaped by social standards and custom. The Amish would remind us that their choice of an alternative lifestyle is not so much a matter of conforming to tradition—for that is inherent in the human experience—but a matter of deciding which traditions are most worthy of embrace.

CULTURAL TRADEOFFS

Tourists are enchanted by the Amish. Social analysts hold them up as models for development, and energy experts herald their efficiency.[7] Others point to the humane character of the Amish social system. Despite these accolades from academics, few have chosen to join them. Few outsiders have chosen to toss aside technological convenience and the delights of individualism and submit themselves to the collective order of Amish life. There is a price to being Amish—a price that few outsiders have been willing to pay. It means giving up self-assertive individualism—submitting to the Ordnung, to religious tradition, to the voice of elders, and to communal wisdom. It means forgoing individual preference in many areas—dress, marriage, transportation, and education. It means limited mobility, little occupational choice, and few possibilities for self-enhancement. It means forgoing many conveniences, restricting friendships, avoiding commercial leisure, unplugging electronic media, and disconnecting from the World Wide Web. It means, in short, inhabiting a different social world, where the group, not the individual, reigns supreme.

It is a world of restricted ideas, where scientific thinking is unacceptable and where the agenda of ideas is controlled. It is a world that in many ways is provincial, narrow, and restrictive—where free choice and individualism are curbed. It means accepting a religious worldview—indeed, a literalist religious worldview with a hot hell and a happy heaven. To give up, to submit, to obey, to respect limits, and to believe are the price of being Amish. For outsiders, it is a high price—a sacrifice few are willing to make. For those on the inside, the price is lower, of course, for it is the bestowed way of life. But in either case, it is costly.

There are benefits that come in return. The Amish offer genuine social security—not an impersonal system that sends computerized monthly checks. Their social security springs into action in the case of fire, death, sickness, senility, or handicap. There is also the benefit of belonging, of being part of a people, of an extended family; of having a niche and knowing it will always be there. There is the security of family with dozens of aunts, uncles, cousins, and siblings surrounding one's play, work, and worship. There is the reward of identity—personal and collective—of knowing who one is and where one fits, regardless of personal or occupational achievement.

There is also the security of tradition, of knowing that things are in order, that things are the way they are supposed to be as handed down from generations before. There is the reward of meaning, of knowing one's life is acceptable to God if one has faithfully followed the teachings of the church. There is the reward of having a permanent place—acreage, trees, a stream—a place where ancestors farmed and fished and where one's offspring will do the same. There is the security of ritual, of predictable routines that tie one into the community via worship, play, family, and work. There is, in short, a stable social "home." The costs of being Amish are high, but the benefits— identity, meaning, and belonging—are precious commodities in the midst of a homeless world.

How does Amish society fare when we consider quality-of-life indicators? Here we have a social system without poverty. Widows, orphans, and the destitute are cared for by the church. The Amish are rarely imprisoned. Here is a society virtually free of crime and violence. Some youth are occasionally arrested for drunken driving, and children are occasionally paddled, but incidents of violent crime and murder are conspicuously absent. Amish suicide and mental illness rates are substantially lower than those in the larger society.[8] Alcohol abuse, present among some youth, is practically nil among adults. Divorce is unheard of. Individuals are not warehoused in bureaucratic institutions—large schools, massive factories, retirement homes, or psychiatric hospitals—but are cared for within the family.[9]

Moreover, the generous resources of social capital in Amish society lower the transaction costs—the need for insurance, formal agreements, litigation, legal costs, and third party brokers. Many of the routine exchanges in Amish society are lubricated with trust and integrity, which reduces the economic cost of transactions. Recycling goods, frugal management, a thrifty lifestyle, and a rejection of consumerism produce scant waste. Energy consumption per capita is remarkably low. Beyond exhaust fumes from diesel power plants and water contamination by manure runoff, the Amish add little to environmental pollution. Personal alienation, loneliness, and meaninglessness are for the most part absent. There are, of course, some unhappy marriages, lonely people, obstinate bishops, cantankerous personalities, and family feuds. But all things considered, the quality-of-life indicators for Amish society as a whole are remarkably robust. The Amish have, indeed, created a humane social system that attends to individual need and generates strong levels of satisfaction.

ON THE OTHER HAND . . .

Despite these accolades, Moderns might argue, this is a lopsided view of the Amish story. Moderns might contend that the Amish are social parasites who feed off the larger social system. They are only able to thrive because they have, fortunately, found themselves in a political system that has been remarkably tolerant of their religious views. The tolerance of the larger culture protects their intolerance. As conscientious objectors, they have avoided the military programs that have protected the very religious freedoms that allow them to be different. Although they expect tolerance from the state for their dissident views, they show little tolerance toward dissidents within their own ranks. Indeed, Moderns might ask if the Amish are using the outside world as a human trash heap when they excommunicate troublemakers and cast them off on the rest of society. Their agricultural achievements and business profits rest firmly on the shoulders of modern science—a science that is off limits for their youth. They have tapped the benefits of science but have contributed little to its development.[10]

Their environmental pollution rate may be commendable, but the diesel trucks that transport products to and from Amish shops add their own fumes to the environment. Besides, what sort of justice allows their horses to chop up roadways without paying gasoline taxes for repairs? It is commendable that they care for their own, but the Amish boycott of Social Security shortchanges the welfare of the destitute in the larger society. In these and other ways, Moderns might argue that the Amish are freeloaders who have directly benefited from the resources of the larger society without contributing their fair share. Indeed, without the benefits of science, higher education, and electronic communication—all of which the Amish eschew—the quality of their life would be dismal in many ways.

AN AMISH REPLY

The Amish would obviously concede that much of this is true—they certainly are dependent on the larger world. Yet this is a rather cockeyed view. Freeloaders? Hardly, they would retort. By what standard are they social parasites when they pay millions in taxes for public schools they will never use? How can they be charged with being free riders when each Amish person annually attracts as much as $30,000 in tourist revenues? Moreover, they pay millions of dollars in federal and state income taxes and use few federal services—even rejecting many forms of subsidies and government "handouts." In many ways the Amish are subsidizing state and federal programs because they are paying into government coffers at the same rate as everyone else while using relatively few public services. They are not tapping Medicare, Medicaid, unemployment insurance, food stamps, or other forms of government aid. Nor are they collecting welfare checks, sitting in penitentiaries, borrowing federal funds for college, using Medicare for expensive surgery, benefiting from farm subsidies, or receiving Social Security checks.

True, they have not contributed directly to scientific achievements, but their tax dollars have supported scientific and medical research as well as the defense budget. Moreover, they have readily cooperated with scientists who have used their tight-knit community to study the genetic transmission of disease. Although the Amish have not provided scientists, hundreds of Amish volunteers have participated in medical studies. Furthermore, their unique presence has fueled a huge tourist industry and a robust regional economy that generates profits for non-Amish entrepreneurs.

Freeloaders? Who is kidding whom? According to Amish calculations, the bottom line shows that they contribute more than they take; they are philanthropists, not parasites, in the larger social system.

Their conscience has not allowed them to participate in military programs, but, they might ask, is it not valuable in the midst of a violent world to create a society where harmony, gentleness, and quiet discipline are the norm rather than hostility? The embodiment of a peaceful social order may be as significant as military threats in nudging the international community toward global harmony. What is so wrong, the Amish ask, with creating a social security system with a human face, where the destitute and helpless are cared for in the context of family, neighborhood, and church? Would the world not be a better place if other groups did likewise?

Besides, the Amish point out, they are quick to help when disasters—fire, storm, and flood—strike their non-Amish neighbors. Moreover, is it not helpful to have a human model, a society that allows us to observe the social impact on people when technology is harnessed, social change is slowed, and the rush of progress is tamed? "What good are the Amish?" asks Marc Olshan. He suggests their most valuable contribution is to teach the rest of us the importance of setting limits.[11]

Such a hypothetical debate between the Amish and their neighbors raises profound questions about the nature of human freedom, the meaning of progress, the role of the individual in the modern world, and the ties between individuals and social systems. The social benefits of Amish society appear nostalgically pleasant, indeed enviable. They come, however, with a high price—the loss of personal freedom. Individual rights, privileges, and freedoms, so fundamental to modern culture, are curtailed in the Amish experience. The right to unlimited self-achievement, to unbridled artistic expression, to free occupational choice, to political participation, to the defense of one's legal rights, to consumerism, to personal expression in dress—in short, the right to be or to do whatever one wants—is limited in Amish life. The communal benefits come at the expense of individual freedom—the cardinal value of modern life.

THE OTHER SIDE OF FREEDOM

There is another side to freedom.[12] Although the Amish are not free *to do* some things, they are free *from* many others. They are not free to buy the latest electrical appliances, but they are free from enormous consumer debt. They are not free to buy the latest car, but they are free from the frustrations of commuter traffic. They are not free to buy the latest convenience, but they are free to enjoy the convenience of walking across the driveway to their work. They are not free to travel on airplanes, but they are free to have lunch at home with their families. They are not free to pursue higher education, but they are free to control the curriculum and organization of their own schools. They are not free to buy the latest fashions, but they are free from the anxiety of what to wear and from endless shopping trips. The Amish are not free to watch television, but they are free from endless commercials. The Amish are not free to pursue many occupations, but they are free from the constraints of boring jobs and administrative policies.

Although the Amish are not free to make up their faces in the latest styles, they are free from the pressure to present a "perfect" face. They are not free to dress as they please, but they are free from agonizing about what they will wear. They are not free to accept Social Security checks, but they are free from worry about who will care for them in old age. They are not free to pick the college of their choice, but they are free from agonizing decisions about college selection and occupational choice. They are not free to discard the traditional ritual of Amish funerals, but they are free from worrying about who will support them in time of grief.

Although the cultural norms of Amish life circumscribe personal freedom, they also lift the burden of choice from the back of the individual. They liberate the individual from the incessant need to decide. In Amish culture, the burden for success and failure leans on the community; in the modern world, the weight of success and failure rests on the individual, who may lack the support of a durable group. The Amish are not as free to make up their own minds, shape their own destinies, and follow wherever their hearts may lead, but they are freer from endless trips to the therapist, freer from the emotional burden of making it on their own—of shouldering the consequences alone.

ARE THE AMISH HAPPY?

What does all this mean for happiness? Which culture—modern or Amish—optimizes the conditions for human fulfillment and best satisfies the yearning for meaning, belonging, and identity? Two recent books have addressed a major riddle of modern life: Why are people so unhappy in an age of plenty?[13] Why have consumerism, entertainment, and technology failed to make us happy? Happiness, of course, is relative. It hinges on cultural expectations, on social values, on the gap between expectations and achievements, and on comparisons with one's social peers.

It would be wrong to assume that the Amish are unhappy because their personal freedom is constrained. Indeed, in an hour-long television special on happiness, ABC interviewed some Amish off camera who reported higher levels of satisfaction with their life than other respondents.[14] What is most troubling, however, is that without all the conveniences of modern life, the Amish might be as happy, if not happier, than the rest of us. That is the fear that torments the modern soul.

One likely reason for their success is the ability of their society to fulfill the basic human needs of identity, belonging, and meaning. The Amish who test the boundaries of their culture may feel the tug of both worlds, but most members do not experience midlife or career crises so typical of modern life. Among Americans the toll of individualism is high, as evinced by the high number of therapists, stress management seminars, wellness centers, lawsuits, and the standard barometers of malaise: divorce, crime, drug abuse, fraud, suicide, and violence. Yet despite the psychic toll, Moderns cherish the exhilaration of individualism. Few would be willing to trade in its thrills for the tranquility, order, and meaning of Amish culture. The Amish provide a social model whereby individual needs are fulfilled, not through the delights of individualism, but in sacrifice and submission to a greater collective good. There are no promises of freewheeling self-fulfillment in Amish life, but the individual is cared for and cherished by a supportive social system—a humane and durable promise.

For "weaker" people, often discarded by the modern system, the Amish setting provides a caring environment where no one slips through the bureaucratic cracks. In the eyes of "stronger" people, the Amish system may feel oppressively tight compared to the pliable fabric of modern culture. Tilted toward the rugged individualist, modern culture easily tramples on the weak. By contrast, Amish culture, tilted toward the community, easily suffocates the strong.

The wisdom distilled in Amish culture suggests that some limits on individualism may, in the long run, serve the deeper needs of the individual better than an unbridled pursuit of self-gratification. In other words, the Amish contend that individuals may not always understand or pursue the things that lead to happiness. Indeed, happiness may be shaped as much by social structures as by individual choice.

OUR COMMON RIDDLE

Some riddles remain. How is it that those who have not been educated beyond the eighth grade have been able to devise such a humane social system? Without consultants or strategic planners, the Amish, in simple and down-to-earth ways, have crafted a social system that not only attracts the attention of tourists and scholars but also raises profound questions about the underpinnings of happiness, freedom, and meaning. Moreover, how is it that, despite the best efforts of the most learned planners and strategists, our modern world is strewn with fragmentation, alienation, and despair? Moderns plan incessantly yet often seem out of control. The Amish, who do little if any strategic planning, seem rather firmly in charge of things.

Side by side, Amish and modern culture tilt in opposite directions—one toward the community and the other toward the individual. Their comparison evokes a common riddle that engulfs the larger human community, both Amish and modern alike. Would it be possible to construct a social "home" where the need for individual expression and the need for community are suspended in a healthy and creative tension? Can we envision a culture where individuals discover their true selves only when they plant their roots in the communal soil of a larger body, where self-fulfillment is achieved in the context of a social mission that transcends selfish interests, where personal identity is firmly grounded in the identity of a larger body, and where the pursuit of profit and pleasure yields to the collective welfare—the common good?

Is it possible to pursue such lofty goals without stifling initiative, without suppressing creativity, and without restricting individual freedom? Can we only have meaningful community at the expense of individual freedom, and must such freedom result in a cancerous debilitation of community? Or is it possible to forge a culture—a social habitat—where the individual and the community are not pitted against each other as adversaries, but where they supplement, complement, and enrich each other? That is the common riddle that begs all of us—Amish and Moderns alike—for a solution.

Such a delicate mix would not only champion the charms of community but would also empower and enable individuals to achieve their highest creative aspirations. Such a "home" would welcome the gifts of mind and body and embrace them—not for selfish ends in themselves but for embellishment of the larger community, not for self-acclaim but for collective celebration, not for personal gain but for corporate enhancement. Can we find a middle ground, a social order that anchors the individual in a larger body and at the same time applauds choice and creative expression? The solution to our common riddle promises to arrest the cancerous growth of individualism as well as to relax the stifling restrictions of traditional life. Hidden within our common riddle is the hope of a new social order, a "home" that taps both the achievements of modernity and the wisdom of Amish life.

Research Procedures

The observations in this book describe the Old Order Amish settlement in Lancaster County, Pennsylvania. The details of social life vary in Amish settlements across the United States, making it unwise to apply the specifics of the Lancaster Amish to other communities. However, although the particulars of practice vary from settlement to settlement, the basic values, philosophy, and worldview of Amish culture described in this book are applicable to other Amish settlements as well.

Various data sources were used for this study: in-depth interviews, primary source documents, ethnographic observations, and three demographic profiles of the Lancaster settlement in 1986, 1993, and 2000. Face-to-face interviews with dozens of Amish were conducted in 1986, 1987, 1993, 1996, and 2000. The informants included males and females, farmers and business owners, mothers and fathers, married and single, teachers, and ordained leaders. Informants were selected to tap a representative cross section of the community. Many interviews involved two sessions; some involved as many as five. A significant portion of the book is based on the notes and transcripts of these interviews. Public officials and non-Amish professionals who relate to the Amish community as lawyers, physicians, accountants, bankers, and veterinarians were also widely consulted.

The Amish are hesitant to publicize minutes of meetings, organizational documents, and policy statements. In many cases generous informants shared copies of materials, personal letters, and other primary sources for which I am deeply grateful. Except for a few who granted permission, I have not revealed or identified informants in the text. Having lived in the Lancaster area all of my life, I have long been familiar with members of the Amish community and am fortunate to have many as friends and acquaintances. These experiences have provided opportunities to observe Amish society firsthand. Throughout the research efforts, the Amish have always been gracious and helpful neighbors who generously shared their time and thoughts with me.

SETTLEMENT PROFILE 1986

A stratified two-stage cluster sample was used to obtain demographic data on a sample of 382 people living in 168 Amish households in twenty districts in 1986. This study provided the primary database for the first edition of the book and is described more fully in that edition.

In 1993 an Amish Enterprise Profile gathered data on Amish enterprises and entrepreneurs in thirteen church districts. Information was gathered on 118 enterprises and in-depth interviews were conducted with thirty-five selected entrepreneurs. The fieldwork was coordinated and conducted by Steven M. Nolt. Some of the findings from the Enterprise Profile have informed the discussion of Amish businesses in Chapter 10. A fuller description of the methods can be found in Kraybill and Nolt (1995:261–64). The results of the study were published in a book (Kraybill and Nolt 1995).

A study conducted in the spring of 2000 provides the primary database for the revised edition of this book. Profile 2000 gathered information on a total of 1,704 individuals living in ten church districts. The districts were purposely selected to represent the total population of 131 church districts as of December 1999. The sample reflected the geographic location, size, and age of the district. Children under 16 years of age were also enumerated. Demographic data were gathered on 888 individuals who were 16 years of age and older. Louise Stoltzfus coordinated all aspects of the fieldwork and recruited informants to assist in each district. The completion rate was 100 percent. Krista Malick keystroked the data and performed the data analysis.

Old Order Amish Lancaster County Settlement Population Estimates, 1880–2010

Date	Districts	Less than 18 Years	18 years and Older	Total
1880	6	400	350	750
1890	6	400	350	750
1900	6	400	350	750
1910	9	600	500	1,100
1920	11	700	650	1,350
1930	15	1,000	850	1,850
1940	18	1,550	1,400	2,950
1950	25	2,200	1,900	4,100
1960	35	3,050	2,700	5,750
1970	46	4,000	3,500	7,500
1980	65	5,650	4,950	10,600
1990	95	8,700	7,700	16,400
2000	131	11,650	10,650	22,300
2010	194	17,150	15,850	33,000

SOURCES: The number of districts is based on listings in *Directory* (1973, 1980, 1996) of the Lancaster Old Order Amish settlement and Amish informants. In 1931 four districts divided to make a total of fifteen, and this number is used for the 1930 calculations. Informant estimates of 125 people per district were used to estimate the population for the years prior to 1940. The 1986 average district size of 163 people was used to estimate the population from 1940 to 1990. The proportion of those 18 years and older (46.8%) to those under 18 years (53.2%) was used to estimate the two age groups from 1940 to 1990 based on the 1986 Profile. The population estimates for 2000 and 2010 are based on the Settlement Profile 2000 data gathered from ten districts that averaged 170 persons, 52 percent of whom were under 18 years. As of 1 January 2000, the Lancaster settlement had 131 districts, including 15 districts that stretched into Chester County and 2 districts in York County. Four districts divided during the year, yielding a total of 135 districts by December 2000. The 2010 estimates are based on current trends. Numbers are rounded to the nearest fifty.

Estimated Amish Population (Old Order and New Order) by State and Province in North America

State/Province	Districts	Adult Members	Children/Adults
Ohio	368	22,100	49,700
Pennsylvania	297	17,800	40,100
Indiana	242	14,500	32,650
Wisconsin	76	4,950	10,250
Michigan	69	4,150	9,300
Missouri	45	2,700	6,100
New York	37	2,200	5,000
Kentucky	38	2,300	5,150
Iowa	36	2,150	4,850
Illinois	31	1,850	4,200
Ontario	24	1,450	3,250
Minnesota	12	700	1,600
Tennessee	11	650	1,500
Delaware	8	500	1,100
Kansas	8	500	1,100
Maryland	6	350	800
Oklahoma	5	300	700
Montana	4	250	550
Virginia	4	250	550
Six states*	10	600	1,350
TOTAL	1,331	80,250	179,800

SOURCE: Raber (2001) and Amish informants.

NOTE: Numbers are rounded to the nearest fifty. The following assumptions were used for the estimates: 60 adult members and 75 unbaptized youth per church across all settlements (135 total population). The actual number of members varies by district and settlement. Lancaster area districts are typically larger than districts in outlying settlements. The estimated national average of 60 members per district is based on the following assumptions: Lancaster Settlement and related districts = 75; Delaware, Indiana, and Ohio districts = 60; Swartzentruber districts = 50; all other districts = 55. The estimate of 75 unbaptized children and youth for 60 adult members (total =135) is based on data from several different settlements.

*The six states are Florida (1), North Carolina (2), Texas (3), Washington (1), West Virginia (2), and Mississippi (1).

A P P E N D I X

Settlements Originating from the Lancaster County Settlement, 1940–2000

Date	Districts	Name	County	State	Origin
1940	5	St. Mary's	St. Mary's	MD	Lancaster
1941	6	Lebanon	Lebanon	PA	Lancaster
1964	0	Gettysburg* (1997)	Adams	PA	St. Mary's
1967	4	Brush Valley	Centre	PA	Lancaster
1968	4	Path Valley	Franklin	PA	St. Mary's
1971	4	Franklin	W. Cumberland, E. Franklin	PA	Lancaster
1973	4	Sugar Valley	Clinton	PA	Lancaster
1973	4	Nittany Valley	Clinton & Centre	PA	Lancaster
1974	2	Montour	Montour & Columbia	PA	Lancaster
1975	2	York	York	PA	Lancaster
1975	2	Perry	Perry	PA	Lancaster
1976	0	Steam Valley* (1991)	Lycoming	PA	Lancaster
1977	2	White Deer	Lycoming & Northumberland	PA	Lancaster
1978	4	Dauphin	Dauphin	PA	Lancaster
1981	2	Romulus	Seneca	NY	Brush Valley
1985	1	Nippenose Valley	Lycoming & Clinton	PA	Lancaster
1989	2	Penns Valley	Centre	PA	Brush Valley
1989	4	Hopkinsville	Christian & Todd	KY	Lancaster
1990	1	Athens	Marathon	WI	Path Valley
1991	0	Burkes Garden* (1999)	Tazewell	VA	St. Mary's
1991	1	Addison	Steuben	NY	St. Mary's
1991	3	Parke	Parke	IN	Lancaster
1992	1	Owen	Clark	WI	Lancaster-Upper Valleys

Date	Districts	Name	County	State	Origin
1992	0	Potter* (1998)	Potter	PA	Lancaster
1994	2	Wayne	Wayne, Randolph & Henry	IN	Lancaster/ Gettysburg
1995	1	Wulff Valley	Buffalo	WI	Path Valley
1995	1	Licking	Texas	MO	Path Valley
1996	1	Abingdon†	Washington	VA	Lancaster
1996	1	Northumberland	Northumberland	PA	Dauphin
1997	1	Indiana	Indiana	PA	Lancaster
1997	1	Charlotte	Charlotte	VA	St. Mary's
1997	1	Moran* (2000)	Moran	TX	Lancaster
1998	1	Fenimore	Grant	WI	Lancaster
1999	1	Plattville	Lafayette	WI	Lancaster
1999	1	Lowville	Lewis	NY	Path Valley
1999	1	Cecilton†	Cecil	MD	Lancaster

SOURCE: Compiled by Donald B. Kraybill in consultation with C. J. Stoltzfus. See also "Outlying Settlements" by C. J. Stoltzfus in *Directory* (1996). New settlements often have settlers coming from several different home settlements. The settlement of origin is considered the source that provided the largest or primary, but not necessarily the first, nucleus of settlers.

*Deceased settlements. Ending date in parentheses.

†Fledgling settlements with five or fewer families and an uncertain future.

APPENDIX E

Scripture Texts for Amish Church Services in the Lancaster Settlement

Date	Scriptures	Date	Scriptures
January 2	Matt. 3–4	July 16	Luke 14–15
January 16	Matt. 5–6	July 30	Luke 16–17
January 30	Matt. 7–8	August 13	Luke 18–19
February 13	Matt. 9–10	August 27	Luke 10, Rom. 12
February 27	Matt. 11–12	September 10	Matt. 13, Gal. 6
March 12	John 14–15	September 24	John 3, Rom. 6
March 26	John 3, Rom. 6		(*Neugeburt*)
	(*Neugeburt*)	October 8	Matt. 18, 1 Cor. 5
April 9	Matt. 18, 1 Cor. 5		(*Ordnungs*)
	(*Ordnungs*)	October 22	*Liebesmahl*
April 23	*Liebesmahl*	November 5	Heb. 11–12
May 7	Heb. 11–12	November 19	Rom. 13, 1 Pet. 2
May 21	Jas. 2–3	December 3	John 10, 1 Cor. 13
June 4	Acts 1–2	December 17	Luke 1–2
June 18	Luke 12–13	December 31	Matt. 24–25
July 2	John 4, Rev. 14		

SOURCE: *The Diary*, December 1999, 36.

NOTE: All the scriptures are from the New Testament. The listed scriptures remain the same each year, but these dates are for the year 2000. Because congregations meet every other week, half of the congregations use the scriptures a week later than the dates listed above. *Liebesmahl* is the communion service (Love Feast).

1 | The Amish Story

1. For readable introductions to the origins of the Anabaptist movement, see Dyck (1993), Klaassen (2001), Loewen and Nolt (1996), Snyder (1995), and Weaver (1987). *The Mennonite Encyclopedia* (1956) covers a wide range of topics related to Anabaptist roots and Amish beginnings.

2. J. E. Kauffman (1975:42).

3. An overview of the suffering and persecution is provided by Dyck (1993:110–13; 1985) and Schowalter (1957). Vivid descriptions of the persecution printed at the end of the *Ausbund* (1984) have been translated from the German by J. E. Kauffman (1975). The classic account of Christian martyrdom and suffering from New Testament times through the Anabaptist persecution was compiled by Braght (1985) in 1660 in the *Martyrs Mirror*.

4. For a discussion of the historical setting and the significance of the Schleitheim Confession of Faith, more properly called the Brotherly Union of a Number of Children of God Concerning Seven Articles, see J. H. Yoder (1973:34–43).

5. Bender (1957:29–54).

6. For a record of his writings, see Menno Simons (1956).

7. The term *Mennist* was first given to Dutch Anabaptist followers of Menno Simons. Eventually the name Mennonite was assumed by other Anabaptist groups as well. However, it was not widely used by the Swiss Anabaptists at the time of the Amish division in 1693.

8. Seguy (1973:182).

9. Hüppi (2000) provides a detailed description of Ammann. Helpful discussions of the identity and background of Jakob Ammann can be found in Baecher (2000), Furner (2000), and Hüppi (2000). The evidence provided by these scholars suggests that Jakob Ammann, a tailor by trade, converted to Anabaptism in 1679. He was probably 49 years old in 1693.

10. Numerous letters exchanged in the controversy have been preserved. They have been translated by Roth (1993), who provides an excellent overview of the issues surrounding the division. Helpful discussions of the context of the Amish division can also be found in Gross (1994), Guth (1995), J. A. Hostetler (1993:25–50), Luthy (1971a), Meyers (1996), Nolt (1992), Roth (1994), and E. Yoder (1987:43–58).

11. Leroy Beachey, in an unpublished paper and in personal conversation, has suggested that Ulrich Miller, an Anabaptist evangelist in the Oberland (highlands) area of Switzerland near Thun, converted many people to Anabaptism, including Jakob Ammann. Thus, Miller, according to Beachey, should be seen as the founder of the Amish movement. Moreover, the primary tension in Switzerland, according to Beachey, was between new converts in the Oberland, where Miller and Ammann lived,

and the more traditional Swiss Brethren who lived in the Emmental Valley under the leadership of Hans Reist.

12. Steven M. Nolt (1992) has written the best overall history of the Amish, including their European origins, North American migration, settlement patterns, and growth in the New World.

13. Nolt (1992:56).

14. J. F. Beiler (1983:17–18). For a discussion of Amish immigration and early settlements, see J. F. Beiler (1976a, 1983); Crowley (1978); G. L. Fisher (1987); J. A. Hostetler (1993:54–72); MacMaster (1985:69–87); Nolt (1992); G. M. Stoltzfus (1954); E. S. Yoder (1987:60–68); and P. Yoder (1987a:286–90). A series of articles about the early Pennsylvania settlements by Amish historian Joseph F. Beiler appeared in *The Diary* in 1972 and 1974. Amish genealogist Amos L. Fisher's (1984) work also provides information on the early settlements.

15. The Dunkards, formally known as Brethren, originated in Germany in 1708. The nickname Dunkard, based on their mode of baptism by immersion, eventually gave way to German Baptist Brethren in 1871. In 1908 they became the Church of the Brethren.

16. Statistics on Lancaster County's agricultural production are available from the Agricultural Committee of the Lancaster Chamber of Commerce and Industry.

17. The Holmes County, Ohio, settlement is somewhat larger than the Lancaster community, but it is divided into various Amish subgroups or affiliations that do not share a common religious discipline. For an excellent (but dated) ethnography of Amish life based on the larger settlements in Indiana, Ohio, and Pennsylvania, see John A. Hostetler's *Amish Society* (1993). See Kraybill (1994b) for a discussion of social change among four groups in the Holmes County settlement.

18. The age, size, and location of the Lancaster settlement have made it a target of numerous studies. For nineteenth-century descriptions of Amish life, see D. Beiler (1888), Gibbons (1869), Umble (1948), and P. Yoder (1979a). Twentieth-century analyses include Bachman (1961), Ericksen et al. (1979), Gallagher (1981), Getz (1946), portions of J. A. Hostetler (1993), Kollmorgen (1942, 1943), Loomis (1979), Loomis and Dyer (1976), and Smith (1961). Rice and Shenk (1947) and Rice and Steinmetz (1956) provide midcentury photographs and interpretations of the Lancaster settlement. The most recent scholarly study has been Tan's (1998) dissertation, which focuses on social capital in Amish society.

19. The Hutterites emerged as a separate branch of Anabaptism in 1528. For a discussion of their origins, see J. A. Hostetler (1997) and Packull (1995). Today they live in communitarian groups in the western United States and in Canada. For a comparison of the Old Order Amish, Hutterites, Mennonites, and Brethren, see Kraybill and Bowman (2001).

20. J. A. Hostetler (1993:91–93).

21. A settlement may have one or several affiliations, and each affiliation may have one or numerous congregations. In the Lancaster Amish settlement the Old Order Amish, New Order Amish, and Beachy Amish represent three different affiliations.

22. The Amish do not maintain population statistics; however, estimates of their population can be calculated by multiplying the known size of church districts in some

settlements by the total number of districts as reported by Raber (2001). Procedures for estimating the population of the Lancaster settlement are described in Appendix B. See Appendix C for North America and Pennsylvania population estimates.

23. I am grateful to C. Nelson Hostetter and Stephen Scott for assistance in identifying the various groups in Lancaster County. The adult membership of the six largest Anabaptist affiliations in Lancaster County include: the Lancaster Mennonite Conference (11,842), the Old Order Amish (9,234), the Church of the Brethren (7,884), the Brethren in Christ (3,117), the Groffdale Old Order Mennonite Conference (2,800), and the Weaverland Old Order Mennonite Conference (2,630).

24. These answers are reported in Ericksen et al. (1979). This comprehensive study of Amish fertility was conducted in the Lancaster Amish settlement. The authors report a completed family size of 6.8, which is quite similar to the 6.6 found in the Lancaster Settlement Profile 1986 and the 6.5 reported in the Lancaster Settlement Profile 2000, both of which are described in Appendix A.

25. The estimate of 90 percent is based on families in the ten-district sample of the Lancaster Settlement Profile 2000, described in Appendix A.

26. Although the Lancaster settlement and the total number of Amish throughout North America are growing, not all settlements prosper. For a discussion of Amish settlements that failed between 1840 and 1960, see Luthy (1986).

27. In the thirty-year period from 1970 to 1999, about 532 families migrated from the Lancaster settlement. Of these, 71 percent (N = 376) settled in other Pennsylvania counties, 12 percent (N = 62) went to Kentucky, 11 percent (N = 56) headed for Indiana, 5 percent (N = 25) settled in Wisconsin, and the remaining thirteen families were scattered in New York, Maryland, Virginia, Ohio, and West Virginia. These migration figures were tabulated from *The Diary* from 1970 to 2000. The totals for each year are shown in Figure 1.4.

28. Numerous analytic concepts have been employed to understand the social organization of Amish society. Typical conceptualizations view the Amish as a sect (Wilson 1970), a folk society, and a *Gemeinschaft*. J. A. Hostetler (1993) suggests that they have formed a "commonwealth" and exemplify a "high context" culture. Loomis and Dyer (1976) use a social systems model. Olshan (1981) has questioned the appropriateness of using the "folk society" model for conceptualizing Amish society. Tan (1998) interprets Amish society from a social capital perspective. All of these conceptual frameworks highlight different aspects of Amish social organization.

29. The sociological literature on modernization is voluminous. My conceptualization of it is indebted to the work of Peter L. Berger (1974, 1977, 1979) and Berger, Berger, and Kellner (1973). Berger's work is anchored in the sociology of knowledge framework developed with Thomas Luckmann in *The Social Construction of Reality* (1966). For a more in-depth analysis of the Amish from a modernization perspective, see Kraybill (1994a).

30. Bellah et al. (1985).

31. I am grateful to Tay Keong Tan for introducing me to *social capital* as an analytical concept for understanding certain aspects of Amish society. Tan's (1998) dissertation on the Lancaster settlement as well as the personal conversations I have had with him have helped to clarify my thinking. Bourdieu (1986), Coleman (1990), and others

make a distinction between *cultural capital* (values, trust, beliefs) and *social capital* (networks and organizational structures). I have used both concepts throughout the text but have emphasized the social dimension. For an introduction to the literature on social capital, see Coleman (1988, 1990), Bourdieu (1986), Fukuyama (1995), Portes (1998), Putnam (2000), Tan (1998), and Woolcock (1998a, 1998b).

32. These tactics are an expansion and elaboration of the defensive structuring practices identified by Siegel (1970).

33. I use the image of negotiation in several ways. In some cases it refers to literal face-to-face bargaining between Amish representatives and government officials—for example, the development of Amish schools, zoning regulations, and the use of bulk tanks to refrigerate milk on farms. In other instances, implicit negotiations between the two cultural systems occur informally and quietly. Negotiation is also a way of understanding controlled and selective social change when some aspects of a new technology are accepted but others are not. For example, using permanent-press fabrics to make traditional Amish clothing is one of many examples of implicitly negotiated cultural agreements. Finally, I also use the metaphor in a symbolic way to capture the dynamic dialogue between Amish life and contemporary culture. See Eaton (1952) for a discussion of controlled acculturation among the Hutterites.

34. These progressive factions eventually affiliated with mainstream Mennonites in the twentieth century: the Conestoga Mennonite Church and the Millwood Mennonite Church. A national series of Amish Ministers' Meetings were held between 1862 and 1878. This was a time of great ferment in Amish communities, especially in the Midwest. Over the course of the consultations, many progressive-minded Amish leaders and their congregations separated from the main Amish body and became known as Amish Mennonites and eventually became Mennonites. The Amish that held to more traditional practices became known as Old Order Amish. Except for a few participants, the Lancaster Amish were largely uninvolved and untouched by this major upheaval. The story of the national Amish ministers meetings as well as the involvement of Lancaster minister "Tennessee" John Stoltzfus is told by Paton Yoder (1979a, 1979b, 1987a, 1991) and Yoder and Estes (1999).

35. This group has had various names at different stages of its evolution, which is discussed in Chapter 8, note 6. For clarity, I have used the term *Peachey church* when referring to this progressive group.

36. An account of this division, told from the New Order perspective, can be found in the *New Order Amish Directory* (1999:127).

2 | The Quiltwork of Amish Culture

1. The literature on Amish quilts is voluminous. Helpful introductions to the world of Amish quilts can be found in Granick (1989); Kraybill, Herr, and Holstein (1996); and Pellman and Pellman (1984).

2. Gordonville (Pa.) scribe Sam Stoltzfus, in *The Diary*, March 1999, 21.

3. Known as the Dordrecht Confession of Faith, the statement contains eighteen articles. It was signed by Flemish and Frisian Mennonite pastors in the Dutch city of

Dordrecht in 1632. Although many Mennonite groups over the years have adhered to the Dordrecht Confession in principle, the Amish have attempted to follow its teachings literally, especially in regard to shunning and footwashing. It is used for Amish instruction classes prior to baptism. The Swiss Brethren never adopted the Dordrecht Confession, which was likely a source of difference between the various factions of Alsatian and Swiss Anabaptists during the division of 1693. For a discussion of the Dordrecht Confession, see *Mennonite Encyclopedia* (1956), vol. 2, s.v. "Dordrecht Confession of Faith," and *Mennonite Encyclopedia* (1956), vol. 1, s.v. "Confessions of Faith." Horst (1982, 1988) and Studer (1984) provide updates on the significance of the Dordrecht Confession. A German and English version of the confession used by the Amish appears in *In Meiner Jugend* (2000).

John Oyer (1996) provides a helpful overview of Amish theology. In 1992, Pathway Publishers, an Amish Press in Aylmer, Canada, revised Mennonite Daniel Kauffman's *One Thousand Questions and Answers on Points of Christian Doctrine* as *One Thousand and One Questions and Answers on the Christian Life*. It includes revisions as well as new material, providing Amish doctrine in question-and-answer format on a variety of topics. Such a rational presentation of Amish views is rare in this oral-based, traditional culture.

4. I am indebted to the insights of Bourdieu (1977) as well as conversations with David Swartz (1997), who has synthesized much of Bourdieu's work, for understanding Gelassenheit as a master disposition in Amish life. In Bourdieu's terms Gelassenheit is *habitus*—a habit-forming, transposable disposition that blends perceptions and action, sentiment, and social structure together. *Habitus*—in our case, Gelassenheit—is a deeply structured cultural grammar for action. As a disposition, it has both structure and propensity that are shaped by early socialization toward action. For another example of the use of Bourdieu's concepts to interpret Amish society, see Reschly's (2000) historical study of the Amish in Iowa.

5. I am grateful to Steven M. Nolt for insight into this important distinction.

6. Friedmann (1956:448–49; 1957:86–88; 1973:66, 124) surveys the Anabaptist use of the term. Cronk's (1977) analysis of Gelassenheit as a redemptive rite in Old Order Amish and Old Order Mennonite communities has influenced my conceptual framework. I am greatly indebted to her work. In a letter to Donald B. Kraybill dated 24 September 1987, Amishman David Luthy noted: "Concerning Gelassenheit, I realize the Amish are not familiar with the term . . . but the Amish are familiar very much with the concept. Your use of it is valid and essential." The explicit use of the word *Gelassenheit* is more pronounced in Hutterite writings and literature.

7. J. A. Hostetler (1993:387–93) offers an excellent analysis of the importance of silence in Amish discourse. Silence is one way of expressing Gelassenheit.

8. *Petition* (1937).

9. Cigars of various sorts and pipes are commonly smoked; however, smoking has declined in recent years. Commercial cigarettes in white wrappers are frowned on as "worldly." Hand-rolled cigarettes in brown wrappers are sometimes used. Tobacco production is dwindling for economic reasons as well as religious convictions.

10. *Rules of a Godly Life* (1983:17).

11. *Guidelines* (1981:64).

12. See Bellah et al. (1985:55–84) for a discussion of the modern preoccupation with finding oneself.

13. *Instruction* (n.d.:16).

14. M. R. Smucker (1988:226–29).

15. J. A. Hostetler (1969:227). For a review of the psychological research on Amish personality types, see Smucker (1988). J. A. Hostetler (1969) reports findings from a variety of personality tests administered to Amish school children in several settlements. An excellent study of the socialization of Amish children is available in Hostetler and Huntington (1992).

16. *Instruction* (n.d.:8–11).

17. *Guidelines* (1981:50). For a collection of source materials used by the Old Order Amish in child rearing and schooling, see J. A. Hostetler (1968).

18. *Instruction* (n.d.:9).

19. For an extended discussion of Old Order understandings of salvation, see Kraybill and Bowman (2001).

20. *Dordrecht* (1976:12, 14).

21. *Guidelines* (1981:47).

22. *Instruction* (n.d.:7–13).

23. *Instruction* (n.d.:26).

24. *Rules of a Godly Life* (1983:26). In 1988 the Amish reprinted a Mennonite booklet, *Pride and Humility,* by Brenneman (1867). For a discussion of the role of humility in Amish and Mennonite culture in the nineteenth century, see Schlabach (1988).

25. There is a deeper reading of this taboo as well. Photography decontextualizes. It pulls images out of context and separates them from their immediate social setting. Photographic images are objective representations that encourage rational reflection and analysis from a distance. Wary of modernity, the Great Separator, the Amish taboo aims to keep people tightly tied to their social context.

For Amish perspectives on photographs when the taboo was evolving in the mid-nineteenth century, see the proceedings of the National Amish Ministers' Meetings compiled by Yoder and Estes (1999). One minister noted that people are tempted to "send their pictures around" (Yoder and Estes 1999:220). Photography not only decontextualizes and separates the individual from a social context, but it also objectifies the individual by creating an object for study and reflection, which encourages a rational, analytical mindset. Instinctively, all of these issues threatened the deeply contextualized culture of Amish life and merited a taboo that was helpfully legitimated by Scripture in Exodus 20:4. For additional discussions of Amish concerns about "graven images," see D. Lehman (1998) and M. Lehman (1993).

26. See, for example, 1 Tim. 2:9 and 1 Pet. 3:3–4.

27. *Rules of a Godly Life* (1983:7).

28. *Dordrecht* (1976:26).

29. *One Thousand* (1992:143–44).

30. J. H. Yoder (1973:38).

31. The Amish also believe that they are not to be "unequally yoked with the world" (2 Cor. 6:14). Moreover, Scripture teaches that they should be "equipped with

the whole armor of God to stand and prevail in this strife torn world." Other scriptures cited in support of separation include John 17:14, Luke 16:15, Titus 2:14. The church is called not to mingle with the world but to "be a light unto it" (Matt. 5:14).

32. *Papers* (1937).

33. Cronk (1977) makes this important point in her study of Gelassenheit.

34. *Rules of a Godly Life* (1983:25).

35. "Editorial" in *Plain Communities Business Exchange,* April 1995, 2.

36. *Standards* (1981:7).

37. *Guidelines* (1981:46).

38. *Instruction* (n.d.:5).

39. The work of two of them from the nineteenth century was recently recognized. The watercolors and other artwork of Amishman Henry Lapp (1862–1904) are an interesting example. Lapp had severe hearing and speech impediments, and thus church leaders may have granted him greater freedom to express his artistic impulses. A discussion of his life and work is recorded in *The Diary* (1982:14:329). Barbara Ebersol (1846–1922) made beautiful and colorful *fraktur* bookplates. Artistic lettering in a Bible was more acceptable than artwork framed for public display. Louise Stoltzfus (1995) provides an overview of the work of both Lapp and Ebersol. Luthy (1995) devotes a book to Barbara Ebersol's life and art. For excellent overviews of the decorative arts of Lancaster's Amish, see Herr (1998) and McCauley and McCauley (1988).

40. A self-trained artist found a ready market for her work in the 1990s.

41. *Standards* (1981:38–39).

42. *Standards* (1981:1).

43. For an analysis of time as a cultural product, see Gleick's (1999) discussion of why everything is accelerating in contemporary culture.

44. *Guidelines* (1981:5).

45. In the first part of the twentieth century, it was customary for Amish families to set their clocks a half-hour ahead of standard time. This "fast half" time was a symbolic reminder of the boundaries between Amish life and modern culture. Very few families continue this practice today.

46. Whether the pace of Amish singing is torturously slow is surely a matter of cultural perspective. It will most likely feel that way to persons who are immersed in the fast pace of modern life. However, an ex-Amish person said, "I experienced the slow pace as uplifting and beautiful."

47. Kraybill and Bowman (2001) develop a more formal definition of Old Order groups that emphasizes tradition (oldness), communal authority (order), and the church's broad scope of control over many dimensions of life.

3 | Symbols of Integration and Separation

1. For an early discussion of the role of symbols in Amish culture, see J. A. Hostetler (1963).

2. D. Yoder (1997) discusses the origin and evolution of the dialect. Beam (1982) has produced an English–Pennsylvania German dictionary. A grammar of the dialect (Frey 1981) is available as well as a reader and grammar (Haag 1982). See Huffines

(1988, 1993) on the Pennsylvania German dialect as well as other changes; and see Louden (1988, 1991a, 1991b, and 1993) and Rohrer (1974) for discussions of the influence of English.

3. *The Diary* (1977:9:30).

4. Although High German is the target language for Amish sacred ritual, in actual practice it is at best only approximated. The *Martyrs Mirror,* the Bible, and other sacred writings used by the Amish are written in the archaic German of Luther's Bible. The spoken German in worship services is highly diluted with the dialect.

5. *In Meiner Jugend,* a devotional reader in German and English, was published by Pathway Publishers in 2000.

6. Recent research has confirmed that Jakob Ammann was a tailor and thus his occupational interests may have encouraged the Amish stress on dress (Hüppi 2000). In the late 1800s, various observers identified Plain dress and strict religious discipline as indicators of Amish identity (Wickersham 1886:168; Ellis and Evans 1883:343). As late as 1924, Klein (1924:368) described Amish dress in great detail and then merely noted, in passing, that the use of automobiles, electric lights, and telephones was considered worldly.

7. Stephen Scott (1986:4) makes the "on-duty" point. See his book for an overview of dress practices among conservative Anabaptist groups.

8. An exception that does cite specific scriptures is the section on dress in *One Thousand* (1992:129–37). This publication uses a variety of Bible verses to make the argument for distinctive dress and gives detailed rationale in the form of answers to specific questions. Such a rational use of Scripture and written apology for practices is not typical among most Amish, who simply see dress standards as an expression of traditional practice.

9. My description of Amish dress is indebted to Sara E. Fisher, who kindly shared an unpublished paper written in 1972 on women's garb, and to Louise Stoltzfus, who drafted a careful summary of dress practices in 2000 related to gender, status, and Plainness. Melvin Gingerich (1970) traced the history of Amish-Mennonite attire through four centuries. The rise and fall of veil wearing among Mennonites in the Lancaster area is analyzed by Kraybill (1987b). Scott (1986) provides the best overall introduction to Amish dress.

10. As the Amish have moved into small towns and boroughs, the horse has created some zoning problems. A lengthy dispute between the borough council of Strasburg and two sisters who wanted to keep their horse in the village continued for several months in 1983. See *Intelligencer* (21 and 28 September 1983, and 12 October 1983) and *New Era* (13 and 14 September 1983, and 14 November 1983) for accounts of the dispute.

11. Letters to the editor, *Intelligencer* (6 July and 10 July 2000).

12. G. L. Fisher (1978:233).

13. For a study of energy conservation on Amish farms, see Johnson, Stoltzfus, and Craumer (1977).

14. A thorough description of the various types of horse-drawn transportation in several Amish and Mennonite settlements was written by Scott (1981).

15. Gibbons (1869:16) noted that at the end of the Civil War the Lancaster Amish

were driving to their worship services in simple farm wagons covered with a yellowish oil cloth. The Amish did not begin using buggies as quickly as did other groups, and they were slow to adopt steel springs to cushion the load on their wagons. By 1880 Amish youth were beginning to drive simple buggies, and tarps in a variety of colors were being stretched over Amish wagons. While a few changes were underway, the Amish were nevertheless maintaining austere standards on their vehicles at the end of the nineteenth century. Whip socks (whip holders) and whips themselves were prohibited, likely to protest the speed symbolized by the dashing horse under whip. Whips are still forbidden. The early Amish buggy and wagon did not have an "easy back" (backrest) on the seat or a dashboard on the front to obstruct flying mud.

16. Although gray is the standard color for the carriage top in the Lancaster area, black, white, and even yellow tops are common in other Amish settlements.

17. The slow-moving vehicle signs were required by law and enforced in June 1977, see *Intelligencer* (30 June 1977). An editorial in the *Intelligencer* (22 August 1988) praised the Amish for using the reflective orange triangles on their buggies and concluded, "We doubt that God will look with disfavor on the Amish for using these symbols."

18. Some Amish groups in other states have resisted the use of reflective triangles. Zook (1993) tells the story of these conflicts.

19. Because of the high demand for carriages, they typically must be ordered a year in advance. Carriage makers, in 2000, agreed on standard prices on carriages and accessories to prevent competition among themselves.

4 | The Social Architecture of Amish Society

1. J. A. Hostetler (1993) describes these in detail. See also Hostetler and Huntington (1992).

2. The role of the Amish wife is described during the wedding ceremony: "The man should know that God has appointed him as head of the woman, that he is to lead, rule and protect her lovingly." The wife "is to honor and respect him and be subject to him . . . she shall be quiet . . . and take good care of the children and housekeeping." Wives are told to conduct themselves submissively and are asked to pledge to "live in subjection to their husband." See *Handbuch* (1978:38–39).

3. L. Stoltzfus (1998).

4. For an excellent discussion of Amish women and feminism, see Olshan and Schmidt (1994). Louise Stoltzfus (1994, 1998) shares valuable insights into the lives and values of Amish women.

5. For an extended discussion of the role of Amish women in business, see Kraybill and Nolt (1995), especially 45–47 and 240–44.

6. "The Hausfrau Diary," in *The Diary*, December 1999, 74.

7. *Recipes for Home Canning and Freezing*, 36. This 36-page booklet names no author or publisher. (Printed by the Gordonville Book Shop. Seventh printing, October 1998.)

8. Huntington (1981) has written an excellent essay on the Amish family. For a description of age roles in the Amish family, see Hostetler and Huntington (1992).

9. More progressive Amish couples are likely to use artificial means of birth control. However, church leaders typically frown on such behavior. For a variety of reasons, older women sometimes undergo sterilization to prevent further births. Various forms of birth control as well as sterilization represent a modernizing trend—a shift from fate to choice.

10. For a description of this small Amish village southeast of Sarasota, see *Intelligencer* (14 January 1987).

11. A household is defined as a living area having separate eating and bathroom facilities. Many extended families have two or three households in the same house. This estimate of the size of the Lancaster church districts is based on the research described in Appendix A.

12. J. A. Hostetler (1993:108).

13. The listing of all the ordinations in the Lancaster settlement is available in *Ein Diener Register* (2000).

14. The leaders are called *Diener* (servant). The *Handbuch* (1978) identifies them as *Volliger Diener* (bishop), *Diener zum Buch* (minister, or servant, of the book), and *Armendiener* (deacon, or servant, to the poor). Their roles are described in *Gemein* (n.d.) and in the *Handbuch* (1978:29–33). Paton Yoder (1987b) provides an excellent review of the ordained offices and notes that the term *bishop* was not used by the Amish until the 1860s.

15. A bishop is not required by church polity to have two districts. Typically a bishop has a "home" district, but he often oversees a second district for several years until the congregation is ready to ordain its own bishop. In some instances a bishop may oversee three districts, and in other cases only one. A bishop usually is responsible for two districts.

16. Schlabach (1988) and Yoder and Estes (1999) provide the best introduction and analysis of these gatherings, which played a key role in the formation of Old Order Amish identity. For a discussion of the role of the Ordnung in the Ministers' Meeting, see J. N. Gingerich (1986). An Amish deacon from the Lancaster area, "Tennessee" John Stoltzfus, participated in the series of Ministers' Meetings. His relationship to the meetings is traced by P. Yoder (1979a, 1979b). See also Yoder and Bender (1979).

17. The progressives in the lower Pequea district formed what eventually became the Millwood Mennonite Church. Progressives in the Conestoga district were the progenitors of what is today the Conestoga Mennonite Church. For primary source materials on these divisions, see P. Yoder (1979a, 1987a). A discussion of the Conestoga division can be found in Mast and Mast (1982). For the Pequea division, see A. N. King (1977).

18. The use of meetinghouses remains a sensitive issue. In the early 1990s an Amishman built a mobile building that could be set up and taken down fairly quickly. It was used at some benefit auctions, and then some districts started using it for weddings. But the bishops "wanted nothing to do with it," said one member, "because they thought it would lead to a church house and larger weddings. So they put it out [banned it] in the fall of 1995."

19. See Beulah Hostetler (1992) for a discussion of this issue in the formation of Old Order group identity.

20. *The Diary* (1975:7:80).

21. For historical background on Amish Aid, see G. L. Fisher (1978:355, 379) and *The Diary* (1973:5, 86).

22. *Directory* (1973:19–24).

23. *The Diary* (1969:1:4; 1976:8:177).

24. For the minutes of the annual meetings, see Steering Committee (1966–2000). Olshan (1993, 1994b) describes the evolution and function of the Steering Committee.

25. *The Diary* (1969:1:4; 1976:8:177).

26. *Rules and Regulations* (1983).

27. *Articles* (1984).

28. The Pequea Bruderschaft Library primarily collects materials related to the Lancaster settlement. The Heritage Historical Library in Aylmer, Ontario, holds a collection of Amish-related materials covering all the settlements in North America.

29. The history and rationale for this program are described in a small pamphlet *Regulations and Guidelines for the Old Order Amish Product Liability Aid,* adopted and established in the fall of 1992. The pamphlet was printed in 2000 by Gordonville Print Shop.

30. A twelfth organization is the Amish Book Committee, which publishes the *Ausbund,* prayer books, and other religious books. It was founded in 1913. A detailed history of its origins is recorded in *The Diary* (1970:2:191–95).

31. The clinic is located south of Strasburg at P.O. Box 128, Strasburg, PA 17579 (717/687-9407).

32. Wagler (n.d.:7).

33. *Standards* (1981:41).

5 | Rites of Redemption and Purification

1. See Kasdorf (1997:136–44), who expands on the orality of Amish culture in her dissertation on Joseph W. Yoder. She notes that even Plato worried that those who rely on writing will lose their memory.

2. There are, of course, ritual variations from settlement to settlement across North America, but within an Amish affiliation, the ritual formulas are firmly established and perpetuated by oral tradition and practice.

3. J. N. Gingerich (1986:181).

4. The Ordnung is the reservoir of "understandings" about expected behavior that have accumulated in Amish culture over time. A minister described the evolution of the Ordnung: "Our fathers' church leaders had a strong desire to hold on to the old way of life, and although much has changed over the years they have been successful in holding the line to the point that we have been separated from the world, which, in time, created a culture different from that of the world. This did not come overnight, nor did it come through rash or harsh commands of our bishops, but by making wise decisions to hold firm to the old-time religion from one time to another, from one generation to another" (J. F. Beiler 1982:353).

5. J. F. Beiler (1982:383).

6. The eighteen articles of the Dordrecht Confession of Faith form the basis of the

instruction classes. The classes emphasize the importance of baptism and communion as the principal components of "true Christian faith." At the end of the instruction period, applicants are asked a series of questions to measure their theological knowledge—for example, "Who has called you?" "Who has redeemed you?" The last session of instruction emphasizes the importance of complying with the Ordnung, and the ministers "make it very clear to the applicants what kind of a covenant they are making" (*Handbuch* 1978:24–26). The Lancaster ministers' manual says the candidates are to be asked several times if they are willing to submit to the order of the church (*Gemein* n.d.:4).

7. J. A. Hostetler (1993:78).

8. Most church districts have a baptismal service every other fall. Youth are typically baptized in their home district but occasionally may be baptized in an adjoining one if they want to be baptized before the next baptismal service in their district.

9. This wording is found in *In Meiner Jugend* (2000:190–91). See also *Handbuch* (1978:26) and *Gemein* (n.d.:6), for variant wording of the vows.

10. *Handbuch* (1978:25) and *Gemein* (n.d.:5–7).

11. The description of the worship service is based on participant observation in worship services in Lancaster County in the spring of 1986 and the summer of 2000.

12. Technically, the worship begins with the first sermon and ends with the benediction. The singing is considered extraneous to the worship service. The ministers are absent (in the counsel room) during the first two songs, and some of the women begin preparing the meal during the last song.

13. The meal typically involves slices of bread, peanut butter, smearcase (cheese spread), pickled vegetables, snitz (dried apple) pie, and coffee. Some districts also serve bologna and cheese. Plates and napkins are not used, and the food is not passed. Several seatings are usually necessary to serve everyone.

14. For background and scholarly sources on the *Ausbund,* consult the *Mennonite Encyclopedia* (1956), vol. 2, s.v. "Ausbund," as well as Bartel (1986), J. A. Hostetler (1993:227–29), Luthy (1971b), Ressler (1986), and Schreiber (1962a). The first known European edition, published in 1564, has been followed by many other editions and printings. The American edition used in the Lancaster settlement includes stories of some forty Swiss Anabaptists who suffered severe persecution between 1645 and 1685. These vivid stories of suffering have been translated and published by J. E. Kauffman (1975). English translations of 69 of the 140 songs of the *Ausbund* along with historical material have been published by the Ohio Amish Library (*Songs* 1998). Bartel (1986) and Durnbaugh (1999) provide helpful discussions of the unique style of Amish singing.

15. Ressler (1978) details the background of this hymn and its use among the Amish and Mennonites.

16. Gibbons (1869:59–69).

17. J. A. Hostetler (1993:278) notes that the speed of singing the "Lob Lied" in different Amish groups across the country ranges from eleven to thirty minutes, depending on their degree of conservatism. The more conservative the group, the slower it is sung.

18. The admonitions toward positive examples, *die Vorstellung,* take up as much as

90 percent of the time with only about 10 percent devoted to *die Abstellung,* things that are not allowed.

19. *Handbuch* (1978:33).

20. Luthy (1975) describes Amish ordination customs across several settlements.

21. *Gemein* (n.d.:10–11).

22. *Handbuch* (1978:33).

23. The use of the lot is based on the account recorded in Acts 1:23–26, where lots were cast to select someone to replace Judas Iscariot.

24. Based on information gathered from her field interviews, Louise Stoltzfus helped to clarify the procedures related to confession as well as shunning.

25. The Lancaster ministers' manual distinguishes between "sins of brotherhood or weakness that can be corrected between brothers . . . and sins of carnality, such as adultery, fornication . . . " The more serious sins, which also include "inordinate living, idleness in useless words, business conduct, and external appearances," are cause for cutting sinners off like a branch until they are willing to be fruitful again. The six-week exclusion is sometimes referred to as "setting someone back from counsel." They are to take no part in Members' Meetings or in communion and should not receive the brotherly greeting, or kiss (*Gemein* n.d.:18–20).

26. *Handbuch* (1978:26–28) and informants.

27. Technically, the *ban* refers to the exclusion of members from communion and the fellowship of the church. The six-week exclusion from communion is sometimes called the *small ban,* in contrast to the *big ban*—excommunication. *Meidung,* or shunning, refers to the social avoidance of those who are excommunicated or excluded from communion. Because the *Bann,* or excommunication, automatically implies *Meidung,* in everyday discourse *Bann* and *Meidung* are sometimes used interchangeably. Such overlap of terminology occurs in the Lancaster County bishop's statement on *Bann und Meidung* in *Bericht* (1943).

28. The Amish process of excommunication and shunning resembles Benedictine language and practice in some ways. See, for example, Benedictine Rules 23 through 29, which cover excommunication and association with the excommunicated. Matthew 18:15–16 and 1 Corinthians 5:5 are highlighted in both Amish and Benedictine practice. See *Rule* (1982:49–53).

29. *Dordrecht* (1976:35).

30. The Moses Hartz controversy at the turn of the century in Lancaster County (discussed in Chapter 8), prompted debate on whether people who left the Amish church for a more progressive Anabaptist church, such as the Mennonites, should be shunned. Those who advocated a strong shunning (*Streng Meidung*) felt that such people should be shunned. More progressive members felt that the shunning should be relaxed in such a case. The debate surrounding the Hartz case was one of the factors leading to the 1910 division. Even after this division, the debate continued to smolder until the Old Order bishops issued a special statement in 1921 in which they argued that they were not practicing a new form of shunning but were merely following the traditional Amish custom as agreed to in a Ministers' Meeting in 1809 and as taught by Bishop David Beiler in 1861. Discussion of the proper application of shunning continued during the first half of the twentieth century, prompting publication of several

statements on it in *Bericht* (1943). The long and heated debates over the use of shunning from 1693 to the present testify to its potent power for social control and its cardinal role in Amish identity and polity.

31. *Dordrecht* (1976:36). Scripture verses that are used to support the practice of shunning, in the Dordrecht Confession of Faith, include 1 Cor. 5:9–11; Rom. 16:17; 2 Thess. 3:14, 15; and Titus 3:10, 11.

32. *Bericht* (1943:2).

33. For a first-person story of shunning by a middle-aged Amish woman, see "Damned: Emma's Choice," which appeared in the *Philadelphia Inquirer Magazine*, 30 January 1994. A collection of stories of ex-Amish has been compiled by Garrett (1998).

34. When a major internal division occurs within the Amish church, members are given a grace period—a time to decide whether they want to leave without the threat of ostracism. The grace period ends if someone who was excommunicated by the Old Order Amish is later accepted into the more liberal group without a confession. In other words, when the splinter group no longer respects the *Bann* that the Old Order Amish apply to their wayward members, the lines are drawn. After that, Old Order members who transfer to the more liberal group are shunned. This was the case in both the 1910 and 1966 divisions in Lancaster County. Thus, Old Order members who joined the New Order Amish in 1966 at the time of the division are not shunned by the Old Order Amish today. However, Old Order members who joined the New Order Amish after the period of grace, are shunned today.

6 | Auctions, Frolics, and Gangs

1. I am grateful to Tay Keong Tan for first introducing me to the concept of *social capital* for interpreting Amish society. His dissertation (Tan 1998) provided the first application of social capital theory to Amish life. Academic definitions of social capital are not always clear. Some suggest that social capital consists of the values and social relationships available to generate common benefits, while others imply that social capital is the resources created by certain values and social structures. I view human values and knowledge as cultural capital, and the social networks, rituals, and structures as social capital. Both forms of capital are the raw materials that produce benefits for both the individual and the community. Social capital can be used to build up the common good or to tear it down as in a violent gang, hate group, or work slowdown.

2. Coleman (1990:653) calls this form of social capital "primordial" because it is rooted in an extended family system that has largely vanished in modern life.

3. There are about 2,500 single youth (16–25 years of age) in the settlement.

4. Township supervisors wrote to an Amish official and asked him "to do all in your power to correct the drinking and drunkenness that presently prevails among Amish youth . . . [since] according to records the last fatal accidents that occurred in Leacock township were either the direct result of, or involved drinking Amish youth." In response to this plea, the Lancaster bishops met and agreed upon five points of an Ordnung that in rare fashion was published in the *Minutes of the Old Order Amish Steering Committee from 1981–1986*, 36–37 (trans. Noah G. Good).

5. My colleague Richard Stevick (2000) makes this important distinction in his study of Amish youth in various settlements across the country. He has conducted the most complete and definitive study of Amish adolescents to date. His careful research and thoughtful suggestions have been most helpful to me in preparing this section on Amish youth.

6. Introduction to the booklet *17th Annual Wood Workers Get Together,* 6 June 1998, Lancaster County.

7. The best description of Amish weddings can be found in Scott (1988). The description in this section is partially based on observations at a wedding attended by the author in November 1998.

8. From an unpublished and undated manuscript, "Ascension Day," by Sam Stoltzfus.

9. Edward T. Hall (1977:85–128) provides an excellent discussion of the difference between low-context and high-context cultures. His analysis of code, context, and meaning has informed and enriched my understanding of the Amish as a high-context culture.

10. *Plain Communities Business Exchange,* August 2000, 15.

11. Personal conversation with an Ohio Amish farmer.

12. From an unpublished and undated manuscript, "Lancaster County's Barn Raising," by Sam Stoltzfus. Other quotes in this section on barn raising are from the same source.

13. For two accounts and reflections by Amish women on death, see E. King (1992) and E. Smucker (1995). King reflects on the murder of her aunt, and Smucker on the accidental death of her son. Bryer (1978, 1979) provides a psychological study of death and dying among the Amish.

14. A funeral director who buries many of the Amish in the Lancaster settlement provided helpful insights into burial practices in an extended interview. See Scott (1988) for a good description of an Amish funeral in central Pennsylvania.

7 | Passing on the Faith

1. For a chronology of Amish court cases involving educational disputes as well as the landmark 1972 U.S. Supreme Court decision, see Keim (1975) and Meyers (1993). Historical overviews of Amish education are provided by Cline (1968:73–121), Ferster (1983), Hostetler and Huntington (1992), and Huntington (1994). Two important source books for documents that trace the rise of Amish schools in the Lancaster settlement are Kinsinger (1997) and C. S. Lapp (1991).

2. Keim (1975:163).

3. Wickersham (1886:168).

4. *The Diary* (1972:4:155).

5. Fisher (1978:312).

6. Harnish (1925).

7. This series of anonymous articles appeared in the *Intelligencer* in four installments in 1931 (19, 20, and 21 February, and 10 March).

8. The East Lampeter Township dispute of 1937 and 1938 is chronicled in two

local Lancaster papers, *Intelligencer Journal* and *New Era*. It also received national press coverage. See especially the *Intelligencer* for 1937: 26 March; 29 April; 13, 15, 27, and 28 May; 12 and 24 June; 3 and 7 July; 20 August; 30 September; 2, 5, and 30 October; 6, 10, and 11 November; 4, 6, 7, 24, and 30 December. For 1938: 4, 9, and 24 February; and 28 June.

9. Because lawyers were involved, the Amish community was divided internally over the East Lampeter Township dispute. However, a substantial portion of Amish residents in the township supported the resistance to the consolidated school. Approximately twenty Amishmen rode the train to the Federal Court Building in Philadelphia to attend a hearing on 12 May 1937 as reported in *Intelligencer* 13 May 1937.

10. Historical documentation of the Amish school movement in Lancaster County is preserved in *The Papers of the Amish School Controversy* (1937–68). This excellent collection of Aaron E. Beiler's papers contains the petitions, correspondence, and minutes of the Old Order Amish School Committee, which first met on 14 September 1937 at the home of Stephen F. Stoltzfus, its first chairman. When Stoltzfus moved to Maryland in 1940, Beiler was appointed chairman and served in that role until his death in 1968 (*Directory* 1973:20–21). A booklet describing the move to Maryland in 1940 was published twenty-five years later (*Amish Moving to Maryland,* 1965). Unless otherwise indicated, this chapter's citations of Amish positions, attitudes, and actions are based on documents in *The Papers* (1937–68). Several documents from this collection were published by Eli M. Shirk (1939) as part of a booklet he prepared on the history of the school controversy. Shirk was an Old Order Mennonite leader who worked closely with the Amish School Committee. Other documents from *The Papers* were compiled and published by C. S. Lapp (1991).

11. *Gemeinden* (1937:4).

12. For documentation related to this case, see Keim (1975:94) and *Intelligencer* (17, 18, and 24 November 1937, 2 December 1937, 29 January 1938, and 1 February 1938).

13. The sale of public one-room schools is reported in *Intelligencer* (10 November 1938). *Directory* (1973) provides a chronological listing of the opening of Amish schools from 1938 to 1973. The first two opened in November 1938.

14. Some three hundred pages of documents and newspaper reports covering the arrests and political struggle in the Lancaster settlement between 1949 and 1955 were compiled by C. S. Lapp (1991).

15. Keim (1975:95).

16. For a review of the court cases that were tested during these years, including several in Lancaster County, see Cline (1968:109–15).

17. "Statement" (1950).

18. *Intelligencer* (30 September 1950).

19. *Intelligencer* (21 September 1950).

20. Smith (1961:247) and Keim (1975:96).

21. The first vocational school classes were held at the Aaron F. Stoltzfus home in Upper Leacock Township. The vocational program was supervised by the Old Order Amish School Committee; see *Directory* (1973:21). It marked the end of the legal battles begun in 1937 and ushered in a new era of peaceful coexistence in Pennsylvania. The vocational school solution became a model for some other localities as well. In some

states legal disputes continued until they were silenced by the Supreme Court decision of 1972, which affirmed the right of the Amish to keep their children out of public high schools. For an excellent discussion of the Supreme Court ruling, see Keim (1975). The vocational program continues in the Lancaster settlement out of respect to the agreement negotiated with the Commonwealth of Pennsylvania between 1953 and 1955. In some other localities the program has been discontinued.

22. Guidelines for the Vocational School Program were spelled out in memorandums from the Pennsylvania Department of Public Instruction (22 September 1955 and 16 January 1956) and are included in *Papers* (1937–68). The program conceived by the Amish was first approved in a joint meeting of the bishops and the school committee on 30 September 1953. A printed version of the principles governing the program was later distributed in pamphlet form (*Vocation* 1956). For another discussion of the vocational school program, see Hostetler and Huntington (1992:40–41). Amish views and vocational school policies can be found in *Vocation* (1956) and *Standards* (1981).

23. *Papers* (9 August 1954).

24. This summary of the reasons behind the protest of consolidated high schools was gleaned from numerous source documents in *Papers* (1937–68).

25. This quote is in the summary paragraph of a four-page review of the history of the Amish School Controversy, covering the years 1937–50. It was likely compiled by Aaron E. Beiler sometime after 18 February 1950, and the statement is probably his. The undated historical review "Repeal from 1947 Enactment" is with Beiler's documents in *Papers* (1937–68).

26. For an extended treatment of Amish schools and childhood socialization, see Hostetler and Huntington (1992). Fisher and Stahl (1986) provide an insider's view of the daily routines and organization of the one-room Amish school. See Esh (1977) for an Amishman's account of the development of Amish schools.

27. *Blackboard Bulletin* (January 2001:16–17). This annual listing of schools shows 158 Amish schools in the Lancaster settlement for the 2000–2001 school year. An average of 30 pupils per school yields a total of 4,740 pupils.

28. *Standards* (1981:2).

29. Pathway Publishers in Aylmer, Ontario, owned and operated by Amish people, is a major supplier of textbooks and teaching aids and is the publisher of the *Blackboard Bulletin,* a monthly teachers magazine with a wide circulation.

30. For a history of the development of the special schools, see *Beginning* (1996), C. S. Lapp (1991:573), and Kinsinger (1997:111–20). Some of the services to these children are provided by the S. June Smith Center in Lancaster.

31. *Standards* (1981:30).

32. *Guidelines* (1981:12).

33. The Old Order Book Society evolved out of the School Committee, which first met in 1937 to protest the new school-attendance laws.

34. *Standards* (1981:31).

35. Hostetler and Huntington (1992:93–95).

36. Outley (1982:45).

37. A record of the negotiations, from the Amish perspective, over a variety of legal issues can be found in Kinsinger (1997).

38. Kinsinger (1997:34).

39. President Bush spoke at the Penn John's School, the last school operated by a local public school board in Lancaster County for mostly Old Order Amish and Mennonite youth.

40. Transcript of the President's Remarks, Office of the Press Secretary, The White House, 22 March 1989.

41. I received more than fifty phone calls from radio, television, and print media (in the United States and abroad) within a two-week period. *New Yorker* and *Time* magazines covered the story as well as the major TV networks.

42. *Philadelphia Magazine* printed an extended story on Amish youth titled "Party On, Amos," August 1997, 137–44.

8 | The Riddles of Technology

1. For extended treatments of the Moses Hartz incident, consult J. A. Hostetler (1993:284–87), Nolt (1992: 204–7), P. Yoder (1987b:103–6), Hartz and Hartz (1965), and Mast and Mast (1982:83–87). The most detailed analysis of this never-ending affair and a list of source documents are provided by Paton Yoder (1991:266–73). Virtually all of the published accounts were written by Mennonites or Amish-Mennonites. Amos J. Stoltzfus (n.d.), who witnessed the episode as a young church member, wrote from an Old Order Amish perspective.

2. The Hartzes were received into the Conestoga Amish-Mennonite congregation after making a "kneeling" confession of failure—one of several options recommended by an out-of-state committee called in to investigate the matter. Old Order Amish preacher David Beiler is typically cited as the person spearheading the renewed shunning of the Hartzes. Paton Yoder (n.d.) points out, however, that a single minister could not have brought about the reversal without the support of others, including the bishops.

3. *Bericht* (1943).

4. The text of the "demand" for a more lenient interpretation of shunning and a threat to secede from the Old Order Amish, dated 29 September 1909, was reprinted in *Bericht* (1943). No names were signed to the "demand," and in their response the bishops curtly noted that "ordinarily one pays little attention to letters without names" (*Bericht* 1943:5). The bishops also argued that their interpretation of shunning simply followed "what the old bishops and ministers taught concerning separation and shunning, some forty, sixty or up to 100 years ago. We want nothing else than to stay in what we have been taught" (*Bericht* 1943:5).

5. The separation began when the dissenting group made its demand on 29 September 1909. The first worship service with ordained ministers present, on 27 February 1910, marks the formal culmination of the division. Thus, I have used the year 1910 in the text to mark this schism. For a chronology of the events surrounding the division, see Glick (1986) and F. E. Lapp (1963). The most extensive discussion, written from the progressive point of view, is included in Elmer Yoder's (1987:103–12) history of the Beachy Amish.

6. Christian J. Beiler (1850–1934) was a spokesman for the dissenting group, but

the name Peachey church was used because Samuel W. Peachey and, in a lesser role, Christian D. Peachey from Mifflin County, Pennsylvania, were instrumental in providing ministerial leadership to the group in its first two years (E. Yoder 1987:108–9). After Christian L. King was ordained bishop on 24 April 1913, the group was sometimes referred to as the King church. With a small following, Christian L. King broke off from Peachey church in 1925 and formed a separate King church, which eventually became defunct. The Peachey church remained a viable group under the leadership of John A. Stoltzfus, who was ordained bishop in April 1926. After that, the Peachey church was sometimes called the "John A. Church," but the Peachey label prevailed until the group began worshiping in the Weavertown Church building in 1930.

The local historian of the group traces the further evolution of the name: "After the church house at Weavertown was acquired it [the group] became known as the Weavertown Amish-Mennonite Church. When the Church joined the Beachy Affiliation it became known as a Beachy Amish-Mennonite denomination" (F. E. Lapp 1963:11). The group affiliated with the Beachy Amish in 1950. For a history of the congregations in that affiliation, see E. Yoder (1987). Today three congregations (Weavertown, Pequea, and Mine Road) represent the growth of the original body. Since 1969, several small groups springing from the Old Order Amish division of 1966 have also affiliated with the Beachy Amish. The membership of all Beachy Amish congregations in Lancaster County today is less than a thousand.

7. E. Yoder (1987:125–27, 351–55).

8. F. E. Lapp (1963), E. Yoder (1987), and Glick (1986), writing from the progressive perspective, emphasize the strict interpretation of shunning as the cause for the division.

9. The written demand of the withdrawing group and the response of the bishops, recorded in *Bericht* (1943), identify strict shunning as the ostensible reason for the division.

10. This perception was confirmed by several leaders and oral historians when asked about the reasons for the 1910 division. Regardless of the actual role of the telephone in the division, its importance in the schism may have increased over time in the Amish mind as a means of diverting attention from the severe enforcement of shunning. Of the Amish use of phones, Amishman John K. Lapp (1986:7) says, "Some were willing to put them away and others were not, so that is when the Kinig gma [Peachey church] started, the phone was one of the issues but I suppose there were some more." Amish minister Joseph Beiler, in the foreword of Gingerich and Kreider (1986:14), says the 1910 schism was "caused by indifferent views in church discipline, most concerning newly invented contraptions that our conservative church leaders could not tolerate." In contrast, oral historians in the progressive group contend that as late as 1916 members of the Peachey church were asked to take out phones when they bought a farm that had them. This suggests that the Peachey church did not accept the phone until at least six years after the division.

11. For an intriguing social history of the Amish and Old Order Mennonite struggle with telephones, see D. Umble (1996).

12. Fletcher (1955:525).

13. One Amishman said: "I remember when the phones came. The church didn't

say anything about them. It was thumbs up. Two of my wife's uncles had the phones in and there were quite a few others that had them and then an issue came up. Two people talking on the phone were gossiping about someone else and it went so far that it became a church issue. They were asked to come to church and make a confession about it. Then the church decided that we just better not allow these phones."

14. J. K. Lapp (1986:7).

15. Fletcher (1955:525).

16. Armstrong and Feldman (1986:65).

17. Some farmers installed phones in sheds near their barns in order to call the artificial inseminator for their cows. This was particularly irksome to some bishops, who were opposed to artificial insemination of dairy cows.

18. Klein (1941:101).

19. Fletcher (1955:62–65).

20. The life story of Isaac Glick is told by his son in a book-length account that provides an overview of many Amish practices in the first two decades of the twentieth century (Glick 1994).

21. The use of Delco and Genco plants by members of the Peachey church was confirmed by several Old Order Amish informants. Surprisingly, an Old Order Amishman remembers taking his batteries to a member of the Peachey church to have them charged.

22. Throughout the text, the distinction between 12-volt and 110-volt current is simplified for the sake of clarity. While the distinction for the most part is correct, there are minor technical variations. As electricity was coming into use, different types of batteries produced various levels of voltage. The Amish had always accepted the simple dry cell battery, but they opposed the Genco and Delco plants, which used wet cell batteries and produced a variety of voltages for electric light bulbs. As electrical technology changed over the years, the Amish continued to accept the use of direct current stored in batteries, which typically is 12-volts. They opposed the use of alternating current taken from the public utility lines, which normally is 110-volts. They opposed electricity from public power lines or in other form—even though home-generated—that could be used to operate standard electrical motors and appliances, rather than to the specific voltage level per se. For all practical purposes, this amounted to a distinction between 12-volt and 110-volt current.

9 | Harnessing the Power of Progress

1. The scooter craze was featured in the 5 June 2000 *Time* magazine as well as in Lancaster's *Intelligencer* of 18 August 2000. National sales of scooters were expected to top 5 million units in 2000.

2. Klein (1941:119).

3. Klein (1941:120). For stories of the arrival of the car in the Lancaster area by a former Amishman, see Glick (1994).

4. Fletcher (1955:525).

5. Fletcher (1955:328).

6. Amish historians and informants are not able to pinpoint a specific date for the

ban on car ownership because the church never seriously considered the issue. By 1917 Mennonite bishops in the Lancaster area were buying cars. It is likely that the Amish consensus against cars had crystallized before this time. The date 1915, however, is an estimate based on conversations with Amish informants. In any event, the car taboo emerged over several years as cars were coming into popular use.

7. Flink (1975:2).

8. Fletcher (1955:330). For a discussion of the social effects of the car, see Allen (1957), who concludes that they are so numerous as to be incalculable!

9. Flink (1975:40).

10. For an Amishman's view of the pros and cons of car ownership, see Wagler (n.d.). Reasons for not owning cars are also provided in *One Thousand* (1992).

11. *New Era* (18 February 1977).

12. A record of the controversy surrounding the PUC regulation of Amish taxis can be found in *Intelligencer* and *New Era*. See especially *New Era* (18 and 22 February 1977, 2 March 1977, 1 November 1977, 21 April 1978) and *Intelligencer* (23 February 1977, 2, 9, and 17 March 1977).

13. *Intelligencer* (1 March 1977).

14. Ivan Glick, in a letter to the author on 26 August 1987, reports that this farmer was Martin Shirk of Churchtown.

15. Tractor use in fields by the Amish was reported by numerous informants and is also documented by Amishman J. K. Lapp (1986:9) in his memoirs.

16. All of the informants living during the first two decades of the twentieth century agree that the Amish church had few if any restrictions on the purchase and use of new farm machinery at that time. Rather than lagging behind their neighbors, Amish farmers often were the first ones in the community to buy new implements as they became available on the public market. For a history of farming practices and equipment use, see Amishman Gideon Fisher's (1978) account of social change on the farm.

17. Similar stories of the tractor to car scenario were given by three other informants. Wagler (n.d.:20) makes the same argument.

18. Evidence against this argument comes from the Old Order Mennonites, who use tractors in the field and continue to drive a horse and carriage on the road. They have maintained the horse infrastructure even though they have only driving horses.

19. At first, tractors were restricted to belt power. In the 1990s, power take off (PTO) attachments were permitted as well.

20. The hay baler brought the first widespread use of gasoline engines. However, some Amish farmers had used "open hopper" engines without radiators on potato diggers before balers came into use.

21. The bishops forbade the use of six mechanical items: combine, forage harvester, barn cleaner, power unit, generator for lights and power, and deep freezer. This list was confirmed by several informants and is explicitly documented in Sam Kauffman's (1962) minutes of the special Ministers' Meeting held 19 December 1962.

22. Hay balers are not self-propelled. This may have contributed to the ease with which they slipped into practice among Amish farmers. The use of any self-propelled equipment would, in the long run, remove the horse from the field and lead to the car.

23. The technology used to farm and harvest tobacco has changed very little since

the early twentieth century. Tobacco production is difficult to mechanize and remains labor intensive. Tobacco farming is on the decline largely because of low tobacco prices and because there are other more profitable sources of farm and nonfarm income. In spring 2001 a tobacco company was signing up Amish farmers to grow a new strain of nicotene-free tobacco. If this venture is successful, tobacco growing may rise again.

24. S. Kauffman (1962).

25. A systematic account of this division has not been written. The best documentary source is the minutes of the special Ministers' Meeting, 19 December 1962, recorded by S. Kauffman (1962). Renno (1985:6–9) has written a brief description of the division, but many of his details are challenged by oral historians.

A brief history from the New Order perspective is available in *New Order* (1999). Abner Beiler (n.d.) has written a short description of the different groups that evolved from the division. See also E. Yoder (1987:354–56) for a description of the offshoot congregations that eventually affiliated with the Beachy Amish. Although six ordained leaders dissented from the bishops' ruling on the six articles, only two ministers actually left the Old Order Amish. The formal separation occurred on 5 June 1966 at a special Ministers' Meeting. One of the ministers eventually rejoined the Old Order Amish. Members of the Old Order Amish were given several months to decide if they wanted to join the New Order group. Members who chose to transfer during this grace period are not shunned. However, members who joined the progressive group after the time of grace are shunned by the Old Order Amish today.

10 | The Transformation of Amish Work

1. For example, Ericksen, Ericksen, and Hostetler (1980:49) argue that "the Old Order Amish culture is largely maintained by the ability of the individual Amish families to establish their children on farms." Meyers (1994), in a study of the impact of nonfarm work in Indiana, concludes that nonfarm work will not bring the demise of their culture.

2. See Reschly (2000) for a discussion of how the Amish developed outstanding farming methods in Europe before they came to North America.

3. *Standards* (1981:49).

4. *Directory* (1977:3).

5. An early history of the evolution of shops written by an Amish historian can be found in *Directory* (1977). An excellent more recent overview of the growth of the businesses was authored by Sam Stoltzfus in the booklet *17th Annual Woodworkers Get Together,* 6 June 1998, Lancaster County. See Kraybill and Nolt (1994, 1995) for an article and a book-length history and analysis of the rise of Amish businesses in the Lancaster settlement.

6. For the history of the expansion into southern Lancaster County, see Kauffman, Petersheim, and Beiler (1992).

7. Kollmorgen (1942:29).

8. *Directory* (1977:3).

9. Martineau and MacQueen (1977:384).

10. Kollmorgen (1942:27).

11. These numbers are provided by the Lancaster County Agricultural Preserve Board. For an excellent discussion of development issues and pressures in Lancaster County, see the six-day series by Ed Klimuska in *New Era* (27 June–2 July 1988). By 2000 some farms were selling for $10,000 per acre; however, the countywide average was not that high.

12. Kollmorgen (1942:23).

13. *Intelligencer* (7 April 1975).

14. Scholarly articles by Martineau and MacQueen (1977) and Ericksen, Ericksen, and Hostetler (1980) discuss the impact of nonfarm occupations on the Amish of Lancaster County. Two series in local newspapers also charted the trend toward nonfarm work (*Intelligencer,* 7 and 8 April 1975, and *New Era,* 30 and 31 July 1987).

15. Schwieder and Schwieder (1975:53).

16. The movement into Lebanon County to the north is told by D. King (1993).

17. A history of the Amish migrations to Centre and Clinton counties (Pennsylvania) as well as a directory of those settlements has been compiled (*Directory,* 1973).

18. *Directory* (1977).

19. In an informal survey of one Lancaster district in 1987, a member reported that among the married men who had not retired, 37 percent were day workers, 19 percent owned their own businesses, 11 percent farmed and had a shop, and 33 percent were full-time farmers (*Die Botschaft,* 15 September 1987).

20. A correspondent for *The Diary* reported in September 2000 that as few as 8 percent of the men were farming in one district and as many as 90 percent in another one.

21. Ed Klimuska's excellent five-part series on the dramatic growth of the quilting industry in Lancaster County appeared in *New Era* (9–13 March 1987) and was reprinted in 1987 in a booklet entitled *Lancaster County: Quilt Capital USA.* See also Kraybill and Nolt (1995:45–57).

22. For an extended discussion of the roles of Amish women in small businesses, see Kraybill and Nolt (1995:45–47, 240–44). The 17 percent level of female ownership is based on data from the Settlement Profile 2000.

23. Meyers (1983b:177) argues that the presence of ethnic support and network systems in occupational settings—more than the type of work per se—is the critical factor in determining whether the shift away from farming will lead to the collapse of Amish society.

24. Several Indiana settlements provide interesting comparisons with Lancaster because many of the Indiana Amish work in large factories owned by non-Amish. In some of the settlements, more than 50 percent of the men work in large factories. Meyers (1983b) conducted a study of stress related to nonfarm occupations in Indiana. He found few stress-related differences between Amish farmers and Amish factory workers. In a more recent article, Meyers (1994) discusses the impact of factory work in several Indiana settlements and concludes that the Amish have adapted in ways that will preserve their culture.

25. The estimates of farms owned and purchased by the Amish are based on a study conducted by Conrad L. Kanagy titled, "Comprehensive Study of Farms Owned by Plain Groups in Lancaster County, PA, 1999." The unpublished report is available

from the author. The estimate of 1,500 farms is based on the Settlement Profile 2000, which found an average of twelve farms per district (12 × 114 in Lancaster County = 1,368).

26. Information regarding the numbers of Amish farms preserved was provided by representatives of the Agricultural Preserve Board and the Lancaster Farmland Trust. Funk (1998) tells the story of land preservation in Lancaster County.

27. For a comparison of Amish businesses in Lancaster County, Pennsylvania, and Indiana County, Pennsylvania, see Kraybill and Kanagy (1996).

28. *New Era* (30 July 1987).

29. For coverage of the zoning problems related to the Amish, see *Intelligencer* (15 and 18 August 1987, 3 March 1988).

30. The hay turner is an advancement over the older hay tedders because it breaks fewer leaves and turns the hay completely upside down. Many farmers now bale high-moisture hay and wrap the bales in plastic to make haylage, which reduces the need for the turner.

31. Sam Stoltzfus, *17th Annual Woodworkers Get Together,* 6 June 1998, 6, 26.

32. Lancaster Settlement Profile (Appendix A). Twelve per district (131) yields a settlement-wide total of 1,572.

33. These estimates were given by knowledgeable non-Amish professionals who work very closely with the Amish in financial matters.

34. The sources of success are explored in depth by Kraybill and Nolt (1995: 218–35).

35. Marc Olshan (1994a) develops this theme in a chapter on Amish cottage industries in New York state.

36. Olshan (1994a:139).

37. On the discrepancy of practices between shops and farms, as well as numerous reader responses, see *Family Life* (April 1987:31–32; June 1987:16–25).

38. *Fortune 500* magazine did a special feature on Amish millionaires in the June 1995 issue.

39. A new bank formed in 1998 in order to provide financial services to the Plain communities of Lancaster County. Home Town Heritage Bank began through conversations with several Amish leaders and financial experts in the larger community. A few Amish people sit on the board of directors, but board members are primarily non-Amish. Not all of its clients are Amish, but Hometown Heritage emphasizes "a simpler way of banking," which appeals to Amish customers. Bank officials, sensitive to Amish culture, have adjusted some of their policies to dovetail with Amish values.

11 | Managing Public Relations

1. Amishman Isaac Glick served as postmaster in the village of Smoketown in the second decade of the twentieth century. See Glick (1994:33) for an account of the Glick family written by Isaac's son Aaron.

2. For the best historical synopsis of the Amish view of the state and participation in government, see Paton Yoder (1993). A volume of essays on conflicts between the Amish and the state was edited by Kraybill (1993).

3. The exemption from Worker's Compensation varies from state to state. The Amish in Pennsylvania are exempt.

4. This intriguing twist is reported by the scribe from Gordonville in *The Diary,* September 2000.

5. Steering Committee (1986:76).

6. Keim (1993:43–66) tells the story of Amish involvements in alternative service during conscription.

7. Steering Committee (1966:1).

8. Olshan (1993:67–68; 1994b:199–214) describes the evolution and role of the National Steering Committee. The minutes of the committee, which are printed periodically, provide a record of the committee's activities. Andrew S. Kinsinger (1997), the first chairman of the Steering Committee, provides an Amish perspective of its development.

9. Amish views of Social Security and a history of their response to it are described by Ferrara (1993:125–44).

10. Kinsinger (1983:596).

11. For a thorough history of the Amish struggle with Social Security, see Ferrara (1993).

12. Cline (1968:145). My discussion of Social Security is heavily indebted to Cline's work and to an Amish informant involved in negotiations with government officials.

13. Cline (1968:164).

14. For a lengthy description of this case and subsequent legal action surrounding it, see Cline (1968:148–55).

15. In some cases, heads of large families with low incomes have inadvertently received "unearned income" checks from the government, but Amish leaders urge members to return them.

16. In recent years some Amish have opened Individual Retirement Accounts (IRAs). The IRS position on this issue was unclear at first, but presently the IRS permits the Amish to have them.

17. For an extended discussion of the Amish reaction to this film as well as a chronology of events, see Hostetler and Kraybill (1988).

18. The agreement was formalized in a letter from Secretary of Commerce Pickard on 12 September 1984.

19. *Intelligencer* (26 January 1985).

20. *Intelligencer* (28 February 1985).

21. "Amish at the Heart of 'Puppy Mill' Debate," *New York Times,* 20 September 1993, A12.

22. *Intelligencer* (14 August 2000).

23. Some of the extensive Lancaster newspaper coverage can be found in *Sunday News* (16 April 2000), *Intelligencer* (12 June 2000), *New Era* (27 June 2000), *Intelligencer* (28 June and 6 July 2000), *New Era* (13 July 2000), *Sunday Patriot News* (23 July 2000), *Sunday News* (23 July 2000), and *Intelligencer* (26 July, and 9, 14, and 16 August 2000).

24. *Intelligencer* (28 June 2000).

25. *Intelligencer* (9 August 2000).

26. *Sunday Patriot News* (8 November 1998). Other accounts of the controversy can be found in *New Era* (21 April 1998), *Intelligencer* (22 April and 17 July), *Sunday News* (2 August 1998), and *Intelligencer* (29 September, 10 October, and 16 November 1998).

27. Hannah B. Lapp, "Labor Department vs. Amish Ways," *Wall Street Journal,* 10 April 1997.

28. The proposed bill, HR 4257, was designed to amend the Fair Labor Standards Act of 1938 so that "certain youth could perform certain work with wood products."

29. Written comments to the House Committee on Education and the Workforce by the chairman of the Old Order Amish Steering Committee, 21 April 1998.

30. Luthy (1994b) tells the story of the growth of tourism from an Amish perspective in several of the larger settlements. L. Stoltzfus (2000) chronicles the historical growth of tourism in Lancaster County.

31. For a history of Amish tourism in Lancaster County, see excellent articles by Luthy (1980, 1994b). The booklet was Steinfeldt's (1937) *The Amish of Lancaster County.* Fisher (1988) describes the rise of tourism from a local Amishman's view. For a creative interpretation of the Amish in the American imagination, see Weaver-Zercher (2001).

32. Estimates from the Pennsylvania Dutch Convention and Visitors Bureau in Lancaster. My estimates of expenditures per Amish person are based on an Amish population of 22,000 (children and adults).

33. *Intelligencer* (28 January 1988).

34. G. Fisher (1978:365).

35. J. Beiler (1976b:482).

36. J. Beiler (1976b:482).

37. *Vogue* magazine, August 1993. For a thorough discussion of the commodification of Amish images in the American culture market, see Weaver-Zercher (2001).

12 | Regulating Social Change

1. Gordonville area scribe in *The Diary,* September 2000.

2. For a structural analysis of social change, see Gallagher's (1981) study of the Lancaster Amish settlement. Other discussions of social change among the Amish in a variety of settlements can be found in Foster (1984a), J. A. Hostetler (1993:387–99), Huntington (1956:1045–55), Meyers (1983b), Nagata (1968), and Olshan (1980). Kraybill and Olshan (1994) provide a number of essays dealing with social change among the Amish of North America. See Kraybill (1994c) for an extended discussion of social change.

3. S. Kauffman (1962:7).

4. My approach to the study of the Amish entrepreneurship is grounded in the growing sociological tradition of cultural analysis that stresses the bona fide role of culture in shaping and regulating social organization.

5. The members of an ethnic group share a common religious, racial, or national background, a sense of peoplehood, and a memory of a common past. Their social

symbols and membership boundaries give them a visible public identity recognized by insiders and outsiders alike. The bulk of the literature on ethnic businesses underscores the important role of cultural resources. The Amish story is unique in that cultural restraints have obstructed and regulated business activity. The formation of business enterprises in this particular ethnic context is a negotiated outcome produced by these two countervailing cultural forces.

6. Howard Rheingold discusses the growing use of cell phones among the Amish in an article in *Wired* magazine, January 1999.

7. This question is addressed at length by Kraybill and Bowman (2001) in their comparative study of four Old Order communities.

8. For additional discussions of Amish survival strategies, see Foster (1984b), J. A. Hostetler (1993), V. Stoltzfus (1973), and Thompson (1981).

13 | Exploring Our Common Riddles

1. Bellah et al. (1985:viii). Other analysts concerned about the debilitating effects of radical individualism include Fukuyama (1995, 1999), Myers (2000), and Putnam (2000).

2. Berger, Berger, and Kellner (1973) develop this theme in *The Homeless Mind.*

3. Hunter's essay "The Modern Malaise" offers a superb review of the social criticism of modernity since 1930 (Hunter and Ainlay 1986). See also Lane (2000) and Myers (2000).

4. Olshan (1981:297) notes that many social scientists ritualistically label the Amish a folk society—a small isolated and traditional group—and thus assume that the Amish are not modern. Berger (1977, 1979), Foster (1984b), and Olshan (1981) contend that choice is central to the modern experience. Olshan (1980, 1981) argues that the Amish are not a folk society because they engage in rational decision making. However, he focuses on their collective decisions and disregards individual choice, which is central to Berger's definition of modernity.

5. The Amish National Steering Committee serves as a quasi–lobby group that intercedes with government officials on behalf of Amish interests. For a record of this group's activities, see Steering Committee (1966–2000) and Olshan (1993, 1994b).

6. This type of rationality corresponds to what Max Weber (1947:115) called *Wert-rational,* rational decisions that are made to uphold or promote absolute religious values.

7. Olshan (1979, 1980) points to the Amish as a model for social development. Berry (1977); Foster (1980, 1981, 1982); and Johnson, Stoltzfus, and Craumer (1977) have described the energy efficiency of Amish culture.

8. In their comprehensive study of mental illness in the Lancaster settlement, Egeland and Hostetter (1983:59) report that major affective mental disorders among the Amish are about half the rate of such disorders in other groups. A study of Amish suicide in the Lancaster area found that the Amish rate was half that of other religious groups and one-third the rate of nonreligious populations (Kraybill, Hostetler, and Shaw 1986:256–57).

9. In severe cases of psychiatric disorder, Amish people are hospitalized. People with mild psychiatric disorders, retardation, and physical disabilities are cared for by the extended family whenever possible.

10. The one area in which they have contributed to science has been through medical research. Hundreds of Amish in the Lancaster area have participated in large medical research projects exploring issues such as the genetic transmission of diabetes, depression, and obesity. Their stable population, extensive family records, and restricted gene pool make them a valuable population for the study of inherited diseases.

11. See Olshan (1994d) for an excellent essay under the title of this question.

12. The notions of freedom and meaning in Amish life are addressed by Olshan (1986). For a perceptive analysis of the Amish plight with modernity, see Enninger (1988).

13. Myers (2000) explores what he calls an *American Paradox—Spiritual Hunger in an Age of Plenty*. Robert Lane (2000) provides extensive documentation in *The Loss of Happiness in Market Democracies*. Both of these analyze the rise of unhappiness in the midst of prosperity.

14. The ABC program was aired on 15 April 1996.

This listing of references includes sources cited in the Notes as well as other select works related to the Amish. Bibliographic information for some sources—pamphlets, newsletters—not appearing in this list are provided in the Notes.

Allen, Francis R.
    1957   "The Automobile." In *Technology and Social Change,* edited by Francis Allen et al. New York: Appleton-Century-Crofts.

Amish Moving to Maryland, The
    1965   Gordonville, Pa.: Printed by A. S. Kinsinger.

Armstrong, Penny, and Sheryl Feldman
    1986   *A Midwife's Story.* New York: Arbor House.

Articles of Incorporation of the Pequea Bruderschaft Library
    1984   Pequea Bruderschaft Library. Intercourse, Pa.

Ausbund, Das ist: Etliche schone christlicher Lieder
    1984   Lancaster, Pa.: Lancaster Press. First ed. in 1564.

Bachman, Calvin G.
    1961   *The Old Order Amish of Lancaster County.* Pennsylvania German Society, vol. 60. A reprint of vol. 49, first published in 1941.

Baecher, Robert
    2000   "Research Note: The 'Patriarche' of Sainte-Marie-aux-Mines." *Mennonite Quarterly Review* 74(1):145–58.

Bartel, Lee R.
    1986   "The Tradition of the Amish in Music." *Hymn* 37(October):20–26.

Beam, C. Richard
    1982   *Pennsylvania German Dictionary.* Schaefferstown, Pa.: Historic Schaefferstown.

Beginning and Development of Parochial Special Schools: 1975–1996, The
    1996   Gordonville, Pa.: Gordonville Print Shop.

Beiler, Abner
    n.d.   "A Brief History of the New Order Amish Church, 1966–1976." Lancaster Mennonite Historical Society Library. Lancaster, Pa.

Beiler, David
    1888   *Das Wahre Christenthum: Eine Christliche Betrachtung nach den Lehren der Heiligen Schrift.* Lancaster, Pa.: Johann Baers and Son.

Beiler, Joseph F.

> 1976a   "Eighteenth-Century Amish in Lancaster County." *Mennonite Research Journal* 17(October):37, 46.
>
> 1976b   "The Tourist Season." *Gospel Herald* (8 June):482.
>
> 1977   "Eighteenth-Century Amish History in Lancaster County, Concluded." *Mennonite Research Journal* 17(April):16.
>
> 1982   "Ordnung." *Mennonite Quarterly Review* 56(October):382–84.
>
> 1983   "A Review of the Founding of Lancaster County Church Settlement." *The Diary* 15(December):17–22.

Bellah, R. N., R. Madsen, W. M. Sullivan, A. Swidler, and S. M. Tipton

> 1985   *Habits of the Heart.* Berkeley and Los Angeles: University of California Press.

Bender, Harold S.

> 1957   "The Anabaptist Vision." In *The Recovery of the Anabaptist Vision,* edited by Guy F. Hershberger. Scottdale, Pa.: Herald Press.

Berger, Peter L.

> 1974   *Pyramids of Sacrifice.* Garden City, N.Y.: Doubleday.
>
> 1977   *Facing Up to Modernity.* New York: Basic Books.
>
> 1979   *The Heretical Imperative.* Garden City, N.Y.: Doubleday.

Berger, Peter L., Brigitte Berger, and Hansfried Kellner

> 1973   *The Homeless Mind.* New York: Random House.

Berger, Peter L., and Thomas Luckmann

> 1966   *The Social Construction of Reality.* Garden City, N.Y.: Doubleday.

Bericht und klare Darstellung von Bann und Meidung wie es angesehen ist bei den Alt Amischen in Lancaster County, PA, Ein (A report and clear statement of the ban and shunning as it is understood by the Old Amish of Lancaster County, PA).

> 1943   Seven-page pamphlet. Translated by Noah G. Good. No publisher.

Berry, Wendell

> 1977   *The Unsettling of America: Culture and Agriculture.* New York: Avon.

Blackboard Bulletin

> 1957–   Aylmer, Ont.: Pathway Publishers. Monthly periodical published for Old Order Amish teachers.

Botschaft, Die

> 1975–   Vols. 1–26 (1975–2000). Lancaster, Pa.: Brookshire Publications and Printing. Described on its masthead as "a weekly newspaper serving Old Order Amish Communities everywhere."

Bourdieu, Pierre

> 1977   *Outline of a Theory of Practice.* Translated by Richard Nice. Cambridge: Cambridge University Press.

1986 "The Forms of Capital." In *Handbook of Theory and Research for Sociology of Education,* edited by J. G. Richardson. New York: Greenwood Press.

Braght, Thieleman J. van
1985 Comp. *The Bloody Theatre; or, Martyrs Mirror.* 14th ed. Scottdale, Pa.: Mennonite Publishing House. Originally published in Dutch (Dordrecht, 1660).

Brenneman, John M.
1867 *Pride and Humility.* Elkhart, Ind.: John F. Funk. Reprinted in 1988. Gordonville, Pa.: Gordonville Print Shop.

Bryer, Kathleen B.
1978 "Attitudes toward Death among Amish Families: Implications for Family Therapy." Master's thesis, Hahnemann Medical College.
1979 "The Amish Way of Death: A Study of Family Support Systems." *American Psychologist* 34(March):255–61.

Buck, Roy
1978 "Boundary Maintenance Revisited: Tourist Experience in an Old Order Amish Community." *Rural Sociology* 43(Summer):221–34.
1979 "Bloodless Theatre: Images of the Old Order Amish in Tourism Literature." *Pennsylvania Mennonite Heritage* 2(July):2–11.

Budget, The
1890– Sugarcreek, Ohio. A weekly newspaper serving Old Order Amish and Mennonite communities.

Christlicher Ordnung, or Christian Discipline
1966 A Collection and Translation of Anabaptist and Amish-Mennonite Church Disciplines (Artikel and Ordnungen) of 1527, 1568, 1607, 1630, 1668, 1688, 1779, 1809, 1837, and 1865, with Historical Explanations and Notes, translated by William R. McGrath. Aylmer, Ont.: Pathway Publishers.

Cline, Paul C.
1968 "Relations between the 'Plain People' and Government in the United States." Ph.D. diss., American University.

Coleman, James S.
1988 "Social Capital in the Creation of Human Capital." *American Journal of Sociology* 94 Supplement: S95–S120.
1990 *Foundations of Social Theory.* Cambridge, Mass: Belknap Press of Harvard University Press.

Cronk, Sandra L.
1977 "Gelassenheit: The Rites of the Redemptive Process in Old Order Amish and Old Order Mennonite Communities." Ph.D. diss., University

of Chicago. Excerpts under the same title appear in *Mennonite Quarterly Review* 55(January 1981):5–44.

Crowley, William K.
1978   "The Old Order Amish: Diffusion and Growth." *Annals of the American Geographers* 63(June):249–64.

Diary, The
1969   Vols. 1–32 (1969–2000). Gordonville, Pa.: Pequea Publishers. A monthly magazine serving Old Order groups.

Directory
1965   *Amish Farm and Home Directory.* Gordonville, Pa.: A. S. Kinsinger.
1973   *Pennsylvania Amish Directory of Lancaster and Chester County Districts.* Gordonville, Pa.: Pequea Publishers.
1977   *Old Order Shop and Service Directory: United States and Canada.* Gordonville, Pa.: Pequea Publishers.
1979   *History and Directory of the Old Order Amish of Brush, Nittany, and Sugar Valleys in Centre and Clinton Counties, Pennsylvania.* Gordonville, Pa.: Pequea Publishers.
1980   *Amish Directory of the Lancaster County Family.* Gordonville, Pa.: Pequea Publishers.
1987   *Address Directory of the Lancaster County Amish.* Soudersburg, Pa.: Eby's Quality Printing.
1988   *Address Book of Lancaster County Amish.* No printer or publisher listed.
1996   *Church Directory of the Lancaster County Amish.* Vols. 1 and 2. Gordonville, Pa.: Pequea Publishers.

Dordrecht Confession of Faith
1976   Aylmer, Ont.: Pathway Publishers. Various printings. Adopted by the Mennonites at a Peace Convention held in Dordrecht, Holland, 21 April 1632.

Durnbaugh, Hedwig T.
1999   "The Amish Singing Style: Theories of Its Origin and Description of Its Singularity." *Pennsylvania Mennonite Heritage* 22(April):24–31.

Dyck, Cornelius J.
1985   "The Suffering Church in Anabaptism." *Mennonite Quarterly Review* 59(January):5–23.
1993   *An Introduction to Mennonite History.* 3rd ed. Scottdale, Pa.: Herald Press.

Eaton, Joseph W.
1952   "Controlled Acculturation: A Survival Technique of the Hutterites." *American Sociological Review* 17:331–40.

Egeland, J., and A. M. Hostetter
  1983   "Amish Study I: Affective Disorders among the Amish, 1976–1980."
         American Journal of Psychiatry 140(January):56–61.

Egeland, J., A. M. Hostetter, and Jean Endicott
  1983   "Amish Study II: Consensus Diagnoses and Reliability Results." *American Journal of Psychiatry* 140(January):62–66.

Egeland, J., A. M. Hostetter, and S. K. Eshleman
  1983   "Amish Study III: The Impact of Cultural Factors on Diagnosis of Bipolar Illnesses." *American Journal of Psychiatry* 140(January):67–71.

Egeland, J., and J. Sussex
  1985   "Suicide and Family Loading for Affective Disorders." *Journal of the American Medical Association* 254:915–18.

Ein Diener Register (1788–2000)
  2000   3rd ed. Millersburg, Pa.: Brookside Printing.

Ellis, Franklin, and Samuel Evans
  1883   *History of Lancaster County, Pennsylvania, with Biographical Sketches of Many of Its Pioneers and Prominent Men.* Philadelphia: Everts and Peck.

Enninger, Werner
  1984   Ed. *Internal and External Perspectives on Amish and Mennonite Life.* Vol. 1. Essen: Unipress.
  1986   Ed. *Internal and External Perspectives on Amish and Mennonite Life.* Vol. 2. Essen: Unipress.
  1988   "Coping with Modernity: Instrumentally and Symbolically, with a Glimpse at the Old Order Amish." *Brethren Life and Thought* 33(Summer):154–70.

Ericksen, Eugene P., J. A. Ericksen, and J. A. Hostetler
  1980   "The Cultivation of the Soil as a Moral Directive: Population Growth, Family Ties, and the Maintenance of Community among the Old Order Amish." *Rural Sociology* 45(Spring):49–68.

Ericksen, Eugene P., J. A. Ericksen, J. A. Hostetler, and G. E. Huntington
  1979   "Fertility Patterns and Trends among the Old Order Amish." *Population Studies* 33(July):255–76.

Esh, Levi A.
  1977   "The Amish Parochial School Movement." *Mennonite Quarterly Review* 51(January):69–75. Reprinted from 1973 *Directory.*

Family Life
  1968– Aylmer, Ont.: Pathway Publishers. A monthly Amish periodical.

Ferrara, Peter J.
>   1993   "Social Security and Taxes." In *The Amish and the State,* edited by Donald B. Kraybill. Baltimore: Johns Hopkins University Press.

Ferster, Herbert V.
>   1983   "The Development of the Amish School System," *Pennsylvania Mennonite Heritage* 6(April):7–14.

Fisher, Amos L.
>   1984   "History of the First Amish Communities in America." *The Diary* 16(September):35–39.

Fisher, Gideon L.
>   1978   *Farm Life and Its Changes.* Gordonville, Pa.: Pequea Publishers.
>   1987   Comp. *Ein Diener Register von Diener Deaconien und Bischof in Lancaster County, 1788 to 1987.* 2nd ed. Gordonville, Pa.: Gordonville Print Shop.
>   1988   "The Early Days of Intercourse." *The Diary* 20(June):31–35.

Fisher, Sara E., and Rachel K. Stahl
>   1986   *The Amish School.* Intercourse, Pa.: Good Books.

Fletcher, S. W.
>   1955   *Pennsylvania Agriculture and Country Life, 1840–1940.* Harrisburg, Pa.: Pennsylvania Historical and Museum Commission.

Flink, James J.
>   1975   *The Car Culture.* Cambridge, Mass.: MIT Press.

Foster, George M.
>   1980   "The Amish and the Ethos of Ecology." *Ecologist* 10(December):331–35.
>   1981   "Amish Society." *Futurist* 15(December):33–40.
>   1982   "Learning from the Amish." *New Roots* 21(Winter):16–21.
>   1984a   "Separation and Survival in Amish Society." *Sociological Focus* 17(January):1–15.
>   1984b   "Occupational Differentiation and Change in an Ohio Amish Settlement." *Ohio Journal of Science* 84(3):74–81.

Frey, J. William
>   1981   *A Simple Grammar of Pennsylvania Dutch.* Lancaster, Pa.: John Baers and Son.

Friedmann, Robert
>   1956   S.v. "Gelassenheit." In *Mennonite Encyclopedia* 2:444–49. Scottdale, Pa.: Herald Press.
>   1957   "The Hutterian Brethren and Community of Goods." In *The Recovery of the Anabaptist Vision,* edited by Guy F. Hershberger. Scottdale, Pa.: Herald Press.
>   1973   *The Theology of Anabaptism.* Scottdale, Pa.: Herald Press.

Fukuyama, Francis
    1995   *Trust: The Social Virtues and the Creation of Prosperity.* New York: Free Press.
    1999   *The Great Disruption: Human Nature and the Reconstruction of Social Order.* New York: Free Press.

Funk, Amos H.
    1998   *My Life and Love for the Land.* Morgantown, Pa.: Masthof Press.

Furner, Mark
    2000   "Research Note: On the Trail of Jacob Ammann." *Mennonite Quarterly Review* 74(October):326–28.

Gallagher Jr., Thomas E.
    1981   "Clinging to the Past or Preparing for the Future? The Structure of Selective Modernization among the Old Order Amish of Lancaster County, Pennsylvania." Ph.D. diss., Temple University.

Garrett, Ottie A.
    1998   Comp. *True Stories of the X-Amish.* Horse Cave, Ky.: Neu Leben Inc.

Gascho, Milton
    1937   "The Amish Division of 1693–1697 in Switzerland and Alsace." *Mennonite Quarterly Review* 11(October):235–66.

Gemeinden, Ein Bericht an Die (A notification to the congregations)
    1937   Translated by Noah G. Good. N.p.

Gemein Ordnungen von Lancaster Co., PA (Church ordinances of Lancaster County, PA)
    n.d.   Translated by Noah G. Good.

Getz, Jane C.
    1946   "The Economic Organization and Practices of the Old Order Amish of Lancaster County, Pennsylvania." *Mennonite Quarterly Review* 20(January):53–80; 20(April):98–127.

Gibbons, Phebe Earle
    1869   "Pennsylvania Dutch." First published in *Atlantic Monthly* in October 1869. Reprinted in *Pennsylvania Dutch and Other Essays.* Philadelphia: Lippincott, 1872, 1874, 1882.

Gingerich, H. F., and R. W. Kreider
    1986   Comp. *Amish and Amish-Mennonite Genealogies.* Gordonville, Pa.: Pequea Publishers.

Gingerich, James Nelson
    1986   "Ordinance or Ordering: *Ordnung* and the Amish Minister Meeting, 1862–1878." *Mennonite Quarterly Review* 60(April):180–99.

Gingerich, Melvin
  1970   *Mennonite Attire Through Four Centuries.* Breinigsville, Pa.: Pennsylvania German Society.

Gleick, James
  1999   *Faster: The Acceleration of Just About Everything.* New York: Pantheon Books.

Glick, Aaron S.
  1986   "A Chronicle of Events Relating to the 1910 Peachey Church Division." Handwritten.
  1987   "Pequea Amish Mennonite Church Twenty-Fifth Anniversary." Mimeo.
  1994   *The Fortunate Years: An Amish Life.* Intercourse, Pa.: Good Books.

Granick, Eve Wheatcroft
  1989   *The Amish Quilt.* Intercourse, Pa: Good Books.

Gross, Leonard
  1994   "Swiss Brethren (Mennonite) Responses to the 1693 Schism." In *Proceedings of the Conference: Tradition and Transition: An Amish Mennonite Heritage of Obedience 1693–1993,* edited by V. Gordon Oyer. Metamora, Ill.: Mennonite Heritage Center.

Guidelines in Regards to the Old Order Amish and Mennonite Parochial Schools
  1981   Gordonville, Pa.: Gordonville Print Shop.

Guth, Hermann
  1995   *Amish Mennonites in Germany: Their Congregations, the Estates Where They Lived, Their Families.* Morgantown, Pa.: Masthof Press.

Haag, Earl C.
  1982   *A Pennsylvania German Reader and Grammar.* State College, Pa.: Pennsylvania State University Press.

Hall, Edward T.
  1977   *Beyond Culture.* New York: Anchor Books.

Handbuch für Bischof (Handbook for bishops)
  1978   Translated by Noah G. Good. Gordonville, Pa.: Gordonville Print Shop. First published in 1935.

Harnish, C. H.
  1925   Letter to the Voters of Upper Leacock Township, 19 October 1925, in *Papers.*

Hartz, Amos, and Susan Hartz
  1965   Comps. *Moses Hartz Family History, 1819–1965.* Elverson, Pa.: by the authors.

Herr, Patricia T.
  1998   *Amish Arts of Lancaster County.* Atglen, Pa.: Schiffer Publishing Ltd.

Hopple, C. Lee
1971,   "Spatial Development of the Southeastern Pennsylvania Plain Dutch
1972   Community to 1970," Parts 1 and 2. *Pennsylvania Folklife* 21(Winter
        1971):18–40; 21(Spring 1972):36–45.

Horst, Irvin B.
1982   "Dordrecht Confession of Faith: 350 Years." *Pennsylvania Mennonite
        Heritage* 5(July):2–8.
1986   "Menno Simons: The Road to a Believer's Church." *Pennsylvania Men-
        nonite Heritage* 9(July):2–8.
1988   Ed. and trans. *Mennonite Confession of Faith* (Dordrecht). Lancaster,
        Pa.: Lancaster Mennonite Historical Society.

Hostetler, Beulah S.
1992   "The Formation of the Old Orders." *Mennonite Quarterly Review* 66
        (January):5–25.
1996   "The Amish and Pietism: Similarities and Differences." In *Les Amish: or-
        igine et particularismes 1693–1993.* Ingersheim: Association Française
        d'Histoire Anabaptiste-Mennonite.

Hostetler, John A.
1963   "The Amish Use of Symbols and Their Function in Bounding the Com-
        munity." *Journal of the Royal Anthropological Institute* 94, pt. 1:11–12.
1968   Ed. "Anabaptist Conceptions of Child Nurture and Schooling: A Collec-
        tion of Source Materials Used by the Old Order Amish." Temple Univer-
        sity, Philadelphia, Pa. Typescript.
1969   "Educational Achievement and Lifestyles in a Traditional Society, the
        Old Order Amish." Temple University, Philadelphia, Pa. Typescript.
1977   "Old Order Amish Survival." *Mennonite Quarterly Review* 51(October):
        352–61.
1979   "The Old Order Amish on the Great Plains." In *Ethnicity on the Great
        Plains,* edited by Fred Leubke. Lincoln: University of Nebraska Press.
1984   "Silence and Survival Strategies among the New and Old Order Amish."
        In *Internal and External Perspectives on Amish and Mennonite Life,* ed-
        ited by Werner Enninger. Vol. 1. Essen: Unipress.
1989   Ed. *Amish Roots: A Treasury of History, Wisdom, and Lore.* Baltimore:
        Johns Hopkins University Press.
1993   *Amish Society.* 4th ed. Baltimore: Johns Hopkins University Press.
1997   *Hutterite Society.* 2d ed. Baltimore: Johns Hopkins University Press.

Hostetler, John A., and Gertrude Enders Huntington
1992   *Amish Children: Education in the Family, School, and Community.* New
        York: Harcourt Brace and Jovanovich.

Hostetler, John A., and Donald B. Kraybill
1988   "Hollywood Markets the Amish." In *Image Ethics: The Moral Rights of
        Subjects in Photography, Film and Television,* edited by John Katz and
        Jay Ruby. New York: Oxford University Press.

Huffines, Marion Lois
  1988   "Pennsylvania German among the Plain Groups: Convergence as a Strategy of Language Maintenance." In *Pennsylvania Mennonite Heritage* 11(July):12–16.
  1993   "Pennsylvania German: Language Persistence and Change in Amish Society." Paper presented at the Young Center, Elizabethtown College, Pa. July.

Hunter, James Davison, and Stephen C. Ainlay
  1986   Eds. *Making Sense of Modern Times: Peter L. Berger and the Vision of Interpretive Sociology.* New York: Routledge and Kegan Paul.

Huntington, Gertrude Enders
  1956   "Dove at the Window: A Study of an Old Order Amish Community in Ohio." Ph.D. diss., Yale University.
  1981   "The Amish Family." In *Ethnic Families in America: Patterns and Variations,* edited by Charles H. Mindel and Robert W. Habenstein. 2nd ed. New York: Elsevier Scientific Publishing.
  1994   "Persistence and Change in Amish Education." In *The Amish Struggle with Modernity,* edited by Donald B. Kraybill and Marc A. Olshan. Hanover: University Press of New England.

Hüppi, John
  2000   "Research Note: Identifying Jacob Ammann." *Mennonite Quarterly Review* 74(October):329–39.

Igou, Brad
  1999   Comp. *The Amish in Their Own Words.* Scottdale, Pa: Herald Press.

In Meiner Jugend: A Devotional Reader in German and English
  2000   Aylmer, Ont.: Pathway Publishers.

Instruction of Youth, The
  n.d.   Gordonville, Pa.: Gordonville Print Shop.

Intelligencer Journal
  1930–   Lancaster, Pa.: Lancaster Newspapers.

Johnson, Warren A., Victor Stoltzfus, and Peter Craumer
  1977   "Energy Conservation in Amish Agriculture." *Science* 198(October 28):373–79.

Kaiser, Grace H.
  1986   *Dr. Frau: A Woman Doctor Among the Amish.* Intercourse, Pa.: Good Books.

Kalberg, Stephen
  1980   "Max Weber's Types of Rationality: Cornerstones for the Analysis of Rationalization Processes in History." *American Journal of Sociology* 85(5): 1145.

Kasdorf, Julia
> 1997 "Fixing Traditions: The Cultural Work of Joseph W. Yoder and His Relationship with the Amish Community of Mifflin County, Pennsylvania." Ph.D. diss., New York University.

Kauffman, John E.
> 1975 Trans. and comp. *Anabaptist Letters from 1635 to 1645*. Translated from the *Ausbund*. Atglen, Pa.

Kauffman, John S., Melvin R. Petersheim, and Ira S. Beiler
> 1992 *Amish History of Southern Lancaster County, 1940–1992*. Elverson, Pa.: Olde Springfield Shoppe.

Kauffman, S. Duane
> 1979 "Miscellaneous Amish-Mennonite Documents." *Pennsylvania Mennonite Heritage* 2(July):12–16.

Kauffman, Sam
> 1962 "Begebenheiten von Eine Lancaster County Diener Versammlung Den 19ten December 1962" (Actions taken at a minister's meeting in Lancaster County on 19 December 1962). Translated by Noah G. Good. Typescript minutes.

Keim, Albert N.
> 1975 Ed. *Compulsory Education and the Amish: The Right Not to Be Modern*. Boston: Beacon Press.
> 1993 "Military Service and Conscription." In *The Amish and the State,* edited by Donald B. Kraybill. Baltimore: Johns Hopkins University Press.

King, Ada Nancy
> 1977 "The Mennonite Church of the Millwood District." *Mennonite Research Journal* 18(July):30–31.

King, David S.
> 1993 *Fifty Years in Lebanon County, Pennsylvania*. Elverson, Pa.: Olde Springfield Shoppe.

King, Emma
> 1992 *Joys, Sorrows, and Shadows*. Elverson, Pa.: Olde Springfield Shoppe.

Kinsinger, Andrew S.
> 1983 "Statement to the Subcommittee on Social Security of the Committee on Ways and Means, U.S. House of Representatives." 9 February 1983. In *Financing Problems of the Social Security System*. Serial 98-5, Washington, D.C.: Government Printing Office.
> 1997 *A Little History of our Parochial Schools and Steering Committee from 1956–1994*. Gordonville, Pa.: Gordonville Print Shop.

Klaassen, Walter
> 2001 *Anabaptism: Neither Protestant nor Catholic*. 3rd ed. Kitchner, Ont.: Pandora Press.

Klein, Frederic Shriver
 1941 *Lancaster County, 1841–1941.* Lancaster, Pa.: Intelligencer Printing.

Klein, H. M. J.
 1924 *Lancaster County, Pennsylvania: A History.* 2 vols. New York: Lewis Historical Publishing.
 1946 *History and Customs of the Amish People.* York, Pa.: Maple Press.

Kollmorgen, Walter M.
 1942 *Culture of a Contemporary Rural Community: The Old Order Amish of Lancaster County, Pennsylvania. Rural Life Studies,* no. 4. Washington, D.C.: U.S. Department of Agriculture.
 1943 "The Agricultural Stability of the Old Order Amish and the Old Order Mennonites of Lancaster County, Pennsylvania." *American Journal of Sociology* 49(November):233–41.

Kraybill, Donald B.
 1987a "At the Crossroads of Modernity: Amish, Mennonites, and Brethren in Lancaster County in 1880." *Pennsylvania Mennonite Heritage* 10(January):2–12.
 1987b "Mennonite Woman's Veiling: The Rise and Fall of a Sacred Symbol." *Mennonite Quarterly Review* 61(July):298–320.
 1988 Review of *Extraordinary Groups: An Examination of Unconventional Lifestyles,* by William M. Kephart. *Mennonite Quarterly Review* 62(January):86–87.
 1993 Ed. *The Amish and the State.* Baltimore: Johns Hopkins University Press.
 1994a "The Amish Encounter with Modernity." In *The Amish Struggle with Modernity,* edited by Donald B. Kraybill and Marc A. Olshan. Hanover: University Press of New England.
 1994b "Plotting Social Change Across Four Affiliations." In *The Amish Struggle with Modernity,* edited by Donald B. Kraybill and Marc A. Olshan. Hanover: University Press of New England.
 1994c "War Against Progress: Coping with Social Change." In *The Amish Struggle with Modernity,* edited by Donald B. Kraybill and Marc A. Olshan. Hanover: University Press of New England.
 1998 "Plain Reservations: Amish and Mennonite Views of Media and Computers." *Journal of Mass Media Ethics* 13(2):99–110.

Kraybill, Donald B., and Carl F. Bowman
 2001 *On the Backroad to Heaven: Old Order Hutterites, Mennonites, Amish, and Brethren.* Baltimore: Johns Hopkins University Press.

Kraybill, Donald B., and Donald R. Fitzkee
 1987 "Amish, Mennonites, and Brethren in the Modern Era." *Pennsylvania Mennonite Heritage* 10(April):2–11.

Kraybill, Donald B., Patricia T. Herr, and Jonathan Holstein
    1996   *A Quiet Spirit: Amish Quilts from the Collection of Cindy Tietze and Stuart Hodosh.* Los Angeles: UCLA Fowler Museum of Cultural History.

Kraybill, Donald B., John A. Hostetler, and D. G. Shaw
    1986   "Suicide Patterns in a Religious Subculture: The Old Order Amish." *International Journal of Moral and Social Studies* 1(Fall):249–63.

Kraybill, Donald B., and Conrad Kanagy
    1996   "From Milk to Manufacturing: The Rise of Entrepreneurship in Two Old Order Amish Communities." *Mennonite Quarterly Review* 70(July): 263–80.

Kraybill, Donald B., and Steven M. Nolt
    1994   "The Rise of Microenterprises." In *The Amish Struggle with Modernity,* edited by Donald B. Kraybill and Marc A. Olshan. Hanover: University Press of New England.
    1995   *Amish Enterprise: From Plows to Profits.* Baltimore: Johns Hopkins University Press.

Kraybill, Donald B., and Marc A. Olshan
    1994   *The Amish Struggle with Modernity.* Hanover: University Press of New England.

Lane, Robert E.
    2000   *The Loss of Happiness in Market Democracies.* New Haven: Yale University Press.

Lapp, Christ S.
    1991   Comp. *Pennsylvania School History: 1690–1990.* Gordonville, Pa.: privately published by the compiler.

Lapp, Ferne E.
    1963   *History of Weavertown Church.* Published privately by Anna Mary Yoder.

Lapp, John K.
    1986   *Remarks of By-Gone Days, A Few Remarks of Old Times.* Gordonville, Pa.: Gordonville Print Shop.

Lehman, Dan W.
    1998   "Graven Images and the (Re)presentation of Amish Trauma." *Mennonite Quarterly Review* 72(October):577–87.

Lehman, Marilyn E.
    1993   "The Taboo on Photography: Its Historical and Social Significance." Paper presented at the Young Center Elizabethtown College, Pa. July.

Loewen, Harry, and Steven M. Nolt
    1996   *Through Fire and Water: An Overview of Mennonite History.* Scottdale, Pa.: Herald Press.

Loomis, Charles P.
1979   "A Farm Hand's Diary." *Mennonite Quarterly Review* 53(July): 235–57.

Loomis, Charles P., and Everett D. Dyer
1976   "The Old Order Amish as a Social System." In *Social Systems: The Study of Sociology,* edited by Charles P. Loomis and Everett D. Dyer. Cambridge, Mass.: Schenkman.

Louden, Mark L.
1988   "Bilingualism and Syntactic Change in Pennsylvania German." Ph.D. diss., Cornell University.
1991a   "Covert Prestige and the Role of English in Plain Pennsylvania German Sociolinguistics." Paper presented at the Annual Meeting of the Linguistic Society of America, Chicago.
1991b   "The Image of the Old Order Amish: General and Sociolinguistic Stereotypes." *National Journal of Sociology* 5(2):111–42.
1993   "Old Order Amish Verbal Behavior as a Reflection of Cultural Convergence." Paper presented at the Young Center, Elizabethtown College, Pa. July.

Luthy, David
1971a   "The Amish Division of 1693." *Family Life* (October):18–20.
1971b   "Four Centuries with the Ausbund." *Family Life* (June):21–22.
1975   "A Survey of Amish Ordination Customs." *Family Life* (March):13–17.
1980   "The Origin of Amish Tourism in Lancaster County, Pennsylvania." *Family Life* (November):31–34.
1986   *The Amish in America: Settlements That Failed, 1840–1960.* Aylmer, Ont.: Pathway Publishers.
1994a   "Appendix: Amish Migration Patterns: 1972–1992." In *The Amish Struggle with Modernity,* edited by Donald B. Kraybill and Marc A. Olshan. Hanover: University Press of New England.
1994b   "The Origin and Growth of Amish Tourism." In *The Amish Struggle with Modernity,* edited by Donald B. Kraybill and Marc A. Olshan. Hanover: University Press of New England.
1995   *Amish Folk Artist, Barbara Ebersol: Her Life, Fraktur, and Death Record Book.* Lancaster, Pa.: Lancaster Mennonite Historical Society.
1996   *Amish Settlements Across America: 1996.* Aylmer, Ont.: Pathway Publishers.

MacMaster, Richard K.
1985   *Land, Piety, Peoplehood.* Vol. 1 of *The Mennonite Experience in America.* Scottdale, Pa.: Herald Press.

Martineau, William H., and Rhonda S. MacQueen
1977   "Occupational Differentiation among the Old Order Amish." *Rural Sociology* 42:383–97.

Mast, J. Lemar, and Lois Ann Mast
  1982   *As Long as Wood Grows and Water Flows.* Morgantown, Pa.: Conestoga
          Mennonite Historical Committee.

Mast, John B.
  1950   Ed. and trans. *The Letters of the Amish Division of 1693–1711.* Oregon
          City, Ore.: Christian J. Schlabach. Printed by Mennonite Publishing
          House: Scottdale, Pa.

McCauley, Daniel, and Kathryn McCauley
  1988   *Decorative Arts of the Amish of Lancaster County.* Intercourse, Pa.: Good
          Books.

Mennonite Encyclopedia, The
  1956   Vols. 1–4. Scottdale, Pa.: Mennonite Publishing House; Hillsboro,
          Kans.: Mennonite Brethren Publishing House; Newton, Kans.: Menno-
          nite Publication Office.
  1990   Vol. 5. Scottdale, Pa.: Herald Press.

Menno Simons
  1956   *The Complete Writings of Menno Simons,* translated by Leonard Ver-
          duin, and edited by John C. Wenger. Scottdale, Pa.: Herald Press.

Meyers, Thomas J.
  1983a   "Amish Origins and Persistence: The Case of Agricultural Innovation."
          Paper presented to the annual meeting of the Rural Sociological Society,
          Lexington, Ky.
  1983b   "Stress and the Amish Community in Transition." Ph.D. diss., Boston
          University.
  1993   "Education and Schooling." In *The Amish and the State,* edited by Don-
          ald B. Kraybill. Baltimore: Johns Hopkins University Press.
  1994   "Lunch Pails and Factories." In *The Amish Struggle with Modernity,* ed-
          ited by Donald B. Kraybill and Marc A. Olshan. Hanover: University
          Press of New England.
  1996   "The Amish Division: A Review of the Literature." In *Les Amish: origine
          et particularismes 1693–1993.* Ingersheim: Association Française d'His-
          toire Anabaptiste-Mennonite.

Myers, David G.
  2000   *The American Paradox: Spiritual Hunger in an Age of Plenty.* New Ha-
          ven: Yale University Press.

Nagata, Judith
  1968   "Continuity and Change among the Old Order Amish of Illinois." Ph.D.
          diss., University of Illinois, Urbana.

New Era, Lancaster
  1930–   Lancaster, Pa.: Lancaster Newspapers.

New Order Amish Directory
  1999   Millersburg, Ohio: Abana Books.

Nolt, Steven M.
  1992   *A History of the Amish.* Intercourse, Pa.: Good Books.
  1994   "Keeping House." In *Proceedings of the Conference: Tradition and Transition: An Amish Mennonite Heritage of Obedience 1693–1993.* Metamora, Ill.: Mennonite Heritage Center.

Olshan, Marc A.
  1979   "The Old Order Amish in New York State." Cornell University, Cornell Rural Sociology Bulletin Series. Bulletin 94. February.
  1980   "The Old Order Amish as a Model for Development." Ph.D. diss., Cornell University.
  1981   "Modernity, the Folk Society, and the Old Order Amish." *Rural Sociology* 46(Summer):297–309.
  1986   "Freedom *vs.* Meaning: Aichinger's 'Bound Man' and the Old Order Amish." In *Internal and External Perspectives on Amish and Mennonite Life,* edited by Werner Enninger. Vol. 2. Essen: Unipress.
  1993   "The National Amish Steering Committee." In *The Amish and the State,* edited by Donald B. Kraybill. Baltimore: Johns Hopkins University Press.
  1994a "Amish Cottage Industries as Trojan Horse." In *The Amish Struggle with Modernity,* edited by Donald B. Kraybill and Marc A. Olshan. Hanover: University Press of New England.
  1994b "Homespun Bureaucracy: A Case Study in Organizational Evolution." In *The Amish Struggle with Modernity,* edited by Donald B. Kraybill and Marc A. Olshan. Hanover: University Press of New England.
  1994c "Modernity, the Folk Society, and the Old Order Amish." In *The Amish Struggle with Modernity,* edited by Donald B. Kraybill and Marc A. Olshan. Hanover: University Press of New England.
  1994d "What Good Are the Amish?" In *The Amish Struggle with Modernity,* edited by Donald B. Kraybill and Marc A. Olshan. Hanover: University Press of New England.

Olshan, Marc A., and Kimberly D. Schmidt
  1994   "Amish Women and the Feminist Conundrum." In *The Amish Struggle with Modernity,* edited by Donald B. Kraybill and Marc A. Olshan. Hanover: University Press of New England.

One Thousand and One Questions and Answers on the Christian Life
  1992   Aylmer, Ont.: Pathway Publishers.

Outley, Nancy Fisher
  1982   "From Amish to Professional and Back Again." In *Perils of Professionalism,* edited by Donald B. Kraybill and Phyllis Pellman Good. Scottdale, Pa.: Herald Press.

Oyer, John S.
    1996   "Is There an Amish Theology?" In *Les Amish: origine et particularismes 1693–1993*. Ingersheim: Association Française d'Histoire Anabaptiste-Mennonite.

Packull, Werner O.
    1995   *Hutterite Beginnings: Communitarian Experiments during the Reformation*. Baltimore: Johns Hopkins University Press.

Papers of the Amish School Controversy, The
    1937–68   Documents Concerning the Old Order Amish School Movement in Lancaster County, Pa., collected by Aaron E. Beiler.

Pellman, Rachel, and Kenneth Pellman
    1984   *The World of Amish Quilts*. Intercourse, Pa: Good Books.

Petition to Our Men in Authority
    1937   A request for changes in the Public School law presented to state officials 17 November 1937. Signed by representatives of thirty-seven Old Order Amish and Old Order Mennonite congregations.

Portes, Alejandro
    1998   "Social Capital: Its Origins and Applications in Modern Sociology." *Annual Review of Sociology* 24:1–24.

Putnam, Robert D.
    2000   *Bowling Alone: The Collapse and Revival of American Community*. New York: Simon & Schuster.

Raber, Ben J.
    1970–   Comp. *The New American Almanac*. Published annually by Ben J. Raber, Baltic, Ohio. Gordonville, Pa.: Gordonville Print Shop. The earlier almanac in German, *Der Neue Amerikanische Kalender*, dates back to 1930.

Renno, John R.
    1985   Comp. *Brief History of the Amish Divisions in Lancaster County*. Danville, Pa.

Reschly, Steven D.
    2000.   *The Amish on the Iowa Prairie, 1840 to 1910*. Baltimore: Johns Hopkins University Press.

Ressler, Martin
    1978   "A Song of Praise." *Pennsylvania Mennonite Heritage* 1(October):10–13.
    1986   "American Continuance of European Origins in Mennonite, Hutterite, and Amish Music Functions." *Pennsylvania Mennonite Heritage* 9(January):6–10.

Revised Regulations and Guidelines for Old Order Amish Liability Aid
    1977   Gordonville, Pa.: Gordonville Print Shop.

Rice, Charles S., and John B. Shenk
  1947   *Meet the Amish: A Pictorial Study of the Amish People.* New Brunswick, N.J.: Rutgers University Press.

Rice, Charles S., and Rollin C. Steinmetz
  1956   *The Amish Year.* New Brunswick, N.J.: Rutgers University Press.

Rohrer, David
  1974   "The Influence of the Pennsylvania German Dialect on Amish English in Lancaster Co." *Mennonite Research Journal* 15(July):34–35.

Roth, John D.
  1993   Trans. and ed. *Letters of the Amish Division: A Sourcebook.* Goshen, Ind.: Mennonite Historical Society.
  1994   "Common Origins of Mennonites and Amish to 1693." In *Tradition and Transition: An Amish Mennonite Heritage of Obedience 1693–1993,* edited by V. Gordon Oyer. Metamora, Ill.: Mennonite Heritage Center.

Rule of St. Benedict in English, The
  1982   Collegeville, Minn.: Liturgical Press.

Rules and Regulations of Old Order Amish Church Aid
  1983   Gordonville, Pa.: Gordonville Print Shop.

Rules of a Godly Life
  1983   Translated by Joseph Stoll from the German, *Geistliches Lustgartlein Frommer Seelen.* LaGrange, Ind.: Edwin L. Lambright.

Schlabach, Theron F.
  1988   *Peace, Faith, Nation: Mennonites and Amish in Nineteenth-Century America.* Vol. 2 of *The Mennonite Experience in America.* Scottdale, Pa.: Herald Press.

Schowalter, Paul
  1957   S.v. "Martyr." In *The Mennonite Encyclopedia* 3:521–25. Scottdale, Pa.: Herald Press.

Schreiber, William I.
  1962a   "The Hymns of the Amish Ausbund in Philological and Literary Perspective." *Mennonite Quarterly Review* 36(January): 37–60.
  1962b   *Our Amish Neighbors.* Chicago: University of Chicago Press.

Schwieder, Elmer, and Dorothy Schwieder
  1975   *A Peculiar People: Iowa's Old Order Amish.* Ames: Iowa State University Press.

Scott, Stephen
  1981   *Plain Buggies: Amish, Mennonite and Brethren Horse-Drawn Transportation.* Intercourse, Pa.: Good Books.
  1986   *Why Do They Dress That Way?* Intercourse, Pa.: Good Books.

1988   *The Amish Wedding and Other Special Occasions of the Old Order Communities.* Intercourse, Pa.: Good Books.

Seguy, Jean
1973   "Religion and Agricultural Success: The Vocational Life of the French Anabaptists from the Seventeenth to the Nineteenth Centuries." *Mennonite Quarterly Review* 47(July):179–224.
1980   "The Bernese Anabaptists in Sainte-Marie-aux-Mines." *Pennsylvania Mennonite Heritage* 3(July):2–9. Translated by Mervin Smucker.

Shirk, Eli M.
1939   Comp. *Report of Committee of Plain People Making Pleas for Leniency from Depressive School Laws.* Ephrata, Pa.

Siegel, Bernard J.
1970   "Defensive Structuring and Environmental Stress." *American Journal of Sociology* 76(July):11–32.

Smith, Elmer L.
1961   *The Amish Today: An Analysis of Their Beliefs, Behavior, and Contemporary Problems.* Pennsylvania German Society, vol. 24. Allentown, Pa.: Schlechters.

Smucker, Esther F.
1995   *Good Night, My Son: A Treasure in Heaven.* Elverson Pa.: Olde Springfield Shoppe.

Smucker, Mervin R.
1988   "How Amish Children View Themselves and Their Families: The Effectiveness of Amish Socialization." *Brethren Life and Thought* 33(Summer):218–36.

Snyder, C. Arnold
1995   *Anabaptist History and Theology: An Introduction.* Kitchener, Ont.: Pandora Press.

Songs of the Ausbund, Vol. 1
1998   Millersburg, Ohio: Ohio Amish Library, Inc.

Standards of the Old Order Amish and Old Order Mennonite Parochial and Vocational Schools of Pennsylvania
1981   Gordonville, Pa.: Gordonville Print Shop.

"Statement of the Bishops of the Old Order Amish Church of Lancaster County Regarding Attendance in Public Schools."
1950   22 February. Typescript.

Steering Committee
1966–2000 *Minutes of the Old Order Amish Steering Committee.* Vols. 1–6. Gordonville, Pa.: Gordonville Print Shop.

Steinfeldt, Bernice
    1937   *The Amish of Lancaster County.* Lancaster, Pa.: Arthur G. Steinfeldt.

Stevick, Richard
    2000   "Amish Youth: The Critical Years." Manuscript.

Stoltzfus, Amos J.
    n.d.   *Ein bericht wie es sich begeben hat das der bahn zwichen die Hausgemein und die Kirchgemein gekommen ist in der Conestoga valley, Lancaster County, Pennsylvania* (A report on how the ban between the house church and the church group came about in the Conestoga Valley, Lancaster County, Pennsylvania). Translated by Noah G. Good.
    1984   *Golden Memories.* Gordonville, Pa.: Pequea Publishers.

Stoltzfus, Grant M.
    1954   "History of the First Amish Mennonite Communities in America." *Mennonite Quarterly Review* 28(October):235–62.

Stoltzfus, Louise
    1994   *Amish Women: Lives and Stories.* Intercourse: Good Books.
    1995   *Two Amish Folk Artists: The Story of Henry Lapp and Barbara Ebersol.* Intercourse, Pa: Good Books.
    1998   *Traces of Wisdom: Amish Women and the Pursuit of Life's Simple Pleasures.* New York: Hyperion.
    2000   *The Story of Tourism in Lancaster County, PA.* Lancaster, Pa.: Pennsylvania Dutch Convention and Visitor's Bureau.

Stoltzfus, Victor
    1973   "Amish Agriculture: Adaptive Strategies for Economic Survival of Community Life." *Rural Sociology* 38(Summer):196–206.
    1977   "Reward and Sanction: The Adaptive Continuity of Amish Life." *Mennonite Quarterly Review* 51(October):308–18.

Studer, Gerald C.
    1984   "The Dordrecht Confession of Faith, 1632–1982." *Mennonite Quarterly Review* 58(October):503–19.

Swartz, David
    1997   *Culture and Power: The Sociology of Pierre Bourdieu.* Chicago: University of Chicago Press.

Tan, Tay Keong
    1998   "Silence, Sacrifice and Shoofly Pies: An Inquiry into Social Capital and Organizational Strategies of the Amish Community in Lancaster County, Pennsylvania." Ph.D. diss., John F. Kennedy School of Government, Harvard University.

Thompson, William E.
    1981   "The Oklahoma Amish: Survival of an Ethnic Subculture." *Ethnicity* 8:476–87.

Umble, Diane Zimmerman
  1994   "Amish on the Line: The Telephone Debates." In *The Amish Struggle with Modernity,* edited by Donald B. Kraybill and Marc A. Olshan. Hanover: University Press of New England.
  1996   *Holding the Line: The Telephone in Old Order Mennonite and Amish Life.* Baltimore: Johns Hopkins University Press.

Umble, John S.
  1948   "Memoirs of an Amish Bishop." *Mennonite Quarterly Review* 22(April):94–115.

Vocation on the Farm
  1956   A Statement of Principles of a Church Vocation in Agricultural Practice by the Old Order Amish Church of Pennsylvania. Strasburg, Pa.: Homsher Printing.

Wagler, David
  n.d.   *Are All Things Lawful?* Aylmer, Ont.: Pathway Publishers.

Weaver, J. Denny
  1987   *Becoming Anabaptist: The Origin and Significance of Sixteenth-Century Anabaptism.* Scottdale, Pa.: Herald Press.

Weaver-Zercher, David
  2001   *The Amish in the American Imagination.* Baltimore: Johns Hopkins University Press.

Weber, Max
  1947   *The Theory of Social and Economic Organization.* New York: Free Press.

Wickersham, James P.
  1886   *A History of Education in Pennsylvania.* Lancaster, Pa.: Inquirer Publishing.

Wilson, Bryan
  1970   *Religious Sects.* New York: McGraw-Hill.

Woolcock, Michael
  1998a   "Social Capital: Its Origins and Applications in Modern Sociology." *Annual Review of Sociology.* Palo Alto, Calif.: Annual Reviews Inc.
  1998b   "Social Capital and Economic Development: Toward a Theoretical Syntheses and Policy Framework." *Theory and Society* 27:151–208.

Yoder, Don
  1997   "Two Worlds in the Dutch Country." *Pennsylvania Folk Life* 46(3): 102–8.

Yoder, Elmer S.
  1987   *The Beachy Amish Mennonite Fellowship Churches.* Hartville, Ohio: Diakonia Ministries.

Yoder, John Howard
 1973 Ed. and trans. *The Legacy of Michael Sattler.* Scottdale, Pa.: Herald Press.

Yoder, Paton
 n.d. "Amish Church Affairs in the Nineteenth Century." Typescript.
 1979a *Eine Wurzel: Tennessee John Stoltzfus.* Lititz, Pa: Sutter House.
 1979b "'Tennessee' John Stoltzfus and the Great Schism in the Amish Church, 1850–1877." *Pennsylvania Mennonite Heritage* 2(July):17–23.
 1987a *Tennessee John Stoltzfus: Amish Church-Related Documents and Family Letters.* Lancaster, Pa.: Lancaster Mennonite Historical Society.
 1987b "The Structure of the Amish Ministry in the Nineteenth Century." *Mennonite Quarterly Review* 61(July):280–97.
 1991 *Tradition and Transition: Amish Mennonites and Old Order Amish, 1800–1900.* Scottdale, Pa.: Herald Press.
 1993 "The Amish View of the State." In *The Amish and the State,* edited by Donald B. Kraybill. Baltimore: Johns Hopkins University Press.

Yoder, Paton, and Elizabeth Bender
 1979 "Baptism as an Issue in the Amish Division of the Nineteenth Century: 'Tennessee' John Stoltzfus." *Mennonite Quarterly Review* 53(October): 306–23.

Yoder, Paton, and Steven R. Estes
 1999 *Proceedings of the Amish Ministers' Meetings 1862–1878.* Goshen, Ind.: Mennonite Historical Society.

Zook, Lee J.
 1993 "Slow-moving Vehicles." In *The Amish and the State,* edited by Donald B. Kraybill. Baltimore: Johns Hopkins University Press.

Photographs by the following photographers appear on the pages listed: Keith Baum, 12, 129; Dennis L. Hughes, 48, 71, 107, 114, 118, 125, 147, 156, 185, 194, 201, 209, 221, 231, 234, 249, 252, 253, 262, 266, 270, 274, 288, 291, 300, 303, 310, 314; Jerry Irwin, 316 (courtesy of the Pennsylvania Dutch Convention and Visitors Bureau); Lucian Niemeyer, 177, 218, 226; Richard K. Reinhold, 14, 20, 35, 42, 59, 85, 159, 181, 282; Charles S. Rice, 163; Blair Seitz, iv, 5 (courtesy of the Lancaster Mennonite Historical Society), 24, 39, 62, 64, 75, 91, 109, 149, 204, 211; Shirley Glick Wenger, 28, 87, 152. A cartoon by Charles Beyl appears on page 214. Drawings by Linda Eberly appear on pages 7, 11, 17, 18, 25, 31, 89, 100, 143, 179, 242, 257, 308. Photographs courtesy of the following sources appear on the pages listed: Lancaster Newspapers, Inc., 170; Wide World Photos, 133.

Donald B. Kraybill's many books on Anabaptist groups include *The Upside-Down Kingdom* (1990), which received the national Religious Book Award, and *The Amish Struggle with Modernity* (1994). He edited the award-winning *The Amish and the State* (1993) and coauthored *Old Order Amish: Their Enduring Way of Life* (1993); *Mennonite Peacemaking: From Quietism to Activism* (1994); and *Amish Enterprise: From Plows to Profits* (1995). His most recent books are *On the Backroad to Heaven: Old Order Hutterites, Mennonites, Amish, and Brethren* (2001) and *Anabaptist World USA* (2001). Kraybill is a professor of sociology and Anabaptist studies at Messiah College in Pennsylvania.